BEST of Knit Picks

PULLOVERS & CARDIGANS

Photography by John Cranford & Amy Cave

Printed in the United States of America

Second Printing, 2020

ISBN 978-1-62767-240-5

Versa Press, Inc.
800-447-7829

www.versapress.com

CONTENTS

CADDINGTON WRAP

by Kate Heppell

FINISHED MEASUREMENTS
50 (52, 55.5, 58.5, 63, 67, 71, 76, 80)" full width, designed to be worn with approx 10" from each side overlap at front

YARN
Knit Picks Capretta™ Superwash (fingering weight, 80% Fine Merino Superwash Wool, 10% Cashmere, 10% Nylon; 460 yards/100g): Bare 27712, 5 (5, 6, 6, 7, 7, 8, 8, 9) hanks

NEEDLES
US 4 (3.5mm) 24" or longer circular needles, plus 60" circulars for border, DPNs for sleeves, or size to obtain gauge

NOTIONS
Yarn Needle
Smooth Contrasting Scrap Yarn
Crochet Hook in the same size or one size larger than gauge needle, or as preferred for Provisional CO

GAUGE
25 sts and 32 rows = 4" in Diamond Pattern, blocked
28 sts and 36 rounds = 4" in Stockinette Stitch in the round, blocked

For pattern support, contact customerservice@knitpicks.com

Caddington Wrap

Notes:

The body of this cardigan is knit in two mirrored pieces from the center back out to the edge in a lace pattern. The first half begins with a Provisional Cast On, from which the second half is picked up. The armholes are worked with scrap yarn, which is then unraveled and the sleeves worked from the live stitches.

It is important to knit a generous swatch of the lace pattern and to wash it and block it before you cast on for this cardigan, as any gauge discrepancies (particularly row gauge) may cause issues with fit. Inch measurements for the length are given throughout the pattern; please note that if your gauge is off and not compensated for, you may need more yarn.

When taking your measurements for this cardigan, pay particular attention to the cross-back measurement. This should be nice and snug to avoid the cardigan falling off the shoulders.

When working the charts, read RS rows (odd numbers) from right to left and WS rows (even numbers) from left to right.

DIRECTIONS

Right Half
Back

Using the Provisional Cast On method, CO 197 (197, 211, 211, 211, 211, 211, 225, 225) sts.

Work in Diamond Pattern from chart until piece measures 6.5 (7.5, 8.25, 8.75, 9, 9, 9, 9.5, 9.5)" from CO edge, remembering to compensate for any changes in gauge during swatch blocking, finishing after a WS row. Make a note of which row you finished on here so that you can work the left half to match.

Armhole

Next Row (RS): Work in pattern for 42 (46, 51, 55, 56, 57, 57, 59, 59) sts, K48 (48, 48, 48, 54, 54, 60, 60, 66) sts using scrap yarn, then slip all of these sts back onto LH needle ready to work again; K across the scrap yarn sts using the working yarn, then work in pattern to end.

Front

Cont in pattern until piece measures 12 (12, 13, 14, 16, 18, 20, 22, 24)" from armhole, remembering to compensate for any changes in gauge during swatch blocking, finishing after a Row 16.

Work Decreasing Diamonds pattern once—rep the red outlined box 10 (10, 11, 11, 11, 11, 11, 12, 12) times each row. Note: If using stitch markers for reps, they will need to be shifted to accommodate the Centered Double Decreases. 142 (142, 156, 156, 156, 156, 156, 170, 170) sts.

BO all sts.

Left Half
Back

Unpick Provisional CO from center back of Right Half and place these sts onto the needles, ready to begin a RS row.

Join yarn. Work in Diamond Pattern from chart until piece measures 6.5 (7.5, 8.25, 8.75, 9, 9, 9, 9.5, 9.5)" from CO edge for the same number of rows as the Right Back, finishing after a WS row.

Armhole

Next Row (RS): Work in pattern for 107 (103, 112, 108, 101, 100, 94, 106, 100) sts, K48 (48, 48, 48, 54, 54, 60, 60, 66) sts using scrap yarn, then slip all of these sts back onto LH needle ready to work again; K across the scrap yarn sts using the working yarn, work in pattern to end.

Front

Cont in pattern until piece measures 12 (12, 13, 14, 16, 18, 20, 22, 24)" from armhole, remembering to compensate for any changes in gauge during swatch blocking, finishing after a Row 16.

Work Decreasing Diamonds pattern once—rep the red outlined box 10 (10, 11, 11, 11, 11, 11, 12, 12) times each row. Note: If using stitch markers for reps, they will need to be shifted to accommodate the Centered Double Decreases. 142 (142, 156, 156, 156, 156, 156, 170, 170) sts.

BO all sts.

Sleeves (work both the same)

Unpick the scrap yarn from both sides of the armhole, placing resulting live sts onto your DPNs.

Join yarn. Starting at underarm with RS facing, PM to indicate the BOR, PU and K 1 st from underarm, K all sts from first side of armhole, PU and K 2 sts from top of armhole, K all sts from second side of armhole, PU and K 1 st from bottom of armhole. Join in the rnd. 100 (100, 100, 100, 112, 112, 124, 124, 136) sts.

Knit 5 (5, 12, 10, 7, 3, 6, 0, 6) rnds.

Dec Rnd: K1, K2tog, K to last 3 sts, SSK, K1. 2 sts dec. Knit 5 (6, 6, 8, 7, 11, 8, 13, 7) rnds. Rep Dec Rnd followed by Knit rnds as established 17 (15, 14, 10, 13, 9, 12, 8, 14) more times. 64 (68, 70, 78, 84, 92, 98, 106, 106) sts.

Next 18 Rnds: Work in 1x1 Rib.

BO in pattern.

Ribbed Edge

Weave in ends. Block to dimensions given in schematic, noting that your current measurements do not include the 2.25" around any edge for the rib except the sleeves.

With long circular needles, PU and K 10 sts per inch around the outer edge, ending with a multiple of 4 sts. Join in the rnd and PM for BOR.

Next 18 Rnds: Work in 2x2 Rib.

BO in pattern.

Finishing

Weave in ends and steam the rib.

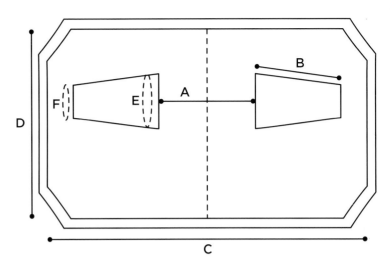

A 13 (15, 16.5, 17.5, 18, 18, 18, 19, 19)"
B 15 (15.25, 15.25, 15.5, 15.5, 16, 16, 16.25, 16.25)"
C 45.5 (47.5, 51, 54, 58.5, 62.5, 66.5, 71.5, 75.5"
D 31.5 (31.5, 33.75, 33.75, 33.75, 33.75, 33.75, 36, 36)"
E 14.25 (14.25, 14.25, 15.75, 16, 16, 17.75, 17.75, 19.5)"
F 9.25 (9.75, 10, 11.25, 12, 13.25, 14, 15.25, 15.25)"

Diamond Decreases Chart

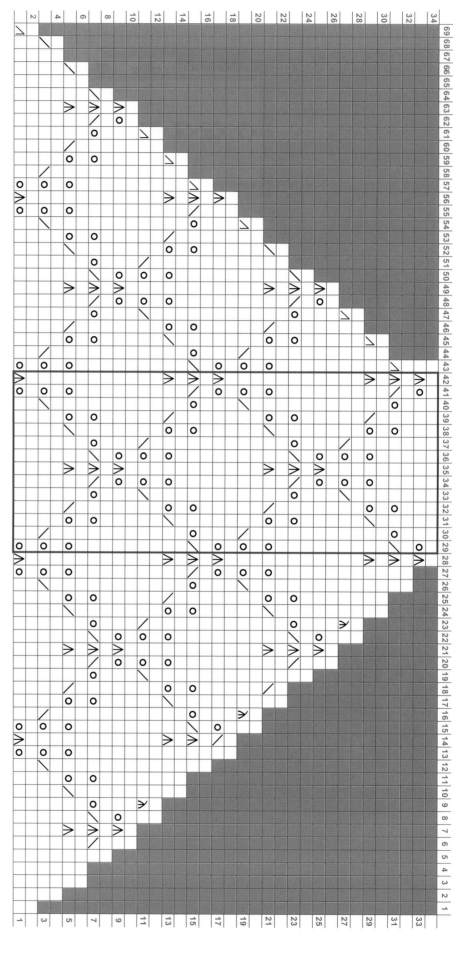

LEGEND

No Stitch
Placeholder—no stitch made

Knit
RS: knit stitch
WS: purl stitch

YO
Yarn over

K2tog
Knit two stitches together as one stitch

SSK
(Slip 1 knit-wise) twice; insert left-hand needle into front of these 2 stitches and knit them together

CDD
Slip first and second stitches together as if to k2tog. Knit 1 stitch. Pass two slipped stitches over the knit stitch

SSSK
(Slip 1 knit-wise) three times; insert left-hand needle from the front to the back of all stitches at the same time and knit them together

K3tog
Knit three stitches together as one stitch

Pattern Repeat

Diamond Chart

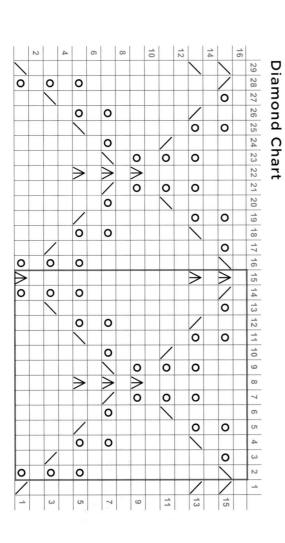

DOGWOOD BLOSSOMS SWEATER

by Kerin Dimeler-Laurence

FINISHED MEASUREMENTS

36 (38, 40, 42, 44, 46, 48)" chest measurement; garment is designed to be worn with 2-4" of positive ease

YARN

Knit Picks Palette™ (fingering weight, 100% Peruvian Highland Wool; 231 yards/50g) (see pg 16 for North Sea colors, pg 36 for Autumn colors, and pg 56 for Midwinter colors)

NEEDLES

US 1 (2.5mm) 32" circular needles or longer circulars for Magic Loop and DPNs, or size to obtain gauge

US 1 (2.25mm) 32" or longer circular needles and DPNs, or one size smaller than those used to obtain gauge

NOTIONS

Yarn Needle
Stitch Markers
Spare DPNs
Cardigan Version: 10 (10, 10, 11, 11, 11, 11) 0.75" Buttons
Sewing Needle and Thread, or size A Crochet Hook for steek

GAUGE

32 sts and 38 rows = 4" in Stranded Stockinette Stitch worked flat and in the round, blocked

For pattern support, contact customerservice@knitpicks.com

Dogwood Blossoms Sweater

Notes:

A new take on a traditional sweater, this Fair Isle sweater features modern palettes and more feminine shaping.

Complete chart sets are given for all three colorways—North Sea starts on pg 16; Autumn on pg 36; Midwinter on pg 56. Directions here apply to all colorways.

For a handy reference, the tables following the charts list each color used in each row of the chart.

DIRECTIONS

Sleeves (make 2 the same)
The sleeves are knit identically for both the pullover and cardigan. Both are worked to the underarm, then are joined tog with steek sts and finished to the top of the sleeve caps.

With MC and smaller needles, CO 72 (72, 76, 80, 80, 84, 88) sts. PM and join in the rnd, being careful not to twist sts. Work in 2x2 Rib for 20 rnds. Switch to larger needles and K one rnd, increasing 2 sts in the rnd. 74 (74, 78, 82, 82, 86, 90) sts.

Begin working from Sleeve chart, following directions for your size. BOR will be underarm side of sleeve. Change colors as shown in chart; leave 6" tails at color changes if you wish to braid ends, or leave short tails and knot every two ends tog firmly, but without disturbing the patterning.

First Sleeve chart ends at Rnd 141; cont to Sleeve Cap chart from there. At Rnd 147, there are 128 (128, 134, 136, 138, 142, 154) sts.

At Rnd 148 in chart, the last 8 (9, 8, 8, 10, 9, 8) sts are bound off for underarm. Cont to BO across the first 8 (9, 8, 8, 10, 9, 8) sts of next rnd. Break yarn and place this sleeve on scrap yarn or a stitch holder.

Joining Sleeves for Steek
Next Rnd: Work to last charted st on one sleeve, PM. CO for steek after last st as follows: (1 st current background color, 1 st current foreground color) three times, 1 st current background color. This 7-st steek will run between the two sleeves.

Instead of joining sleeve back to other side of itself, PM and K next rnd of second sleeve onto same needle directly after steek. After last st of this sleeve, CO another 7-st steek, PM and join to next rnd of first sleeve. The two sleeves are now linked tog in the rnd.

Cont working from chart, following color changes and decs for your size and working steek sts in a 1x1 checkerboard pattern. After last rnd, BO all sts with either current color. Set aside.

Pullover Version
Body
With MC and smaller needles, CO 288 (304, 320, 336, 352, 368, 384) sts. PM and join in the rnd, being careful not to twist sts. Work in 2x2 Rib for 20 rnds.

Switch to larger needles and K one rnd plain in MC, PM after 144 (152, 160, 168, 176, 184, 192) sts to mark right underarm.

Begin working from Pullover Body chart, following directions for your size. BOR is under left arm. Change colors as shown in chart; leave 6" tails at color changes if you wish to braid ends, or leave short tails and knot every two ends tog firmly, but without disturbing the patterning.

Armscyes Shaping
At Rnd 133 in chart, sts are bound off for armscyes. Work in pattern until 5 (7, 9, 12, 9, 10, 10) sts before right underarm M; BO next 10 (14, 18, 24, 18, 20, 20) sts in pattern. Work to 5 (7, 9, 12, 9, 10, 10) sts before end of rnd (left underarm M) and BO those last sts of rnd, plus first 5 (7, 9, 12, 9, 10, 10) sts of next rnd.

On next rnd, steek sts are CO to join armscyes. Work across front of sweater in pattern, following decs. After first bound-off st of right armscye, PM and CO a 7-st steek as done for sleeves. Join to first live st of back and work across in pattern. PM and CO another 7-st steek at left armscye; join to front and begin next rnd.

At Row 135 (137, 140, 139, 140, 141, 143), 2 sts are bound off to begin neckline. Work across front of sweater, binding off 2 center sts as shown in chart. On next rnd, work from chart to first bound-off st, PM, and CO 7-st steek as done for sleeves and armscyes. PM and join to right side of front; cont around in pattern.

Cont working from chart, following color changes and decs and working the 3 steeks in a 1x1 checkerboard pattern with current colors.

Shoulder Shaping
The shoulders are shaped with short rows. They are worked back and forth across both shoulders on one side of garment.

On Rnd 210 (210, 214, 217, 219, 222, 227) of chart, BO right armscye steek, back neck, and left armscye steek as shown. Remainder of shoulders will be worked flat.

Cont working each shoulder from chart, working W&Ts where indicated and purling in pattern across WS rows. On the back, attach yarn for each shoulder with RS facing, and cont working from chart; note that back right shoulder is worked as the front left, and back left is worked as the front right.

After each shoulder is complete, work across all shoulder sts in pattern, picking up wraps and working them tog with the st they wrap. Break yarn, leaving an 18" tail.

Join Shoulders
Turn sweater inside out. Place matching shoulders on needles, holding one side in front of the other, right sides together. Perform a 3-Needle BO across all sts using yarn tail in either of the current colors. Rep for other shoulder.

Cardigan Version

Body

With MC and smaller needles, CO 295 (311, 327, 343, 359, 375, 391) sts. PM and join in the rnd, being careful not to twist sts.

Rnd 1: K7, PM to mark edge of center steek; it will be cut between these two Ms. Work around remaining sts in 2x2 Rib. K7, (K2, P2) to end for next 19 rnds. Switch to larger needles and K one rnd plain in MC, PM after 79 (83, 87, 91, 95, 99, 103) sts to mark right underarm and after 223 (235, 247, 259, 271, 283, 295) sts to mark left underarm.

Next Rnd: Begin working from Cardigan Body Repeat chart. Work from chart between Ms; follow colored line for your size. Work the 7 center steek sts (not shown on chart) in a checkerboard pattern, alternating current colors every st.

Armscyes Shaping

Move to Cardigan Armscye and Neck Shaping charts. At Rnd 133 in chart, sts are bound off for armscyes. Work in pattern until 5 (7, 9, 12, 9, 10, 10) sts before right underarm M; BO next 10 (14, 18, 24, 18, 20, 20) sts in pattern. Work to 5 (7, 9, 12, 9, 10, 10) sts before left underarm M and BO next 10 (14, 18, 24, 18, 20, 20) sts in pattern, then cont in pattern to end of rnd.

On next rnd, steek sts are CO to join armscyes. Work across front of sweater in pattern, following decs. After first bound-off st of right armscye, PM and CO a 7-st steek as done for sleeves. Join to first live st of back and work across in pattern. PM and CO another 7-st steek at left armscye; join to front and begin next rnd.

Because of center front steek, neck line begins with decs on either side of steek instead of binding off.

Shoulders

Work Shoulder Shaping and Join Shoulders exactly as for Pullover Version (previous page).

Steeks

Using a crochet hook appropriate to your yarn weight, follow steps in diagram in Glossary and crochet chain up the steek. Work a crochet chain around every steek: sleeve cap, armscyes, neck placket, neck, and back neck. With very sharp scissors, cut each steek open.

Set in Sleeves

With RSs facing out, set sleeves into armscye openings, making sure that the center of each sleeve cap is placed at the shoulder seam. Pin in place. Using yarn needle and yarn, begin at underarm and sew sleeves into armscyes.

Neckband & Button Bands

The neckband and button bands are picked up and knit as one long strip of ribbing around the entire front opening.

Pullover

Sts are picked up around neck with RS facing, starting at point of V-neck, up right edge of neckline, around back and finally down left edge of neck. Neckline is worked in the rnd.

With MC and smaller needles, PU and K one st from point of

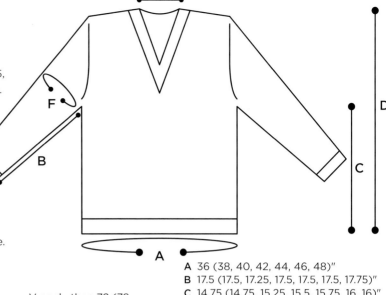

A 36 (38, 40, 42, 44, 46, 48)"
B 17.5 (17.5, 17.25, 17.5, 17.5, 17.5, 17.75)"
C 14.75 (14.75, 15.25, 15.5, 15.75, 16, 16)"
D 23.5 (23.5, 24.5, 25, 25.5, 26, 26.5)"
E 9 (9, 9.5, 10, 10 10.5, 11)"
F 16 (16, 16.75, 17, 17.25, 17.75, 19.25)"
G 7.25 (7.25, 7.5, 7.25, 7.5, 7.25, 7.25)"

V-neck, then 78 (78, 79, 83, 83, 85, 90) sts up right side of neck, 58 (58, 60, 60, 60, 60, 58) sts across back of neck, 78 (78, 79, 83, 83, 85, 90) sts down left edge of neckline, and one st from point of V-neck. 216 (216, 220, 228, 228, 232, 240) sts. PM and join in the rnd.

Rnd 1: K1, (P2, K2) to last 3 sts, P2, K1.
Rnd 2: SSK, work in established rib to last 2 sts, K2tog. 2 sts dec.
Rep Rnd 2 eight more times. On next rnd, BO all sts in rib.

Cardigan

Sts are picked up for button bands and neck with RS facing, starting at bottom of right edge of cardigan, around back of neck and finally down left edge of cardigan. This band is worked flat as one piece.

With MC and smaller needles, PU and K 114 (116, 123, 126, 128, 131, 132) sts up right side of body, 78 (78, 80 ,83, 83, 86, 90) sts up right side of neck, 58 (58, 60, 60, 60, 60, 58) sts across back of neck, 78 (78, 80 ,83, 83, 86, 90) sts down left edge of neckline, and 114 (116, 123, 126, 128, 131, 132) sts down left edge of body. 442 (446, 466, 478, 482, 494, 502) sts.

Row 1: (P2, K2) to last 2 sts, P2.
Row 2: (K2, P2) to last 2 sts, K2.
Rep Rows 1-2 once, then Row 1 once more.

Next Row, work Buttonholes: K1, (K1, P2, K1, SSK, YO twice, K2tog, K1, P2, K1) 10 (10, 10, 11, 11, 11, 11) times, work in established rib to end.
Next Row: Work in established rib, knitting into front of first YO and into back of second YO in each double YO. Work in established rib for four more rows; BO in rib.

Finishing

Weave in ends that will show; for others, it's fine to knot the ends and cut them short. If desired, sew bias tape or other stabilizer along cut steek edges. Wash and block. For cardigan, sew buttons opposite buttonholes.

Dogwood Blossoms:
NORTH SEA COLORWAY

YARN COLORS

3 balls:
MC Asphalt Heather 24243

2 balls each:
Pool 23723
Navy 24001
Tidepool Heather 24007

1 ball each:
Celestial 24582
Clarity 25548
Sky 23724
Tranquil 25094
Sagebrush 25549
Teal 24000
Rainforest Heather 24008
White 23728
Mist 23733
Silver 24586
Ash 23731

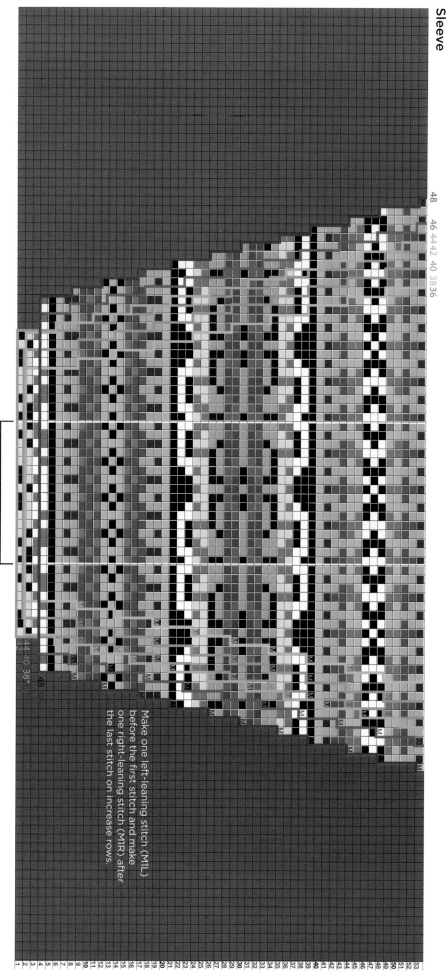

Sleeve

All sizes: repeat these four times, then continue on to stitch 109 of the chart.

*Sizes 36 and 38 share the same stitch count and shaping instructions until the sleeve cap; use the line marked 38 for both sizes.

Make one left-leaning stitch (M1L) before the first stitch and make one right-leaning stitch (M1R) after the last stitch on increase rows.

Clarity □
Sky
Pool
Celestial
Navy

Sagebrush
Tranquil
Tidepool Heather
Teal
Rainforest Heather

White □
Mist
Silver
Ash
Asphalt Heather

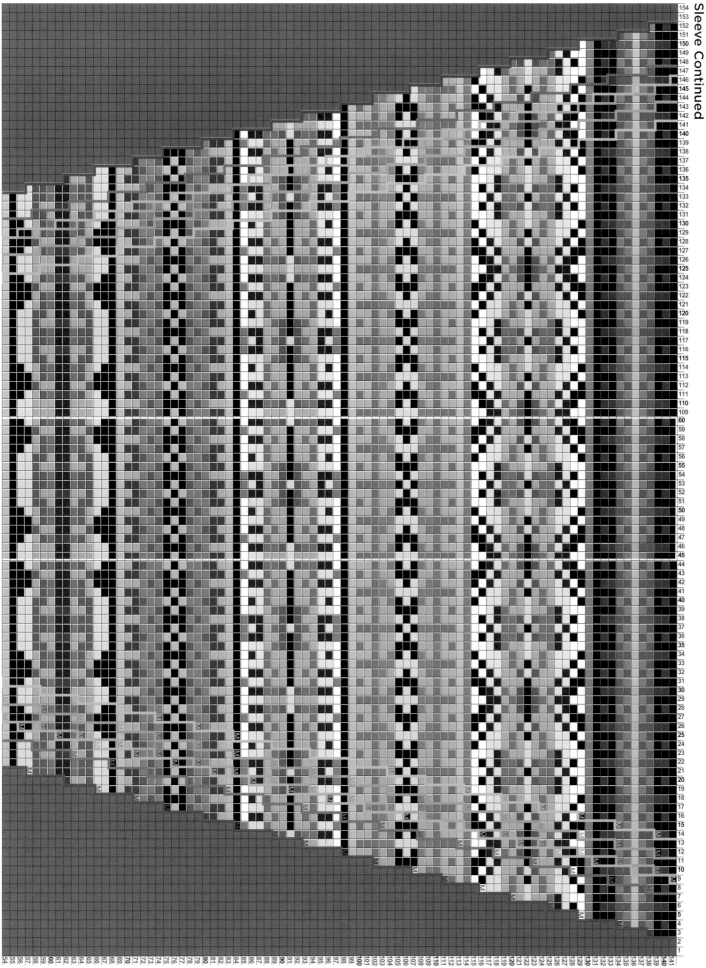

Sleeve Cap (Left Side)

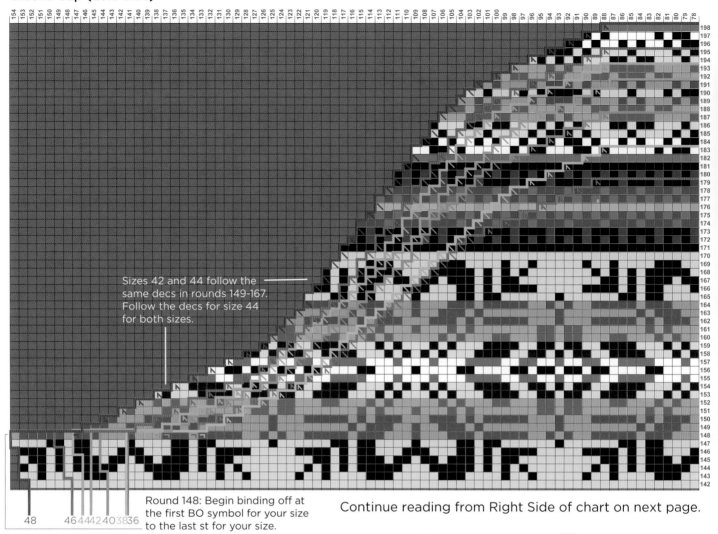

Sizes 42 and 44 follow the same decs in rounds 149-167. Follow the decs for size 44 for both sizes.

Round 148: Begin binding off at the first BO symbol for your size to the last st for your size.

48 46 44 42 40 38 36

Continue reading from Right Side of chart on next page.

Reading Charts
All charts are read from right to left, bottom to top, as all pieces are worked in the round.

Binding Off
Because there are many sizes represented in each chart, not all bind-off marks are shown. When sts are bound off, they will still appear in the row in which they are bound off, but not in subsequent rows.

However, sts removed by decs will not appear in the row from which they are removed. When a set of bound-off sts is followed by decs on the next round, those removed sts will widen the area of 'No Stitch' above the bound-off sts.

Where bound-off sections cross over the end/beginning of a round, the BO sts will appear at the end of the first round and then over the first several sts of the following round. When these are followed immediately by a dec, the st that remains on the RH needle after the last bound off st becomes part of the dec. For instance, if a BO st is followed directly by a K3tog, slip the st back to the LH needle and knit it together with the following two sts.

	Clarity		White
	Sky		Mist
	Pool		Silver
	Celestial		Ash
	Navy		Asphalt Heather
	Sagebrush		Teal
	Tranquil		Rainforest Heather
	Tidepool Heather		

No decreases in the round following BO

Bound off stitches

A double decrease in the row following the BO results in two 'no stitch' spaces next to those left by the BO sts.

Bound off stitches

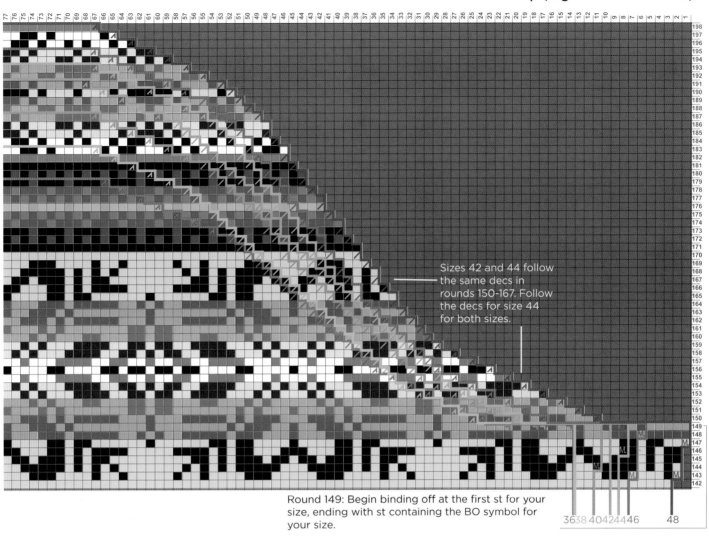

Sizes 42 and 44 follow the same decs in rounds 150-167. Follow the decs for size 44 for both sizes.

Round 149: Begin binding off at the first st for your size, ending with st containing the BO symbol for your size.

3638 40424446   48

LEGEND

No Stitch
Placeholder—no stitch made

Knit
RS: knit stitch
WS: purl stitch

M1
Make one stitch, following instructions on chart

K2tog
Knit two stitches together as one stitch

SSK
(Slip 1 knit-wise) twice; insert left-hand needle into front of these 2 stitches and knit them together

K3tog
Knit three stitches together as one stitch

SSSK
(Slip 1 knit-wise) three times; insert left-hand needle from the front to the back of all stitches at the same time and knit them together

Wrap and Turn (W&T)
Wrap and turn for short row, following pattern instructions

BO
Bind off 1 stitch

Pullover Body Repeat: Sizes 36″, 40″, 44″, 48″

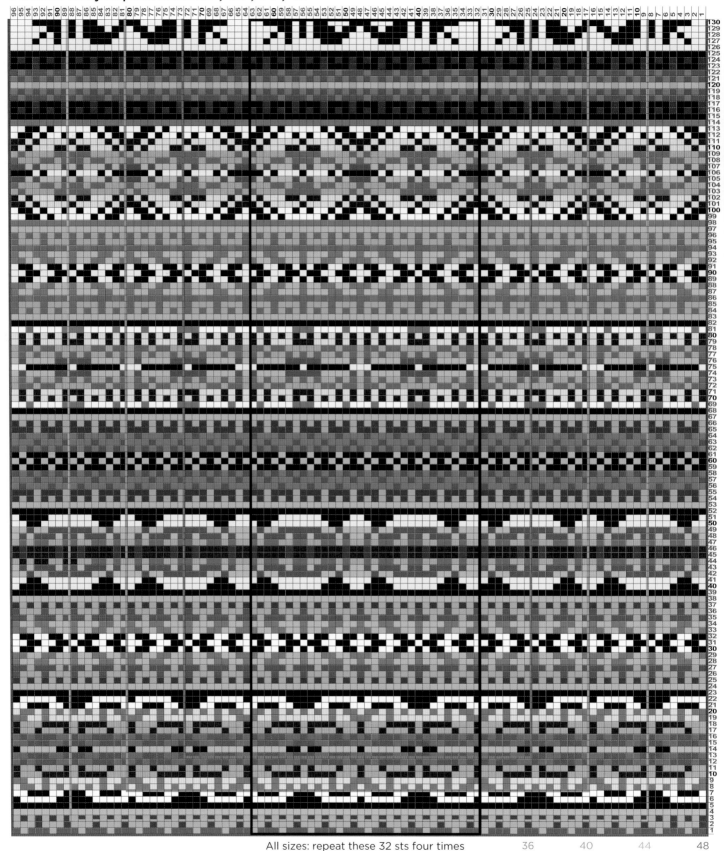

All sizes: repeat these 32 sts four times   36   40   44   48

Read this chart from the first st and row outlined in your size, from right to left, until the last outlined st in your size. Work this chart across the front and again across the back for a given round.

After completing this chart, move on to the Pullover Armscye and Neck Shaping chart for your size.

Pullover Body Repeats: Sizes 38″, 42″, 46″

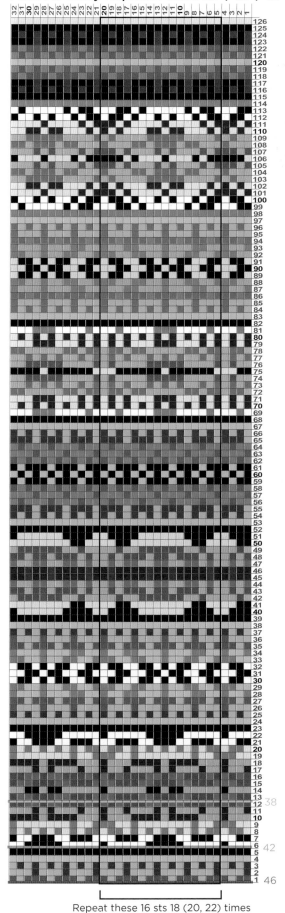

Clarity

Sky

Pool

Celestial

Navy

Sagebrush

Tranquil

Tidepool Heather

Teal

Rainforest Heather

White

Mist

Silver

Ash

Asphalt Heather

Repeat these 16 sts 18 (20, 22) times

Pullover Armscye and Neck Shaping: Sizes 36″, 40″, 44″, 48″ (Left Side)

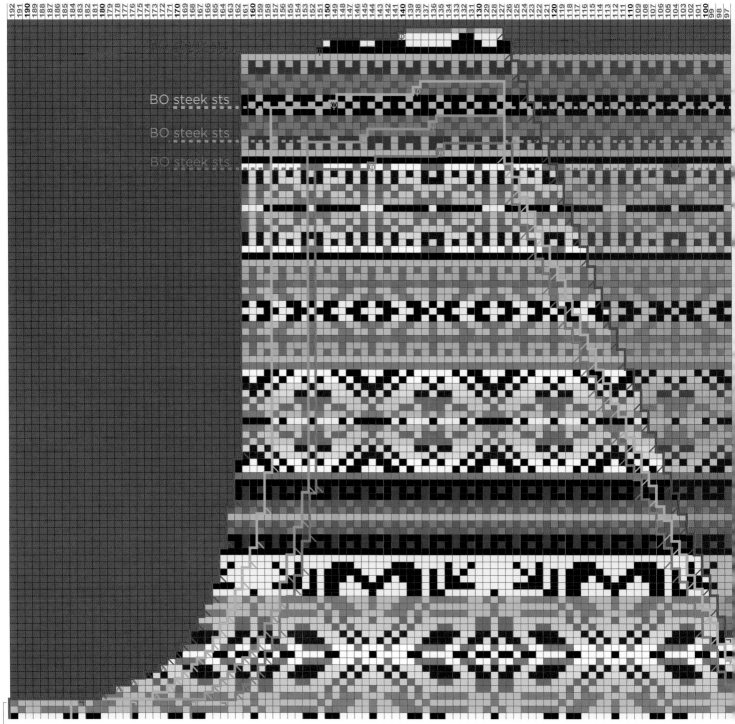

BO steek sts

BO steek sts

BO steek sts

Round 133: Begin binding off at st containing the BO symbol for your size, ending with the last st for your size.

Continue reading from Right Side of chart on next page.

This chart shows both the front and back of the sweater. For the front, follow neck decs as shown; for the back, work across the whole back in pattern until the bind-off at the back neck.

Sizes 40 and 44 share the same pattern of neck decs; follow decs for size 44 for both sizes.

Pullover Armscye and Neck Shaping: Sizes 36″, 40″, 44″, 48″ (Right Side—start here)

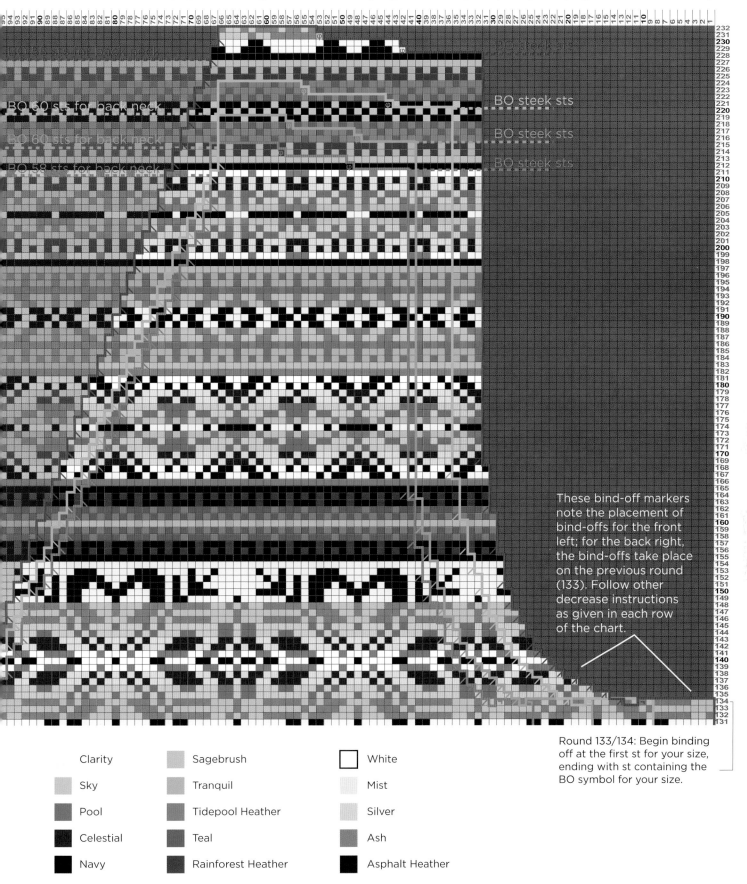

BO 60 sts for back neck

BO 60 sts for back neck

BO 58 sts for back neck

BO steek sts

BO steek sts

BO steek sts

These bind-off markers note the placement of bind-offs for the front left; for the back right, the bind-offs take place on the previous round (133). Follow other decrease instructions as given in each row of the chart.

Round 133/134: Begin binding off at the first st for your size, ending with st containing the BO symbol for your size.

	Clarity		Sagebrush		White
	Sky		Tranquil		Mist
	Pool		Tidepool Heather		Silver
	Celestial		Teal		Ash
	Navy		Rainforest Heather		Asphalt Heather

Pullover Armscye and Neck Shaping: Sizes 38″, 42″, 46″ (Left Side)

Round 133: Begin binding off at st containing the BO symbol for your size, ending with the last st for your size.

Continue reading from Right Side of chart on next page.

This chart shows both the front and back of the sweater. For the front, follow neck decs as shown; for the back, work across the whole back in pattern until the bind-off at the back neck.

Pullover Armscye and Neck Shaping: Sizes 38″, 42″, 46″ (Right Side—start here)

BO 58 sts for back neck

BO 58 sts for back neck

BO 58 sts for back neck

BO steek sts

BO steek sts

BO steek sts

These bind-off markers note the placement of bind-offs for the front left; for the back right, the bind-offs take place on the previous row (133). Follow other decrease instructions as given in each row of the chart.

Round 133/134: Begin binding off at the first st for your size, ending with st containing the BO symbol for your size.

	Clarity		Sagebrush		White
	Sky		Tranquil		Mist
	Pool		Tidepool Heather		Silver
	Celestial		Teal		Ash
	Navy		Rainforest Heather		Asphalt Heather

Cardigan Body Repeat (Left Side)

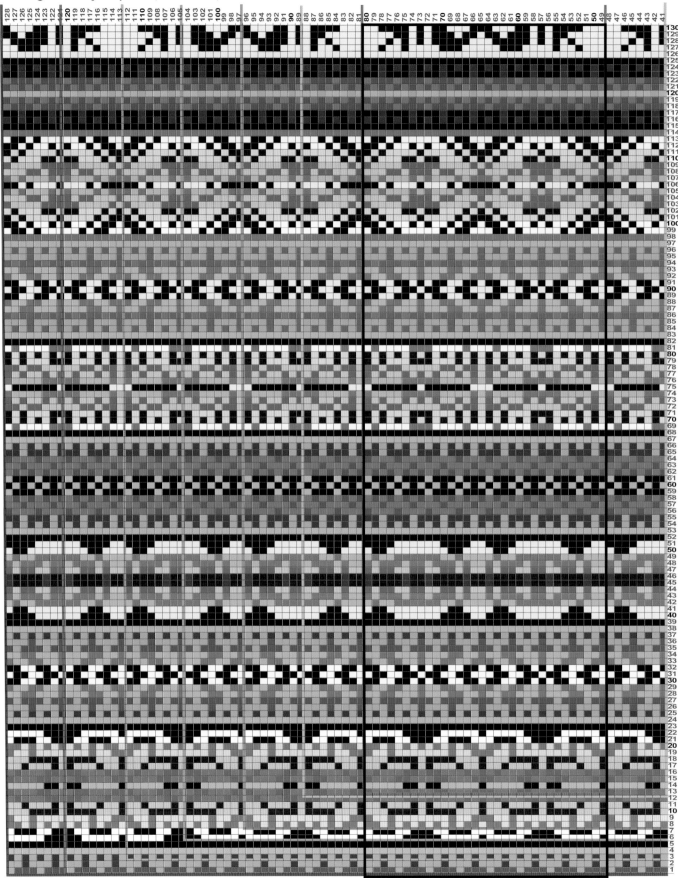

Continue reading from Right Side of chart on next page.

All sizes: repeat these 32 sts nine times

Cardigan Body Repeat (Right Side—start here)

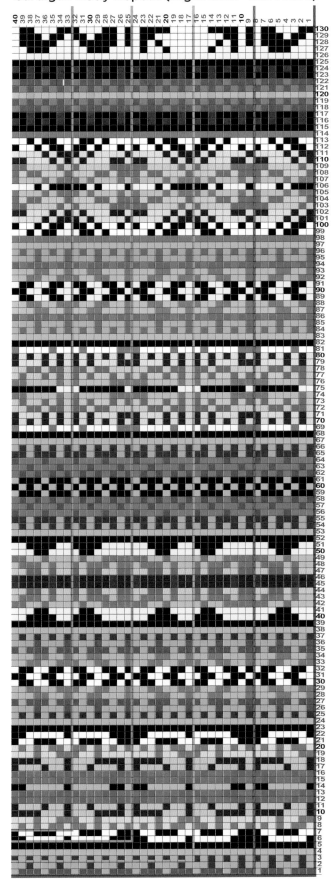

Read this chart from the first st and row outlined in your size, from right to left, until the last outlined st in your size. Note that size 36 is an even repeat of the center 32-st repeat.

Work this chart across the front and again across the back for a given round.

After completing this chart, move on to the Cardigan Armscye and Neck Shaping chart for your size.

	Clarity		White
	Sky		Mist
	Pool		Silver
	Celestial		Ash
	Navy		Asphalt Heather
	Sagebrush		
	Tranquil		
	Tidepool Heather		
	Teal		
	Rainforest Heather		

Cardigan Armscye and Neck Shaping: All Sizes (Right Side, second half)

Continue reading from Right Side of chart on next page.

Cardigan Armscye and Neck Shaping: All Sizes (Right Side—start here)

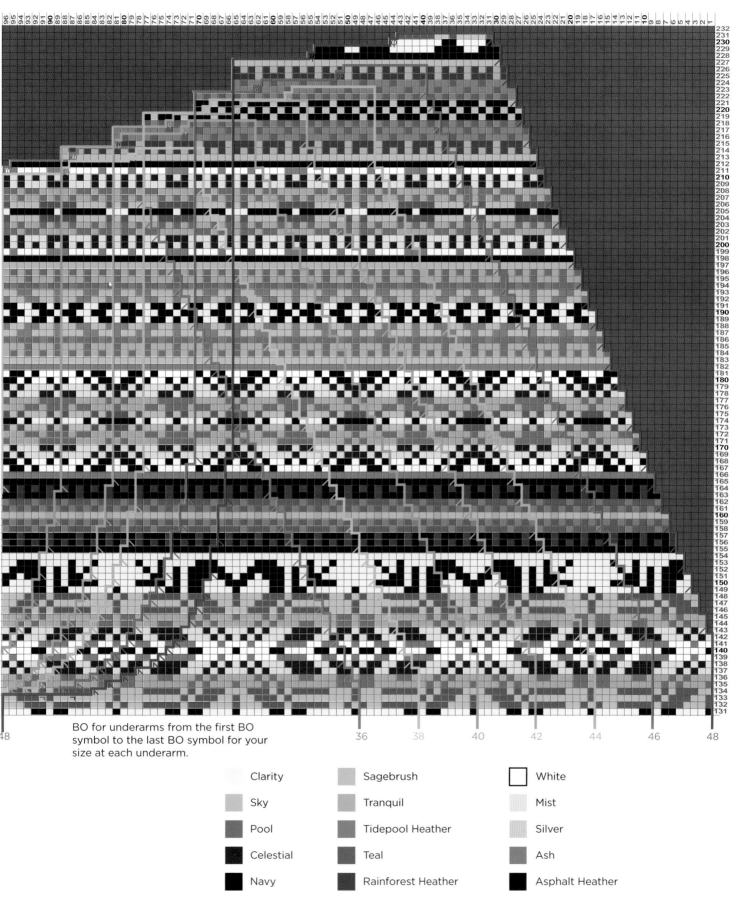

BO for underarms from the first BO symbol to the last BO symbol for your size at each underarm.

Clarity	Sagebrush	White
Sky	Tranquil	Mist
Pool	Tidepool Heather	Silver
Celestial	Teal	Ash
Navy	Rainforest Heather	Asphalt Heather

Cardigan Armscye and Neck Shaping: All Sizes (Left Side, second half—end here)

Continue reading from Left Side, first half of chart.

Cardigan Armscye and Neck Shaping: All Sizes (Left Side, first half)

Continue reading from Right Side, second half of chart.

	Clarity		Sagebrush		White
	Sky		Tranquil		Mist
	Pool		Tidepool Heather		Silver
	Celestial		Teal		Ash
	Navy		Rainforest Heather		Asphalt Heather

Colors used for each row

Row	Color 1	Color 2
1	Mist	Celestial
2	Mist	Celestial
3	White	Tidepool Heather
4	White	Tidepool Heather
5		Navy
6		Sagebrush
7	Rainforest Heather	Tranquil
8	Rainforest Heather	Tranquil
9	Teal	Tranquil
10	Teal	Tidepool Heather
11	Teal	Tidepool Heather
12	Sagebrush	Navy
13	Sagebrush	Navy
14	Sagebrush	Navy
15	Teal	Tidepool Heather
16	Teal	Tidepool Heather
17	Teal	Tranquil
18	Rainforest Heather	Tranquil
19	Rainforest Heather	Tranquil
20		Sagebrush
21		Navy
22	White	Navy
23	White	Navy
24	Mist	Tidepool Heather
25	Mist	Tidepool Heather
26	Silver	Tidepool Heather
27	Silver	Tidepool Heather
28	Ash	Celestial
29	Ash	Celestial
30	Asphalt Heather	Pool
31	Ash	Pool
32	Ash	Sky
33	Silver	Pool
34	Silver	Pool
35	Mist	Tidepool Heather
36	Mist	Tidepool Heather
37	White	Navy
38	White	Navy
39		Navy
40		Sagebrush
41	Rainforest Heather	Tranquil
42	Teal	Tranquil
43	Teal	Tranquil
44	Sagebrush	Tidepool Heather
45	Sagebrush	Tidepool Heather
46	White	Navy
47	White	Navy
48	White	Navy
49	Sagebrush	Tidepool Heather
50	Sagebrush	Tidepool Heather
51	Teal	Tranquil
52	Teal	Tranquil
53	Rainforest Heather	Tranquil
54		Sagebrush
55		Asphalt Heather
56	Clarity	Asphalt Heather
57	Clarity	Asphalt Heather
58	Sky	Ash
59	Sky	Ash
60	Pool	Silver
61	Celestial	Celestial
62	Celestial	Celestial
63	Pool	Silver
64	Sky	Ash
65	Sky	Ash
66	Clarity	Asphalt Heather
67	Clarity	Asphalt Heather
68		Asphalt Heather
69		Sagebrush
70	Rainforest Heather	Tranquil
71	Rainforest Heather	Tranquil
72	Teal	Tidepool Heather
73	Teal	Tidepool Heather
74	Teal	Tidepool Heather
75	Sagebrush	Navy
76	Sagebrush	Navy
77	Sagebrush	Navy
78	Teal	Tidepool Heather
79	Teal	Tidepool Heather
80	Teal	Tidepool Heather
81	Rainforest Heather	Tranquil
82	Rainforest Heather	Tranquil
83		Tranquil
84		Navy
85	White	Navy
86	Mist	Celestial
87	Mist	Celestial
88	Silver	Sky
89	Silver	Clarity
90	Ash	Clarity
91	Asphalt Heather	Sky
92	Ash	Celestial
93	Silver	Celestial
94	Silver	Pool
95	Mist	Celestial
96	Mist	Celestial
97	White	Tidepool Heather
98		Sagebrush
99		Navy
100	Pool	Tidepool Heather
101	Pool	Tranquil
102	Pool	Tranquil
103	Sky	Tranquil
104	Sky	Tidepool Heather
105	Clarity	Tidepool Heather
106	Clarity	Tidepool Heather
107	Clarity	Navy
108	Sky	Navy
109	Sky	Tidepool Heather
110	Pool	Tidepool Heather
111	Pool	Pool
112	Pool	Pool
113		Tidepool Heather
114		Tidepool Heather
115	White	Navy
116	White	Navy
117	Mist	Celestial
118	Mist	Celestial
119	Silver	Pool
120	Silver	Pool
121	Ash	Clarity
122	Asphalt Heather	Clarity
123	Ash	Sky
124	Silver	Pool
125	Silver	Pool
126	Mist	Celestial
127	Mist	Celestial
128	White	Navy
129	White	Navy
130		Tidepool Heather
131		Navy
132	Rainforest Heather	Navy
133	Rainforest Heather	Navy
134	Teal	Tidepool Heather
135	Teal	Tidepool Heather
136	Sagebrush	Tranquil
137	Teal	Tidepool Heather
138	Teal	Tidepool Heather
139	Rainforest Heather	Navy
140	Rainforest Heather	Navy
141		Navy
142		Clarity
143	Asphalt Heather	Clarity
144	Asphalt Heather	Clarity
145	Asphalt Heather	Clarity
146	Asphalt Heather	Clarity
147	Asphalt Heather	Clarity
148	Ash	Clarity
149	Ash	Sky
150	Ash	Sky
151	Silver	Pool
152	Silver	Pool
153	Mist	Celestial
154	Mist	Celestial
155	White	Tidepool Heather
156	White	Tidepool Heather
157	White	Navy
158	Mist	Celestial
159	Mist	Celestial
160	Silver	Pool
161	Silver	Pool
162	Ash	Sky
163	Ash	Sky
164	Ash	Sky
165	Asphalt Heather	Sky
166	Asphalt Heather	Clarity
167	Asphalt Heather	Clarity
168	Asphalt Heather	Clarity
169	Asphalt Heather	Clarity
170		Clarity
171		Navy
172	Rainforest Heather	Navy
173	Rainforest Heather	Navy
174	Teal	Tidepool Heather
175	Teal	Tidepool Heather
176	Sagebrush	Tranquil
177	Teal	Tidepool Heather
178	Teal	Tidepool Heather
179	Rainforest Heather	Navy
180	Rainforest Heather	Navy
181	Silver	Navy
182		Tidepool Heather
183	White	Navy
184	White	Navy
185	Mist	Celestial
186	Mist	Celestial
187	Silver	Pool
188	Silver	Pool
189	Ash	Clarity
190	Asphalt Heather	Clarity
191	Ash	Sky
192	Silver	Pool
193	Silver	Pool
194	Mist	Celestial
195	Mist	Celestial
196	White	Navy
197	White	Navy
198		Tidepool Heather

NORTH SEA BODY

Colors used for each row

Row	Color 1	Color 2
1	Teal	Tranquil
2	Rainforest Heather	Tranquil
3	Rainforest Heather	Tranquil
4		Sagebrush
5		Navy
6	White	Navy
7	White	Navy
8	Mist	Tidepool Heather
9	Mist	Navy
10	Silver	Celestial
11	Silver	Celestial
12	Ash	Pool
13	Ash	Pool
14	Asphalt Heather	Sky
15	Ash	Pool
16	Ash	Pool
17	Silver	Celestial
18	Silver	Celestial
19	Mist	Tidepool Heather
20	Mist	Pool
21	White	Pool
22	White	Navy
23		Navy
24		Sagebrush
25	Rainforest Heather	Tranquil
26	Teal	Tranquil
27	Teal	Tranquil
28	Sagebrush	Tidepool Heather
29	Sagebrush	Tidepool Heather
30	White	Navy
31	White	Navy
32	White	Navy
33	Sagebrush	Tidepool Heather
34	Sagebrush	Tidepool Heather
35	Teal	Tidepool Heather
36	Teal	Tranquil
37	Rainforest Heather	Tranquil
38		Tranquil
39		Sagebrush
40	Clarity	Asphalt Heather
41	Clarity	Asphalt Heather
42	Sky	Asphalt Heather
43	Sky	Ash
44	Pool	Ash
45	Celestial	Silver
46	Celestial	Rainforest Heather
47	Pool	Silver
48	Sky	Ash
49	Sky	Ash
50	Clarity	Asphalt Heather
51	Clarity	Asphalt Heather
52		Asphalt Heather
53		Sagebrush
54	Rainforest Heather	Tranquil
55	Rainforest Heather	Tidepool Heather
56	Teal	Navy
57	Teal	Tidepool Heather
58	Teal	Tidepool Heather
59	Sagebrush	Navy
60	Sagebrush	Navy
61	Pool	Celestial
62	Teal	Celestial
63	Pool	Tidepool Heather
64	Teal	Tidepool Heather
65	Rainforest Heather	Tranquil
66	Pool	Tranquil
67		Sagebrush
68	White	Navy
69	White	Navy
70	Mist	Tidepool Heather
71	Mist	Celestial
72	Silver	Pool
73	Silver	Pool
74	Ash	Sky
75	Asphalt Heather	Clarity
76	Ash	Sky
77	Silver	Pool
78	Silver	Pool
79	Mist	Celestial
80	Mist	Celestial
81	White	Tidepool Heather
82		Navy
83		Sagebrush
84	Pool	Tranquil
85	Pool	Tranquil
86	Pool	Tidepool Heather
87	Sky	Tidepool Heather
88	Sky	Tidepool Heather
89	Clarity	Navy
90	Clarity	Navy
91	Clarity	Navy
92	Sky	Tidepool Heather
93	Ash	Tidepool Heather
94	Pool	Silver
95	Rainforest Heather	Tranquil
96	Rainforest Heather	Tranquil
97	Silver	Sagebrush
98		Tidepool Heather
99	White	Navy
100	White	Navy
101	Mist	Celestial
102	Mist	Celestial
103	Silver	Pool
104	Silver	Pool
105	Ash	Sky
106	Asphalt Heather	Clarity
107	Ash	Sky
108	Silver	Pool
109	Silver	Pool
110	Mist	Celestial
111	Mist	Celestial
112	White	Asphalt Heather
113	White	Asphalt Heather
114		Sagebrush
115		Tidepool Heather
116	Rainforest Heather	Navy
117	Rainforest Heather	Navy
118	Teal	Tidepool Heather
119	Teal	Tidepool Heather
120	Sagebrush	Tranquil
121	Teal	Tidepool Heather
122	Teal	Tidepool Heather
123	Rainforest Heather	Tidepool Heather
124	Rainforest Heather	Navy
125		Navy
126		Clarity
127	Asphalt Heather	Clarity
128	Asphalt Heather	Clarity
129	Asphalt Heather	Clarity
130	Asphalt Heather	Clarity
131	Asphalt Heather	Clarity
132	Ash	Clarity
133	Ash	Sky
134	Ash	Sky
135	Silver	Sky
136	Silver	Pool
137	Mist	Celestial
138	Mist	Tidepool Heather
139	White	Navy
140	White	Navy
141	White	Tidepool Heather
142	Mist	Celestial
143	Mist	Celestial
144	Silver	Pool
145	Silver	Pool
146	Ash	Sky
147	Ash	Sky
148	Ash	Sky
149	Ash	Clarity
150	Asphalt Heather	Clarity
151	Ash	Clarity
152	Ash	Clarity
153	Asphalt Heather	Clarity
154		Celestial
155		Navy
156	Rainforest Heather	Navy
157	Rainforest Heather	Navy
158	Teal	Sagebrush
159	Teal	Navy
160	Sagebrush	Tranquil
161	Teal	Tidepool Heather
162	Teal	Tidepool Heather
163	Rainforest Heather	Tidepool Heather
164	Rainforest Heather	Navy
165		Navy
166		Tidepool Heather
167	White	Navy
168	White	Navy
169	Mist	Celestial
170	Mist	Celestial
171	Silver	Pool
172	Silver	Pool
173	Ash	Sky
174	Asphalt Heather	Clarity
175	Ash	Sky
176	Silver	Pool
177	Silver	Pool
178	Mist	Celestial
179	Mist	Celestial
180	White	Navy
181	White	Navy
182		Tidepool Heather
183		Sagebrush
184	Pool	Tranquil
185	Pool	Tranquil
186	Pool	Tidepool Heather
187	Sky	Tidepool Heather
188	Sky	Tidepool Heather
189	Clarity	Navy
190	Clarity	Navy
191	Clarity	Navy
192	Sky	Tidepool Heather
193	Sky	Tidepool Heather
194	Pool	Tidepool Heather
195	Pool	Tranquil
196	Pool	Tranquil
197		Sagebrush
198		Navy
199	White	Navy
200	Mist	Celestial
201	Mist	Celestial
202	Silver	Pool
203	Silver	Pool
204	Ash	Sky
205	Asphalt Heather	Clarity
206	Ash	Sky
207	Silver	Pool
208	Silver	Pool
209	Mist	Celestial
210	Mist	Celestial
211	White	Tidepool Heather
212		Navy
213		Tranquil
214	Rainforest Heather	Tranquil
215	Rainforest Heather	Tranquil
216	Teal	Tidepool Heather
217	Teal	Tidepool Heather
218	Teal	Tidepool Heather
219	Sagebrush	Navy
220	Sagebrush	Navy
221	Sagebrush	Navy
222	Teal	Tidepool Heather
223	Teal	Tidepool Heather
224	Teal	Tidepool Heather
225	Rainforest Heather	Tranquil
226	Rainforest Heather	Tranquil
227		Sagebrush
228		Asphalt Heather
229	Clarity	Asphalt Heather
230	Clarity	Asphalt Heather
231	Sky	Ash
232	Sky	Ash

Dogwood Blossoms:
AUTUMN COLORWAY

YARN COLORS

3 balls:
MC Garnet Heather 24015

2 balls each:
Mongoose 25084
Merlot Heather 24014
Hazelnut 24563

1 ball each:
Almond 24560
Doe 24240
Bison 24562
Masala 24248
Orange 24554
Golden Heather 24005
Kumquat Heather 25008
Rose Hip 24556
Raspberry Heather 24247
Serrano 24553
Pimento 24246

Sleeve

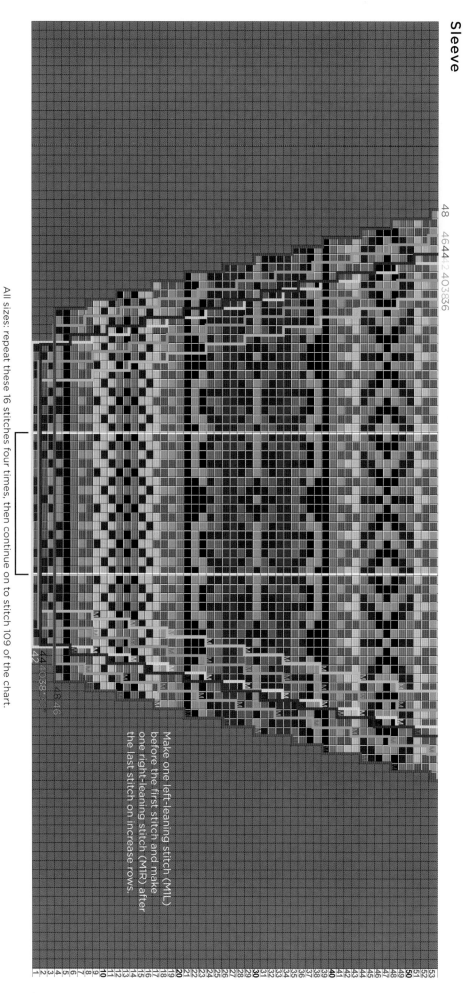

All sizes: repeat these 16 stitches four times, then continue on to stitch 109 of the chart.

*Sizes 36 and 38 share the same stitch count and shaping instructions until the sleeve cap; use the line marked 38 for both sizes.

Make one left-leaning stitch (M1L) before the first stitch and make one right-leaning stitch (M1R) after the last stitch on increase rows.

Almond

Doe

Mongoose

Bison

Merlot Heather

Hazelnut

Masala

Orange

Golden Heather

Kumquat Heather

Rose Hip

Raspberry Heather

Serrano

Pimento

Garnet Heather

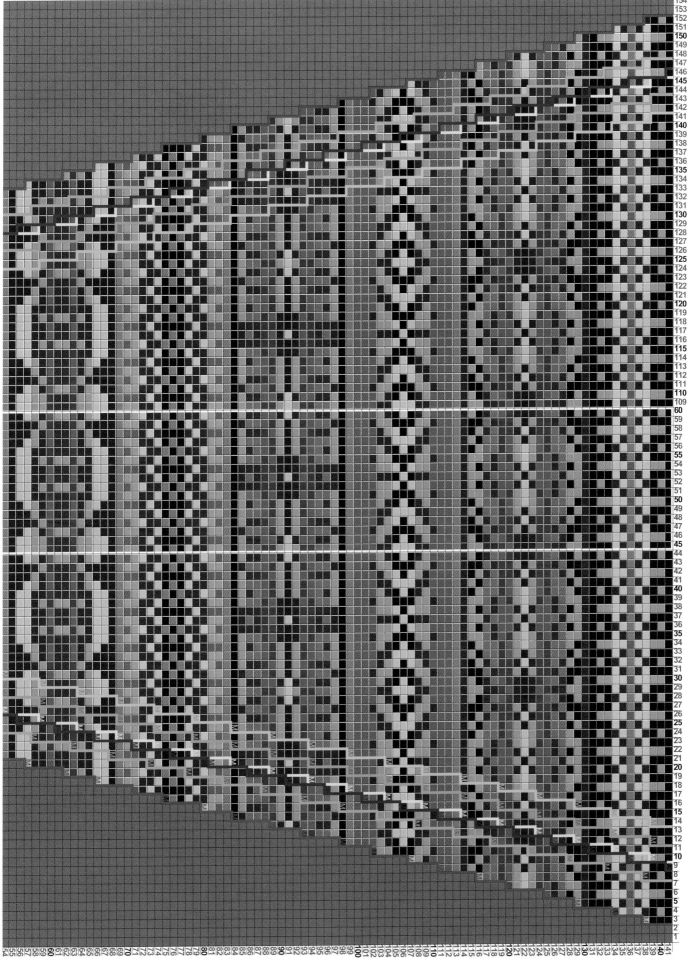

Sleeve Cap (Left Side)

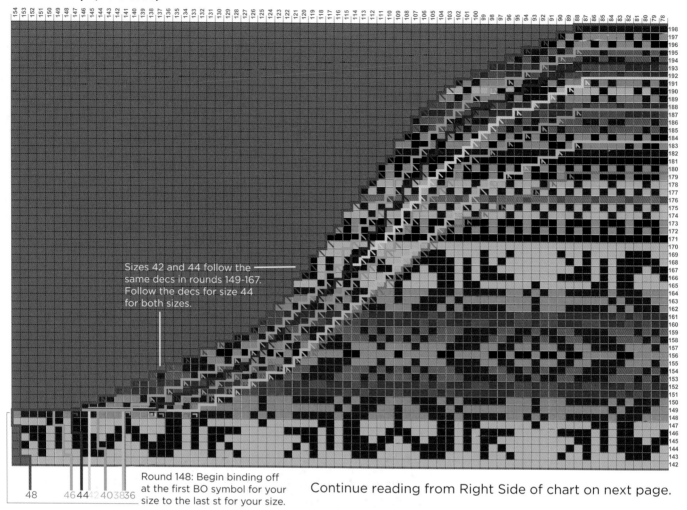

Sizes 42 and 44 follow the same decs in rounds 149-167. Follow the decs for size 44 for both sizes.

Round 148: Begin binding off at the first BO symbol for your size to the last st for your size.

48   46 44 42 40 38 36

Continue reading from Right Side of chart on next page.

Reading Charts

All charts are read from right to left, bottom to top, as all pieces are worked in the round.

Binding Off

Because there are many sizes represented in each chart, not all bind-off marks are shown. When sts are bound off, they will still appear in the row in which they are bound off, but not in subsequent rows.

However, sts removed by decs will not appear in the row from which they are removed. When a set of bound-off sts is followed by decs on the next round, those removed sts will widen the area of 'No Stitch' above the bound-off sts.

Where bound-off sections cross over the end/beginning of a round, the BO sts will appear at the end of the first round and then over the first several sts of the following round. When these are followed immediately by a dec, the st that remains on the RH needle after the last bound off st becomes part of the dec. For instance, if a BO st is followed directly by a K3tog, slip the st back to the LH needle and knit it together with the following two sts.

	Almond		Golden Heather
	Doe		Kumquat Heather
	Mongoose		Rose Hip
	Bison		Raspberry Heather
	Merlot Heather		Serrano
	Hazelnut		Pimento
	Masala		Garnet Heather
	Orange		

No decreases in the round following BO

Bound off stitches

A double decrease in the row following the BO results in two 'no stitch' spaces next to those left by the BO sts.

Bound off stitches

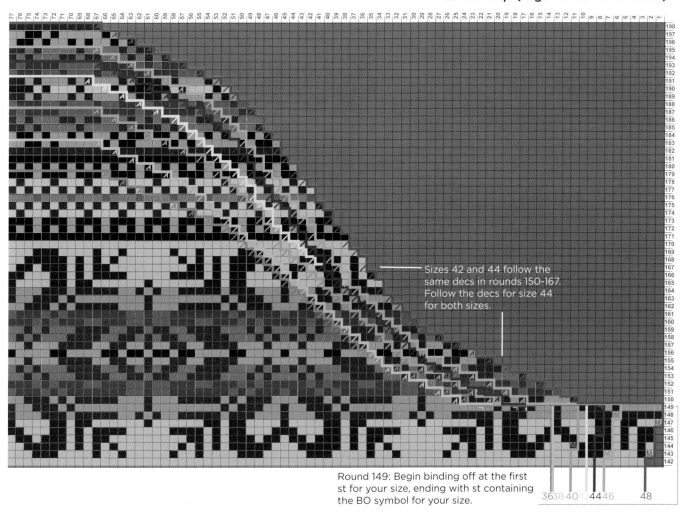

Sizes 42 and 44 follow the same decs in rounds 150-167. Follow the decs for size 44 for both sizes.

Round 149: Begin binding off at the first st for your size, ending with st containing the BO symbol for your size.

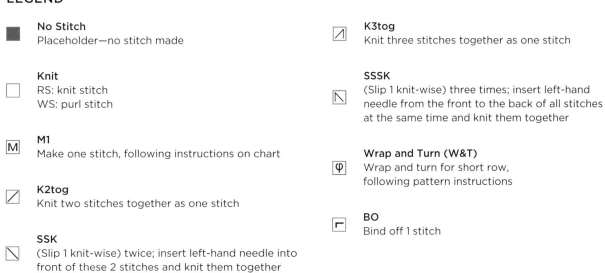

LEGEND

No Stitch
Placeholder—no stitch made

Knit
RS: knit stitch
WS: purl stitch

M1
Make one stitch, following instructions on chart

K2tog
Knit two stitches together as one stitch

SSK
(Slip 1 knit-wise) twice; insert left-hand needle into front of these 2 stitches and knit them together

K3tog
Knit three stitches together as one stitch

SSSK
(Slip 1 knit-wise) three times; insert left-hand needle from the front to the back of all stitches at the same time and knit them together

Wrap and Turn (W&T)
Wrap and turn for short row, following pattern instructions

BO
Bind off 1 stitch

Pullover Body Repeat: Sizes 36", 40", 44", 48"

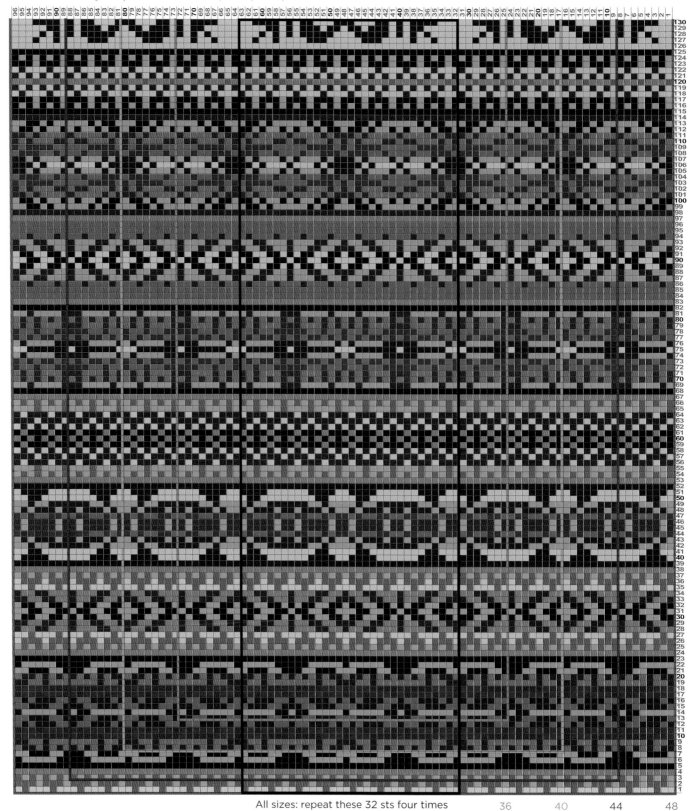

All sizes: repeat these 32 sts four times

36   40   44   48

Read this chart from the first st and row outlined in your size, from right to left, until the last outlined st in your size. Work this chart across the front and again across the back for a given round.

After completing this chart, move on to the Pullover Armscye and Neck Shaping chart for your size.

Pullover Body Repeats: Sizes 38", 42", 46"

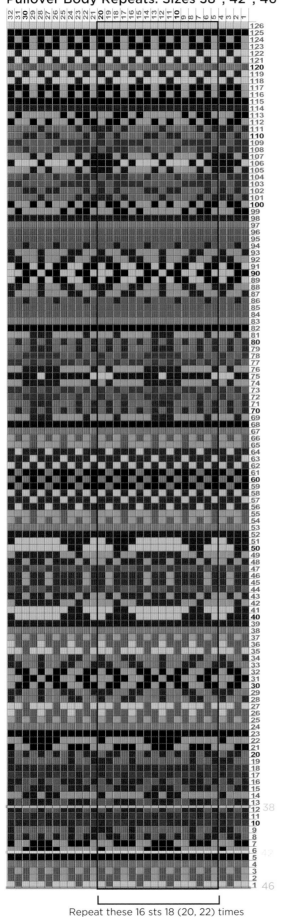

Repeat these 16 sts 18 (20, 22) times

Almond		Golden Heather	
Doe		Kumquat Heather	
Mongoose		Rose Hip	
Bison		Raspberry Heather	
Merlot Heather		Serrano	
Hazelnut		Pimento	
Masala		Garnet Heather	
Orange			

Pullover Armscye and Neck Shaping: Sizes 36″, 40″, 44″, 48″ (Left Side)

Round 133: Begin binding off at st containing the BO symbol for your size, ending with the last st for your size.

Continue reading from Right Side of chart on next page.

This chart shows both the front and back of the sweater. For the front, follow neck decs as shown; for the back, work across the whole back in pattern until the bind-off at the back neck.

Sizes 40 and 44 share the same pattern of neck decs; follow decs for size 44 for both sizes.

Pullover Armscye and Neck Shaping: Sizes 36″, 40″, 44″, 48″ (Right Side—start here)

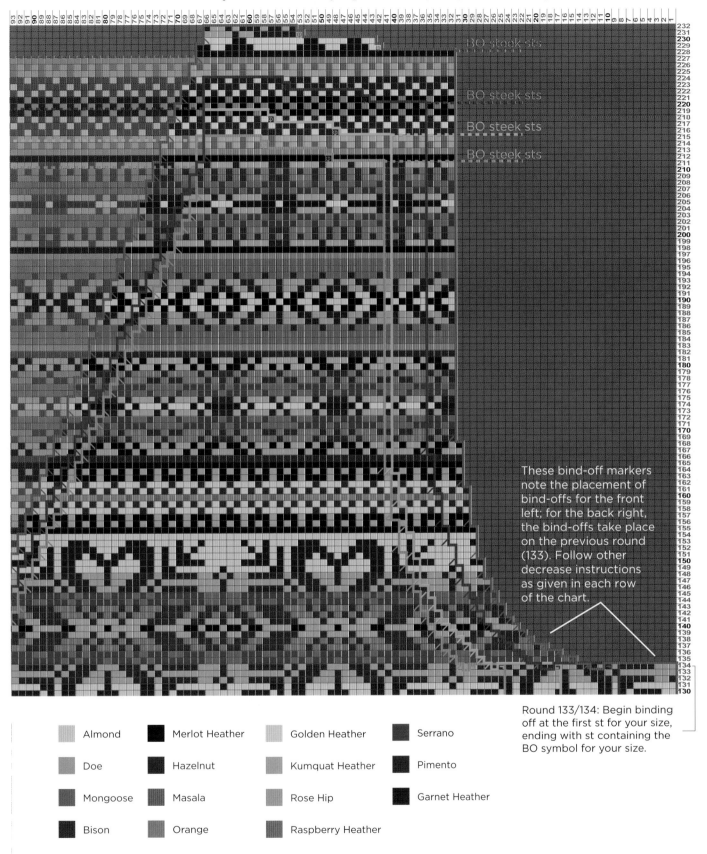

BO steek sts

BO steek sts

BO steek sts

BO steek sts

These bind-off markers note the placement of bind-offs for the front left; for the back right, the bind-offs take place on the previous round (133). Follow other decrease instructions as given in each row of the chart.

Round 133/134: Begin binding off at the first st for your size, ending with st containing the BO symbol for your size.

	Almond		Merlot Heather		Golden Heather		Serrano
	Doe		Hazelnut		Kumquat Heather		Pimento
	Mongoose		Masala		Rose Hip		Garnet Heather
	Bison		Orange		Raspberry Heather		

Pullover Armscye and Neck Shaping: Sizes 38", 42", 46" (Left Side)

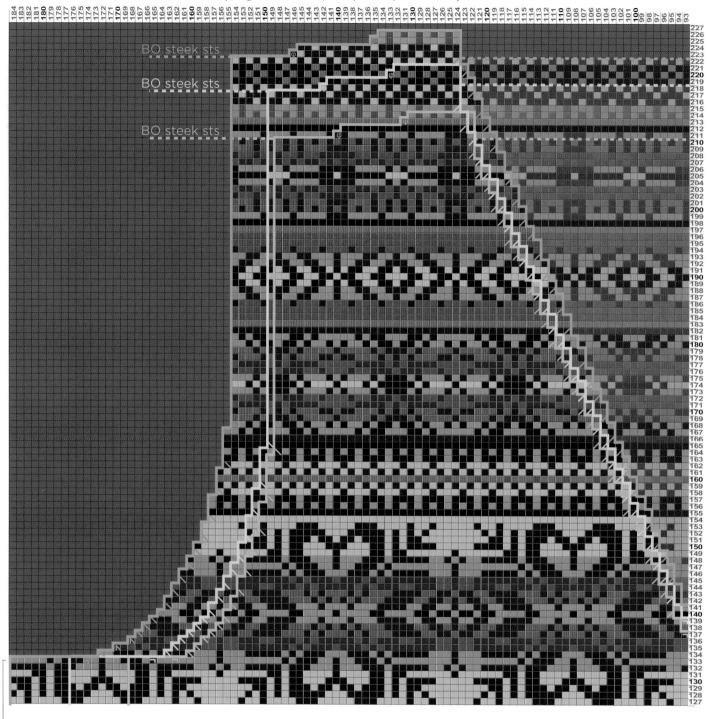

BO steek sts

BO steek sts

BO steek sts

Round 133: Begin binding off at st containing the BO symbol for your size, ending with the last st for your size.

Continue reading from Right Side of chart on next page.

This chart shows both the front and back of the sweater. For the front, follow neck decs as shown; for the back, work across the whole back in pattern until the bind-off at the back neck.

Pullover Armscye and Neck Shaping: Sizes 38″, 42″, 46″ (Right Side—start here)

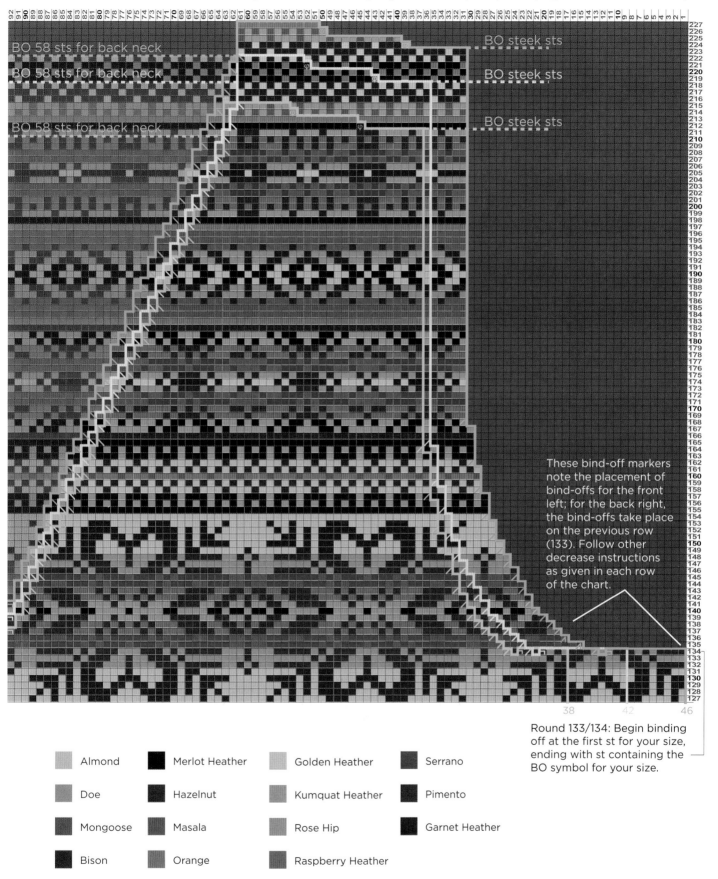

BO 58 sts for back neck

BO 58 sts for back neck

BO 58 sts for back neck

BO steek sts

BO steek sts

BO steek sts

These bind-off markers note the placement of bind-offs for the front left; for the back right, the bind-offs take place on the previous row (133). Follow other decrease instructions as given in each row of the chart.

Round 133/134: Begin binding off at the first st for your size, ending with st containing the BO symbol for your size.

	Almond		Merlot Heather		Golden Heather		Serrano
	Doe		Hazelnut		Kumquat Heather		Pimento
	Mongoose		Masala		Rose Hip		Garnet Heather
	Bison		Orange		Raspberry Heather		

Cardigan Body Repeat (Left Side)

Continue reading from Right Side of chart on next page.

All sizes: repeat these 32 sts nine times

Cardigan Body Repeat (Right Side—start here)

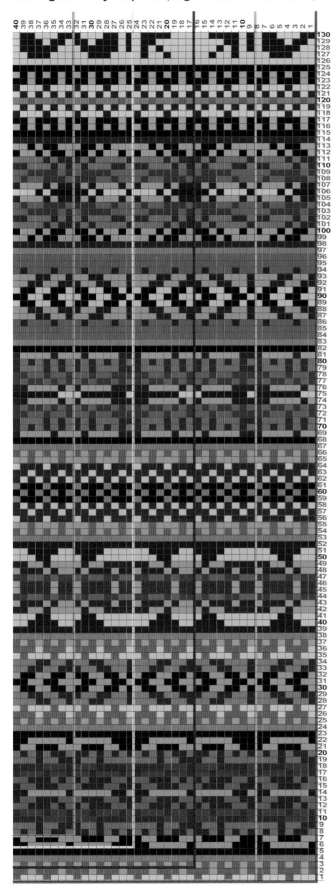

Read this chart from the first st and row outlined in your size, from right to left, until the last outlined st in your size. Note that size 36 is an even repeat of the center 32-st repeat.

Work this chart across the front and again across the back for a given round.

After completing this chart, move on to the Cardigan Armscye and Neck Shaping chart for your size.

Almond		Golden Heather
Doe		Kumquat Heather
Mongoose		Rose Hip
Bison		Raspberry Heather
Merlot Heather		Serrano
Hazelnut		Pimento
Masala		Garnet Heather
Orange		

Continue reading from Right Side of chart on next page.

Cardigan Armscye and Neck Shaping: All Sizes (Right Side—start here)

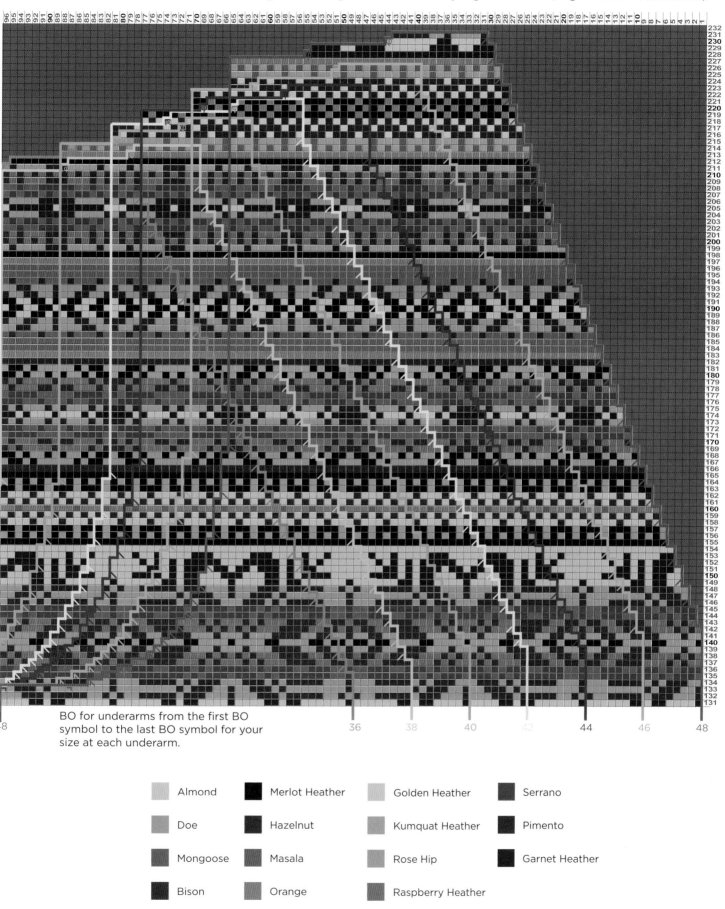

BO for underarms from the first BO symbol to the last BO symbol for your size at each underarm.

Almond

Doe

Mongoose

Bison

Merlot Heather

Hazelnut

Masala

Orange

Golden Heather

Kumquat Heather

Rose Hip

Raspberry Heather

Serrano

Pimento

Garnet Heather

Cardigan Armscye and Neck Shaping: All Sizes (Left Side, second half—end here)

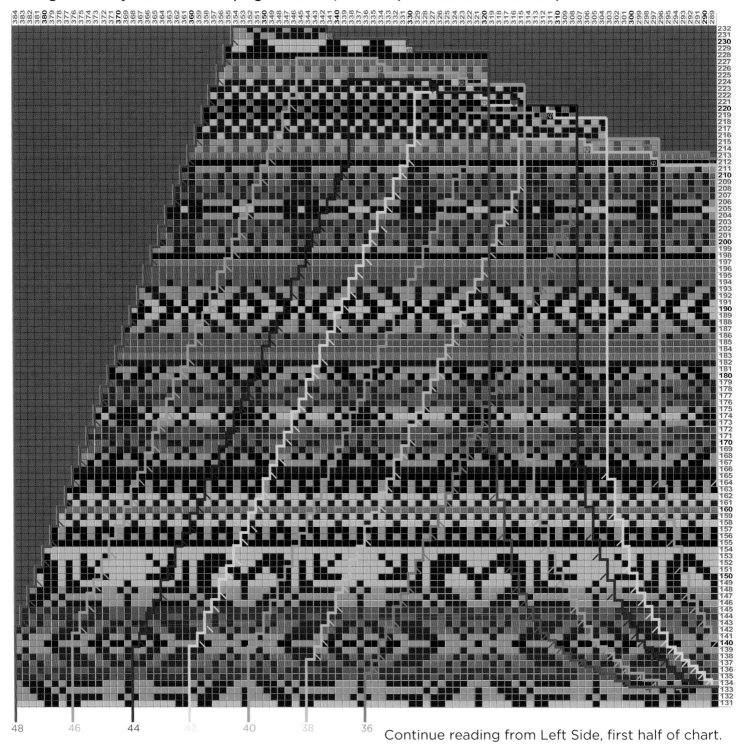

Continue reading from Left Side, first half of chart.

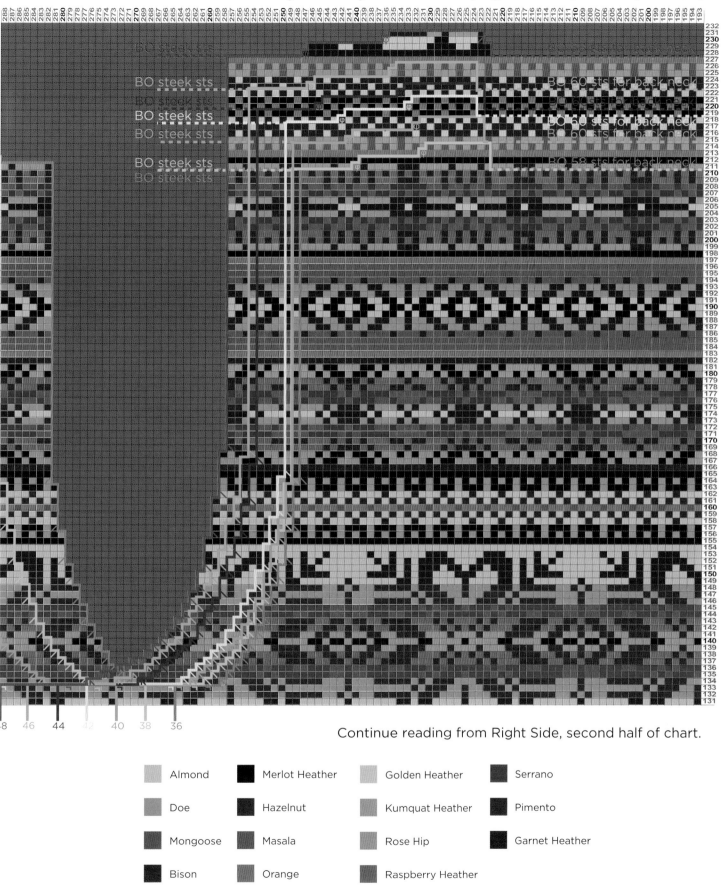

Continue reading from Right Side, second half of chart.

	Almond		Merlot Heather		Golden Heather		Serrano
	Doe		Hazelnut		Kumquat Heather		Pimento
	Mongoose		Masala		Rose Hip		Garnet Heather
	Bison		Orange		Raspberry Heather		

Colors used for each row

Row	Color 1	Color 2
1	Raspberry Heather	Bison
2	Raspberry Heather	Bison
3	Rose Hip	Hazelnut
4	Rose Hip	Hazelnut
5	Orange	Merlot Heather
6	Orange	Orange
7	Kumquat Heather	Masala
8	Kumquat Heather	Masala
9	Golden Heather	Hazelnut
10	Golden Heather	Hazelnut
11	Golden Heather	Hazelnut
12	Orange	Merlot Heather
13	Orange	Merlot Heather
14	Orange	Merlot Heather
15	Golden Heather	Hazelnut
16	Golden Heather	Hazelnut
17	Golden Heather	Masala
18	Kumquat Heather	Masala
19	Kumquat Heather	Masala
20	Orange	Orange
21	Rose Hip	Merlot Heather
22	Rose Hip	Merlot Heather
23	Rose Hip	Merlot Heather
24	Raspberry Heather	Hazelnut
25	Raspberry Heather	Hazelnut
26	Serrano	Bison
27	Serrano	Bison
28	Pimento	Mongoose
29	Pimento	Mongoose
30	Garnet Heather	Doe
31	Pimento	Mongoose
32	Pimento	Mongoose
33	Serrano	Bison
34	Serrano	Bison
35	Raspberry Heather	Hazelnut
36	Raspberry Heather	Hazelnut
37	Rose Hip	Merlot Heather
38	Rose Hip	Merlot Heather
39	Orange	Orange
40	Orange	Orange
41	Kumquat Heather	Masala
42	Golden Heather	Masala
43	Golden Heather	Hazelnut
44	Orange	Hazelnut
45	Orange	Hazelnut
46	Rose Hip	Merlot Heather
47	Rose Hip	Merlot Heather
48	Rose Hip	Merlot Heather
49	Orange	Hazelnut
50	Orange	Hazelnut
51	Golden Heather	Hazelnut
52	Golden Heather	Masala
53	Kumquat Heather	Masala
54	Orange	Masala
55	Almond	Garnet Heather
56	Almond	Garnet Heather
57	Almond	Garnet Heather
58	Doe	Pimento
59	Doe	Serrano
60	Mongoose	Serrano
61	Bison	Kumquat Heather
62	Bison	Kumquat Heather
63	Mongoose	Serrano
64	Doe	Serrano
65	Pimento	Pimento
66	Almond	Garnet Heather
67	Almond	Garnet Heather
68	Almond	Garnet Heather
69	Kumquat Heather	Orange
70	Kumquat Heather	Masala
71	Kumquat Heather	Masala
72	Golden Heather	Hazelnut
73	Golden Heather	Hazelnut
74	Golden Heather	Hazelnut
75	Orange	Merlot Heather
76	Orange	Merlot Heather
77	Orange	Merlot Heather
78	Golden Heather	Masala
79	Golden Heather	Hazelnut
80	Golden Heather	Hazelnut
81	Kumquat Heather	Masala
82	Kumquat Heather	Masala
83	Rose Hip	Bison
84	Rose Hip	Mongoose
85	Rose Hip	Mongoose
86	Raspberry Heather	Bison
87	Raspberry Heather	Bison
88	Serrano	Mongoose
89	Serrano	Mongoose
90	Pimento	Doe
91	Garnet Heather	Almond
92	Pimento	Doe
93	Serrano	Mongoose
94	Serrano	Mongoose
95	Raspberry Heather	Bison
96	Raspberry Heather	Bison
97	Rose Hip	Hazelnut
98	Doe	Merlot Heather
99	Doe	Masala
100	Mongoose	Masala
101	Mongoose	Hazelnut
102	Mongoose	Hazelnut
103	Doe	Doe
104	Doe	Doe
105	Almond	Merlot Heather
106	Almond	Merlot Heather
107	Almond	Merlot Heather
108	Doe	Doe
109	Doe	Doe
110	Mongoose	Hazelnut
111	Mongoose	Hazelnut
112	Mongoose	Masala
113	Doe	Masala
114	Doe	Hazelnut
115	Rose Hip	Hazelnut
116	Rose Hip	Merlot Heather
117	Raspberry Heather	Bison
118	Raspberry Heather	Bison
119	Serrano	Mongoose
120	Serrano	Mongoose
121	Pimento	Doe
122	Garnet Heather	Almond
123	Pimento	Doe
124	Serrano	Mongoose
125	Serrano	Mongoose
126	Raspberry Heather	Bison
127	Raspberry Heather	Bison
128	Rose Hip	Merlot Heather
129	Rose Hip	Hazelnut
130	Orange	Hazelnut
131	Serrano	Merlot Heather
132	Kumquat Heather	Merlot Heather
133	Kumquat Heather	Merlot Heather
134	Golden Heather	Hazelnut
135	Golden Heather	Hazelnut
136	Orange	Merlot Heather
137	Golden Heather	Hazelnut
138	Golden Heather	Hazelnut
139	Kumquat Heather	Merlot Heather
140	Kumquat Heather	Masala
141	Kumquat Heather	Masala
142	Garnet Heather	Almond
143	Garnet Heather	Almond
144	Garnet Heather	Almond
145	Garnet Heather	Almond
146	Garnet Heather	Almond
147	Garnet Heather	Almond
148	Pimento	Doe
149	Pimento	Doe
150	Pimento	Doe
151	Serrano	Mongoose
152	Serrano	Mongoose
153	Raspberry Heather	Bison
154	Raspberry Heather	Bison
155	Rose Hip	Merlot Heather
156	Rose Hip	Merlot Heather
157	Rose Hip	Merlot Heather
158	Raspberry Heather	Bison
159	Raspberry Heather	Bison
160	Serrano	Mongoose
161	Serrano	Mongoose
162	Pimento	Doe
163	Pimento	Doe
164	Pimento	Doe
165	Garnet Heather	Almond
166	Garnet Heather	Almond
167	Garnet Heather	Almond
168	Garnet Heather	Almond
169	Garnet Heather	Almond
170	Almond	Almond
171	Golden Heather	Hazelnut
172	Kumquat Heather	Masala
173	Kumquat Heather	Masala
174	Golden Heather	Hazelnut
175	Golden Heather	Hazelnut
176	Orange	Merlot Heather
177	Golden Heather	Hazelnut
178	Golden Heather	Hazelnut
179	Kumquat Heather	Masala
180	Kumquat Heather	Masala
181	Kumquat Heather	Masala
182	Rose Hip	Hazelnut
183	Rose Hip	Merlot Heather
184	Rose Hip	Merlot Heather
185	Raspberry Heather	Bison
186	Raspberry Heather	Bison
187	Serrano	Mongoose
188	Pimento	Doe
189	Garnet Heather	Almond
190	Garnet Heather	Almond
191	Pimento	Doe
192	Serrano	Mongoose
193	Serrano	Mongoose
194	Raspberry Heather	Bison
195	Raspberry Heather	Bison
196	Rose Hip	Merlot Heather
197	Rose Hip	Merlot Heather
198	Rose Hip	Hazelnut

Colors used for each row

Row	Colors
1	Golden Heather, Masala
2	Kumquat Heather, Masala
3	Kumquat Heather, Masala
4	Merlot Heather
5	Rose Hip, Merlot Heather
6	Rose Hip, Merlot Heather
7	Rose Hip, Merlot Heather
8	Raspberry Heather, Hazelnut
9	Raspberry Heather, Hazelnut
10	Serrano, Bison
11	Serrano, Bison
12	Pimento, Mongoose
13	Pimento, Mongoose
14	Garnet Heather, Doe
15	Pimento, Mongoose
16	Pimento, Mongoose
17	Serrano, Bison
18	Serrano, Bison
19	Raspberry Heather, Hazelnut
20	Raspberry Heather, Hazelnut
21	Rose Hip, Merlot Heather
22	Rose Hip, Merlot Heather
23	Merlot Heather
24	Orange
25	Kumquat Heather, Masala
26	Golden Heather, Masala
27	Golden Heather, Masala
28	Orange, Hazelnut
29	Orange, Hazelnut
30	Rose Hip, Merlot Heather
31	Rose Hip, Merlot Heather
32	Rose Hip, Merlot Heather
33	Orange, Hazelnut
34	Orange, Hazelnut
35	Golden Heather, Masala
36	Golden Heather, Masala
37	Kumquat Heather, Masala
38	Orange
39	Garnet Heather
40	Almond, Garnet Heather
41	Almond, Garnet Heather
42	Doe, Pimento
43	Doe, Pimento
44	Mongoose, Serrano
45	Bison, Kumquat Heather
46	Bison, Serrano
47	Mongoose, Serrano
48	Doe, Pimento
49	Doe, Pimento
50	Almond, Garnet Heather
51	Almond, Garnet Heather
52	Orange
53	Masala
54	Kumquat Heather, Masala
55	Kumquat Heather, Masala
56	Golden Heather, Hazelnut
57	Golden Heather, Hazelnut
58	Golden Heather, Hazelnut
59	Orange, Merlot Heather
60	Orange, Merlot Heather
61	Orange, Hazelnut
62	Golden Heather, Hazelnut
63	Golden Heather, Hazelnut
64	Golden Heather, Hazelnut
65	Kumquat Heather, Masala
66	Kumquat Heather, Masala
67	Orange
68	Hazelnut
69	Rose Hip, Merlot Heather
70	Raspberry Heather, Bison
71	Raspberry Heather, Bison
72	Serrano, Mongoose
73	Serrano, Mongoose
74	Pimento, Doe
75	Garnet Heather, Almond
76	Pimento, Doe
77	Serrano, Mongoose
78	Serrano, Mongoose
79	Raspberry Heather, Bison
80	Raspberry Heather, Bison
81	Rose Hip, Hazelnut
82	Merlot Heather
83	Orange
84	Mongoose, Masala
85	Mongoose, Masala
86	Mongoose, Masala
87	Doe, Hazelnut
88	Doe, Hazelnut
89	Almond, Merlot Heather
90	Almond, Merlot Heather
91	Almond, Merlot Heather
92	Doe, Hazelnut
93	Doe, Hazelnut
94	Mongoose, Masala
95	Mongoose, Masala
96	Mongoose, Masala
97	Orange
98	Hazelnut
99	Rose Hip, Merlot Heather
100	Rose Hip, Merlot Heather
101	Raspberry Heather, Bison
102	Raspberry Heather, Bison
103	Serrano, Mongoose
104	Serrano, Mongoose
105	Pimento, Doe
106	Pimento, Almond
107	Pimento, Doe
108	Serrano, Mongoose
109	Serrano, Mongoose
110	Raspberry Heather, Bison
111	Raspberry Heather, Bison
112	Rose Hip, Merlot Heather
113	Rose Hip, Merlot Heather
114	Hazelnut
115	Merlot Heather
116	Kumquat Heather, Merlot Heather
117	Kumquat Heather, Hazelnut
118	Golden Heather, Hazelnut
119	Golden Heather, Masala
120	Orange, Hazelnut
121	Golden Heather, Hazelnut
122	Golden Heather, Hazelnut
123	Kumquat Heather, Hazelnut
124	Kumquat Heather, Merlot Heather
125	Merlot Heather
126	Almond
127	Garnet Heather, Merlot Heather
128	Garnet Heather, Merlot Heather
129	Garnet Heather, Merlot Heather
130	Garnet Heather, Hazelnut
131	Garnet Heather, Hazelnut
132	Pimento, Bison
133	Pimento, Doe
134	Pimento, Doe
135	Serrano, Mongoose
136	Serrano, Almond
137	Raspberry Heather, Bison
138	Raspberry Heather, Doe
139	Rose Hip, Mongoose
140	Rose Hip, Hazelnut
141	Rose Hip, Hazelnut
142	Raspberry Heather, Bison
143	Raspberry Heather, Bison
144	Serrano, Mongoose
145	Serrano, Mongoose
146	Pimento, Doe
147	Pimento, Doe
148	Pimento, Almond
149	Garnet Heather, Almond
150	Garnet Heather, Almond
151	Garnet Heather, Almond
152	Garnet Heather, Almond
153	Garnet Heather, Almond
154	Almond
155	Almond, Mongoose
156	Kumquat Heather, Mongoose
157	Kumquat Heather, Mongoose
158	Golden Heather, Doe
159	Golden Heather, Doe
160	Orange, Doe
161	Golden Heather, Hazelnut
162	Golden Heather, Hazelnut
163	Golden Heather, Merlot Heather
164	Kumquat Heather, Hazelnut
165	Merlot Heather
166	Merlot Heather, Hazelnut
167	Rose Hip, Merlot Heather
168	Rose Hip, Merlot Heather
169	Serrano, Bison
170	Raspberry Heather, Bison
171	Raspberry Heather, Mongoose
172	Serrano, Mongoose
173	Pimento, Doe
174	Garnet Heather, Merlot Heather
175	Pimento, Merlot Heather
176	Serrano, Mongoose
177	Serrano, Mongoose
178	Raspberry Heather, Bison
179	Rose Hip, Bison
180	Rose Hip, Merlot Heather
181	Rose Hip, Merlot Heather
182	Hazelnut
183	Orange
184	Mongoose, Masala
185	Mongoose, Masala
186	Mongoose, Masala
187	Doe, Hazelnut
188	Doe, Hazelnut
189	Almond, Merlot Heather
190	Almond, Merlot Heather
191	Almond, Merlot Heather
192	Doe, Hazelnut
193	Doe, Hazelnut
194	Mongoose, Masala
195	Mongoose, Masala
196	Mongoose, Masala
197	Orange
198	Merlot Heather
199	Rose Hip, Hazelnut
200	Raspberry Heather, Bison
201	Raspberry Heather, Bison
202	Serrano, Mongoose
203	Serrano, Mongoose
204	Pimento, Doe
205	Pimento, Almond
206	Pimento, Doe
207	Serrano, Mongoose
208	Serrano, Mongoose
209	Raspberry Heather, Bison
210	Raspberry Heather, Bison
211	Rose Hip, Merlot Heather
212	Orange
213	Masala
214	Kumquat Heather, Masala
215	Kumquat Heather, Masala
216	Golden Heather, Hazelnut
217	Golden Heather, Hazelnut
218	Golden Heather, Hazelnut
219	Orange, Merlot Heather
220	Orange, Merlot Heather
221	Orange, Merlot Heather
222	Golden Heather, Hazelnut
223	Golden Heather, Hazelnut
224	Golden Heather, Hazelnut
225	Kumquat Heather, Masala
226	Kumquat Heather, Masala
227	Orange
228	Garnet Heather
229	Almond, Garnet Heather
230	Almond, Garnet Heather
231	Doe, Pimento
232	Doe, Pimento

Dogwood Blossoms:
MIDWINTER COLORWAY

YARN COLORS

3 balls:
MC Eggplant 24255

2 balls each:
Celestial 24582
Navy 24001
Marine Heather 24010

1 ball each:
Jay 24581
Bluebell 24578
Chicory 24577
Calypso Heather 24009
Caribbean 25095
French Lavender 24575
Aster 24576
Pennyroyal 25090
Hyacinth 23721
Huckleberry Heather 24259
Mulberry 24571

Sleeve

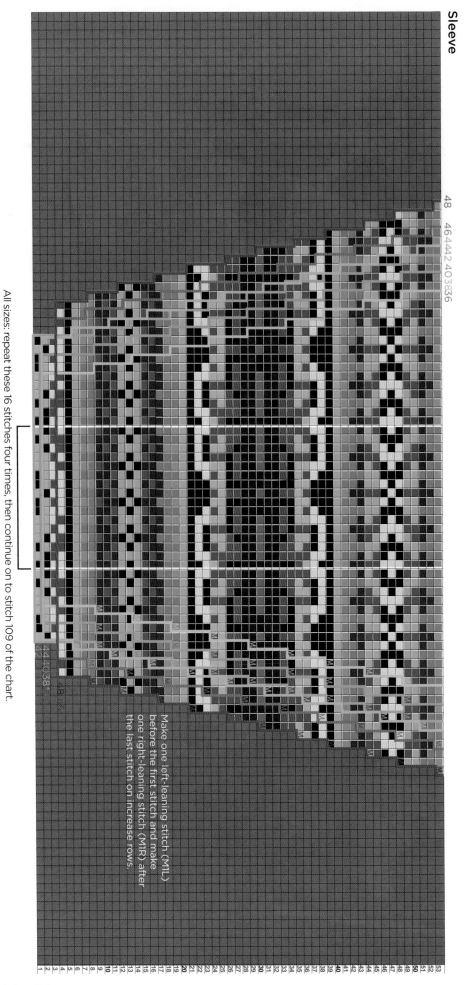

All sizes: repeat these 16 stitches four times, then continue on to stitch 109 of the chart.

*Sizes 36 and 38 share the same stitch count and shaping instructions until the sleeve cap; use the line marked 38 for both sizes.

Make one left-leaning stitch (M1L) before the first stitch and make one right-leaning stitch (M1R) after the last stitch on increase rows.

■ Bluebell	■ Navy
■ Chicory	■ Marine Heather
■ Celestial	■ Calypso Heather
■ Jay	■ Caribbean

■ French Lavender	■ Huckleberry Heather
■ Aster	■ Mulberry
■ Pennyroyal	■ Eggplant
■ Hyacinth	

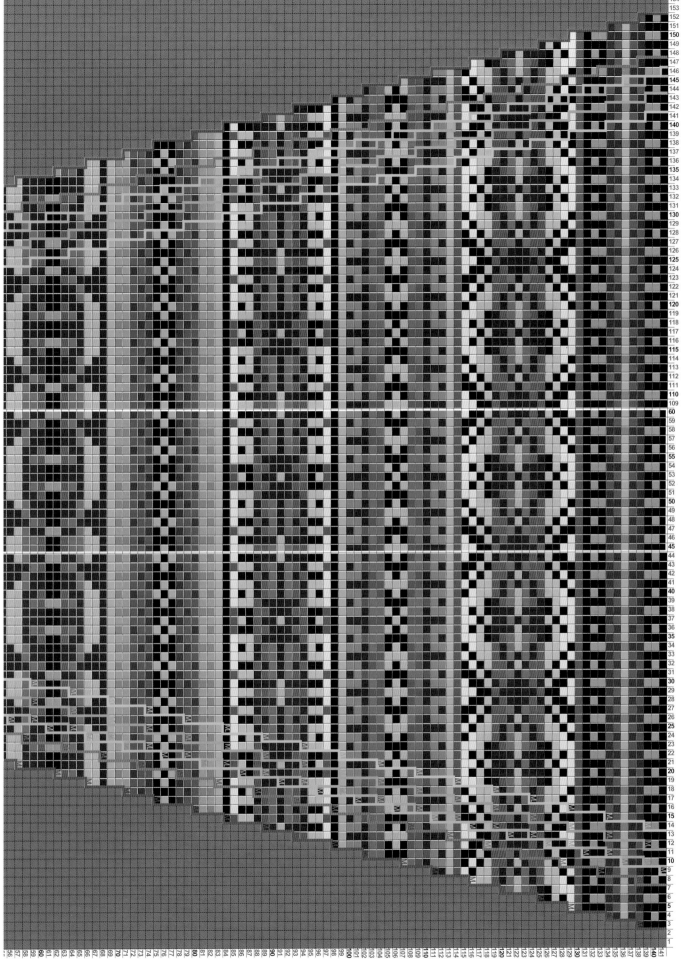

Sleeve Cap (Left Side)

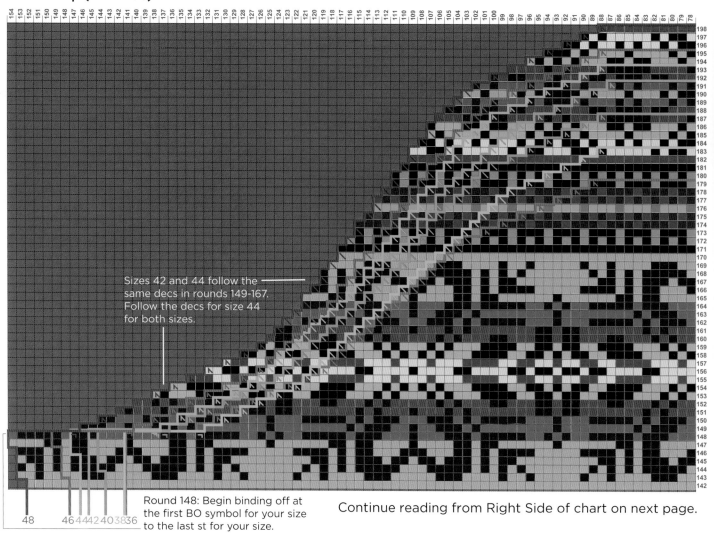

Sizes 42 and 44 follow the same decs in rounds 149-167. Follow the decs for size 44 for both sizes.

Round 148: Begin binding off at the first BO symbol for your size to the last st for your size.

Continue reading from Right Side of chart on next page.

Reading Charts

All charts are read from right to left, bottom to top, as all pieces are worked in the round.

Binding Off

Because there are many sizes represented in each chart, not all bind-off marks are shown. When sts are bound off, they will still appear in the row in which they are bound off, but not in subsequent rows.

However, sts removed by decs will not appear in the row from which they are removed. When a set of bound-off sts is followed by decs on the next round, those removed sts will widen the area of 'No Stitch' above the bound-off sts.

Where bound-off sections cross over the end/beginning of a round, the BO sts will appear at the end of the first round and then over the first several sts of the following round. When these are followed immediately by a dec, the st that remains on the RH needle after the last bound off st becomes part of the dec. For instance, if a BO st is followed directly by a K3tog, slip the st back to the LH needle and knit it together with the following two sts.

Bluebell · French Lavender · Chicory · Aster · Celestial · Pennyroyal · Jay · Hyacinth · Navy · Huckleberry Heather · Marine Heather · Mulberry · Calypso Heather · Eggplant · Caribbean

No decreases in the round following BO

Bound off stitches

A double decrease in the row following the BO results in two 'no stitch' spaces next to those left by the BO sts.

Bound off stitches

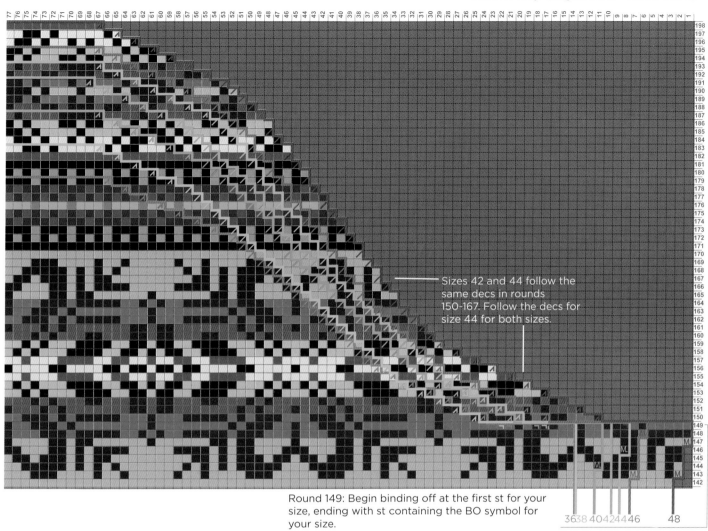

Sizes 42 and 44 follow the same decs in rounds 150-167. Follow the decs for size 44 for both sizes.

Round 149: Begin binding off at the first st for your size, ending with st containing the BO symbol for your size.

36 38 40 42 44 46 48

LEGEND

No Stitch
Placeholder—no stitch made

Knit
RS: knit stitch
WS: purl stitch

M1
Make one stitch, following instructions on chart

K2tog
Knit two stitches together as one stitch

SSK
(Slip 1 knit-wise) twice; insert left-hand needle into front of these 2 stitches and knit them together

K3tog
Knit three stitches together as one stitch

SSSK
(Slip 1 knit-wise) three times; insert left-hand needle from the front to the back of all stitches at the same time and knit them together

Wrap and Turn (W&T)
Wrap and turn for short row, following pattern instructions

BO
Bind off 1 stitch

Pullover Body Repeat: Sizes 36", 40", 44", 48"

All sizes: repeat these 32 sts four times

36   40   44   48

Read this chart from the first st and row outlined in your size, from right to left, until the last outlined st in your size. Work this chart across the front and again across the back for a given round.

After completing this chart, move on to the Pullover Armscye and Neck Shaping chart for your size.

Pullover Body Repeats: Sizes 38", 42", 46"

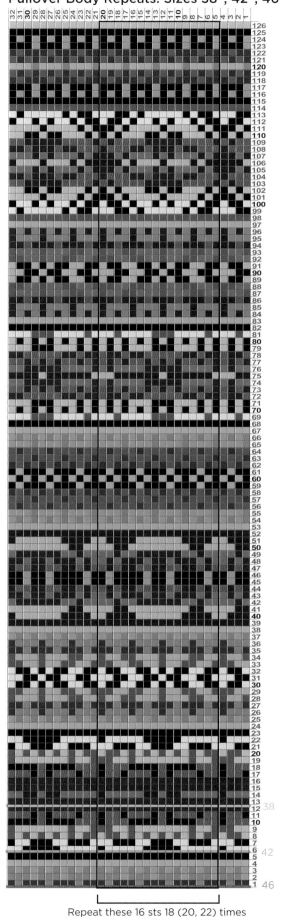

Bluebell

Chicory

Celestial

Jay

Navy

Marine Heather

Calypso Heather

Caribbean

French Lavender

Aster

Pennyroyal

Hyacinth

Huckleberry Heather

Mulberry

Eggplant

Repeat these 16 sts 18 (20, 22) times

Pullover Armscye and Neck Shaping: Sizes 36", 40", 44", 48" (Left Side)

Round 133: Begin binding off at st containing the BO symbol for your size, ending with the last st for your size.

Continue reading from Right Side of chart on next page.

This chart shows both the front and back of the sweater. For the front, follow neck decs as shown; for the back, work across the whole back in pattern until the bind-off at the back neck.

Sizes 40 and 44 share the same pattern of neck decs; follow decs for size 44 for both sizes.

Pullover Armscye and Neck Shaping: Sizes 36″, 40″, 44″, 48″ (Right Side—start here)

BO 58 sts for back neck

BO 60 sts for back neck

BO 60 sts for back neck

BO 58 sts for back neck

BO steek sts

BO steek sts

BO steek sts

BO steek sts

These bind-off markers note the placement of bind-offs for the front left; for the back right, the bind-offs take place on the previous round (133). Follow other decrease instructions as given in each row of the chart.

Round 133/134: Begin binding off at the first st for your size, ending with st containing the BO symbol for your size.

Bluebell	Navy	French Lavender	Huckleberry Heather
Chicory	Marine Heather	Aster	Mulberry
Celestial	Calypso Heather	Pennyroyal	Eggplant
Jay	Caribbean	Hyacinth	

Pullover Armscye and Neck Shaping: Sizes 38″, 42″, 46″ (Left Side)

BO steek sts

BO steek sts

BO steek sts

Round 133: Begin binding off at st containing the BO symbol for your size, ending with the last st for your size.

Continue reading from Right Side of chart on next page.

This chart shows both the front and back of the sweater. For the front, follow neck decs as shown; for the back, work across the whole back in pattern until the bind-off at the back neck.

Pullover Armscye and Neck Shaping: Sizes 38″, 42″, 46″ (Right Side—start here)

BO 58 sts for back neck

BO steek sts

BO 58 sts for back neck

BO steek sts

BO 58 sts for back neck

BO steek sts

These bind-off markers note the placement of bind-offs for the front left; for the back right, the bind-offs take place on the previous row (133). Follow other decrease instructions as given in each row of the chart.

Round 133/134: Begin binding off at the first st for your size, ending with st containing the BO symbol for your size.

	Bluebell		Navy		French Lavender		Huckleberry Heather
	Chicory		Marine Heather		Aster		Mulberry
	Celestial		Calypso Heather		Pennyroyal		Eggplant
	Jay		Caribbean		Hyacinth		

Cardigan Body Repeat (Left Side)

Continue reading from Right Side of chart on next page.　　All sizes: repeat these 32 sts nine times

Cardigan Body Repeat (Right Side—start here)

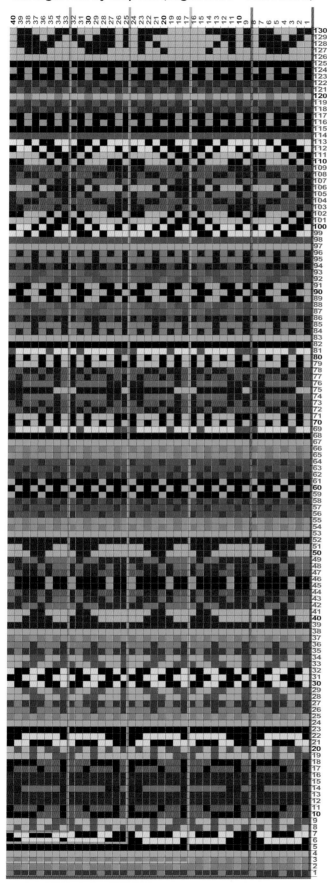

Read this chart from the first st and row outlined in your size, from right to left, until the last outlined st in your size. Note that size 36 is an even repeat of the center 32-st repeat.

Work this chart across the front and again across the back for a given round.

After completing this chart, move on to the Cardigan Armscye and Neck Shaping chart for your size.

Bluebell	French Lavender
Chicory	Aster
Celestial	Pennyroyal
Jay	Hyacinth
Navy	Huckleberry Heather
Marine Heather	Mulberry
Calypso Heather	Eggplant
Caribbean	

Cardigan Armscye and Neck Shaping: All Sizes (Right Side, second half)

BO 58 sts for back neck

BO 60 sts for back neck

BO 60 sts for back neck
BO 60 sts for back neck

BO 58 sts for back neck

BO steek sts

BO steek sts

BO steek sts
BO steek sts

BO steek sts

BO steek sts

BO steek sts
BO steek sts

Continue reading from Right Side of chart on next page.

Cardigan Armscye and Neck Shaping: All Sizes (Right Side—start here)

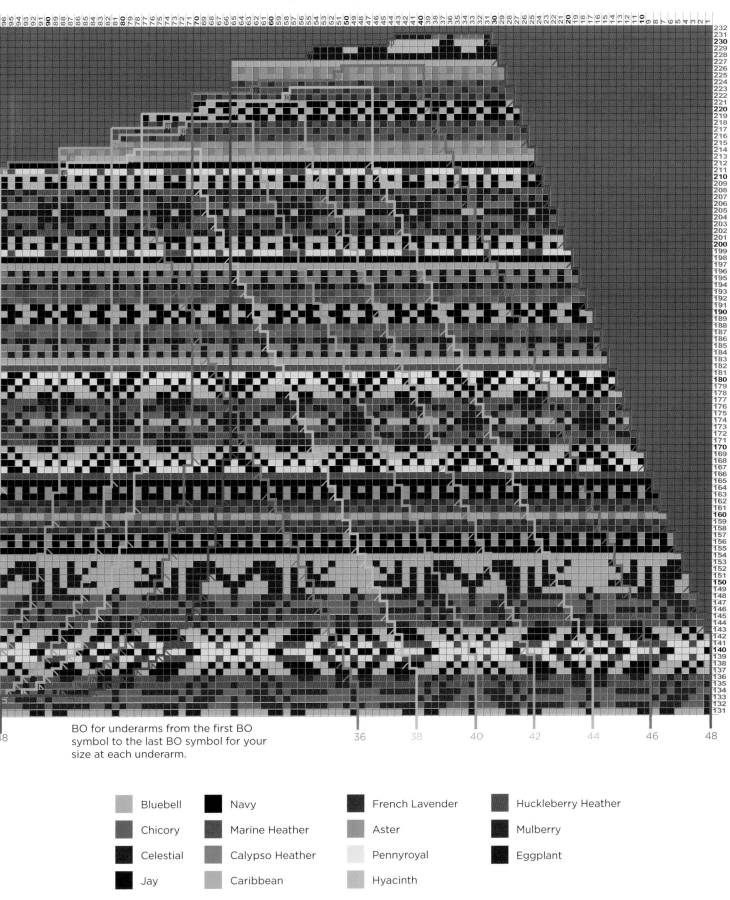

BO for underarms from the first BO symbol to the last BO symbol for your size at each underarm.

	Bluebell		Navy		French Lavender		Huckleberry Heather
	Chicory		Marine Heather		Aster		Mulberry
	Celestial		Calypso Heather		Pennyroyal		Eggplant
	Jay		Caribbean		Hyacinth		

Cardigan Armscye and Neck Shaping: All Sizes (Left Side, second half—end here)

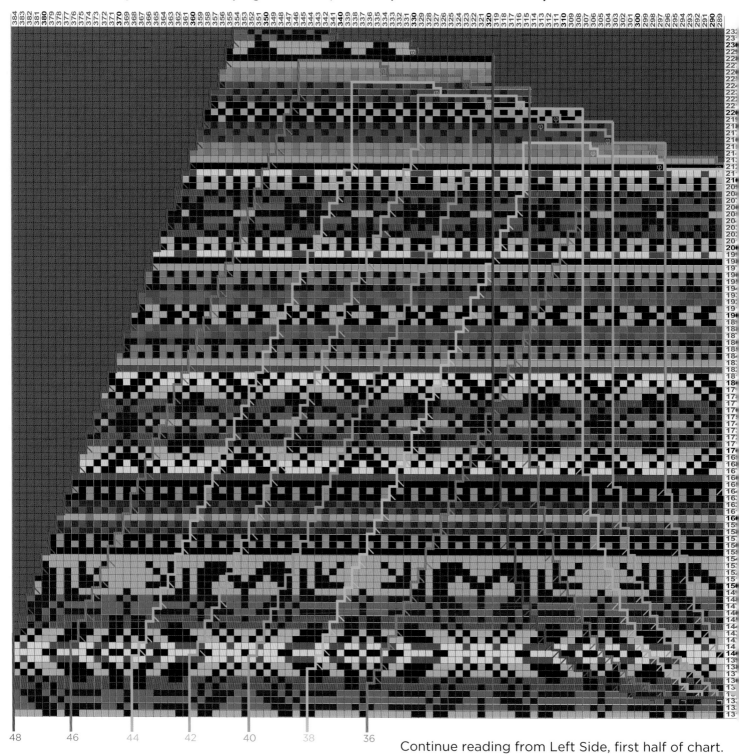

Continue reading from Left Side, first half of chart.

Continue reading from Right Side, second half of chart.

	Bluebell		Navy		French Lavender		Huckleberry Heather
	Chicory		Marine Heather		Aster		Mulberry
	Celestial		Calypso Heather		Pennyroyal		Eggplant
	Jay		Caribbean		Hyacinth		

Colors used for each row

Row	Color 1	Color 2
77	Caribbean	Navy
76	Caribbean	Navy
75	French Lavender	Navy
74	Caribbean	Marine Heather
73	French Lavender	Marine Heather
72	French Lavender	Marine Heather
71	Aster	Navy
70	Aster	Calypso Heather
69		Caribbean
16	French Lavender	Marine Heather
15	French Lavender	Marine Heather
14	Caribbean	Navy
13	Caribbean	Navy
12	Caribbean	Navy
11	French Lavender	Marine Heather
10	French Lavender	Marine Heather
9	French Lavender	Marine Heather
8	Aster	Calypso Heather
7	Aster	Calypso Heather
6		Caribbean
5		Navy
4	Pennyroyal	Marine Heather
3	Pennyroyal	Marine Heather
2	Hyacinth	Jay
1	Hyacinth	Jay
68		Eggplant
67	Bluebell	Eggplant
66	Bluebell	Eggplant
65	Chicory	Mulberry
64	Chicory	Mulberry
63	Celestial	Huckleberry Heather
62	Jay	Aster
61	Jay	Aster
60	Celestial	Huckleberry Heather
59	Chicory	Mulberry
58	Chicory	Mulberry
57	Bluebell	Eggplant
56	Bluebell	Eggplant
55	Navy	Eggplant
54	Navy	Caribbean
53	Aster	Calypso Heather
52	French Lavender	Calypso Heather
51	French Lavender	Marine Heather
50	Caribbean	Marine Heather
49	Caribbean	Marine Heather
48	Pennyroyal	Navy
47	Pennyroyal	Navy
46	Pennyroyal	Navy
45	Caribbean	Marine Heather
44	Caribbean	Marine Heather
43	French Lavender	Calypso Heather
42	French Lavender	Calypso Heather
41	Aster	Caribbean
40		Caribbean
39		Navy
38	Pennyroyal	Navy
37	Pennyroyal	Navy
36	Hyacinth	Marine Heather
35	Hyacinth	Marine Heather
34	Huckleberry Heather	Jay
33	Huckleberry Heather	Jay
32	Mulberry	Celestial
31	Mulberry	Celestial
30	Eggplant	Chicory
29	Mulberry	Celestial
28	Mulberry	Celestial
27	Huckleberry Heather	Jay
26	Huckleberry Heather	Jay
25	Hyacinth	Marine Heather
24	Hyacinth	Marine Heather
23	Pennyroyal	Navy
22	Pennyroyal	Navy
21	Pennyroyal	Navy
20		Caribbean
19	Aster	Calypso Heather
18	Aster	Calypso Heather
17	French Lavender	Calypso Heather
138	French Lavender	Marine Heather
137	French Lavender	Marine Heather
136	Caribbean	Calypso Heather
135	French Lavender	Marine Heather
134	French Lavender	Marine Heather
133	Aster	Navy
132	Aster	Navy
131		Navy
130		Marine Heather
129	Pennyroyal	Navy
128	Pennyroyal	Navy
127	Hyacinth	Jay
126	Hyacinth	Jay
125	Huckleberry Heather	Celestial
124	Huckleberry Heather	Celestial
123	Mulberry	Chicory
122	Eggplant	Bluebell
121	Mulberry	Chicory
120	Huckleberry Heather	Celestial
119	Huckleberry Heather	Celestial
118	Hyacinth	Jay
117	Hyacinth	Jay
116	Pennyroyal	Navy
115	Pennyroyal	Navy
114	Caribbean	Marine Heather
113		Caribbean
112	Celestial	Calypso Heather
111	Celestial	Calypso Heather
110	Celestial	Marine Heather
109	Chicory	Marine Heather
108	Chicory	Navy
107	Bluebell	Navy
106	Bluebell	Navy
105	Bluebell	Navy
104	Chicory	Marine Heather
103	Chicory	Marine Heather
102	Celestial	Marine Heather
101	Celestial	Calypso Heather
100	Celestial	Calypso Heather
100		Caribbean
99		Caribbean
98		Navy
97	Pennyroyal	Marine Heather
96	Hyacinth	Jay
95	Hyacinth	Jay
94	Huckleberry Heather	Celestial
93	Huckleberry Heather	Celestial
92	Mulberry	Chicory
91	Eggplant	Bluebell
90	Mulberry	Chicory
89	Huckleberry Heather	Celestial
88	Huckleberry Heather	Celestial
87	Hyacinth	Jay
86	Hyacinth	Jay
85	Pennyroyal	Marine Heather
84		Navy
83		Caribbean
82	Aster	Calypso Heather
81	Aster	Calypso Heather
80	French Lavender	Marine Heather
79	French Lavender	Marine Heather
78	French Lavender	Marine Heather
198		Marine Heather
197	Pennyroyal	Navy
196	Pennyroyal	Navy
195	Hyacinth	Jay
194	Hyacinth	Jay
193	Huckleberry Heather	Celestial
192	Huckleberry Heather	Celestial
191	Mulberry	Chicory
190	Eggplant	Bluebell
189	Mulberry	Chicory
188	Huckleberry Heather	Celestial
187	Huckleberry Heather	Celestial
186	Hyacinth	Jay
185	Hyacinth	Jay
184	Pennyroyal	Navy
183	Pennyroyal	Navy
182		Marine Heather
181		Navy
180	Aster	Navy
179	Aster	Navy
178	French Lavender	Marine Heather
177	French Lavender	Marine Heather
176	Caribbean	Calypso Heather
175	French Lavender	Marine Heather
174	French Lavender	Marine Heather
173	Aster	Navy
172	Aster	Navy
171		Navy
170		Bluebell
169		Bluebell
168	Eggplant	Bluebell
167	Eggplant	Bluebell
166	Eggplant	Bluebell
165	Eggplant	Bluebell
164	Mulberry	Chicory
163	Mulberry	Chicory
162	Mulberry	Chicory
161	Huckleberry Heather	Celestial
160	Huckleberry Heather	Celestial
159	Hyacinth	Jay
158	Hyacinth	Jay
157	Pennyroyal	Navy
156	Pennyroyal	Navy
155	Pennyroyal	Navy
154	Hyacinth	Jay
153	Hyacinth	Jay
152	Huckleberry Heather	Celestial
151	Huckleberry Heather	Celestial
150	Mulberry	Chicory
149	Mulberry	Chicory
148	Mulberry	Chicory
147	Eggplant	Bluebell
146	Eggplant	Bluebell
145	Eggplant	Bluebell
144	Eggplant	Bluebell
143	Eggplant	Bluebell
142	Eggplant	Bluebell
141		Bluebell
140	Aster	Navy
139	Aster	Navy

MIDWINTER BODY

Colors used for each row

Row	Color 1	Color 2
1	French Lavender	Calypso Heather
2	Aster	Calypso Heather
3	Aster	Caribbean
4	Caribbean	
5	Navy	
6	Pennyroyal	Navy
7	Pennyroyal	Navy
8	Hyacinth	Marine Heather
9	Hyacinth	Marine Heather
10	Huckleberry Heather	Jay
11	Huckleberry Heather	Jay
12	Mulberry	Celestial
13	Mulberry	Celestial
14	Eggplant	Chicory
15	Mulberry	Celestial
16	Huckleberry Heather	Celestial
17	Huckleberry Heather	Jay
18	Hyacinth	Jay
19	Hyacinth	Jay
20	Hyacinth	Jay
21	Pennyroyal	Navy
22	Pennyroyal	Navy
23	Navy	
24	Caribbean	
25	Aster	Calypso Heather
26	French Lavender	Calypso Heather
27	French Lavender	Calypso Heather
28	Caribbean	Marine Heather
29	Caribbean	Marine Heather
30	Pennyroyal	Navy
31	Pennyroyal	Navy
32	Pennyroyal	Navy
33	Caribbean	Marine Heather
34	Caribbean	Marine Heather
35	French Lavender	Calypso Heather
36	French Lavender	Calypso Heather
37	Aster	Calypso Heather
38	Caribbean	
39	Eggplant	
40	Bluebell	Eggplant
41	Bluebell	Eggplant
42	Chicory	Mulberry
43	Chicory	Mulberry
44	Celestial	Huckleberry Heather
45	Jay	Aster
46	Jay	Aster
47	Celestial	Huckleberry Heather
48	Chicory	Mulberry
49	Chicory	Mulberry
50	Bluebell	Eggplant
51	Bluebell	Eggplant
52	Eggplant	
53	Caribbean	
54	Aster	Caribbean
55	Aster	Calypso Heather
56	French Lavender	Marine Heather
57	French Lavender	Marine Heather
58	French Lavender	Marine Heather
59	Caribbean	Navy
60	Caribbean	Navy
61	Caribbean	Navy
62	French Lavender	Marine Heather
63	French Lavender	Marine Heather
64	French Lavender	Marine Heather
65	Aster	Calypso Heather
66	Aster	Calypso Heather
67	Caribbean	
68	Navy	
69	Pennyroyal	Marine Heather
70	Hyacinth	Jay
71	Hyacinth	Jay
72	Huckleberry Heather	Celestial
73	Huckleberry Heather	Celestial
74	Mulberry	Chicory
75	Eggplant	Bluebell
76	Mulberry	Chicory
77	Huckleberry Heather	Celestial
78	Huckleberry Heather	Celestial
79	Hyacinth	Jay
80	Hyacinth	Jay
81	Pennyroyal	Marine Heather
82	Navy	
83	Caribbean	
84	Celestial	Calypso Heather
85	Celestial	Calypso Heather
86	Celestial	Marine Heather
87	Chicory	Marine Heather
88	Chicory	Marine Heather
89	Bluebell	Navy
90	Bluebell	Navy
91	Bluebell	Navy
92	Chicory	Marine Heather
93	Chicory	Marine Heather
94	Celestial	Marine Heather
95	Celestial	Calypso Heather
96	Celestial	Calypso Heather
97	Caribbean	
98	Marine Heather	
99	Pennyroyal	Navy
100	Pennyroyal	Navy
101	Hyacinth	Jay
102	Hyacinth	Jay
103	Huckleberry Heather	Celestial
104	Huckleberry Heather	Celestial
105	Mulberry	Chicory
106	Eggplant	Bluebell
107	Mulberry	Chicory
108	Huckleberry Heather	Celestial
109	Huckleberry Heather	Celestial
110	Hyacinth	Jay
111	Hyacinth	Jay
112	Pennyroyal	Navy
113	Pennyroyal	Navy
114	Navy	
115	Caribbean	
116	Aster	Calypso Heather
117	Aster	Calypso Heather
118	French Lavender	Marine Heather
119	French Lavender	Marine Heather
120	Caribbean	Navy
121	French Lavender	Marine Heather
122	French Lavender	Marine Heather
123	Aster	Calypso Heather
124	Aster	Calypso Heather
125	Caribbean	
126	Navy	
127	Eggplant	Bluebell
128	Eggplant	Bluebell
129	Eggplant	Bluebell
130	Eggplant	Bluebell
131	Hyacinth	Jay
132	Mulberry	Chicory
133	Mulberry	Chicory
134	Mulberry	Chicory
135	Huckleberry Heather	Celestial
136	Huckleberry Heather	Celestial
137	Hyacinth	Jay
138	Hyacinth	Jay
139	Pennyroyal	Navy
140	Pennyroyal	Navy
141	Pennyroyal	Navy
142	Hyacinth	Jay
143	Hyacinth	Jay
144	Huckleberry Heather	Jay
145	Huckleberry Heather	Jay
146	Mulberry	Chicory
147	Mulberry	Chicory
148	Mulberry	Chicory
149	Eggplant	Bluebell
150	Eggplant	Bluebell
151	Eggplant	Bluebell
152	Eggplant	Bluebell
153	Eggplant	Bluebell
154	Caribbean	
155	Navy	
156	Aster	Calypso Heather
157	Aster	Calypso Heather
158	French Lavender	Marine Heather
159	French Lavender	Marine Heather
160	Caribbean	Navy
161	French Lavender	Marine Heather
162	French Lavender	Marine Heather
163	Aster	Calypso Heather
164	Aster	Calypso Heather
165	Navy	
166	Marine Heather	
167	Pennyroyal	Navy
168	Pennyroyal	Navy
169	Hyacinth	Jay
170	Hyacinth	Jay
171	Huckleberry Heather	Celestial
172	Huckleberry Heather	Celestial
173	Mulberry	Chicory
174	Eggplant	Bluebell
175	Mulberry	Chicory
176	Huckleberry Heather	Celestial
177	Huckleberry Heather	Celestial
178	Hyacinth	Jay
179	Hyacinth	Jay
180	Pennyroyal	Navy
181	Pennyroyal	Navy
182	Navy	
183	Caribbean	
184	Celestial	Calypso Heather
185	Celestial	Calypso Heather
186	Celestial	Marine Heather
187	Chicory	Marine Heather
188	Chicory	Marine Heather
189	Bluebell	Navy
190	Bluebell	Navy
191	Bluebell	Navy
192	Chicory	Marine Heather
193	Chicory	Marine Heather
194	Celestial	Marine Heather
195	Celestial	Calypso Heather
196	Celestial	Calypso Heather
197	Caribbean	
198	Navy	
199	Pennyroyal	Marine Heather
200	Hyacinth	Jay
201	Hyacinth	Jay
202	Huckleberry Heather	Celestial
203	Huckleberry Heather	Celestial
204	Mulberry	Chicory
205	Eggplant	Bluebell
206	Mulberry	Chicory
207	Huckleberry Heather	Celestial
208	Huckleberry Heather	Celestial
209	Hyacinth	Jay
210	Hyacinth	Jay
211	Pennyroyal	Marine Heather
212	Navy	
213	Caribbean	
214	Aster	Calypso Heather
215	Aster	Calypso Heather
216	French Lavender	Marine Heather
217	French Lavender	Marine Heather
218	French Lavender	Marine Heather
219	Caribbean	Navy
220	Caribbean	Navy
221	Caribbean	Navy
222	French Lavender	Marine Heather
223	French Lavender	Marine Heather
224	French Lavender	Marine Heather
225	Aster	Calypso Heather
226	Aster	Calypso Heather
227	Caribbean	
228	Eggplant	
229	Bluebell	Eggplant
230	Bluebell	Eggplant
231	Chicory	Mulberry
232	Chicory	Mulberry

EDELE CARDIGAN

by Kerin Dimeler-Laurence

FINISHED MEASUREMENTS
32 (36, 40, 44, 48, 52, 56, 60, 64)"
finished bust measurement

YARN
Knit Picks Gloss™ (DK weight, 70%
Merino Wool, 30% Silk; 123 yards/50g):
Kenai 27016, 10 (12, 14, 15, 16, 18, 19, 20,
22) balls

NEEDLES
US 5 (3.75mm) DPNs and straight
needles or 32-60" circular needles,
or size to obtain gauge

US 4 (3.5mm) DPNs or preferred method
for working in the round, or one size
smaller than those used to obtain gauge

NOTIONS
Yarn Needle
Stitch Markers
Six or Seven 0.75" Buttons
Stitch Holders or Scrap Yarn
Optional: Crochet Hook (for belt loops)

GAUGE
23 sts and 36 rows = 4" in Snowflake
Pattern worked flat and in the round,
blocked

For pattern support, contact customerservice@knitpicks.com

Edele Cardigan

Notes:

This cardigan echoes a simpler time. The basic shaping and all-over pattern are coupled with afterthought pockets and optional belt detail.

All references to Right and Left are as worn, unless otherwise indicated.

This pattern is offered in numerous sizes, so you may find it helpful to highlight the numbers for your size throughout the pattern before beginning. Reading through the pattern will also allow you to spot the "at the same time" instructions which appear several places in this pattern.

The charts are followed from bottom to top. When knitting in the round, read each row as a RS row, from right to left. When knitting flat, read RS rows from right to left, and WS rows from left to right. On round 1, begin at the stitch noted for your size, and work across to the last st for your size. Extra stitches are shown in this chart to aid with shaping.

Twisted Rib (worked in the rnd over an even number of sts)
Rnd 1: (P1, K1 TBL) around.
Rnd 2: (P1, K1) around.
Rep Rnds 1-2 for pattern.

Twisted Rib (worked flat over an even number of sts)
Row 1 (RS): (P1, K1 TBL) across.
Row 2 (WS): (P1, K1) across.
Rep Rows 1-2 for pattern

DIRECTIONS

Sleeves (make 2 the same)
The sleeves are knit identically and are worked in the rnd to the sleeve caps. You can knit them separately or at the same time. The sleeve caps are worked flat.

With smaller needles, loosely CO 44 (48, 50, 52, 54, 60, 64, 66, 66) sts. PM and join in the rnd, being careful not to twist sts. Work in Twisted Rib for 2".
Switch to larger needles and begin working from Sleeve chart, following rep instructions for your size.

Increases
Work incs as instructed for your size through the sleeve, maintaining pattern throughout.

Inc Rnd: KFB, work in pattern to last st, KFB. 2 sts added.

Sizes 44" and 52" Only: Work an Inc Rnd on the next rnd.

All Sizes
While maintaining pattern, work Inc Rnd every 8 (8, 7, 7, 5 & 11, 5 & 11, 4, 4, 3 & 7) rnds 18 (19, 22, 23, 14, 15, 37, 38, 21) times. 80 (86, 94, 100, 110, 122, 138, 142, 150) sts.
Work 16 (8, 8, 1, 9, 1, 14, 8, 13) rnds in pattern.

Sleeve Cap
On next rnd, sts are bound off for sleeve cap.
Work in pattern to 4 (2, 2, 2, 2, 3, 3, 2, 2) sts before end of rnd. BO the last 4 (2, 2, 2, 2, 3, 3, 2, 2) sts of rnd and the first 4 (2, 2, 2, 2, 3, 3, 2, 2) sts of next rnd. Begin working back and forth in pattern while shaping sleeve cap.

For these directions, references to left and right are as oriented; right is the beginning of a row, and left is the end of a row.

Double Dec Row: K3tog or P3tog TBL at right edge; SSSK or P3tog at left edge. 2 sts dec at each edge. 4 sts total dec.
Dec Row: K2tog or P2tog TBL at right edge; SSK or P2tog at left edge. 1 st dec at each edge. 2 sts total dec.

Size 32: Work a Double Dec Row every row two times; work a Dec Row every row four times, then every other row 14 times, then every row two times; work a Double Dec Row every row two times. 16 sts remain.

Size 36: Work a Double Dec Row; work a Dec Row every row nine times, then every other row three times, (work two rows in pattern, work a Dec Row) three times, work a Dec Row every other row six times, then every row five times; work a Double Dec Row every row two times. 18 sts remain.

Size 40: Work a Double Dec Row; work a Dec Row every row nine times, then every other row three times, (work two rows in pattern, work a Dec Row) four times, work a Dec Row every other row four times, then every row five times; work a Double Dec Row every row four times. 20 sts remain.

Size 44: Work a Double Dec Row; work a Dec Row every row seven times, then every other row seven times, (work two rows in pattern, work a Dec Row) three times, work a Dec Row every other row five times, then every row eight times; work a Double Dec Row every row three times. 20 sts remain.

Size 48: Work a Double Dec Row every row 3 times; work a Dec Row every row seven times, then every other row seven times, (work two rows in pattern, work a Dec Row) five times, work a Dec Row every other row three times, then every row eight times; work a Double Dec Row every row three times. 22 sts remain.

Size 52: Work a Double Dec Row every row three times; work a Dec Row every row nine times, then every other row eight times, (work two rows in pattern, work a Dec Row) three times, work a Dec Row every other row three times, then every row eight times; work a Double Dec Row every row five times. 22 sts remain.

Size 56: Work a Double Dec Row, (work a Double Dec Row, work a Dec Row) three times; work a Dec Row every row eight times, then every other row 16 times, then every row five times; work a Double Dec Row every row six times. 28 sts remain.

Size 60: Work a Double Dec Row, (work a Double Dec Row, work a Dec Row) three times; work a Dec Row every row seven times, then every other row six times, (work two rows in pattern, work a Dec Row) three times, work a Dec Row every other row seven times, then every row seven times; work a Double Dec Row every row five times. 36 sts remain.

Size 64: (Work a Double Dec Row, work a Dec Row) four times; work a Dec Row every row nine times, then every other row nine times, (work two rows in pattern, work a Dec Row) four times, work a Dec Row every other row six times, then every row five times; work a Double Dec Row every row four times. 40 sts remain.

All Sizes: BO remaining sts.

Pocket (optional, make 2 the same)
The pockets are worked as a small flap of fabric that is joined to the body of the sweater at a given point.

Using larger needles, CO 27 sts. Work flat in St st for 5".
Last Row (RS): K2tog, K to last 2 sts, K2tog. 25 sts.
Break yarn and place live sts on scrap yarn or a stitch holder.

Body
The body is worked flat in one piece. Optional waist details or belt loops are added at the end.

With smaller needles, loosely CO 204 (228, 252, 272, 296, 320, 340, 364, 388) sts. PM after first 10 sts to mark Buttonhole Band, then after another 46 (52, 58, 63, 69, 75, 80, 86, 92) sts to mark right underarm, after a further 92 (104, 116, 126, 138, 150, 160, 172, 184) sts to mark left underarm, and before last 10 sts to mark Button Band.

Work in Twisted Rib for 3". At the same time follow the Buttonhole Band instructions.

Buttonhole Band
Maintain Twisted Rib over Buttonhole Band and Button Band throughout.
After 1" of knitting and then every 3" up to the neckline, work across Buttonhole Band on RS as follows: P1, K1 TBL, K2tog, YO twice, P2tog, K1 TBL, P1, K1 TBL.
On the next row, (P1, K1) into the double YO.

Switch to larger needles and begin working from Snowflake chart between Buttonhole Band and Button Band, following instructions for your size. Work in pattern for 14 (14.5, 15, 15, 15.5, 16, 16, 16.5, 16.5)" or desired length, maintaining Buttonhole pattern.

At the same time, attach pockets: After body measures 6" long, on next RS row, work in pattern for 18 (20, 20, 22, 22, 24, 24, 26, 26) sts. *Without working them, Sl the next 25 sts onto a stitch holder or scrap yarn. Place one pocket on a spare needle and hold it behind cardigan with RS of pocket facing WS of cardigan. Knit directly across the 25 sts of pocket in Snowflake pattern; cont in pattern from next live st around body* to 43 (45, 45, 47, 47, 49, 49, 51, 51) sts before end of row. Rep pocket directions from * to * to attach second pocket. Cont in pattern.

Armscyes & Neckline
On next row, begin decreasing for neckline and bind off for armscyes. Shaping for both sections happens at the same time; read both sections before proceeding.

Armscyes
On next RS row, work from chart to 2 (2, 3, 3, 3, 5, 5, 8, 12) sts before first underarm M. BO next 4 (4, 6, 6, 6, 10, 10, 16, 24) sts in pattern, removing M. Rep at other underarm. 8 (8, 12, 12, 12, 20, 20, 32, 48) sts removed.

Place 88 (100, 110, 120, 132, 140, 150, 156, 160) Back sts on stitch holder or scrap yarn.

Cont across both fronts in pattern, attaching a new ball of yarn at armscye edge of Right front, and following decs at armscyes as given below. Maintain armscye edge st in St st to shoulder; this will serve as a selvage. All decs happen over the 2 or 3 sts next to this selvage st. For these directions, references to left and right are as oriented; right is the beginning of a row, and left is the end of a row.

Armscye Double Dec: K3tog or P3tog TBL at right edge; SSSK or P3tog at left edge. 2 sts dec at each edge. 4 sts total dec.
Armscye Dec: K2tog or P2tog TBL at right edge; SSK or P2tog at left edge. 1 st dec at each edge. 2 sts total dec.

Size 32: Work an Armscye Dec every row two times, work one row in pattern, work an Armscye Dec, (work two rows in pattern, work an Armscye Dec) two times, work three rows in pattern, work an Armscye Dec, work seven rows in pattern, work an Armscye Dec. 7 sts dec from each armscye.

Size 36: Work an Armscye Dec every row three times, work an Armscye Dec every other row three times, work two rows in pattern, work an Armscye Dec, (work three rows in pattern, work an Armscye Dec) two times, work five rows in pattern, work an Armscye Dec, work ten rows in pattern, work an Armscye Dec. 11 sts dec from each armscye.

Size 40: Work an Armscye Double Dec, work an Armscye Dec every row four times, work an Armscye Dec every other row three times, (work two rows in pattern, work an Armscye Dec) two times, work three rows in pattern, work an Armscye Dec, work five rows in pattern, work an Armscye Dec, work eight rows in pattern, work an Armscye Dec. 14 sts dec from each armscye.

Size 44: Work an Armscye Double Dec, work an Armscye Dec every row five times, work an Armscye Dec every other row four times, work two rows in pattern, work an Armscye Dec, (work three rows in pattern, work an Armscye Dec) two times, work five rows in pattern, work an Armscye Dec, work ten rows in pattern, work an Armscye Dec. 16 sts dec from each armscye.

Size 48: Work an Armscye Double Dec every row two times, work an Armscye Dec every row seven times, work an Armscye Dec every other row three times, (work two rows in pattern, work an Armscye Dec) three times, work five rows in pattern, work an Armscye Dec, work seven rows in pattern, work an Armscye Dec. 19 sts dec from each armscye.

Size 52: Work an Armscye Double Dec every row two times, work an Armscye Dec every row six times, work an Armscye Dec every other row two times, (work two rows in pattern, work an Armscye Dec) three times, (work three rows in pattern, work an Armscye Dec) two times, work seven rows in pattern, work an Armscye Dec. 18 sts dec from each armscye.

Size 56: Work an Armscye Double Dec every row three times, work an Armscye Dec every row seven times, work an Armscye Dec every other row four times, (work two rows in pattern, work an Armscye Dec) two times, (work three rows in pattern, work an Armscye Dec) two times, work six rows in pattern, work an Armscye Dec. 22 sts dec from each armscye.

Size 60: Work an Armscye Double Dec every row four times, work an Armscye Dec every row seven times, work an Armscye Dec every other row five times, work two rows in pattern, work an Armscye Dec, (work three rows in pattern, work an Armscye Dec) two times, work six rows in pattern, work an Armscye Dec. 24 sts dec from each armscye.

Size 64: Work an Armscye Double Dec every row five times, work an Armscye Dec every row eight times, work an Armscye Dec every other row four times, (work two rows in pattern, work an Armscye Dec) three times, work three rows in pattern, work an Armscye Dec, work eight rows in pattern, work an Armscye Dec. 27 sts dec from each armscye.

Work armscye edges straight, maintaining selvage st, to end of Neckline and Shoulder directions.

Neckline
The neckline decs happen between Body and Buttonhole Band or Button Band. Start counting with the WS row after armscye BO as the first row.

Neckline Dec (RS): on Right front, work across first 9 sts of Buttonhole Band, SSK the last Buttonhole Band st tog with first st of Body. On Left front, work across to 1 st before Button Band, P2tog TBL over last st of Body and first st of Button Band.

Work a Neckline Dec every 4th row 18 (19, 20, 21, 22, 24, 26, 26, 25) times. After all Neckline and Armscye shaping is complete, 19 (20, 21, 23, 25, 28, 27, 28, 28) sts remain between Armscyes and front Bands.

Work across fronts for 5 (9, 9, 9, 9, 15, 9, 13, 17) rows.

Shoulder Shaping
Short Row 1 (RS): Work across Left front and then Right front in pattern to 6 (6, 7, 7, 8, 9, 9, 9, 9) sts before end of Right shoulder, W&T.
Short Row 2 (WS): Work across fronts in pattern to 6 (6, 7, 7, 8, 9, 9, 9, 9) sts before end of Left shoulder, W&T.

Short Row 3: Work across Left front and then Right front in pattern to 6 (6, 7, 7, 8, 9, 9, 9, 9) before wrapped st on Right shoulder, W&T.
Short Row 4: Work across Right front and then Left front in pattern to 6 (6, 7, 7, 8, 9, 9, 9, 9) sts before wrapped st on Left shoulder, W&T.

Next Row: Finish front shoulders by knitting back across RS of Left front to Button Band. Break yarn on Left front, leaving 18-24" tail. Leave yarn attached at Buttonhole Band on Right front; place both Bands on stitch holders or scrap yarn. Place remaining 19 (20, 21, 23, 25, 28, 27, 28, 28) Front shoulder sts on each side on separate stitch holders or scrap yarn.

Back
Place live Back sts on the needles, ready to begin a RS row. The Back Armscyes are worked in the same manner as the front. Maintain armscye edge st in St st to shoulder; this will serve as a selvage. All decs happen over the 2 or 3 sts next to this selvage st. For these directions, references to left and right are as oriented; right is the beginning of a row, and left is the end of a row.

Armscye Double Dec: K3tog or P3tog TBL at right edge; SSSK or P3tog at left edge. 2 sts dec at each edge. 4 sts total dec.
Armscye Dec: K2tog or P2tog TBL at right edge; SSK or P2tog at left edge. 1 st dec at each edge. 2 sts total dec.

Follow Front Armscye Dec directions for your size, using Armscye Dec and Armscye Double Dec instructions given above. 14 (22, 28, 32, 38, 36, 44, 47, 54) sts dec; 74 (48, 82, 88, 94, 104, 106, 108, 106) sts remaining.
Work across Back in pattern, maintaining a 1-st selvage at each armscye, for 55 (48, 53, 51, 59, 74, 74, 78, 74) rows.

Shoulder Shaping
Short Row 1 (RS): Work across in pattern to 6 (6, 7, 7, 8, 9, 9, 9) sts before end of Left shoulder, W&T.
Short Row 2 (WS): Work across in pattern to 6 (6, 7, 7, 8, 9, 9, 9) sts before end of Right shoulder, W&T.
Short Row 3: Work across in pattern to 6 (6, 7, 7, 8, 9, 9, 9, 9) before wrapped st on Left shoulder, W&T.
Next Row: Work across WS of Left shoulder for 7 (8, 7, 9, 9, 10, 9, 10, 10) sts, so that a total of 19 (20, 21, 23, 25, 28, 27, 28, 28) sts are on LH needle, then BO the next 36 (38, 40, 42, 44, 48, 52, 52, 50) sts across neck. Cont in pattern to 6 (6, 7, 7, 8, 9, 9, 9, 9) sts before wrapped st on Right shoulder, W&T.
Next Row: Work across RS of Right shoulder; break yarn, leaving 18-24" tail.

Join Shoulders
With RS facing, use the 18-24" yarn tail to graft the 19 (20, 21, 23, 25, 28, 27, 28, 28) sts of the shoulders tog. Use Kitchener stitch to join the two sets of live shoulder sts. PU wraps and graft them with the sts they wrap. Rep at other shoulder.

Collar
Place the 10 live sts of Buttonhole Band back on the needles, ready to begin a RS row. Work across first row, ending with a KFB. 11 sts.

Work in established Twisted Rib for 56 (60, 62, 66, 68, 74, 80, 80, 78) rows. Break yarn, leaving 12″ tail; use this tail to graft the live sts of the two bands tog.

Finishing

Sew Down Collar
Whipstitch selvage edge of collar down across bound-off sts of the back neck.

Sew In Sleeves
Pin each sleeve into armscye at underarm and shoulder seam. Sew sleeves starting at underarms. Using Mattress Stitch, and starting at center of underarm, stitch sleeve in place halfway to shoulder. Do the same up the other side. Cont seaming up both sides of sleeve to top of shoulder. Rep for second sleeve.

Pocket Border
Place the 25 held pocket sts back on the needles, and PU 1 st from body fabric at either edge. 27 sts.
Attach yarn and work in Twisted Rib for 1″.
BO all sts in pattern. Using the yarn tails, stitch short edges of border to body of cardigan.
Turn cardigan inside out. Whipstitch edges of pocket fabric down to WS of cardigan, being careful not to let sts show on RS.
Rep for second pocket.

Final Touches
Sew buttons on opposite buttonholes.

To make optional belt loops, use a crochet hook to pull a loop of yarn through to RS of fabric, 5″ below armscye along underarm. Chain stitch for 2″, then pass crochet chain back through Body to WS about 1.5″ lower.
Fasten off ends and rep on other side.

Weave in ends, wash, and block.

A 32 (36, 40, 44, 48, 52, 56, 60, 64)″
B 17 (17.5, 18, 18, 18.5, 19, 19, 19.5, 19.5)″
C 25.5 (26.5, 27.5, 27.75, 28.75, 30.5, 31, 31.5, 31)″
D 19.75 (19.75, 20, 20, 20, 20.5, 20, 19.75, 19.75)″
E 7.75 (8.25, 8.75, 9, 9.5, 10.5, 11.25, 11.5, 11.5)″
F 14 (15, 16.25, 17.5, 19.25, 21.25, 24, 24.75, 26)″
G 6.25 (6.5, 7, 7.25, 7.75, 8.25, 9, 9, 8.75)″

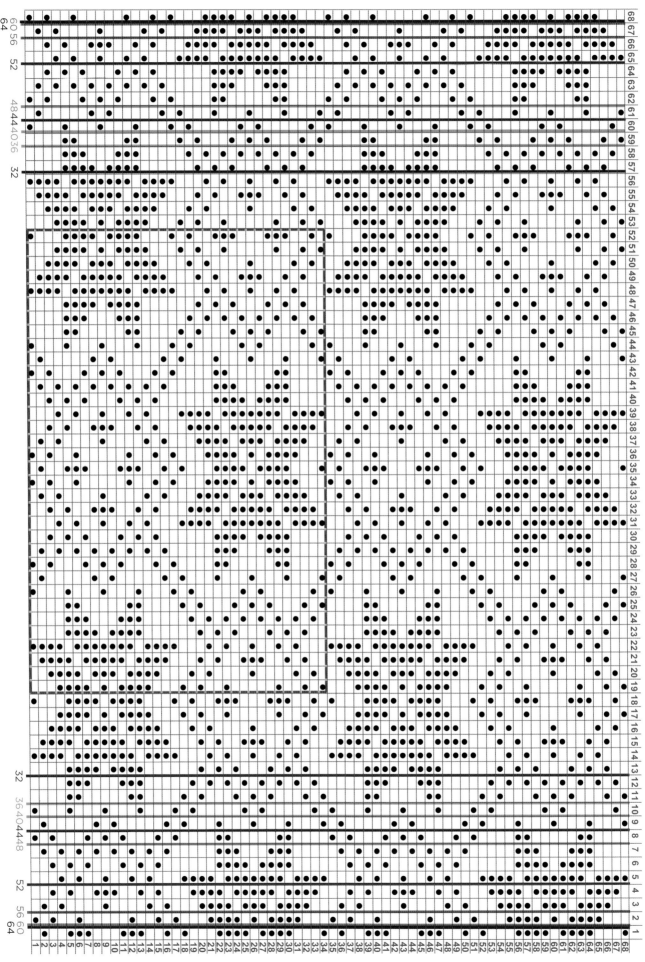

Snowflake

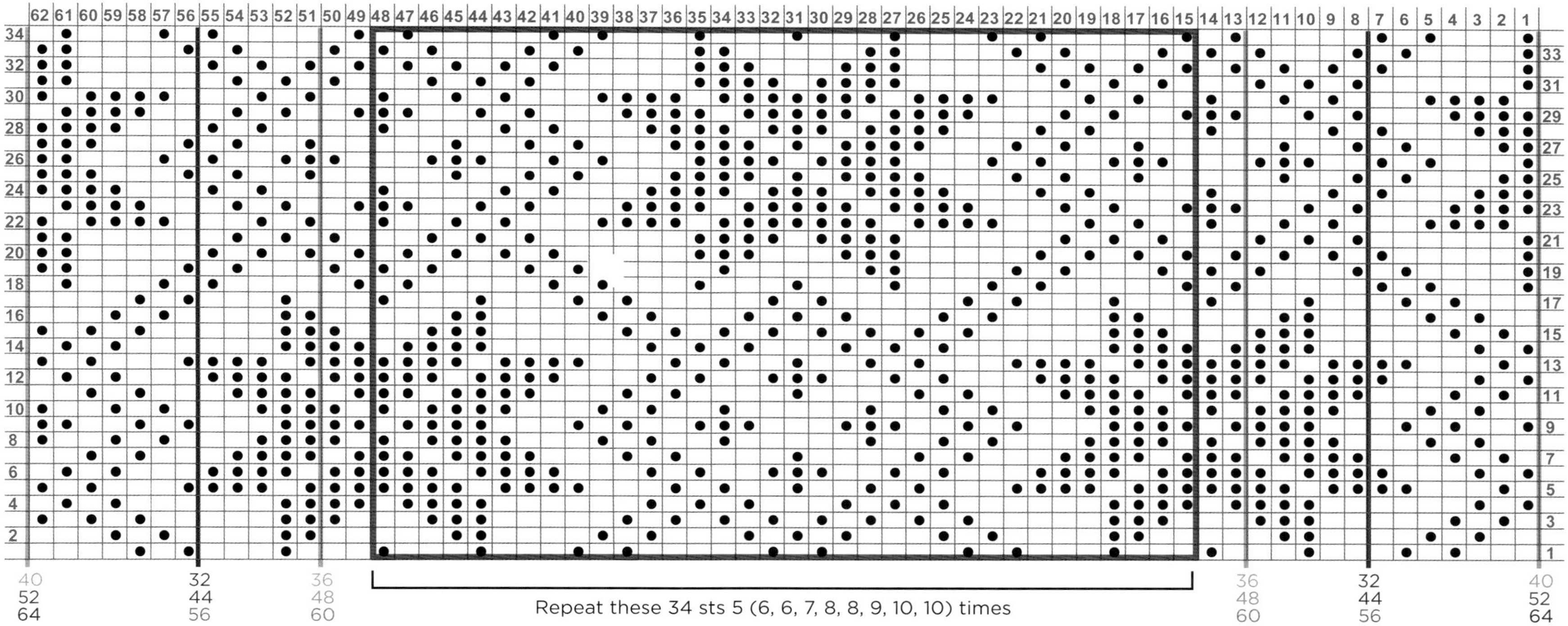

Repeat these 34 sts 5 (6, 6, 7, 8, 8, 9, 10, 10) times

LEGEND

Knit
☐ RS: knit stitch
WS: purl stitch

Purl
● RS: purl stitch
WS: knit stitch

☐ **Pattern Repeat**

	32"	52"
	36"	56"
	40"	60"
	44"	64"
	48"	

Edele Cardigan **85**

HARLEY PULLOVER

by Jenny Williams

FINISHED MEASUREMENTS

36 (40.25, 44.25, 48.25, 51.75, 56.5)"
finished bust measurement; garment
is meant to be worn with up to 4" of
positive ease

YARN

Knit Picks Swish™ (DK weight,
100% Fine Superwash Merino Wool;
123 yards/50g): Marble Heather 24636,
11 (12, 12, 13, 14, 15) skeins

NEEDLES

US 5 (3.75mm) DPNs or long circular
needles for Magic Loop, and 24" or
longer circulars, or size to obtain gauge

NOTIONS

Yarn Needle
12 Stitch Markers in 3 Colors (A, B & C,
4 of each color)
Locking Stitch Marker or Safety Pin
Cable Needle
Optional: Crochet Hook (to pick up sts)
Scrap Yarn or Extra Circular Cables

GAUGE

22 sts and 33 rows = 4" in Stockinette
Stitch worked in the round, blocked

For pattern support, contact customerservice@knitpicks.com

Harley Pullover

Notes:

This pullover begins with the key design element: the collar. Knitted flat, the collar is seamed up the back, stitches are picked up along the edge, and the body of the sweater is worked from the top down in the round. The braid cable is repeated down the center of both raglan sleeves, which are worked in the round. The 4-stitch cables mark each raglan and then follow both sides of the torso down to the hem. A 4" vent at the bottom, knitted flat, lends comfort to the overall positive ease of the design. The drawstring hem at the collar is sewn in place and a 2 stitch drawstring I-cord is threaded through.

When working a chart in the round, read each row from right to left, as a RS row. When working flat, read RS rows from right to left, and WS rows from left to right.

DIRECTIONS

CO 35 sts.
Next Row (WS): P across.

Collar

Work reps of Collar Chart beginning with Row 1 for 11.25 (11. 5, 11.75, 12, 12.25, 12.75)", ending on a WS row.

Drawstring Eyelets

Step 1 (RS): Work sts 1–27 of Collar Chart, BO 2 sts, work remainder of chart.
Step 2: Work sts 35–30 of Collar Chart, CO 2 sts using the Cabled Cast On, work remainder of chart.

Work Collar Chart for 4 more rows, ending on a WS row. Work Steps 1 and 2 once more. Cont working Collar Chart until collar is 23.25 (23.75, 24.25, 24.75, 25.25, 26.25)" from CO edge and space between drawstring eyelets falls precisely in center of collar when folded in half. BO all sts.

Block collar to a length of 24.25 (24.75, 25.25, 25.75, 26.25, 27.25)", again making sure space between drawstring eyelets falls in center of collar, and allow to dry thoroughly. Using the yarn needle, sew CO edge and BO edge of collar together with RSs together. Left edge with drawstring eyelets now becomes top edge of collar. Right edge of collar now becomes bottom edge, and sts will be picked up around it.

Upper Sweater

Pick Up Stitches

Along RS, bottom edge of collar, attach locking st marker or safety pin 4.75 (5, 5, 5, 5.25, 5.5)" to right of center between the drawstring eyelets, to mark BOR. Periodically move this M as you work, continuing to mark BOR.

When picking up sts, you may find it easiest to use a crochet hook to pull each st through the collar, and then slide it onto the RH needle.
PU and K 132 (135, 138, 140, 143, 149) sts evenly around collar, divided into the following segments:
Front Right Raglan: PU and K 11 sts, PM Color B.

Chest Panel: PU and K 30 (32, 33, 34, 36, 39) sts, PM Color A, (make sure these sts are centered just beneath the space between drawstring eyelets).
Front Left Raglan: PU and K 11 sts, PM B.
Left Sleeve Front: PU and K 1 st, PM C.
Braid: PU and K 17 sts, PM C.
Left Sleeve Back: PU and K 1 st, PM A.
Back Left Raglan: PU and K 11 sts, PM B.
Back Panel: PU and K 20 (21, 23, 24, 25, 28) sts, PM A.
Back Right Raglan: PU and K 11 sts, PM B.
Right Sleeve Back: PU and K 1 st, PM C.
Braid: PU and K 17 sts, PM C.
Right Sleeve Front: PU and K 1 st, PM A.

Work Upper Sweater

Join yarn to begin working in the rnd. Color A and B Ms indicate beginning and end of a Raglan Chart section respectively. Color C Ms indicate beginning and end of a Braid Chart section.

When increasing, Color A Ms indicate an inc st in front of the M, while Color B Ms indicate an inc st past or beyond the M. SMs as you come to them. Incs are written for each size individually in order to make raglan seams as even as possible. Inc rnd definitions follow the individual sizing section.

Size 36": Work 1 Body & Sleeve Inc Rnd followed by 1 Regular Rnd five times. Work 1 Body & Sleeve Inc Rnd followed by 2 Regular Rnds 21 times. Work 1 Sleeve Only Inc Rnd followed by 1 Regular Rnd three times. 220 sts inc. 352 sts.

Sizes 40.25" and 44.25": Work 1 Body & Sleeve Inc Rnd followed by 1 Regular Rnd 14 (25) times. Work 1 Body & Sleeve Inc Rnd followed by 2 Regular Rnds 16 (7) times. Work 1 (2) Body Only Inc Rnd(s) followed by 2 Regular Rnds 1 (2) time(s). 244 (272) sts inc. 379 (410) sts.

Size 48.25": Work 1 Body & Sleeve Inc Rnd followed by 1 Regular Rnd 33 times. Work 1 Body Only Inc Rnd followed by 1 Regular Rnd four times. Work 2 Body Only Inc Rnd followed by 2 Regular Rnds two times, work 2 Regular Rnds. 296 sts inc. 436 sts.

Size 51.75": Work 1 Body & Sleeve Inc Rnd followed by 1 Regular Rnd 35 times. Work 1 Body Only Inc Rnd followed by 1 Regular Rnd ten times. 320 sts inc. 463 sts.

Size 56.5": Work 2 Body & Sleeve Inc Rnds followed by 1 Regular Rnd five times. Work 1 Body & Sleeve Inc Rnd followed by 1 Regular Rnd 27 times. Work 1 Body Only Inc Rnd followed by 1 Regular Rnd 13 times. 348 sts inc. 497 sts.

Body & Sleeve Inc Rnd: Work Raglan Chart to M B, KFB, K to 1 st before M A, KFB, work Raglan Chart to M B, KFB, K to M C, work Braid Chart to next M C, K to 1 st before M A, KFB, work Raglan Chart to M B, KFB, K to 1 st before M A, KFB, work Raglan Chart to M B, KFB, K to M C, work Braid Chart to next M C, K to 1 st before M A, KFB. 8 sts inc.

Body Only Inc Rnd: Work Raglan Chart to M B, KFB, K to 1 st before M A, KFB, work Raglan Chart to M B, K to M C, work Braid Chart to next M C, K to M A, work Raglan Chart to M B, KFB, K to 1 st before M A, KFB, work Raglan Chart to M B, K to M C, work Braid Chart to next M C, K to M A. 4 sts inc.

Sleeve Only Inc Rnd: Work Raglan Chart to M B, K to M A, work Raglan Chart to M B, KFB, K to M C, work Braid Chart to next M C, K to 1 st before M A, KFB, work Raglan Chart to M B, K to M A, work Raglan Chart to M B, KFB, K to M C, work Braid Chart to next M C, K to 1 st before M A, KFB. 4 sts inc.

Regular Rnd: Work Raglan Chart to M B, K to M A, work Raglan Chart to M B, K to M C, work Braid Chart to next M C, K to M A, work Raglan Chart to M B, K to M A, work Raglan Chart to M B, K to M C, work Braid Chart to next M C, K to M A.

Divide Body & Sleeves
Remove M A, work Raglan Chart to M B, K to M A, work Raglan Chart to M B and remove M. Place next 77 (79, 83, 85, 89, 93) sts on scrap yarn or extra circular cable. These sts will later become the left sleeve. Remove M A, join and work Raglan Chart to M B, K to M A, work Raglan Chart to M B and remove M. Place next 77 (79, 83, 85, 89, 93) sts on scrap yarn or extra circular cable. These sts will later become the right sleeve. PM for BOR.

Sweater Body
Join and work body of sweater in established pattern which includes 2 sets of Raglan Chart sts under each arm. 198 (221, 244, 266, 285, 311) sts total for body. Work in pattern for 8 (8, 8.5, 8.75, 9, 9)" from armhole, ending at BOR M.

Hip Shaping
*Work 1 Inc Rnd followed by 23 (13, 13, 7, 5, 5) rnds in established pattern; rep from * 0 (1, 1, 2, 3, 3) more times. 202 (229, 252, 278, 301, 327) sts.

Inc Rnd:
Work Raglan Chart to M B, KFB, K to 1 st before M A, KFB, work Raglan Chart twice to M B, KFB, K to 1 st before M A, KFB, work Raglan Chart once to beginning of rnd. 4 sts inc.

Vents (worked flat)
To eliminate first P st, K2tog and work Raglan Chart to M B, K to M A, work Raglan Chart once and K2tog over last 2 sts, eliminating a second P st. Place remaining 96 (109, 121, 134, 145, 158) sts on scrap yarn or extra circular cable.
Turn, and cont working front 104 (118, 129, 142, 154, 167) sts in established pattern flat for 1" from beginning of vent, ending on a WS row.

Front Bottom Ribbing
Row 1 (RS): Work Raglan Chart (minus beginning P st), K2 (1, 6, 11, 3, 0), *K5 (4, 4, 3, 4, 5), M1; work from * 15 (23, 23, 32, 31, 29) times total, K to M A, work Raglan Chart (minus ending P st). 119 (141, 152, 174, 185, 196) sts.
Row 2 (WS): Work Raglan Chart (minus beginning P st), work Raglan Chart across row 9 (11, 12, 14, 15, 16) times, work Raglan Chart (minus ending P st).

Cont in established pattern for 3" from beginning of ribbing. BO all sts.

Back Bottom Ribbing
Move back ribbing 96 (109, 121, 134, 145, 158) sts from scrap yarn to live needles. To eliminate first P st, K2tog and work Raglan Chart to M B, K to M A, work Raglan Chart once and K2tog over last 2 sts, eliminating a second P st.
Turn, and cont working back 94 (107, 119, 132, 143, 156) sts in established pattern flat for 1" from beginning of vent, ending on a WS row.

Row 1 (RS): Work Raglan Chart (minus beginning P st), K0 (7, 3, 8, 13, 8), *K5 (3, 4, 3, 3, 4), M1; work from * 14 (23, 22, 31, 31, 29) times total, K to M A, work Raglan Chart (minus ending P st). 108 (130, 141, 163, 174, 185) sts.
Row 2 (WS): Work Raglan Chart (minus beginning P st), work Raglan Chart across row 8 (10, 11, 13, 14, 15) times, work Raglan Chart (minus ending P st).
Cont in established pattern for 3" from beginning of ribbing. BO all sts.

Sleeves
Sleeves can be worked with DPNs or circular needles using Magic Loop method. Move left sleeve from scrap yarn to live needles. 77 (79, 83, 85, 89, 93) sts. PM to mark BOR and join yarn to begin working in the rnd. Remove other Ms as you come to them.

Work in established pattern, including Braid Chart at center of sleeve. As you go, K2tog over first 2 sts of rnd and K2tog TBL over last 2 sts of rnd every 6th rnd 4 (5, 7, 6, 6, 6) times. 69 (69, 69, 73, 77, 81) sts.
Cont in established pattern for 14.5 (15, 15.5, 15.5, 15.5, 15.5)" from armpit.

Cuff
Setup Rnd: *K17 (17, 17, 24, 38, 78), K2tog; rep from * to last st, K1. 65 (65, 65, 70 75, 80) sts.
Rnd 1: *Work 2/2 RC, as illustrated in Raglan Chart, P1; rep from * across the rnd 13 (13, 13, 14, 15, 16) times.
Rep Rnd 1 for 4.5", working three plain rnds between cable rnds as in the Raglan Chart.
BO all sts.

Work right sleeve as for left, substituting 2/2 LC for 2/2 RC.

I-cord Drawstring
Using DPNs, CO 2 sts. *Sl sts to right end of needle. K2; rep from * for 43" or desired length.

Finishing
Weave in ends. Fold drawstring hem in half with WS tog, and sew in place along inside of collar. Block to Schematic measurements. Thread drawstring through left drawstring eyelet, around back of collar and through right eyelet.

LEGEND

☐ **Knit**
RS: knit stitch
WS: purl stitch

◉ **Purl**
RS: purl stitch
WS: knit stitch

C2 Over 2 Right (2/2 RC)
Sl2 to CN, hold in back. K2, K2 from CN

C2 Over 2 Left (2/2 LC)
Sl2 to CN, hold in front. K2, K2 from CN

C3 Over 2 Right P (3/2 RPC)
Sl2 to CN, hold in back, K3, P2 from CN

C3 Over 2 Left P (3/2 LPC)
Sl3 to CN, hold in front. P2, K3 from CN

C3 Over 3 Right (3/3 RC)
Sl3 to CN, hold in back. K3, K3 from CN

C3 Over 3 Left (3/3 LC)
Sl3 to CN, hold in front. K3, K3 from CN

Collar Chart

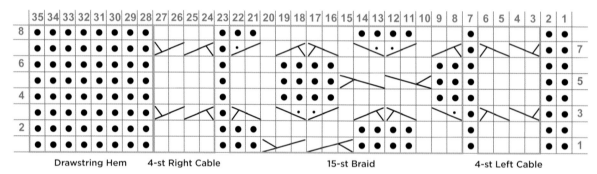

Drawstring Hem · 4-st Right Cable · 15-st Braid · 4-st Left Cable

Braid Chart

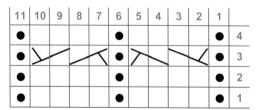

Raglan Chart

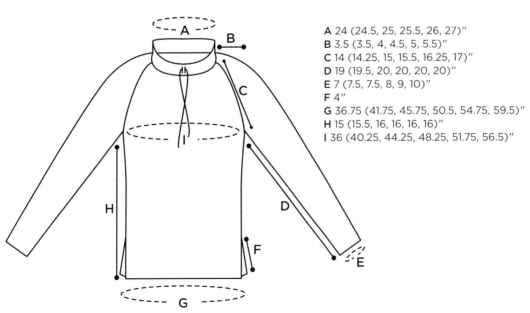

A 24 (24.5, 25, 25.5, 26, 27)″
B 3.5 (3.5, 4, 4.5, 5, 5.5)″
C 14 (14.25, 15, 15.5, 16.25, 17)″
D 19 (19.5, 20, 20, 20, 20)″
E 7 (7.5, 7.5, 8, 9, 10)″
F 4″
G 36.75 (41.75, 45.75, 50.5, 54.75, 59.5)″
H 15 (15.5, 16, 16, 16, 16)″
I 36 (40.25, 44.25, 48.25, 51.75, 56.5)″

LOFOTEN PULLOVER

by Kerin Dimeler-Laurence

FINISHED MEASUREMENTS

36 (38, 40, 42, 44, 46, 48)″ chest circumference; garment is meant to be worn with 4″ of ease

YARN

Knit Picks Wool of the Andes™ (sport weight, 100% Peruvian Highland Wool; 137 yards/50g) (see pg 102 for Autumn colors and pg 114 for Black colors)

NEEDLES

US 5 (3.75 mm) 32″ or longer circular needles for Magic Loop method, and spare DPNs, or size to obtain gauge
US 4 (3.5mm) 24-32″ circulars, or one size smaller than those used to obtain gauge

NOTIONS

Yarn Needle
Stitch Markers
Optional: Grosgrain Ribbon
Sewing Thread to match MC, and Needle
3 Clasps or a 6-8″ non-separating Zipper
Optional: Six 0.5″ Buttons to match clasp
Size D Crochet Hook for steeks and embellishment

GAUGE

25 sts and 30 rounds = 4″ in Stockinette Stitch and Stranded Stockinette Stitch on larger needles in the round, blocked

For pattern support, contact customerservice@knitpicks.com

Lofoten Pullover

Notes:

In admiration of the classic Norwegian ski sweater, the Lofoten Pullover incorporates modern details alongside traditional motifs and bright splashes of color. In addition to set-in shoulders, you'll also find knitted facings around the cuffs and placket, as well as a ribbed hem for a comfortable fit. This quintessential pullover is ideal for adventurous knitters and boasts an exciting array of techniques, including colorwork, steeks, surface crochet, and more.

You may need different size needles for St st and stranded St st; be sure to swatch in the round for both before beginning.

Because there are many different sizes shown on some of the charts, you may want to use a pen or pencil to outline your size and scratch out any stitches beyond that line.

The Cuff pattern on the sleeves mimics the embroidered cuffs on the original Lusekofte sweaters. Both sleeves are knit identically. A facing is knit for the cuff, then a turning row, and the patterned outer layer of the sleeve begins thereafter. The facing is turned under, reinforcing the cuff. At the shoulder, the sleeves are joined together as one with steeks to make the shoulder sections simpler to complete. This is quite different from most shoulder constructions, but will allow you to maintain knitting in the round to the very top of the sleeves.

The neck is a two-stage process. First, stitches for the placket are bound off and a steek is worked between the two halves; then, as the neckline itself decreases, a new steek is cast on between the sides. This will aid in the ease of finishing the garment.

Though most modern Norwegian sweaters use a machine-sewn steek, the thickness of this sweater's fabric does not lend well to this technique. Instead, use a crochet-chain or hand-sewn steek (see Glossary).

Crochet chain embroidery finishes the look of the neckline and seams. Work this crochet chain in exactly the same way as in a crocheted steek. The only difference is that this is purely for looks, and not for stability!

DIRECTIONS

Sleeves (make 2 the same)

With smaller needles and scrap yarn, provisionally CO 54 (54, 58, 58, 58, 62, 62) sts. PM and join in the rnd. Switch to MC and work in St st for 3.5". Purl one rnd.

Switch to larger needles and begin working from Bracelet Charts, being sure to select the chart corresponding to your size. (Though it looks like the chart should start from the center, work it right to left as usual. This will place the vertical lines on the outside of the wrist when worn.) There are two decs towards end of Bracelet section.

After Rnd 25 of Bracelet Chart, begin working sleeve in St st in MC. Work in St st through the following Inc rnd, then switch to Sleeve Cap Chart (see Beginning of Rnd directions on the Sleeve Cap Chart page).

Note: for longer sleeves, keep knitting in St st after the incs, but before Sleeve Cap Chart, until desired length. Every four rnds adds approx .5". Sleeve Cap Chart adds 1" to length of sleeve from cuff to underarm. For largest sizes, more of MC may need to be purchased to lengthen sleeves and body.

Inc Rnd: M1L in pattern, K to end of rnd, M1R in pattern. Work Inc Rnds in pattern as follows:

Size 36: Every 5th and 11th rnd eight times. 32 sts inc. 84 sts total.

Size 38: Every 5th rnd 17 times. 34 sts inc. 86 sts total.

Size 40: Every 5th rnd 17 times. 34 sts inc. 90 sts total.

Size 42: On the 3rd rnd, then every 5th rnd 18 times. 38 sts inc. 94 sts total.

Size 44: Every 5th rnd 19 times. 38 sts inc. 94 sts total.

Size 46: On the 1st and 3rd rnd, then every 5th rnd 19 times. 42 sts inc. 102 sts total.

Size 48: On the 5th rnd, then every 4th rnd 22 times. 46 sts inc. 106 sts total.

Work 10 (14, 16, 10, 11, 9, 14) rnds plain.
Work both sleeves through St st portion and through Rnd 7 of Sleeve Cap Chart corresponding to your size.
On Rnd 8 of Sleeve Cap Chart, BO for underarms: work to 6 (5, 6, 5, 5, 7, 6) sts before end of rnd. BO 13 (11, 13, 11, 11, 15, 13) sts across last sts of this rnd and first sts of next, removing M.

Join Sleeves for Steek

Next Rnd: Work to last charted st on one sleeve. CO for steek after last st as follows:
(1 st MC, 1 st C1) three times, 1 st MC. This 7-st steek will run between the two sleeves.

Instead of joining the sleeve back to other side of itself, PM and K next rnd of second sleeve onto same needle directly after steek. After last st of this sleeve, CO another 7-st steek, PM and join to next rnd of first sleeve. The two sleeves are now linked together in the rnd.

Follow Sleeve Cap Chart for your size, working all decs as shown. Work first and last st of steeks in MC, and work in a checkerboard pattern, alternating MC and C1, over the five sts between.
After last rnd of Sleeve Cap Chart, BO all sts using MC.

Body

The body is knit in one piece, with steeks across armscyes and front neck placket. With MC and smaller needles, CO 228 (240, 252, 264, 276, 288, 300) sts. PM and join in the rnd, being careful not to twist sts. Work in 2x2 Rib for 2".

Color Pattern

Switch to larger needles. Attach C1 and begin working from Lower Band and Body Chart.

After completing Rnds 1-23, begin working body in St st in MC. Work until body measures 14 (14.5, 15, 15.5, 16, 15.5, 15)" from CO. Note: Especially with smaller sizes, you can increase length of body for a better fit. Work solid colored body until it is 1" below desired length.

Begin Chest Chart

Next rnd, begin working from Chest Chart. This begins approx 1" below break for armscyes. PM after 57 (60, 63, 66, 69, 72, 75) sts to mark center front, and another after 114 (120, 126, 132, 138, 144, 150) sts from BOR; this marks right underarm. BOR is under left arm.

(Though all incs, decs, and BOs are noted in your chart, some are repeated below for greater detail.) Ms are added on either side of steeks to help you follow the pattern—these are optional.

In center of chest below neck placket, there is space in which you can monogram the sweater. Choose two characters from Monogram Chart and place them in this space; sizes 46 and 48 have enough space for two lines of characters.

Break for Sleeves

On Rnd 9 of your chart, BO for armscyes. Work until 4 (4, 4, 5, 6, 6, 7) sts before right underarm M. BO 8 (8, 8, 10, 12, 12, 14) sts, removing M. Work in pattern across back until 4 (4, 4, 5, 6, 6, 7) sts before end of rnd; BO 9 (9, 9, 11, 13, 13, 15) sts, removing M.
Work from Rnd 10 across front of sweater, noting that there are decs at armscyes on this rnd. At right underarm, PM and CO 6 sts in alternating colors across gap. PM and rejoin to back of garment and cont Rnd 10 to left underarm; PM and CO 6 sts in alternating colors across gap, PM after third st to mark new BOR. PM and join to front.
Begin working from Rnd 11. Two steeks have been created.

Work from Chest and Back Charts, following decs at armscyes and working steeks in a 1x1 checkerboard pattern.

Neck Placket and Steek

On Rnd 20 (21, 21, 24, 25, 29, 31) of Chest chart, work in pattern to 6 sts before center front M. BO next 12 sts loosely in alternating colors. Cont around in pattern.

On next rnd, work in pattern to center front, PM, and CO 6 sts in alternating colors across gap. PM and join to other side; cont in the rnd.

Shape Neck

On Rnd 53 (55, 59, 63, 65, 70, 72), BO for neck as follows. Work to 4 (5, 5, 5, 5, 6, 5) sts before center neck steek. BO 4 (5, 5, 5, 5, 6, 5) sts, 6 steek sts, and then 4 (5, 5, 5, 5, 6, 5) sts after steek. Cont in pattern around.

Next Rnd: Work to last st before bound off neck sts. CO a new 7-st steek between sides of neck, in the same way other steeks have been CO. This steek will run up neckline for remainder of sweater. (As you shape neckline, note that there may be some decs in neckline area while also working short-row shoulders.)

Shoulder Shaping

Shoulders are shaped with short rows. They are worked back and forth across both shoulders on one side of garment.

First short row is worked across right side of front. At the same time, neckline in back is bound off. On last rnd before short rows begin, work across front, BO armscye steek sts, and work to st 61 (59, 60, 64, 63, 62, 62) of Back Chart. (Note: this is only referring to a st on the chart, not how many sts across back you will knit.) BO next 28 (32, 30, 22, 24, 26, 26) sts, cont across back, BO steek sts at next armscye, and cont to next rnd of front.

Note that even though you will be working back and forth, row numbers still appear along right side of chart.
At st indicated on front, W&T. (You may wrap with one or both colors, as you wish.) On next row, purl in pattern to st indicated, W&T. Cont in this manner until last row; break yarns. With RS facing, attach C4 at edge of left armscye (not where you left off!) and work one row, picking up wraps and knitting them with the sts they wrap. Break yarn.

Turn your work so that back is facing you. Attach both MC and C1, and work across shoulders to first bound-off st. CO a 7-st steek, and cont across row. Work back and forth in short rows as done for front. After last charted row, break yarns. With RS facing, attach C4 at edge of right armscye (not where you left off!) and work one row, picking up wraps and knitting them with the sts they wrap. Do not break yarn.

Place all front and back shoulder sts on needles so that the two needle tips are pointing out of left armscye, with front of sweater facing you and RS out. Using C4 from Back, perform a 3-Needle BO across left shoulder, neck steeks, and right shoulder. This will give a decorative seam to the shoulders. Break yarn.

Steeks

Once you have chosen a method of steeking, sew or crochet around every steek: sleeve cap, armscyes, neck placket, neck, and back neck. With very sharp scissors, cut each steek open.

Neckbands & Collar

With RS facing and using MC, PU and K 29 (30, 33, 34, 35, 36, 37) sts up right edge (as worn) of neck placket; PU sts between body sts and first steek st.
Work in St st for five more rows.
Next Row (RS): P across, to create a turning row.
Work in St st for 6 more rows.
BO all sts, leaving a generous 12" tail.
Turn band under along turning row, trapping loose steek ends inside. Using yarn tail, whipstitch bound-off edge to WS of picked-up edge. Weave in this end.

Rep this band on left edge; before weaving in end, use it to whipstitch both neckbands to center edge above monogram.

Collar

With RS facing, using MC, PU and K sts as follows for collar: PU 10 (11, 11, 11, 11, 12, 11) sts from top of right neckband and bound-off collar sts, 20 (20, 19, 19, 19, 18, 20) sts up neckline to shoulder join, 6 (6, 6, 9, 9, 9, 9) sts down slope of back right shoulder, 28 (32, 30, 22, 24, 26, 26) across back, 6 (6, 6, 9, 9, 9, 9) sts up slope of back left shoulder, 20 (20, 19, 19, 19, 18, 20) sts down slope of neckline, and 10 (11, 11, 11, 11, 12, 11) sts across bound-off sts and left neckband; 100 (106, 102, 100, 102, 104, 106) sts total. PM and CO a 7-st steek after last picked up st; PM and join to first st on other side of collar.

Next Rnd: Begin working from Collar Chart, noting that you may not end after a full chart rep. After last rnd, BO all sts.

Using steek finishing method of your choice, prepare and cut steek. Fold steek sts behind collar sts, and then fold collar towards inside of sweater along turning row. Using MC, sew folded ends of collar shut, and then sew bound off edge to WS of picked up sts. Weave in ends.

Finishing

Turn sleeves inside out. Weave in or tie off ends. Fold cuff facing down along turning row to cover inside of Bracelet. Unravel Provisional CO and place sts onto DPNs or circulars. Using MC, carefully stitch down each st to its corresponding st on inside of sleeve, being careful not to disrupt color pattern on RS. Weave in this end. Rep on second sleeve.

Turn body inside out. Weave in or tie off ends.

Turn both body and sleeves RS out. Pin one sleeve in place at underarm and at top. Using MC and Mattress Stitch, sew sleeve into armscye from top of shoulder to underarm, then back up to top on the other side. Be sure to sew between last patterned st and first st of steeks, where applicable. Rep for second sleeve.

Tie off ends of yarn used to sew, but do not weave them in. This will allow you to adjust seam later, if necessary.

Wash and block sweater to finished measurements.

Embellishment

With C4, work a crochet chain around base of collar (where sts were picked up), then along picked-up beginnings of neckbands, and finally around sleeve seams. To finish them, pass a single strand of yarn through last loop in front, then pass that strand back through fabric to WS. Weave this end back through WS of crochet chain

Cuff Buttons (optional)

Sew three buttons to each cuff on outer edge. Line them up with Rows 5, 13, and 21 of Bracelet Chart, up center column of sts.

Closures

Clasps

Sew three clasps to neckband. Place first clasp under line of embroidery on collar, and a second just above bottom of neckband. Place the third halfway between top clasp and bottom clasp. Clasps should be situated so that, when closed, the two neckband edges just touch each other.

Zipper

Pin zipper to neckbands so the loose top end of zipper tape is folded behind the rest of the zipper and the zipper's teeth are visible from RS of garment. Closed end of zipper should be below the split in the neckband. Following manufacturer's directions, sew zipper tape to underside of neckbands.

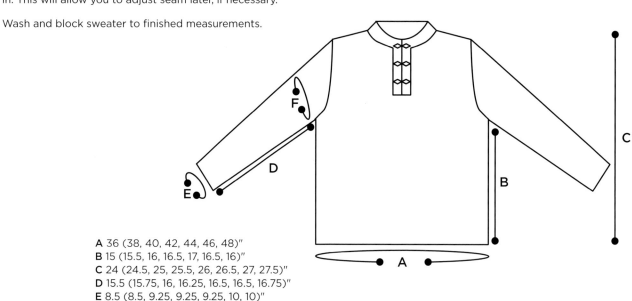

A 36 (38, 40, 42, 44, 46, 48)"
B 15 (15.5, 16, 16.5, 17, 16.5, 16)"
C 24 (24.5, 25, 25.5, 26, 26.5, 27, 27.5)"
D 15.5 (15.75, 16, 16.25, 16.5, 16.5, 16.75)"
E 8.5 (8.5, 9.25, 9.25, 9.25, 10, 10)"
F 13.5 (13.75, 14.5, 15, 15, 16.25, 17"

Lofoten:

AUTUMN COLORWAY

YARN COLORS

8 (9, 9, 10, 10, 11, 12) skeins:
MC Bramble Heather 25278

3 (3, 3, 4, 4, 5, 5) skeins:
C1 Oyster Heather 25276

1 skein each:
C2 Thyme 25280
C3 Pumpkin 25295
C4 Saffron 25284

LEGEND

▦	**No Stitch** Placeholder—no stitch made	
☐	**Knit** Knit stitch	
⊡	**Purl** Purl stitch	
◿	**K2tog** Knit two stitches together as one stitch	
◺	**SSK** (Slip 1 knit-wise) twice; insert left-hand needle into front of these 2 stitches and knit them together	
◹	**K3tog** Knit three stitches together as one stitch	
◺	**SSSK** (Slip 1 knit-wise) three times; insert left-hand needle from the front to the back of all stitches at the same time and knit them together	
φ	**Wrap and Turn (W&T)** Wrap and turn for short row, following pattern instructions	

■	MC
☐	C1
▨	C2
▤	C3
■	C4
☐	36″
☐	38″
☐	40″
☐	42″
☐	44″
☐	46″
☐	48″

Lower Band and Body Chart

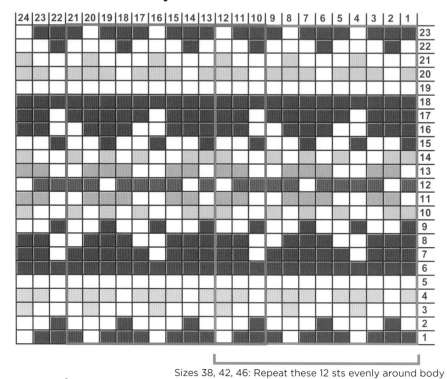

Note: this chart is worked in the Body section, after the Sleeve Cap Chart.

Sizes 38, 42, 46: Repeat these 12 sts evenly around body

Sizes 36, 40, 44, 48: Repeat these 12 sts evenly around body

Bracelet Charts

These charts represent every st around the cuffs of each size. After the 25 rounds of the bracelet pattern, cont the sleeves in St st in the main color.

Sizes 36" & 38": 54 sts

Sizes 40", 42" & 44": 58 sts

Sizes 46" & 48": 62 sts

Sleeve Cap Chart (36", 40", 44", 48")

After the sleeve has been worked in Stockinette stitch, the sleeve cap patterning begins. All decreases are included in this chart.

Note: Bound-off stitches are not represented by a symbol on this chart because of the overlap between sizes. Follow the bind-off instructions as written in the pattern.

Beginning of Round

The patterning shown here on rounds 1-4 should match up with the same patterning (in reversed orientation) as in rounds 22-25 of the Bracelet Chart.

After round 4, begin working from the chart as shown for your size; no additional moving of stitches is needed. Work in the round, following color pattern and steek instructions.

Begin working these rounds from that point in the pattern that corresponds to where you would be in the border pattern. This may or may not be the first stitch shown for your size! An example is shown to the right.

If your border round lines up here...

...Begin Round 1 of the chart here.

Begin Round 1 here.

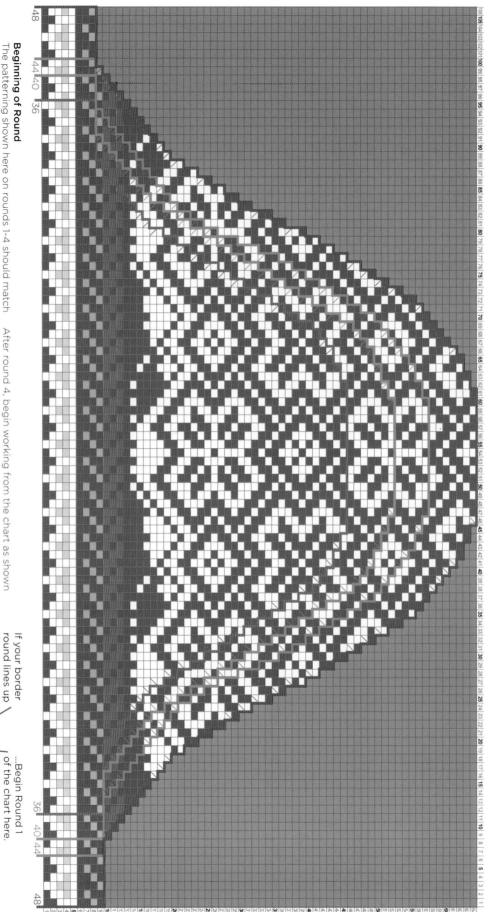

Sleeve Cap Chart (38", 42", 46")

After the sleeve has been worked in Stockinette stitch, the sleeve cap patterning begins. All decreases are included in this chart.

Note: Bound-off stitches are not represented by a symbol on this chart because of the overlap between sizes. Follow the bind-off instructions as written in the pattern.

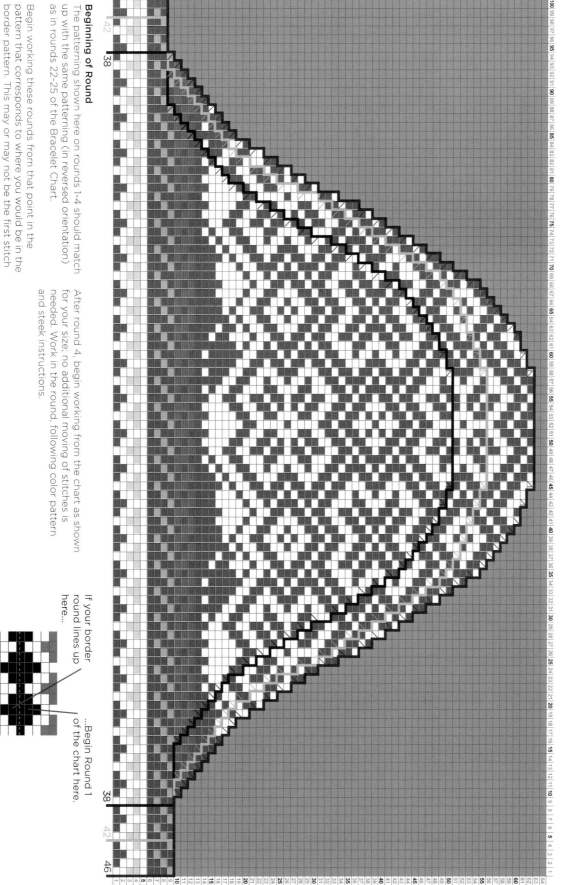

Beginning of Round

The patterning shown here on rounds 1-4 should match up with the same patterning (in reversed orientation) as in rounds 22-25 of the Bracelet Chart.

After round 4, begin working from the chart as shown for your size; no additional moving of stitches is needed. Work in the round, following color pattern and steek instructions.

Begin working these rounds from that point in the pattern that corresponds to where you would be in the border pattern. This may or may not be the first stitch shown for your size! An example is shown to the right.

If your border round lines up here...

...Begin Round 1 of the chart here.

Begin Round 1 here.

Chest Chart (Left Side)

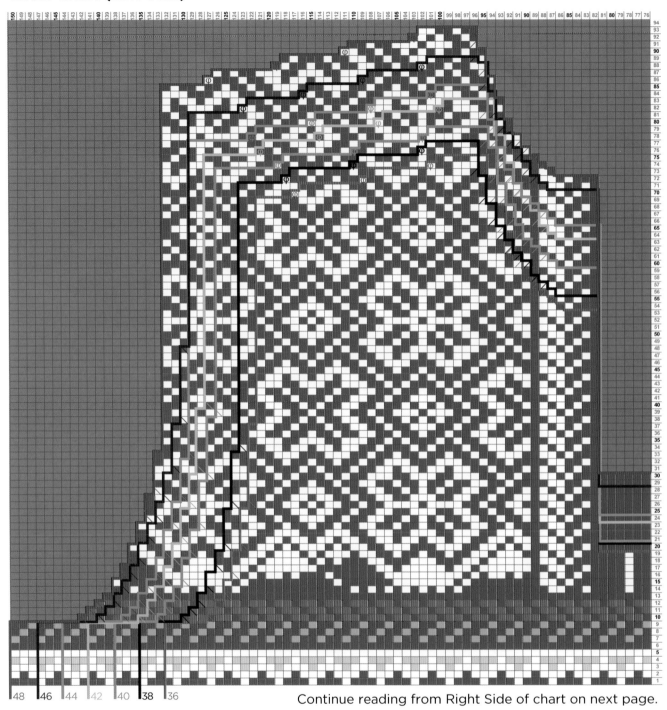

Continue reading from Right Side of chart on next page.

Chart Directions

Work from this chart starting with the stitch corresponding to your size, but read the 'Beginning of Round' instructions before proceeding.

Follow the chart for your size, working all decreases as given. When you reach the end of the chart for your size, read across the same row on the Back Chart to complete the round.

Steeks are not represented on the chart; follow the pattern directions for their placement.

Between stitches 70-81 and after row 13, work a two-character monogram; see Monogram Chart for more instructions.

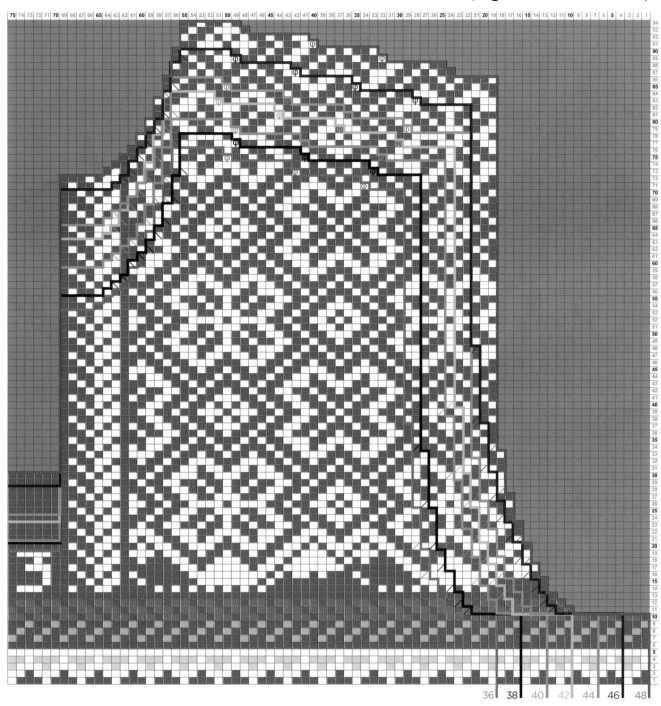

Beginning of Round

The patterning shown here on rounds 1-4 should match up with the same patterning (in reversed orientation) as in rounds 20-23 of the Lower Band and Body Chart. Begin working these rounds from that point in the pattern that corresponds to where you would be in the border pattern. This may or may not be the first stitch shown for your size!

After round 4, begin working from the chart as shown for your size; no additional moving of stitches is needed. Work in the round, following color pattern and steek instructions.

Back Chart (Left Side)

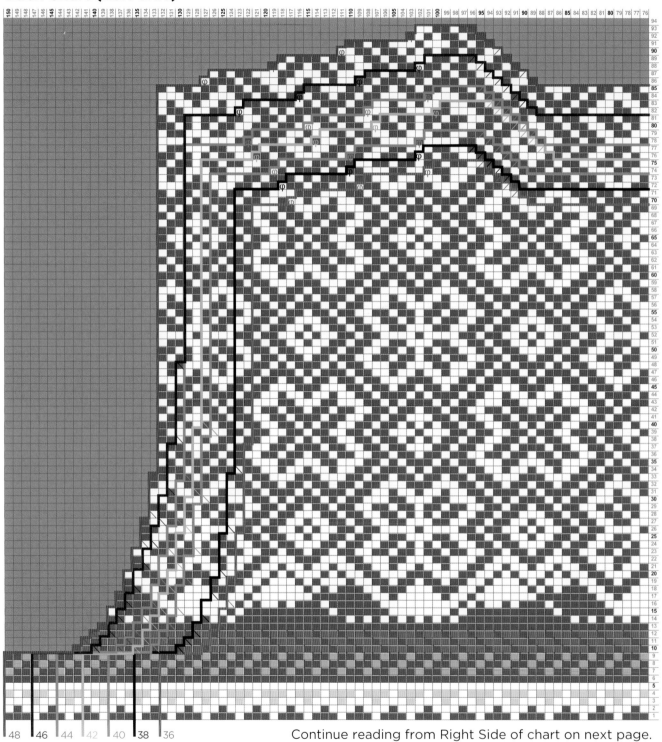

Continue reading from Right Side of chart on next page.

Back Chart (Right Side—start here)

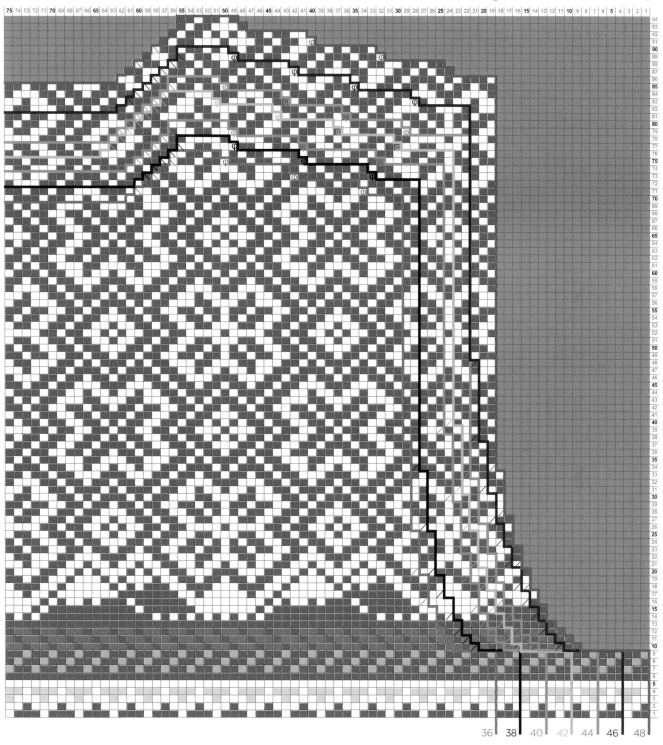

Monogram Chart

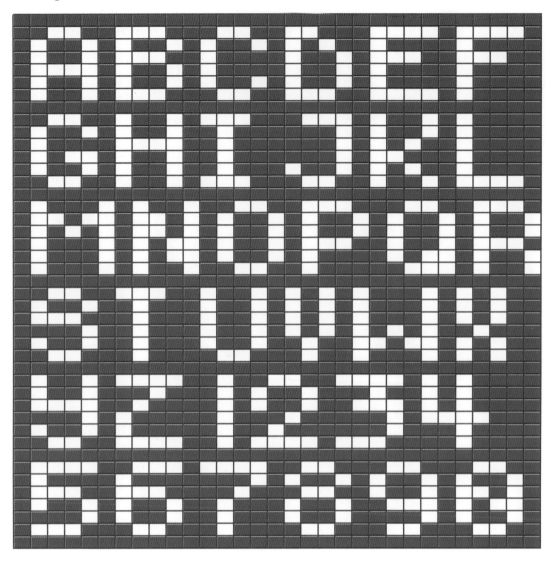

For a personal touch, add a monogram to your sweater. In the center of the chest below the neck placket, there is a small section worked in MC. This section is wide enough for two characters on the above chart, and sizes 46 and 48 can also fit two rows. Use the characters shown in the Chest Chart as a placement guide. Most characters are four stitches across, but if you are using characters that are fewer or more stitches, be sure to check their placement in the grid! Use the sample grid at right to chart your monogram. Work from this sample chart over stitches 70-81 and over rows 13 and above, ending where your size indicates.

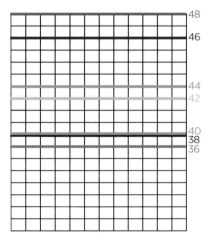

Collar Chart

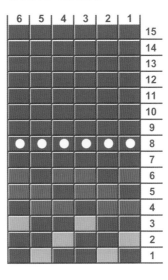

2nd Colorway

Lofoten:

BLACK COLORWAY

YARN COLORS

8 (9, 9, 10, 10, 11, 12) skeins:
MC Coal 25268

3 (3, 3, 4, 4, 5, 5) skeins:
C1 White 25269

1 skein each:
C2 Haze Heather 25657
C3 Thirst Heather 25960
C4 Peapod 25959

LEGEND

■ **No Stitch**
Placeholder—no stitch made

□ **Knit**
Knit stitch

⊡ **Purl**
Purl stitch

◪ **K2tog**
Knit two stitches together as one stitch

◩ **SSK**
(Slip 1 knit-wise) twice; insert left-hand needle into front of these 2 stitches and knit them together

◪ **K3tog**
Knit three stitches together as one stitch

◪ **SSSK**
(Slip 1 knit-wise) three times; insert left-hand needle from the front to the back of all stitches at the same time and knit them together

φ **Wrap and Turn (W&T)**
Wrap and turn for short row, following pattern instructions

■ MC
□ C1
▦ C2
▦ C3
▦ C4
□ 36″
□ 38″
□ 40″
□ 42″
□ 44″
□ 46″
□ 48″

Lower Band and Body Chart

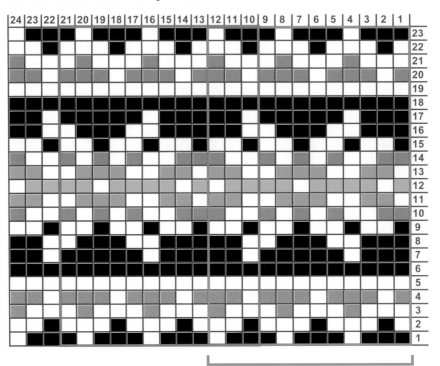

Note: this chart is worked in the Body section, after the Sleeve Cap Chart.

Sizes 38, 42, 46: Repeat these 12 sts evenly around body

Sizes 36, 40, 44, 48: Repeat these 12 sts evenly around body

Bracelet Charts

These charts represent every st around the cuffs of each size. After the 25 rounds of the bracelet pattern, cont the sleeves in St st in the main color.

Sizes 36″ & 38″: 54 sts

Sizes 40″, 42″ & 44″: 58 sts

Sizes 46″ & 48″: 62 sts

Sleeve Cap Chart (36", 40", 44", 48")

After the sleeve has been worked in Stockinette stitch, the sleeve cap patterning begins. All decreases are included in this chart.

Note: Bound-off stitches are not represented by a symbol on this chart because of the overlap between sizes. Follow the bind-off instructions as written in the pattern.

Beginning of Round

The patterning shown here on rounds 1-4 should match up with the same patterning (in reversed orientation) as in rounds 22-25 of the Bracelet Chart.

After round 4, begin working from the chart as shown for your size; no additional moving of stitches is needed. Work in the round, following color pattern and steek instructions.

Begin working these rounds from that point in the pattern that corresponds to where you would be in the border pattern. This may or may not be the first stitch shown for your size! An example is shown to the right.

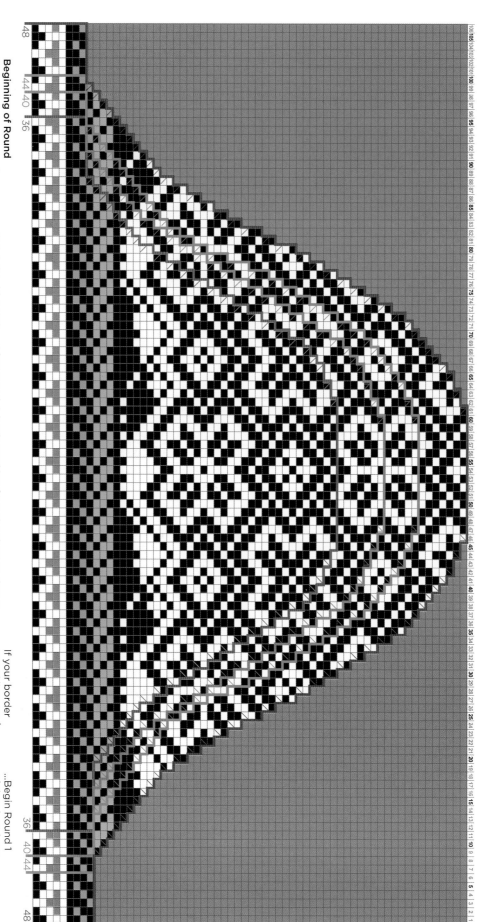

If your border round lines up here...

...Begin Round 1 of the chart here.

Sleeve Cap Chart (38", 42", 46")

After the sleeve has been worked in Stockinette stitch, the sleeve cap patterning begins. All decreases are included in this chart.

Note: Bound-off stitches are not represented by a symbol on this chart because of the overlap between sizes. Follow the bind-off instructions as written in the pattern.

Beginning of Round

The patterning shown here on rounds 1-4 should match up with the same patterning (in reversed orientation) as in rounds 22-25 of the Bracelet Chart.

After round 4, begin working from the chart as shown for your size; no additional moving of stitches is needed. Work in the round, following color pattern and steek instructions.

Begin working these rounds from that point in the pattern that corresponds to where you would be in the border pattern. This may or may not be the first stitch shown for your size! An example is shown to the right.

If your border round lines up here...

...Begin Round 1 of the chart here.

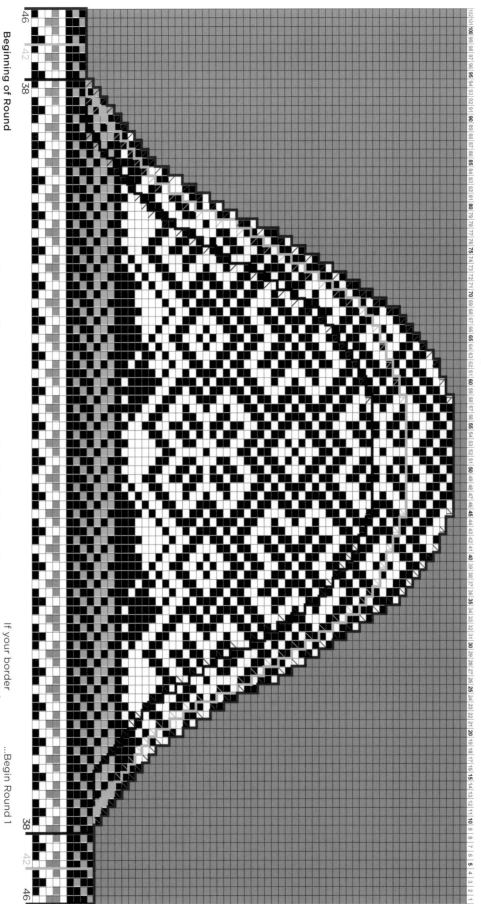

Chest Chart (Left Side)

Continue reading from Right Side of chart on next page.

Chart Directions

Work from this chart starting with the stitch corresponding to your size, but read the 'Beginning of Round' instructions before proceeding.

Follow the chart for your size, working all decreases as given. When you reach the end of the chart for your size, read across the same row on the Back Chart to complete the round.

Steeks are not represented on the chart; follow the pattern directions for their placement.

Between stitches 70-81 and after row 13, work a two-character monogram; see Monogram Chart for more instructions.

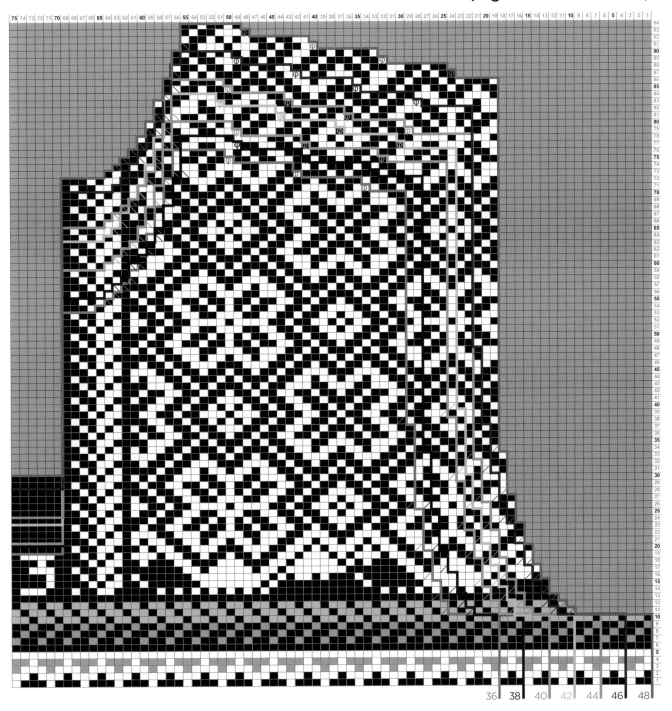

Beginning of Round

The patterning shown here on rounds 1-4 should match up with the same patterning (in reversed orientation) as in rounds 20-23 of the Lower Band and Body Chart. Begin working these rounds from that point in the pattern that corresponds to where you would be in the border pattern. This may or may not be the first stitch shown for your size!

After round 4, begin working from the chart as shown for your size; no additional moving of stitches is needed. Work in the round, following color pattern and steek instructions.

Back Chart (Left Side)

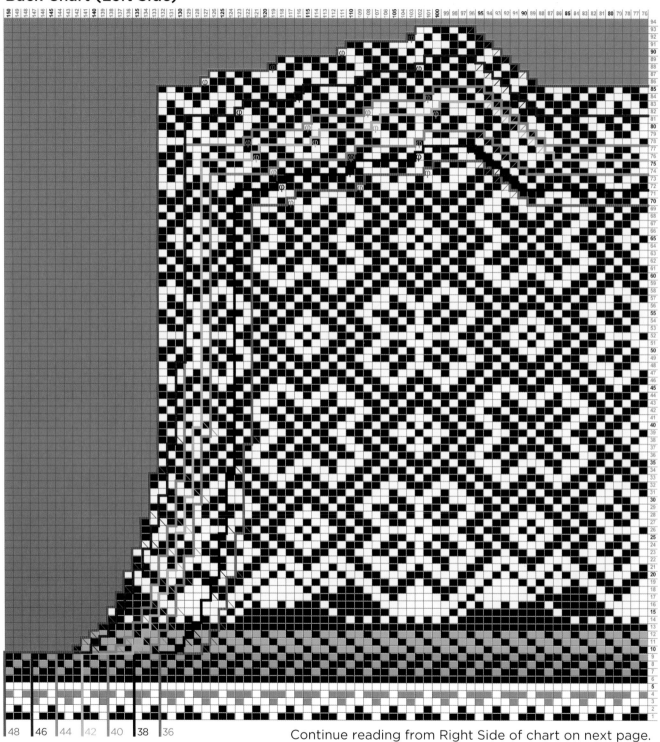

Continue reading from Right Side of chart on next page.

Monogram Chart

For a personal touch, add a monogram to your sweater. In the center of the chest below the neck placket, there is a small section worked in MC. This section is wide enough for two characters on the above chart, and sizes 46 and 48 can also fit two rows. Use the characters shown in the Chest Chart as a placement guide. Most characters are four stitches across, but if you are using characters that are fewer or more stitches, be sure to check their placement in the grid! Use the sample grid at right to chart your monogram. Work from this sample chart over stitches 70-81 and over rows 13 and above, ending where your size indicates.

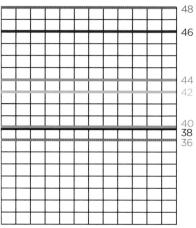

Collar Chart

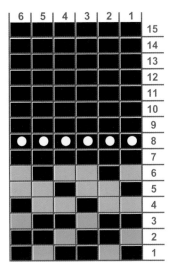

MORAINE PULLOVER

by Kerin Dimeler-Laurence

FINISHED MEASUREMENTS
32 (36, 40, 44, 48, 52)" finished bust measurement

YARN
Knit Picks Palette™ (fingering weight, 100% Peruvian Highland Wool; 231 yards/50g) (see pg 130 for Atmosphere colors and pg 150 for Forest colors)

NEEDLES
US 3 (3.25mm) 32-60" circular needles, plus spare needles of same size, and DPNs or long circulars for Magic Loop, or size to obtain gauge

US 2 (3mm) 32-60" circular needles and DPNs or long circulars for Magic Loop, or one size smaller than those used to obtain gauge

NOTIONS
Yarn Needle
Stitch Markers
Scrap Yarn or Stitch Holders
Sewing Needle and Thread for steek

GAUGE
32 sts and 38 rounds = 4" in Stranded Stockinette Stitch in the round, blocked

For pattern support, contact customerservice@knitpicks.com

Moraine Pullover

Notes:

Combining classic style with modern colors and motifs, the Moraine Pullover blurs the line between foreground and background. This bottom-up raglan style pullover features a clever, all-over patterning with bold color repeats that are sure to catch your eye.

Columns of flowers bow into faux princess seams, while the actual shaping takes place along the sides. The sleeves and the body of the pullover both begin with corrugated ribbing and are worked in the round, then joined together at the armscyes. A steek is cast on across the neckline so the sweater can be worked in the round to the end. Finally, the pullover is finished off with a curved V-neck that also features a simple band of corrugated ribbing. A true classic with a twist, the Moraine Sweater is sure to be a treat for any knitter looking to explore colorwork knitting!

All references to Right and Left are as worn. Splice yarn ends together where possible—this will save time in finishing. Where colors are repeated after a few rounds, carry the unused color up the inside of the work—this will make for fewer ends to weave in. Unless indicated otherwise, MC in these directions refers to the color called for in the charts.

Read through the pattern first so you become familiar with the places where there are instructions in the pattern occurring at the same time you are working from one or more charts and other "at the same time" instructions.

All charts are worked in the rnd, followed from bottom to top, rounds read from right to left.

DIRECTIONS

Sleeves (make 2 the same)
With MC and smaller needles, loosely CO 64 (68, 72, 80, 84, 88) sts. PM and join in the rnd, being careful not to twist sts. Work in 2x2 Rib for two rnds.

On next rnd, begin Corrugated Ribbing. Attach C11 and begin patterning: K2 in MC, P2 in C11, following color order in Corrugated Ribbing chart and referencing Color Progression legend. Cont working in this manner for the 18 rnds of chart.

Next Rnd: Work 2x2 Rib in MC only.
Next Rnd: Switch to larger needles and K all in MC.

On next rnd, begin working from Sleeve Part 1 chart, following shaping directions for your size and changing colors as indicated in charts. Sleeve chart is broken into three parts; begin with Part 1.

On second-to-last rnd for your size in Sleeve Part 3, BO for armscyes: Work in pattern to 5 (5, 5, 6, 6, 7) sts before end of rnd. K the next st in MC—this 1 st of MC will become half of the raglan dec 'stripe'. BO last 4 (4, 4, 5, 5, 6) sts, then first 4 (4, 4, 5, 5, 6) sts of next rnd. K1 in MC to create the other 'stripe', then work around in pattern to last st for your

size. Place remaining 104 (108, 112, 118, 122, 128) sleeve sts on stitch holder or scrap yarn.

Body
All shaping in the Body occurs at the underarms, just as done in the sleeves.

Hem
With MC and smaller needles, loosely CO 272 (296, 328, 360, 396, 436) sts. PM and join in the rnd, being careful not to twist sts. Work in 2x2 Rib for two rnds.

On next rnd, begin Corrugated Ribbing. Attach C11 and begin patterning: K2 in MC, P2 in C11, following color order in Corrugated Ribbing chart and referencing Color Progression legend. Cont working in this manner for the 18 rnds of chart.

Next Rnd: Work 2x2 Rib in MC only.
Next Rnd: Switch to larger needles and K all in MC, PM after 136 (148, 164, 180, 198, 218) sts to mark right underarm. Beginning of rnd is at left underarm.

Torso
On next rnd, begin working from Lower Body chart, following shaping directions for your size and changing colors as indicated in charts. This chart is repeated on front (first half of sts) and back (second half of sts) of sweater.

Cont working in pattern as established to second-to-last rnd for your size.
On next rnd, sts are bound off for armscyes. *Work in pattern to 5 (5, 5, 6, 6, 7) sts before next underarm M. K1 in MC (this will establish first half of raglan 'stripe')*; with MC, BO next 8 (8, 8, 10, 10, 12) sts, removing M. K1 in MC; rep from * to *. With MC, BO last 4 (4, 4, 5, 5, 6) sts of this rnd and first 4 (4, 4, 5, 5, 6) sts of next rnd, K1 in MC. 252 (272, 300, 328, 356, 392) sts.

Join Body and Sleeves
Place one sleeve on a spare set of needles. Maintain one St st in current color on either side of each of the four Ms that will note the raglan dec points. Work all decs in pattern as given.

Beginning at st 1, work Raglan and Neckline Part 1 chart on rnd indicated for your size to first bound-off st of body. *PM and begin knitting across sleeve: K across Raglan Sleeve Part 1 in pattern as established to last st.* PM, and work across back of Body in Body pattern as established to first bound-off st. Place second sleeve on spare needles; rep from * to *. PM to mark BOR; this is front of left shoulder. 460 (488, 524, 564, 600, 648) sts on needles; 104 (108, 112, 118, 122, 128) sts across each sleeve and 126 (136, 150, 164, 178, 196) sts across both front and back of body. PM after st 63 (68, 75, 82, 89, 98) of Front to mark center neck.

Raglan Decreases
The sleeves and body are dec'd together. Follow decs as given for your size in Raglan charts. Work all decs in pattern color, and maintain 'stripes' flanking the Ms.

On rnd noted for your size, begin working from Neckline directions at the same time as maintaining Raglan Decs.

Neckline

After binding off for neckline, a steek is CO across gap.

On rnd highlighted in chart, BO sts for neckline: Work in pattern to 1 st before center front M. BO next 2 sts in pattern, removing M. Cont around Body in pattern.

On next rnd, CO steek sts: Work in pattern to first bound-off st of the neckline. CO 7 sts in alternating colors. Join to next live st, and cont in pattern.

Over next several rnds, more sts will be dec at neckline. See notes for Raglan and Neckline charts for which dec to work on a given rnd.

After all neckline and Raglan shaping is complete, 78 (82, 80, 88, 94, 94) sts remain around sleeves and back. With MC, BO steek and remaining sts.

Finishing

Steek

To finish sweater, steek must first be sewn and cut.
Then, collar is picked up and knit on.
Use Glossary instructions to prepare steeking, then, with very sharp scissors, carefully cut along center cut line.

Collar Trim

A simple band of Corrugated Ribbing finishes off neckline. With MC and smaller needles, PU and K 48 (50, 46, 51, 56, 56) sts across back neck, 12 (14, 14, 16, 16, 16) sts across left sleeve, 52 (55, 61, 65, 70, 72) sts down left edge of neckline including 1 from BO at center front, PM and PU and K 52 (55, 61, 65, 70, 72) sts up right side, and 12 (14, 14, 16, 16, 16) sts across right sleeve to first picked up st at back neck. Join in the rnd. 176 (188, 196, 212, 228, 232) sts.

Corrugated Ribbing Setup: K 0 (3, 1, 0, 2, 0) sts and PM to mark BOR. *K1 in MC, P2 in C11, K1 in MC; rep from * to end of rnd. There should be a K st on either side of center M.

Neckline Ribbing: Attach C10. Work in Corrugated Ribbing as established to 2 sts before center M. K2tog with MC, SM, SSK with MC, work in Corrugated Ribbing as established to end of rnd.

Rep Neckline Ribbing as established, maintaining MC and moving to C9, C8, C7, and C6, working one rnd in each CC; at the same time, work decs as given above on every other rnd.

Break C6. Work one rnd in ribbing in MC. BO all sts loosely.

Using yarn tails or short pieces of MC, graft bound-off sts of underarms closed.

Weave in ends. Wash and block.

A 32(36, 40, 44, 48, 52)"
B 16 (16.5, 17, 17.7, 17.7, 18.2)"
C 23.5 (24.4, 25.5, 27, 27.7, 28.5)"
D 17.5 (18.5, 18, 18, 18.25, 18.25)"
E 8 (8.5, 9, 10, 10.5, 11)"
F 13 (13.5, 14, 14.75, 15.25, 16)"

Moraine:
ATMOSPHERE COLORWAY

YARN COLORS

3 balls:
MC Jay 24581

2 balls each:
C7 Rooibos Heather 25551
C8 Lantana 24572
C9 Mulberry 24571
C10 French Lavender 24575

1 ball each:
C1 Marine Heather 24010
C2 Spruce 25535
C3 Seafaring 26048
C4 Tranquil 25094
C5 Pistachio 25550
C6 Hazelnut 24563
C11 Chicory 24577

LEGEND

■ **No Stitch**
Placeholder—no stitch made

□ **Knit**
Knit stitch

◪ **K2tog**
Knit two stitches together as one stitch

◩ **SSK**
(Slip 1 knit-wise) twice; insert left-hand needle into front of these 2 stitches and knit them together

[MR] **M1R**
Make one right-leaning stitch

[M̲] **M1L**
Make one left-leaning stitch

[⌐] **BO**
Bind off 1 stitch

▢ **Pattern Repeat**

Color Progression

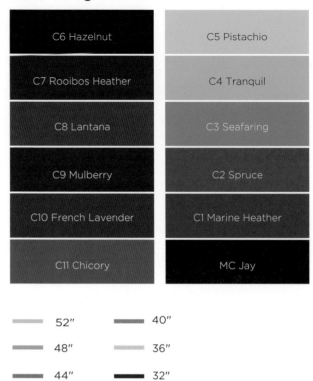

C6 Hazelnut	C5 Pistachio
C7 Rooibos Heather	C4 Tranquil
C8 Lantana	C3 Seafaring
C9 Mulberry	C2 Spruce
C10 French Lavender	C1 Marine Heather
C11 Chicory	MC Jay

— 52"   — 40"
— 48"   — 36"
— 44"   — 32"

Corrugated Ribbing

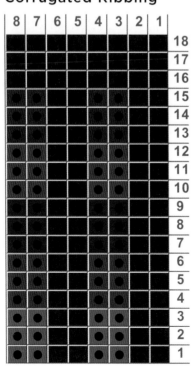

Sleeves

Though the charts are broken up into several sections, the sleeves have a simple shape: all of the actual increasing of the sleeves takes place at the beginning and end of the round, while the other shaping shown across the middle serves to shift the floral patterns across the sleeve from the center to the back—this does not affect the shape of the sleeve, only the patterning.

Begin with Part 1, starting at the round noted for your size, then move on to Part 2, then Part 3.

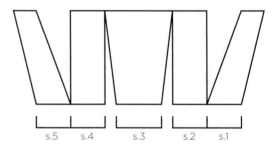

s.1) All Sizes: Work incs as shown; work to the last st marked for your size. Note: Several sizes share the same size lines in this section; note the size numbers with each line.
s.2) All Sizes: Work decs over the first st of this section and the last st of section 1.
s.3) Starting at the first st noted for your size, work M1 incs after the last st of section 2 and before the first st of section 4.
s.4) All Sizes: Work decs over the last st of section 4 and the first st of section 5.
s.5) Starting at the first st noted for your size, work to end of chart, increasing as shown. Note: Several sizes share the same size lines in this section; note the size numbers with each line.

All charts are followed from bottom to top, and rounds read from right to left.

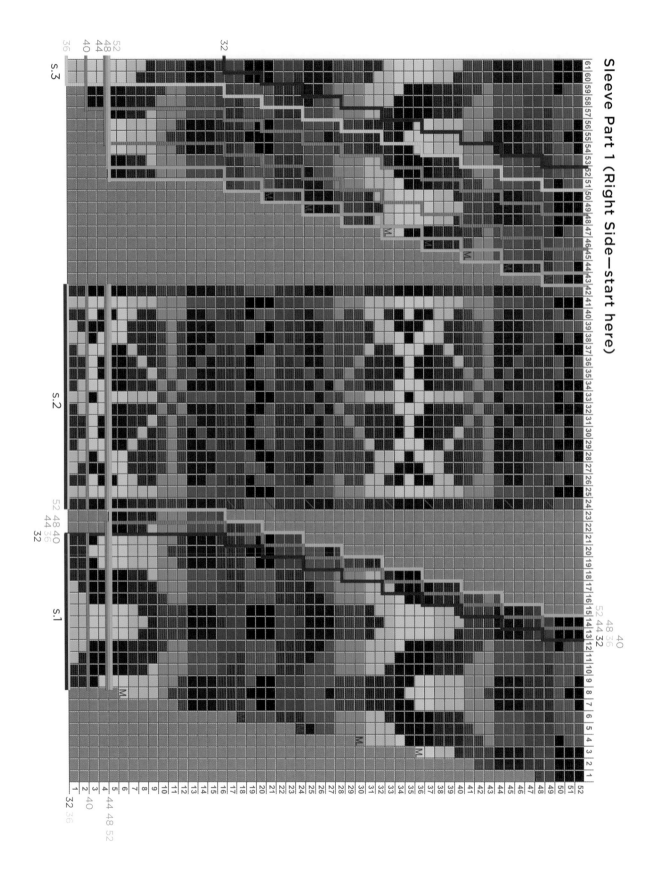

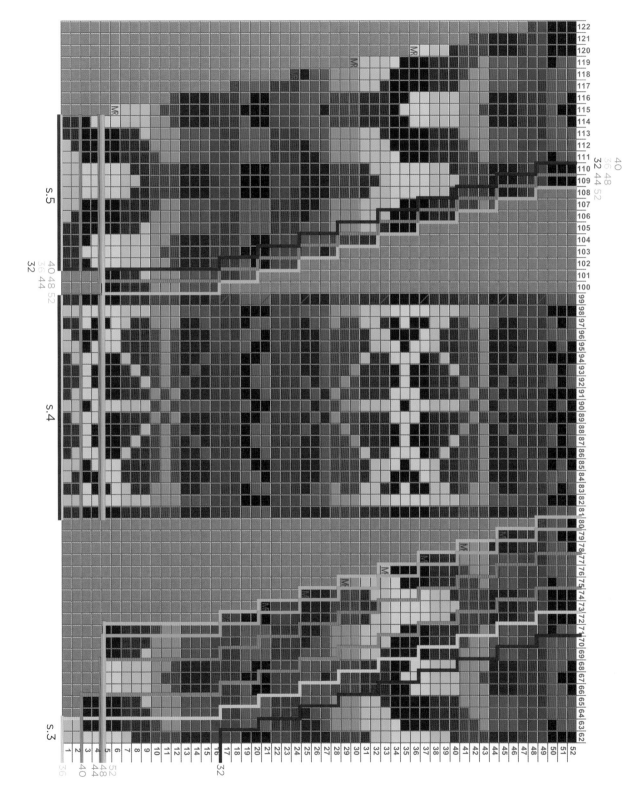

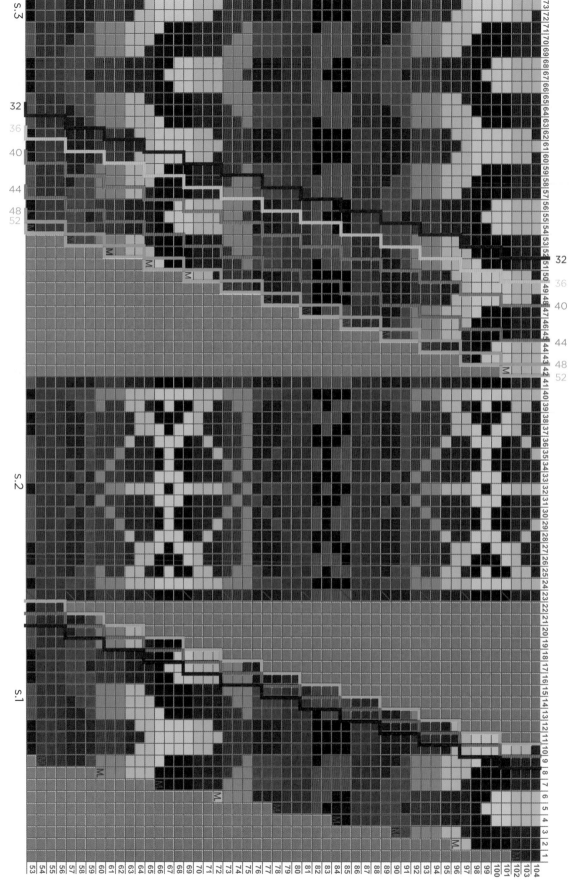

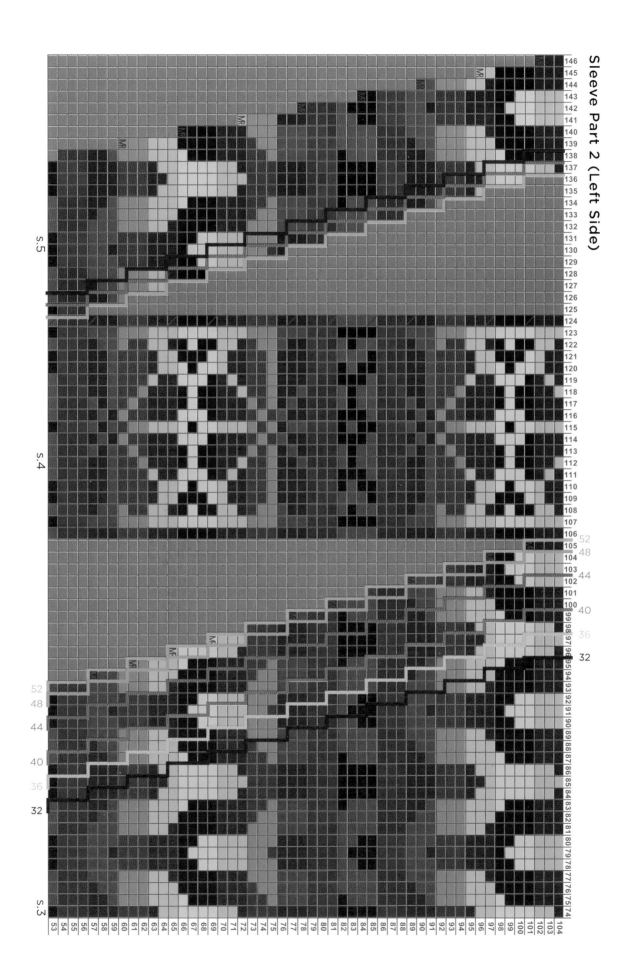

Sleeve Part 3 (Right Side—start here)

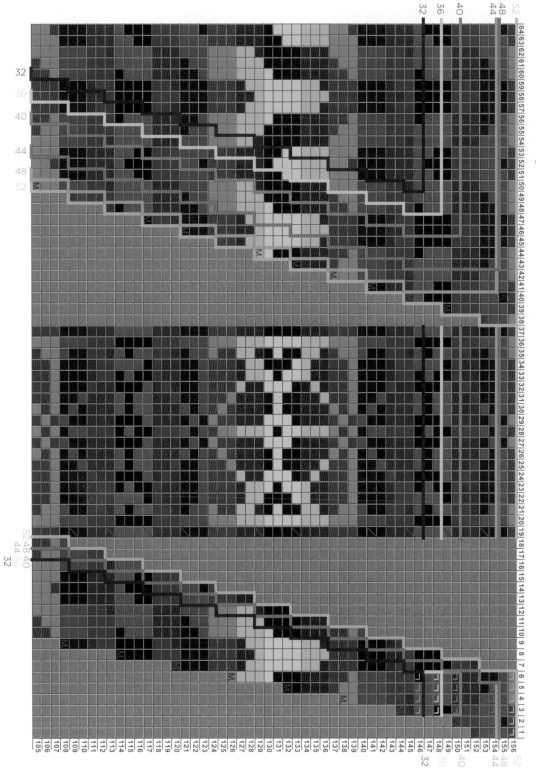

All sizes: repeat these
12 sts three times.

Lower Body (Left Side)

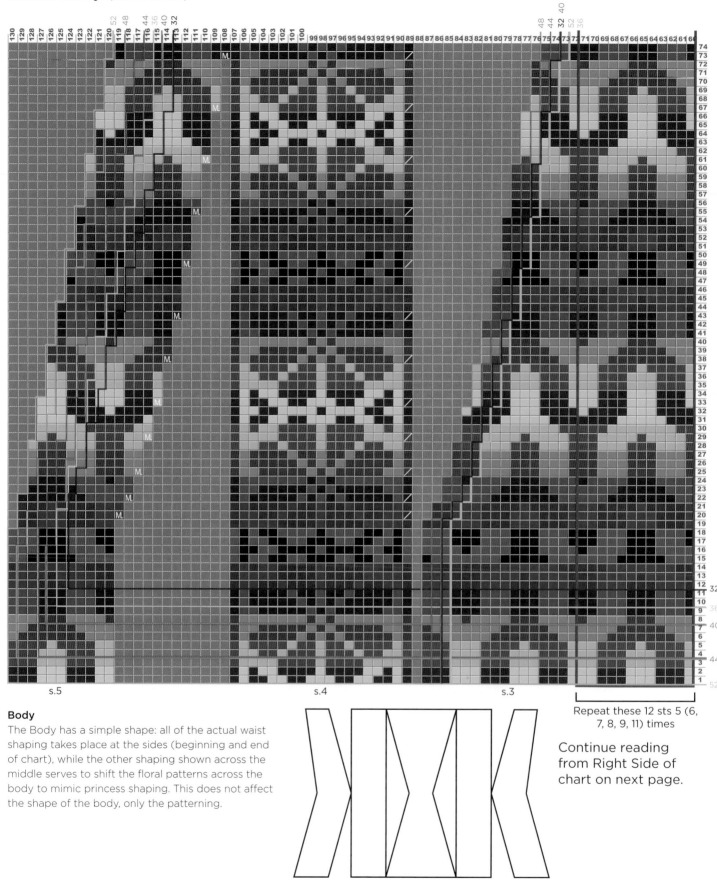

Body

The Body has a simple shape: all of the actual waist shaping takes place at the sides (beginning and end of chart), while the other shaping shown across the middle serves to shift the floral patterns across the body to mimic princess shaping. This does not affect the shape of the body, only the patterning.

s.5 s.4 s.3 s.2 s.1

Repeat these 12 sts 5 (6, 7, 8, 9, 11) times

Continue reading from Right Side of chart on next page.

Lower Body (Right Side—start here)

Section Shaping

s.1.) All Sizes: Beginning at the first row and st for your size, work decs and incs shown; work to the last st in this section. Note: The decs and incs at the side seams are only marked by the outline of your size. K2tog at the beginning and SSK at the end of the chart.

s.2.) All Sizes, Lower Body Chart: Work decs over the last st of this section and the last st of section 3. Upper Chart: Work decs over the first st of this section and the last st of section 1.

s.3.) All Sizes, Upper Chart: Starting at the first st noted for your size, work M1 incs after the last st of section 2 and before the first st of section 4.

s.4.) All Sizes Lower Body Chart: Work decs over the first st of section 4 and the last st of section 3. Upper Chart: Work decs over the last st of section 4 and the first st of section 5.

s.5.) Starting at the first st, work to the last st noted for your size, increasing and decreasing as shown. Note: The decs and incs at the side seams are only marked by the outline of your size. M1R at the beginning and M1L at the end of the chart.

Upper Body (Left Side)

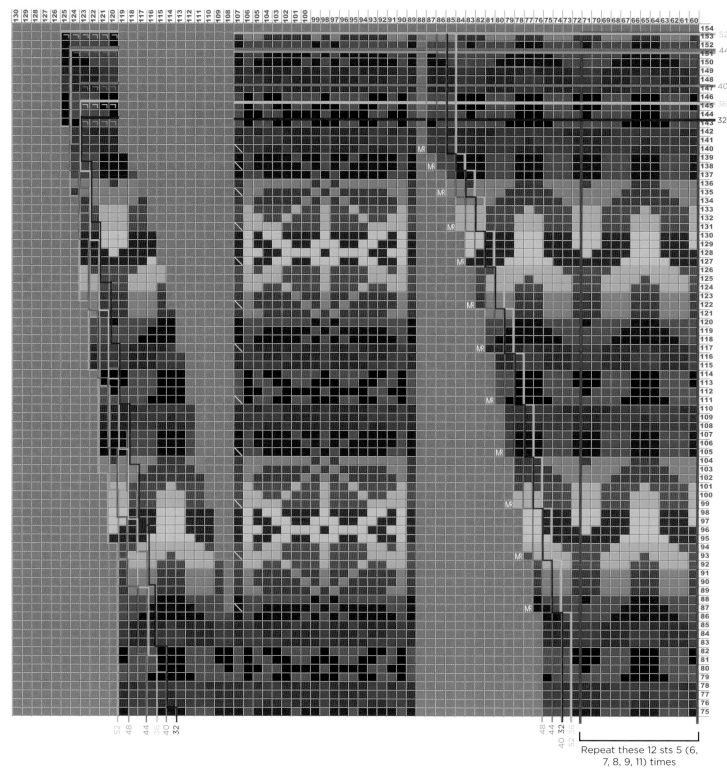

Repeat these 12 sts 5 (6, 7, 8, 9, 11) times

Continue reading from Right Side of chart on next page.

Upper Body (Right Side—start here)

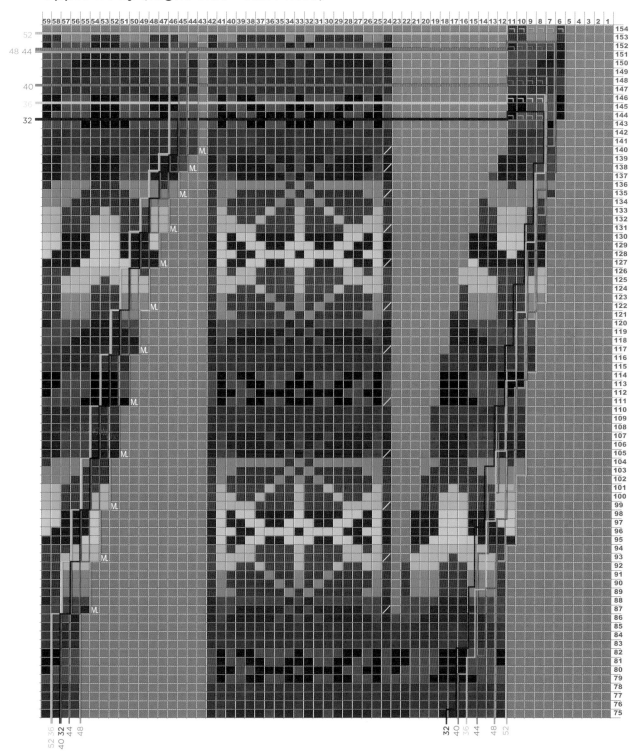

Raglan and Neckline Charts (beginning on next page)

Work these charts over the body of the raglan yoke.
Begin with Part 1, then move on to Part 2, then Part 3, then Part 4.
Both the front and the back are shown; the center decs (dotted lines) are worked across the front and form the neckline and should be worked on either side of the steek.
On the Left (as worn) neckline edge, SSK the last two neckline sts together; on the Right (as worn) neckline edge, K2tog the first two sts of the neckline.

Work decs in the first and last sts; where there is a shift in the line demarcating your size, work an SSK over st 1 and the first st for your size, and work a K2tog over the last st for your size and the last charted st.

All sizes: Start with st 1 on the round noted for your size, then move to the first st marked for your size. Work to the last st marked for your size, following repeat instructions, then work the last charted st.

After all neckline sts have been decreased, there are still several rounds that are worked over the sleeves and back only.

Raglan and Neckline Part 1 (Right Side—start here)

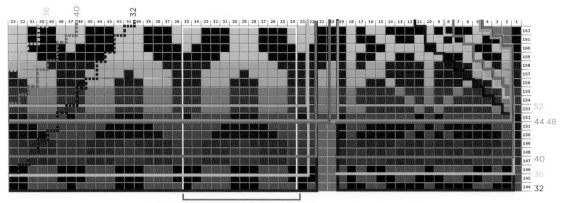

Repeat these 12 sts 2 (2, 3, 3, 4, 5) times

Raglan and Neckline Part 1 (Left Side)

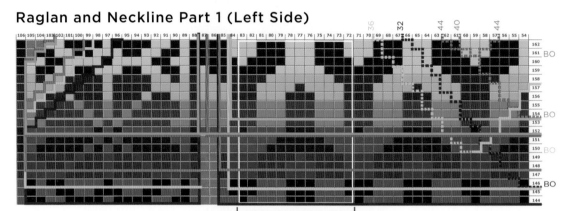

Repeat these 12 sts 2 (3, 3, 4, 4, 5) times

Raglan and Neckline Part 2 (Right Side—start here)

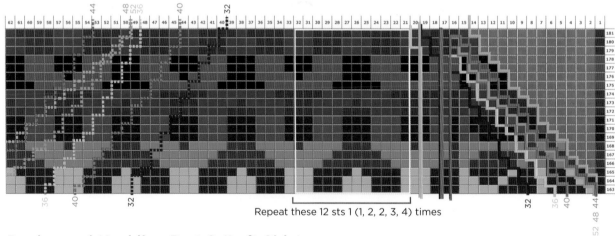

Repeat these 12 sts 1 (1, 2, 2, 3, 4) times

Raglan and Neckline Part 2 (Left Side)

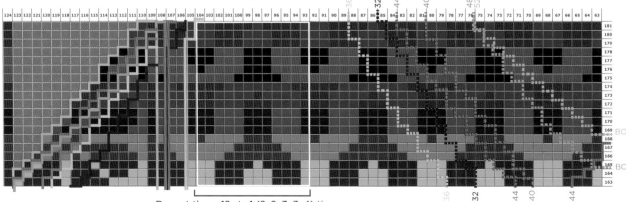

Repeat these 12 sts 1 (2, 2, 3, 3, 4) times

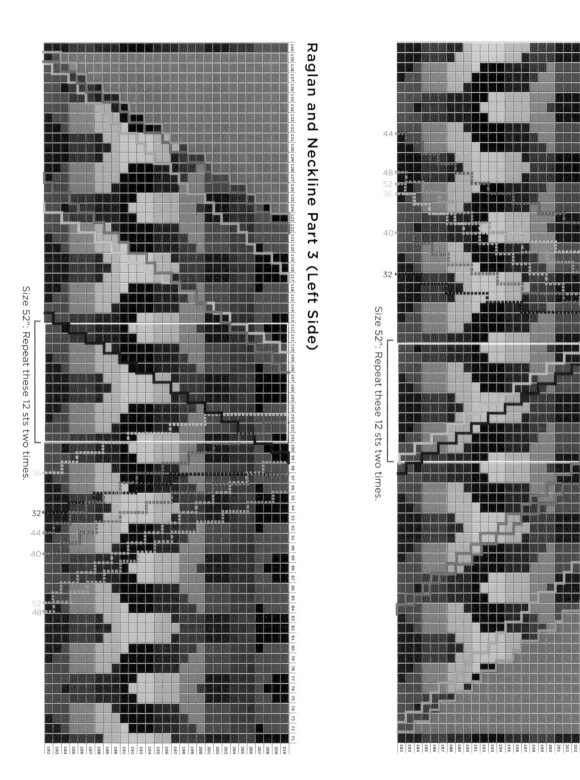

Raglan and Neckline Part 3 (Right Side—start here)

Size 52": Repeat these 12 sts two times.

Raglan and Neckline Part 3 (Left Side)

Size 52": Repeat these 12 sts two times.

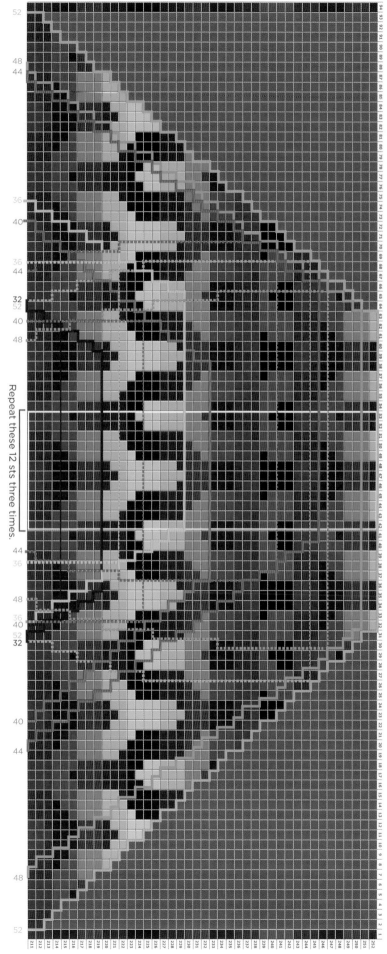

Repeat these 12 sts three times.

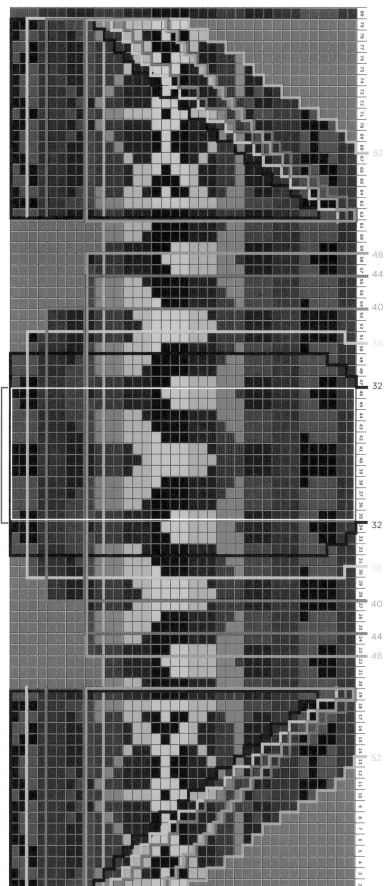

Repeat these 12 sts five times.

Work these charts over the sleeves of the raglan yoke.
Begin with Part 1, then move on to Part 2, then Part 3.

Work decs in the first and last sts; where there is a shift in the line demarcating your size, work an SSK over st 1 and the first st for your size, and work a K2tog over the last st for your size and the last charted st.

All sizes: Start with st 1, then move to the first st marked for your size. Work to the last st marked for your size, following repeat instructions, then work the last charted st.

Raglan Sleeve Part 2

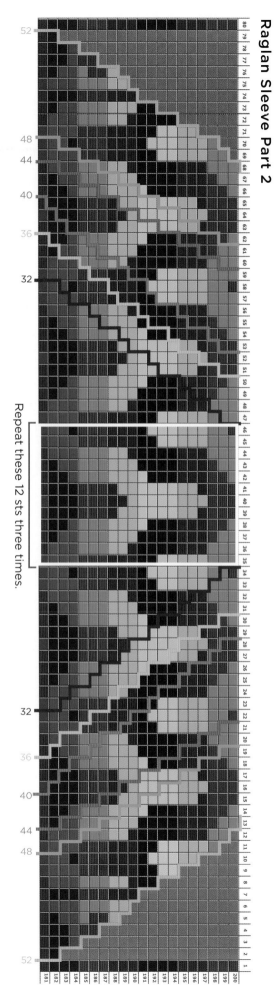

Repeat these 12 sts three times.

Moraine: Atmosphere Colorway

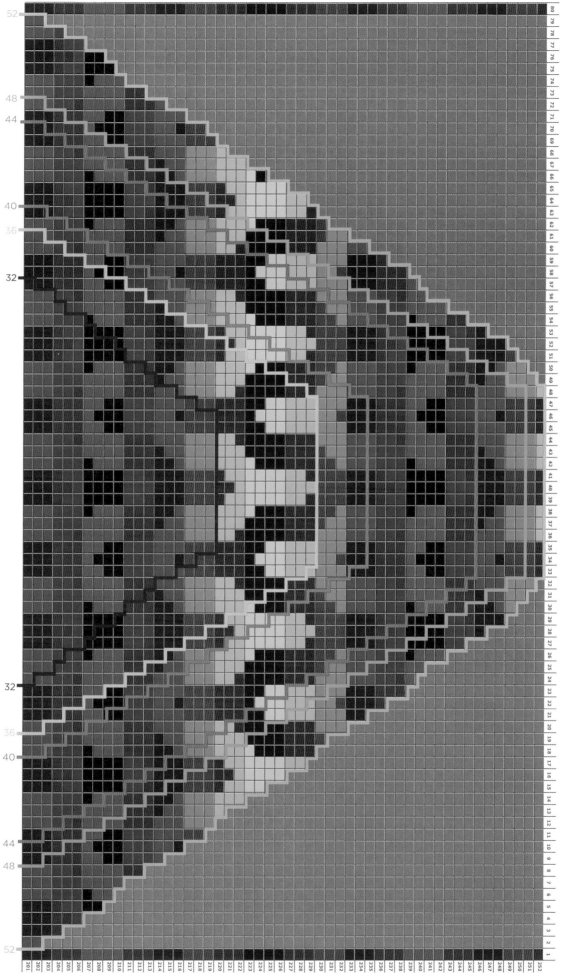

Moraine:

FOREST COLORWAY

YARN COLORS

3 balls:
MC Midnight Heather 25540

2 balls each:
C7 Larch Heather 25543
C8 Caper 25545
C9 Lichen 26047
C10 Green Tea Heather 24258

1 ball each:
C1 Douglas Fir Heather 26046
C2 Aurora Heather 25537
C3 Ivy 23999
C4 Spearmint 24253
C5 Celadon Heather 24254
C6 Bittersweet Heather 24239
C11 Sea Grass 26049

LEGEND

⬜ **No Stitch**
Placeholder—no stitch made

⬜ **Knit**
Knit stitch

◿ **K2tog**
Knit two stitches together as one stitch

◺ **SSK**
(Slip 1 knit-wise) twice; insert left-hand needle into front of these 2 stitches and knit them together

Ⓜ️ᴿ **M1R**
Make one right-leaning stitch

Ⓜ️ᴸ **M1L**
Make one left-leaning stitch

⌐ **BO**
Bind off 1 stitch

⬜ **Pattern Repeat**

Color Progression

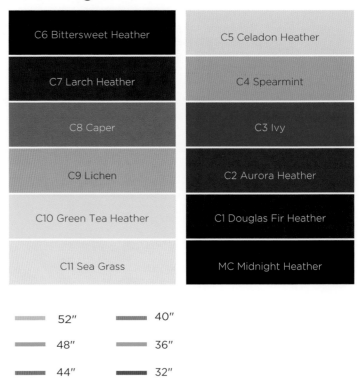

C6 Bittersweet Heather	C5 Celadon Heather
C7 Larch Heather	C4 Spearmint
C8 Caper	C3 Ivy
C9 Lichen	C2 Aurora Heather
C10 Green Tea Heather	C1 Douglas Fir Heather
C11 Sea Grass	MC Midnight Heather

52"		40"	
48"		36"	
44"		32"	

Corrugated Ribbing

(Chart columns 8 7 6 5 4 3 2 1; rows 1–18, read bottom to top.)

Sleeves

Though the charts are broken up into several sections, the sleeves have a simple shape: all of the actual increasing of the sleeves takes place at the beginning and end of the round, while the other shaping shown across the middle serves to shift the floral patterns across the sleeve from the center to the back—this does not affect the shape of the sleeve, only the patterning.

Begin with Part 1, starting at the round noted for your size, then move on to Part 2, then Part 3.

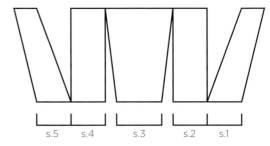

s.5   s.4   s.3   s.2   s.1

s.1) All Sizes: Work incs as shown; work to the last st marked for your size. Note: Several sizes share the same size lines in this section; note the size numbers with each line.
s.2) All Sizes: Work decs over the first st of this section and the last st of section 1.
s.3) Starting at the first st noted for your size, work M1 incs after the last st of section 2 and before the first st of section 4.
s.4) All Sizes: Work decs over the last st of section 4 and the first st of section 5.
s.5) Starting at the first st noted for your size, work to end of chart, increasing as shown. Note: Several sizes share the same size lines in this section; note the size numbers with each line.

All charts are followed from bottom to top, and rounds read from right to left.

Sleeve Part 1 (Right Side—start here)

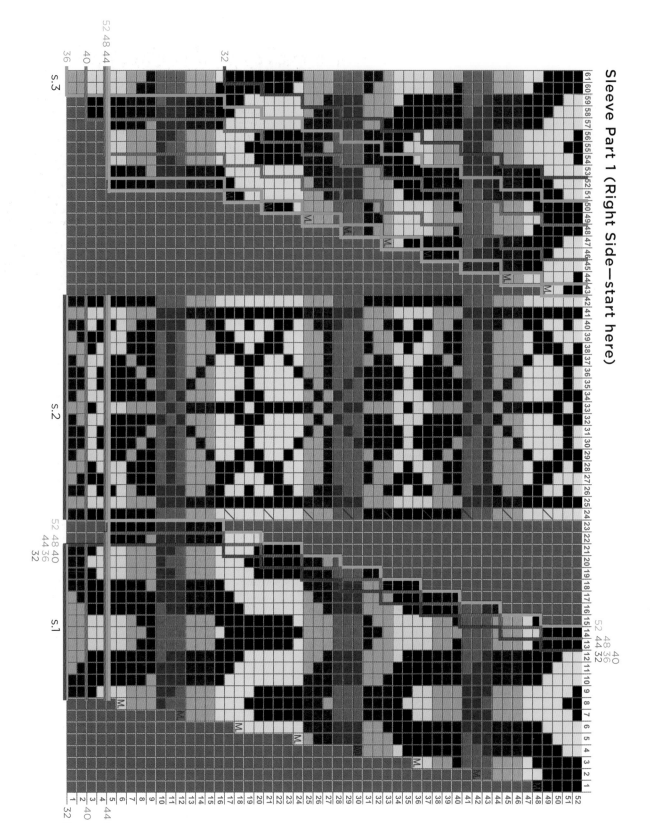

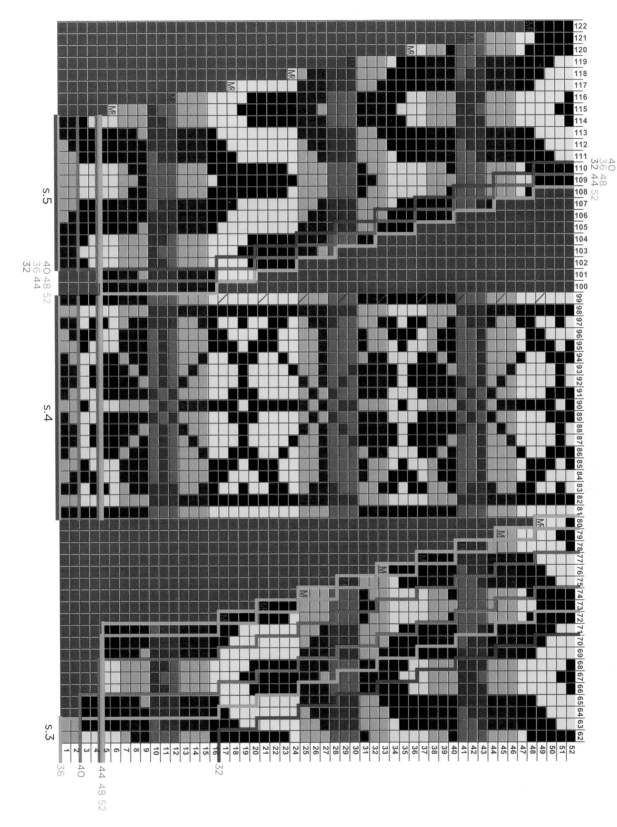

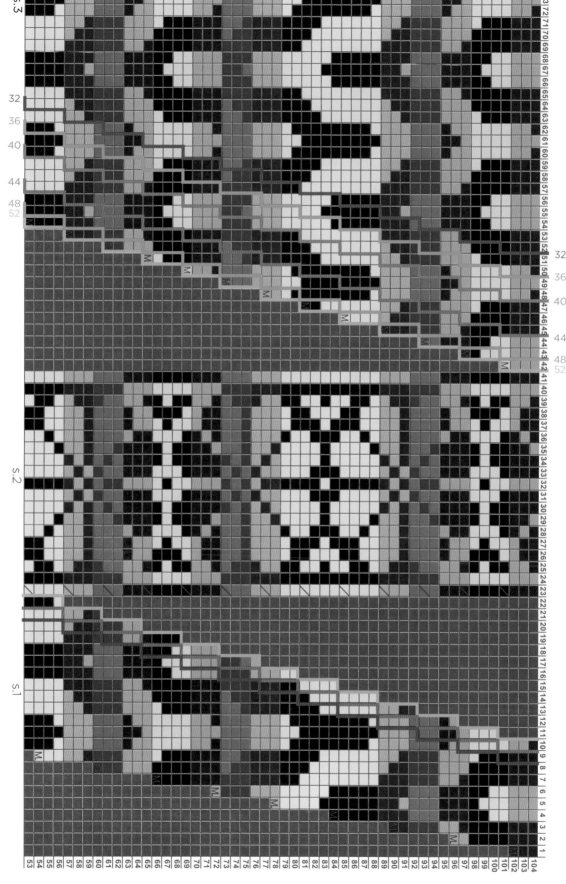

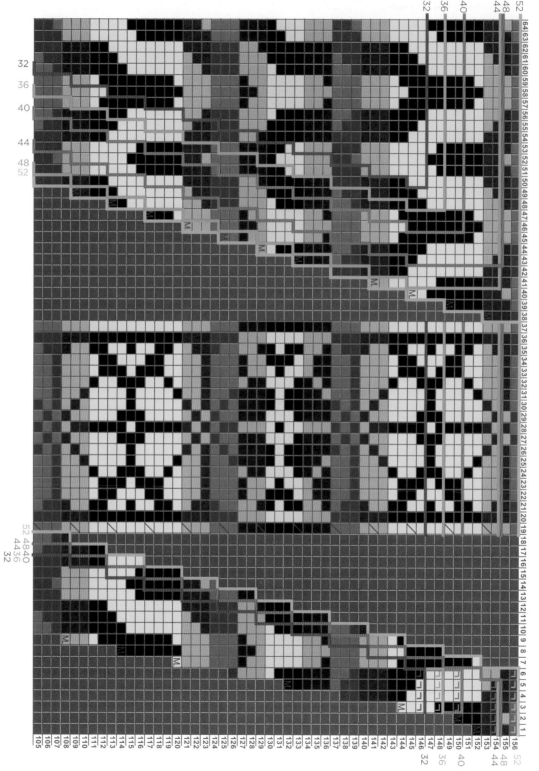

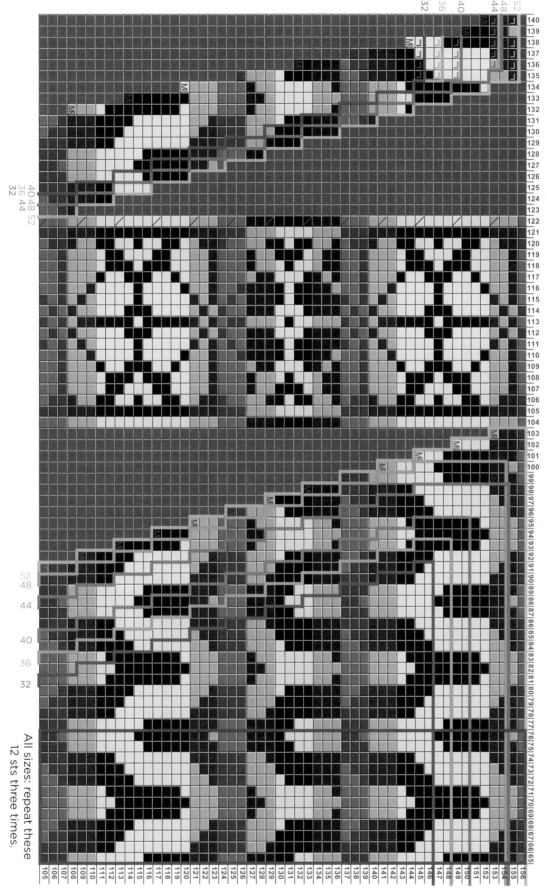

All sizes: repeat these
12 sts three times.

Lower Body (Left Side)

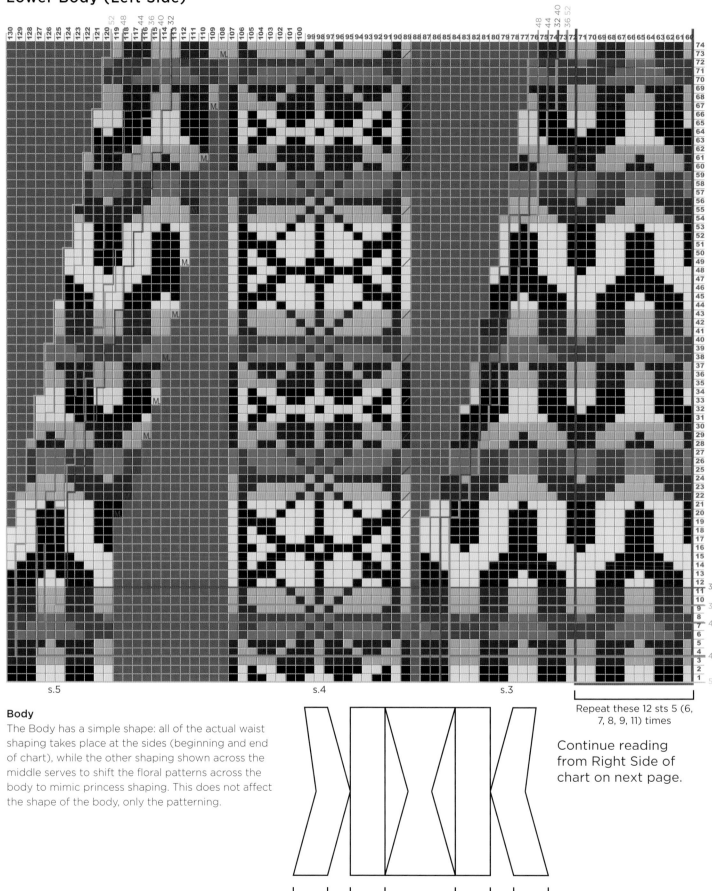

Repeat these 12 sts 5 (6, 7, 8, 9, 11) times

Continue reading from Right Side of chart on next page.

Body

The Body has a simple shape: all of the actual waist shaping takes place at the sides (beginning and end of chart), while the other shaping shown across the middle serves to shift the floral patterns across the body to mimic princess shaping. This does not affect the shape of the body, only the patterning.

Lower Body (Right Side—start here)

Section Shaping

s.1.) All Sizes: Beginning at the first row and st for your size, work decs and incs shown; work to the last st in this section. Note: The decs and incs at the side seams are only marked by the outline of your size. K2tog at the beginning and SSK at the end of the chart.

s.2.) All Sizes, Lower Body Chart: Work decs over the last st of this section and the last st of section 3. Upper Chart: Work decs over the first st of this section and the last st of section 1.

s.3.) All Sizes, Upper Chart: Starting at the first st noted for your size, work M1 incs after the last st of section 2 and before the first st of section 4.

s.4.) All Sizes Lower Body Chart: Work decs over the first st of section 4 and the last st of section 3. Upper Chart: Work decs over the last st of section 4 and the first st of section 5.

s.5.) Starting at the first st, work to the last st noted for your size, increasing and decreasing as shown. Note: The decs and incs at the side seams are only marked by the outline of your size. M1R at the beginning and M1L at the end of the chart.

Upper Body (Left Side)

Repeat these 12 sts 5 (6, 7, 8, 9, 11) times

Continue reading from Right Side of chart on next page.

Upper Body (Right Side—start here)

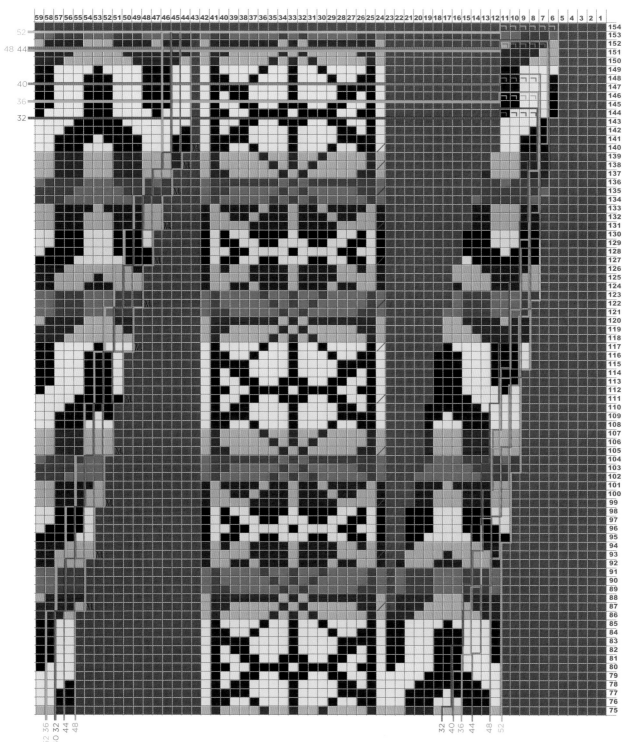

Raglan and Neckline Charts (beginning on next page)

Work these charts over the body of the raglan yoke.
Begin with Part 1, then move on to Part 2, then Part 3, then Part 4.
Both the front and the back are shown; the center decs (dotted lines) are worked across the front and form the neckline and should be worked on either side of the steek.
On the Left (as worn) neckline edge, SSK the last two neckline sts together; on the Right (as worn) neckline edge, K2tog the first two sts of the neckline.

Work decs in the first and last sts; where there is a shift in the line demarcating your size, work an SSK over st 1 and the first st for your size, and work a K2tog over the last st for your size and the last charted st.

All sizes: Start with st 1 on the round noted for your size, then move to the first st marked for your size. Work to the last st marked for your size, following repeat instructions, then work the last charted st.

After all neckline sts have been decreased, there are still several rounds that are worked over the sleeves and back only.

Raglan and Neckline Part 1 (Right Side—start here)

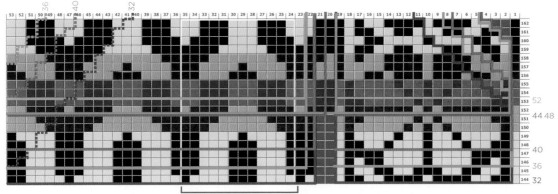

Repeat these 12 sts 2 (2, 3, 3, 4, 5) times

Raglan and Neckline Part 1 (Left Side)

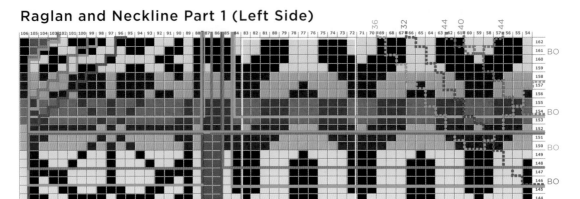

Repeat these 12 sts 2 (3, 3, 4, 4, 5) times

Raglan and Neckline Part 2 (Right Side—start here)

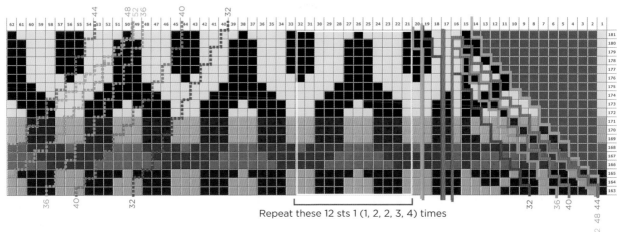

Repeat these 12 sts 1 (1, 2, 2, 3, 4) times

Raglan and Neckline Part 2 (Left Side)

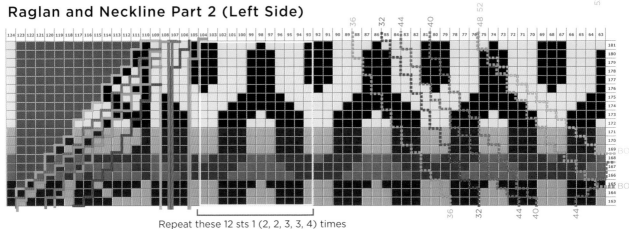

Repeat these 12 sts 1 (2, 2, 3, 3, 4) times

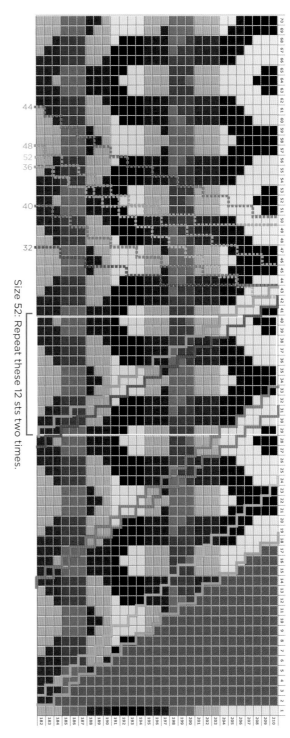

Raglan and Neckline Part 3 (Right Side—start here)

Size 52: Repeat these 12 sts two times.

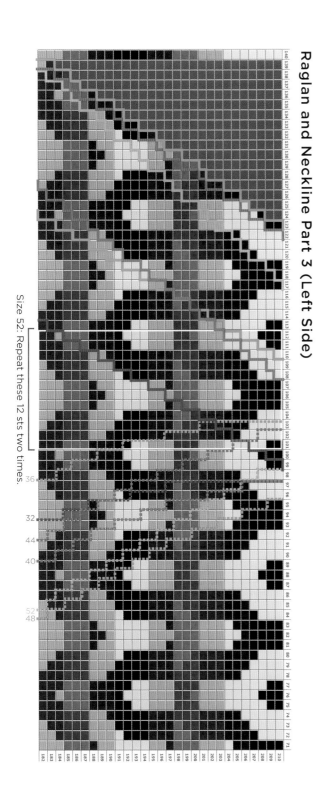

Raglan and Neckline Part 3 (Left Side)

Size 52: Repeat these 12 sts two times.

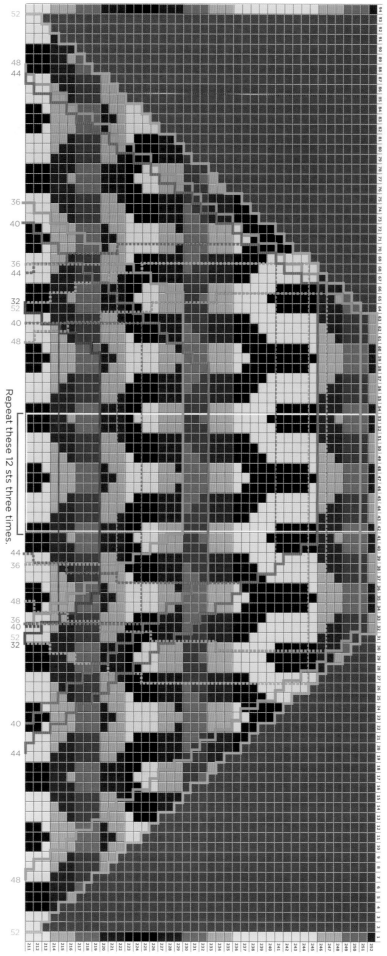

Repeat these 12 sts three times.

Raglan Sleeve Part 1

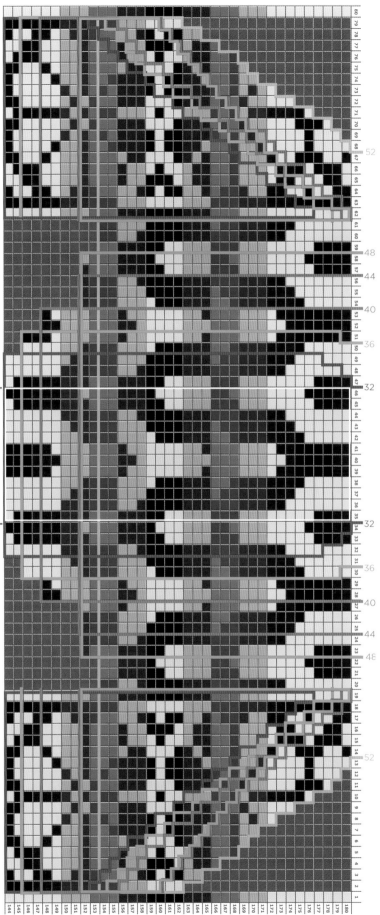

Work these charts over the sleeves of the raglan yoke. Begin with Part 1, then move on to Part 2, then Part 3.

Work decs in the first and last sts; where there is a shift in the line demarcating your size, work an SSK over st 1 and the first st for your size, and work a K2tog over the last st for your size and the last charted st.

Repeat these 12 sts five times.

All sizes: Start with st 1, then move to the first st marked for your size. Work to the last st marked for your size, following repeat instructions, then work the last charted st.

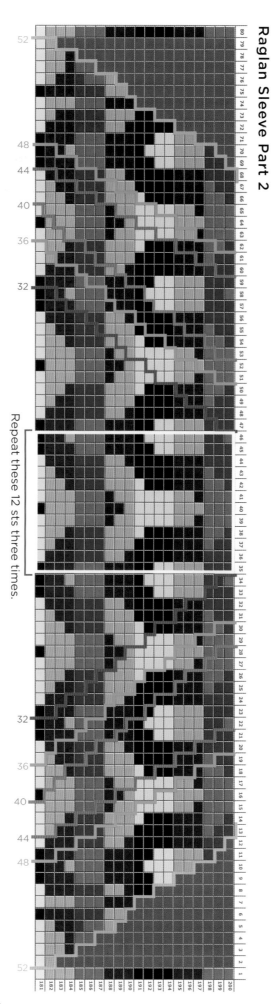

Repeat these 12 sts three times.

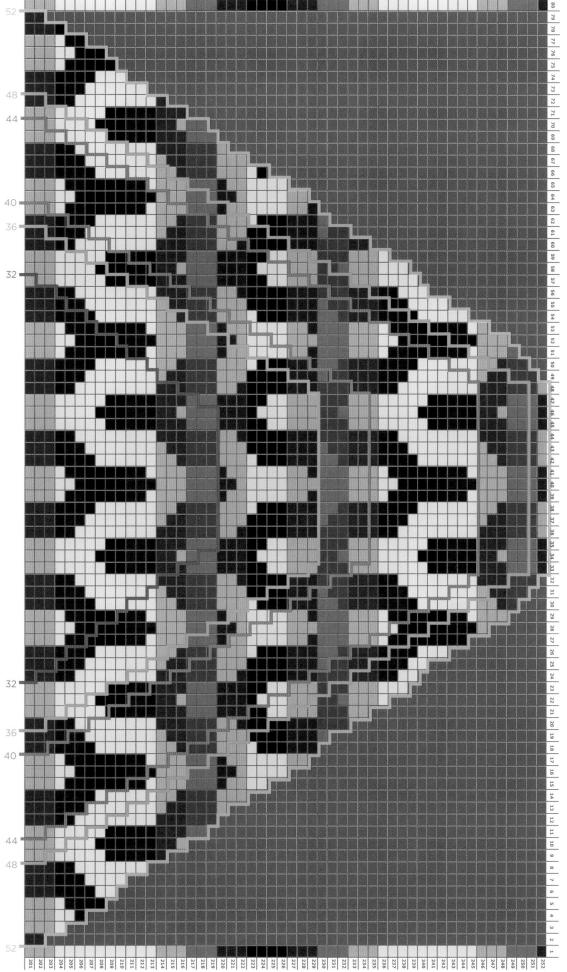

OAKWOOD PONCHO

by Nikki Wagner

FINISHED MEASUREMENTS

42 (45, 46)" actual finished measurements; to fit bust sizes 28-38 (40-50, 52-62)", with 10" of positive ease

YARN

Knit Picks Wool of the Andes™ Tweed (worsted weight, 80% Peruvian Highland Wool, 20% Donegal Tweed; 110 yards/50g): MC Down Heather 25458, 12 (15, 16) skeins; C1 North Pole Heather 25964, 2 skeins; C2 Flagstone Heather 25457 1 skein; C3 Wellies Heather 25968, 1 skein

NEEDLES

US 8 (5mm) 24" or longer circular needles, or size to obtain gauge

NOTIONS

Yarn Needle
2 Stitch Markers
2 Stitch Holders
Size F Crochet Hook, to add fringe

GAUGE

17 sts and 26 rows = 4" in Stockinette Stitch, blocked

For pattern support, contact customerservice@knitpicks.com

Oakwood Poncho

Notes:

A truly unique knit, the Oakwood Poncho will take you from days on the trail to evenings sipping a glass of wine. Knit in both Stockinette and Brioche stitch, this gorgeous, easy garment will keep you stitching, as you dream of the occasions for which it will come in handy.

This poncho is knit in Stockinette Stitch with the exception of two columns located on the front inside edges, which are knit in Brioche Stitch. A short row is added after every other right side Brioche Stitch row. The first stitch of every Stockinette Stitch row is a slip-stitch. Single-stranded fringe is added at the bottom edges.

The color block section on the fronts is worked in intarsia. However, with the first color change row of each stair-step pattern, you'll float working strands of yarn over 9 stitches on the wrong side. Use a separate main color skein of yarn for the Brioche Column.

The poncho is worked from the bottom of the back to the bottom of the front. Charts are worked at the color blocking sections of the piece. The charts are followed from bottom to top, with RS rows (odd numbers) read from right to left, and WS rows (even numbers) read from left to right.

Brioche Bind Off
BO the Brioche sts in rib pattern, working the YO and K sts as same st.

Slip 1 Stitch, Yarn Over (Sl1yo)
WYIF, Sl 1 P-wise, then bring yarn over right needle.

Brioche Stitch (BRK)
K the YO and st tog as one.

DIRECTIONS

Back
With C1, loosely CO 178 (190, 196) sts. Work St st for 3". Then, break C1 and, with MC, work St st until entire piece measures 28 (30, 31)", ending on a WS row.

Separate Right and Left Front Sides
Next Row (RS): K76 (82, 85); these are the Right Front sts, do not cut yarn. Sl next 26 sts to stitch holder (these sts will be reserved for neck). Sl remaining 76 (82, 85) sts to second stitch holder for Left Front side.

Right Front
Return to Right Front sts; with WS facing, work Setup Row.

Setup Row (WS): *Sl1yo, K1; rep from * seven more times, P1, PM, P to end of row. 17 sts in Brioche Column; 59 (65, 68) sts in St st.

Row 1 (RS): K to M, SM, K1, *Sl1yo, BRK; rep from * seven more times.
Short Row 1: *Sl1yo, BRK; rep from * seven more times, W&T.

Short Row 2: WYIF, Sl wrapped st P-wise, *Sl1yo, BRK; rep from * seven more times.
Row 2 (WS): *Sl1yo, BRK; rep from * seven more times, work wrap tog with wrapped st as P2tog, SM, P to end of row.
Row 3: Rep Row 1.
Row 4: *Sl1yo, BRK; rep from * seven more times, P1, SM, P to end of row.
Rep Rows 1-4, with Short Rows included, until piece measures 16 (18, 19)" from beginning of Brioche Column. End on Row 4.

Right Front Color Blocking
Right Front color blocking is worked 9 sts across over 4 rows in a diagonal stair-step pattern; add a new color after 20 rows. Color blocking is worked in intarsia. Float working yarns across each new 9-st stair step as needed. Work Right Side Chart in St st and change colors accordingly. The pattern below incorporates color block chart with established Brioche st pattern.

Row 1 (RS): WIth MC, K5 (11, 14), PM, work Row 1 from Right Side Chart, remove M, with MC K1, *Sl1yo, BRK; rep from * seven more times.
Short Row 1: With MC *Sl1yo, BRK; rep from * seven more times, W&T.
Short Row 2: With MC yarn in front, Sl wrapped st P-wise, *Sl1yo, BRK; rep from * seven more times.
Row 2 (WS): With MC *Sl1yo, BRK; rep from * seven more times, work wrap tog with wrapped st as P2tog, work next even row from Right Side Chart, SM, with MC P to end of row.
Row 3: With MC K to M, SM, work next odd row from Right Side Chart, with MC K1, *Sl1yo, BRK; rep from * seven more times.
Row 4: With MC *Sl1yo, BRK; rep from * seven more times, P1, work next even row from Right Side Chart, SM, with MC P to end of row.
Row 5: With MC K to M, SM, work next odd row from Right Side Chart, with MC K1, Sl1yo, BRK; rep from * seven more times.
Short Row 1: With MC *Sl1yo, BRK; rep from * seven more times, W&T.
Short Row 2: With MC yarn in front, Sl wrapped st P-wise, *Sl1yo, BRK; rep from * seven more times.
Row 6: With MC *Sl1yo, BRK; rep from * seven more times, work wrap tog with wrapped st as P2tog, work next even row from Right Side Chart, SM, with MC P to end of row.
Row 7: Rep Row 5.
Row 8: With MC *Sl1yo, BRK; rep from * seven more times, P1, work next even row from Right Side Chart, SM, with MC P to end of row.
Rep Rows 5-8, with Short Rows, through Row 80 of Right Side Chart.

With MC, BO all sts on Right Front, using Brioche Bind Off for Brioche Column.

Left Front

Starting with a new ball of MC yarn, with WS facing, Sl 76 (82, 85) sts from second stitch holder.

Setup Row (WS): P until 17 sts remain, PM, P1 *Sl1yo, K1; rep from * seven more times.

Short Row 1: *Sl1yo, BRK; rep from * seven more times, W&T.
Short Row 2: WYIF, Sl wrapped st P-wise, *Sl1yo, BRK; rep from * seven more times
Row 1 (RS): *Sl1yo, BRK; rep from * seven more times, work wrap tog with wrapped st as a K2tog, SM, K to end.
Row 2: P to M, SM, P1, *Sl1yo, BRK; rep from * seven more times.
Row 3: *Sl1yo, BRK; rep from * seven more times, K1, SM, K to end.
Row 4: Rep Row 2.
Rep (Short Rows, Rows 1-4) until piece measures 16 (18, 19)" from beginning of Brioche Column. End on WS Short Row 2.

Left Front Color Blocking

Left Front color blocking is worked same as Right Front: 9 sts across over 4 rows in a diagonal stair-step pattern; add a new color after 20 rows. Color blocking is worked in intarsia. Float working yarns across each new 9-st stair step as needed. Work Left Side Chart in St st and change colors accordingly. The pattern below incorporates the color block chart with established Brioche st pattern.

Row 1 (RS): With MC *Sl1yo, BRK; rep from * seven more times, work wrap tog with wrapped st as a K2tog, remove M, work Row 1 from Left Side Chart, PM, with MC K to end of row.
Row 2 (WS): With MC P to M, SM, work next even row from Left Side Chart, with MC P1, *Sl1yo, BRK; rep from * seven more times.
Row 3: With MC *Sl1yo, BRK; rep from * seven more times, K1, work next odd row from Left Side Chart, SM, with MC K to end of row.
Row 4: With MC P to M, SM, work next even row from Left Side Chart, with MC P1, *Sl1yo, BRK; rep from * seven more times.
Short Row 1: With MC *Sl1yo, BRK; rep from * seven more times, W&T.
Short Row 2: With MC Sl wrapped st, *Sl1yo, BRK; rep from * seven more times.

Row 5: With MC *Sl1yo, BRK; rep from * seven more times, work wrap tog with wrapped st as a K2tog, work next odd row from Left Side Chart, SM, with MC K to end of row.
Row 6: With MC P to M, SM, work next even row from Left Side Chart, with MC P1, *Sl1yo, BRK; rep from * seven more times.
Row 7: With MC *Sl1yo, BRK; rep from * seven more times, K1, work next odd row from Left Side Chart, SM, with MC K to end of row.
Row 8: Rep Row 6.
Short Row 1: With MC *Sl1yo, BRK; rep from * seven more times, W&T.

Short Row 2: With MC Sl wrapped st, *Sl1yo, BRK; rep from * seven more times.
Rep (Rows 5-8, Short Rows), through Row 80 of Left Side Chart.

With MC, BO all sts on Left Front, using Brioche Bind Off for Brioche Column.

Neck

To PU sts from edge, Sl RH needle through 2 edge sts and work them tog as 1 st.
With RS facing, Sl all sts from stitch holder onto needle. Then PU and K 1 st from Row 1 of Brioche Column on Right Front. 27 sts.

Starting with RS, the neck will be worked as follows in St st:
Row 1 (RS): K2tog, K11, CDD, K11, PU and K 1 st from Row 1 of Brioche Column on Left Front. 25 sts.
Row 2 (WS): P2tog, P23, PU and P 1 st from Row 2 of Brioche Column on Right Front.
Row 3: K2tog, K10, CDD, K10, PU and K 1 st from Row 2 of Brioche Column on Left Front. 23 sts.
Row 4: P2tog, P21, PU and P 1 st from Row 3 of Brioche Column on Right Front.

Bind Off Neck Stitches

*K2tog, move resulting st to LH needle; rep from * to last st. PU 1 st from Row 3 of Brioche Column on Left Front and place st on LH needle, K2tog. Pull yarn through resulting st to fasten off.

Finishing

Weave in ends; block to diagram measurements.
Add fringe after piece has been blocked and dried.

Fringe

With MC cut 330 (354, 366) 10" strands of yarn; one strand per fringe.

Back Fringe: Fold one strand of yarn in half. With RS facing, insert crochet hook through back of first st on backside CO edge. Pull folded end of yarn strand through st, about half an inch (do not pull all the way through). With crochet hook, pull the ends of the strand through the folded loop and pull tight.
Rep this process for each st along backside CO edge.

Front Fringe: Work as for Back Fringe, beginning with first st on Right Front, along BO edge. Rep for each st along Right Front and Left Front BO edges.

Steam block Fringe if necessary.

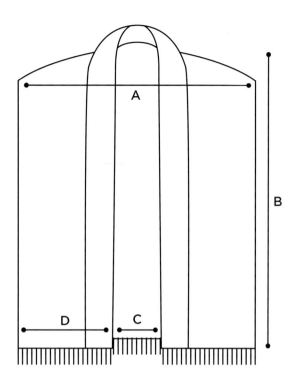

A 42 (45, 46)"
B 28 (30, 31)"
C 5"
D 18.5 (20, 20.5)"

LEGEND

Knit
☐ RS: knit stitch
WS: purl stitch

▢ MC

▢ C1

▢ C2

▢ C3

Right Side Chart

Left Side Chart

PRINCESS PULLOVER

by Kerin Dimeler-Laurence

FINISHED MEASUREMENTS
32 (36, 40, 44, 48, 52, 56, 60, 64)"
finished bust measurement

YARN
Knit Picks Galileo™ (sport weight, 50%
Merino Wool, 50% Viscose from Bamboo;
131 yards/50g): Gem 26104, 13 (13, 14, 15,
16, 17, 18, 19, 20) balls

NEEDLES
US 3 (3.25mm) DPNs and 24-48" circular
needles, or long circulars for Magic Loop,
or size to obtain gauge

US 2 (2.75mm) DPNs and 24-48" circular
needles, or long circulars for Magic Loop,
or one size smaller than those used
to obtain gauge

NOTIONS
Yarn Needle
Stitch Markers
Scrap Yarn or Stitch Holders
Crochet Hook for Provisional CO
Scrap Yarn for Provisional CO

GAUGE
31 sts and 38 rounds = 4" over Cable
Pattern in the round, blocked
24 sts and 38 rounds = 4" in Stockinette
Stitch in the round, blocked

For pattern support, contact customerservice@knitpicks.com

Princess Pullover

Notes:

A twist on a classic Aran pullover, this sweater has a feminine touch. Its gorgeous shaping is designed to flatter. Crafted in Knit Picks Galileo, you're sure to have eyes turning toward you: a vibrant, modern princess.

The sleeves begin at the wrist and are increased to the underarm. Turned hems allow them to lie flat. The body begins with the same turned hem as the sleeves. All of the waist shaping is worked in the Cable Panel. The charts are worked in the round; read each chart row from right to left as a RS row. All references to Right and Left are as worn, unless otherwise noted.

Join Hem

Unravel Provisional CO and place sts on spare needle. Hold these sts in back of working needle, and work across row in pattern, working one st from front needle and one from back K-wise tog as one. This is worked like a 3-Needle Bind Off, without binding off.

DIRECTIONS

Sleeves (make 2 the same)

Provisionally CO 60 (60, 62, 64, 68, 74, 78, 80, 82) sts onto smaller needles.

Setup Row: Attach working yarn and K across.
Join in the rnd, being careful not to twist sts.
Knit nine rnds, then purl one rnd (the turning rnd).
Switch to larger needles.

Start Pattern: K7 (7, 8, 9, 11, 14, 16, 17, 18), work from Rnd 1 of Sleeve chart over next 46 sts, K to end.

Cont working in pattern as established, with St st flanking central 46-st motif, through the first 8 rnds. On next rnd (9th rnd of patterning), unravel Provisional CO and place sts on spare needles; work in pattern around sleeve, joining hem.

Sleeve Increases

Inc Rnd: K1, M1L, work in pattern to last st, M1R, K1. 2 sts inc.
Cont in pattern as established, working an Inc Rnd every 12 (10, 9, 8, 6, 5, 4 & 9, 4, 4) rnds 13 (16, 18, 20, 27, 28, 16, 36, 38) times. 86 (92, 98, 104, 122, 130, 142, 152, 158) sts on the needles.

Knit 5 (2, 1, 3, 15, 12, 9, 22, 6) rnds in pattern.

Sleeve Cap Shaping

On next rnd, sts are bound off at base of sleeve cap. Cap is then worked flat (back and forth) to end. Sleeve cap should begin on what will be a WS row (odd-numbered on chart)—work an extra rnd if needed to be ready to work a WS row.

Work to 4 (6, 6, 6, 7, 5, 4, 4, 3) sts before end of rnd. BO last 4 (6, 6, 6, 7, 5, 4, 4, 3) sts of rnd, then first 6 (8, 8, 8, 9, 7, 6, 6, 5) sts of next rnd. Work in pattern to last 3 sts of rnd, SSSK. You are now working flat over 74 (76, 82, 88, 104, 116, 130, 140 148) sts.

Shape the caps as follows:

Double Dec Row

RS: K3tog, work in pattern to last 3 sts, SSSK. 2 sts dec at each edge.

WS: P3tog TBL, work in pattern to last 3 sts, P3tog. 2 sts dec at each edge.

Single Dec Row

RS: K2tog, work in pattern to last 2 sts, SSK. 1 st dec at each edge.

WS: P2tog TBL, work in pattern to last 2 sts, P2tog. 1 st dec at each edge.

Work a Double Dec Row every row 2 (2, 1, 1, 3, 3, 5, 2, 0) times; work a Single Dec Row every row 4 (5, 6, 4, 5, 3, 7, 15, 16) times, then every other row 7 (3, 6, 5, 3, 7, 4, 2, 8) times, then every third row 3 (6, 5, 7, 4, 7, 7, 3, 4) times, then every other row 6 (2, 3, 3, 9, 9, 6, 12, 9) times, then every row 5 (2, 3, 6, 2, 3, 8, 7, 9) times; work a Double Dec Row every row 1 (3, 3, 2, 3, 3, 3, 4, 4) times.

After last row of Sleeve Cap, BO remaining 12 (20, 20, 26, 34, 34, 34, 38, 40) sts.

Body

Provisionally CO 264 (296, 320, 340, 372, 396, 420, 456, 484) sts onto smaller needles.

Setup Row: Attach working yarn and K across.
PM and join in the rnd, being careful not to twist sts.
Knit nine rnds, then purl one rnd (the turning rnd).
Switch to larger needles.

Start Pattern: *K13 (14, 17, 21, 26, 26, 30, 39, 45), work from first rnd for your size of Cable Panel chart over next 106 (120, 126, 128, 134, 146, 150, 150, 152) sts, K13 (14, 17, 21, 26, 26, 30, 39, 45)*, PM to mark right underarm, rep from * to * across back.

Cont working in pattern as established, with St st flanking central cable panel, through the first 8 rnds for your size. On next rnd (9th rnd of patterning for your size), unravel Provisional CO and place sts on spare needles; work in pattern around body, joining hem.

Work as established, working St st up sides of Body and Cable Panels on front and back. Rep Rnds 153-160 of Center Panel chart through armhole, neck, and back.
At rnd noted for your size, BO for armholes, then work reps of Center Panel, armhole, and neckline decs at the same time. 118 (234, 146, 156, 172, 184, 196, 214, 228) sts each on front and back; 236 (268, 292, 312, 344, 368, 392, 428, 456) sts total.

Armholes

At rnd in Center Panel chart noted for your size, sts are bound off at each armhole: Work to 2 (2, 2, 3, 3, 5, 7, 9, 11) sts before right underarm M, BO next 4 (4, 4, 6, 6, 10, 14, 18, 22) sts, removing M; rep at left underarm M. 114 (130, 142, 150, 166, 174, 182, 196, 206) sts remain across both Front and Back.

Place Back sts on scrap yarn or a stitch holder, to work flat across Front sts only. After this, Front and Back are worked flat, separately, to the shoulders.

Front
Setup Row (RS): Work one row plain.

Armhole Double Dec Row
RS: K3tog, work in pattern to last 3 sts, SSSK. 2 sts dec at each edge.
WS: P3tog TBL, work in pattern to last 3 sts, P3tog. 2 sts dec at each edge.

Armhole Single Dec Row
RS: K2tog, work in pattern to last 2 sts, SSK. 1 st dec at each edge.
WS: P2tog TBL, work in pattern to last 2 sts, P2tog. 1 st dec at each edge.

Work an Armhole Double Dec Row every row 1 (1, 1, 2, 4, 2, 4, 7, 7) times; work an Armhole Single Dec Row every row 4 (4, 5, 7, 6, 6, 7, 7, 11) times, then every other row 2 (3, 4, 3, 6, 5, 2, 5, 6) times, then every third row 2 (0, 3, 3, 2, 3, 4, 2, 2) times; follow additional instructions for your size below.

Sizes 32", 40", 44", 48", and 64": Work 6 (6, 6, 3, 5) rows in pattern, then work an Armhole Single Dec Row. 92 (112, 114, 120, 138) sts remain across front.
Size 36": Work an Armhole Double Dec Row every fourth row two times; work seven rows in pattern, work an Armhole Single Dec Row. 102 sts remain across front.
Size 52": Work four rows in pattern, work an Armhole Single Dec Row, work seven rows in pattern, work an Armhole Single Dec Row. 134 sts remain across front.
Size 56": Work an Armhole Single Dec Row every fifth row two times. 136 sts remain across front.
Size 60": Work an Armhole Double Dec Row every fourth row two times. 136 sts remain across front.

Work 15 (7, 13, 17, 22, 25, 26, 32, 33) rows in pattern.

Neckline
On next RS row, sts are BO at front neck to form neckline: Work in pattern for 40 (41, 46, 47, 49, 54, 55, 55, 56) sts, BO next 12 (20, 20, 20, 22, 26, 26, 26, 26) sts; work in pattern to end. Follow neckline decrease directions below; attach a second ball of yarn at left neckline edge and work both sides of neckline together.

Neckline Double Dec Row
RS: Work in pattern to last 3 sts of left neck edge, SSSK. Using second ball of yarn, at right neck edge, K3tog, work in pattern across right shoulder. 4 sts dec.
WS: Work in pattern to last 3 sts of right neck edge, P3tog. P3tog TBL, work in pattern across left shoulder. 4 sts dec.

Neckline Dec Row
RS: Work in pattern to last 2 sts of left neck edge, SSK. K2tog, work in pattern across right shoulder. 2 sts dec.
WS: Work in pattern to last 2 sts of right neck edge, P2tog. P2tog TBL, work in pattern across left shoulder. 2 sts dec.

Shape Neckline
Work a Neckline Double Dec Row every row 4 (3, 2, 5, 2, 4, 3, 3, 3) times; work a Neckline Single Dec Row every row 2 (5, 5, 5, 6, 2, 4, 4, 5) times, then every other row 4 (3, 4, 3, 4, 4, 5, 6, 4) times, then every third row 2 (2, 2, 3, 3, 3, 2, 2, 3) times. 16 (16, 15, 17, 17, 17, 17, 18, 18) sts dec from each Front side. 24 (25, 31, 26, 32, 37, 38, 37, 38) sts remain on each shoulder.

Short Rows
A set of short rows finishes off the shoulders.
Short Row 1 (RS): Work in pattern to 7 (8, 9, 9, 10, 11, 11, 11, 12) sts before end of right shoulder, W&T.
Short Row 2 (WS): Work in pattern to 7 (8, 9, 9, 10, 11, 11, 11, 12) sts before end of left shoulder, W&T.
Short Row 3: Work in pattern to 7 (8, 9, 9, 10, 11, 11, 11, 12) sts before last wrapped st, W&T.
Short Row 4: Work in pattern to 7 (8, 9, 9, 10, 11, 11, 11, 12) sts before wrapped st, W&T.
Next Row (RS): K across all sts, picking up wrapped sts and knitting them together with the sts they wrap.

Break yarn and put shoulders on stitch holders or scrap yarn.

Back
Sl 114 (130, 142, 150, 166, 174, 182, 196, 206) Back sts onto needles, and attach yarn ready to begin a RS row. Work through Armhole shaping directions as for Front. 92 (102, 112, 114, 120, 134, 136, 136, 138) sts remain.

Work 47 (42, 47, 51, 57, 64, 68, 70, 73) rows in pattern.

Neckline
On next RS row, sts are bound off at back neck to form neckline: Work in pattern for 25 (26, 32, 27, 33, 38, 39, 38, 39) sts, BO next 42 (50, 48, 60, 54, 58, 58, 60, 60) sts; work in pattern to end.

Next Row (WS): Work in pattern to 2 sts before neckline edge of left shoulder, P2tog. Attach a new ball of yarn at right shoulder; P2tog TBL across first 2 sts, then work in pattern to end. 24 (25, 31, 26, 32, 37, 38, 37, 38) sts remain on each shoulder.

Work Short Rows section as for Front, working Back left shoulder as for Front right and Back right as Front left; do not break yarn.

Join Shoulders
Turn body inside out, and join shoulders tog using working yarn from Back, with 3-Needle Bind Off technique.

Finishing
Set in Sleeves
With right sides facing out, set sleeves into armhole openings, making sure that center of each sleeve cap is placed at shoulder seam and that seam under sleeve and bound-off sts of armhole are centered. Pin in place. Using yarn needle and yarn, begin at underarm and sew sleeves into armholes, using Mattress stitch.

Collar

Collar is worked as a rolled crew neck. Use smaller needles. With RS facing and starting at right shoulder seam, PU and K 2 sts into first bound-off st at back neck, 42 (50, 48, 60, 54, 58, 58, 60, 60) sts across bound-off sts at back neck, 2 sts up to left shoulder seam, and 42 (50, 48, 60, 54, 58, 58, 60, 60) sts around front neckline edge back to right shoulder. 88 (104, 100, 124, 112, 120, 120, 124, 124) sts. PM and join in the rnd.

Work in 2x2 Rib for 2″. Break yarn, leaving a tail of approx 2 yards. Fold collar towards inside. Using yarn tail, whipstitch the live sts to back of picked up row.

Weave in ends. Wash and block to measurements.

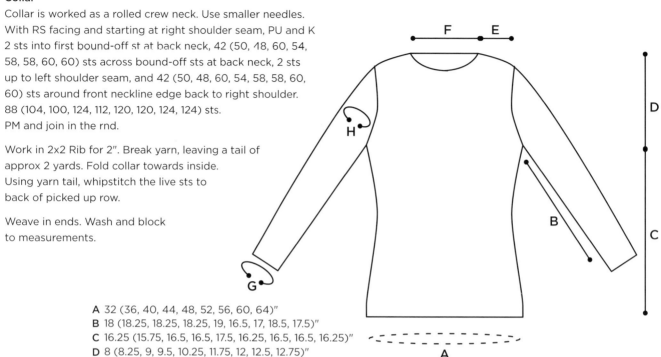

A 32 (36, 40, 44, 48, 52, 56, 60, 64)″
B 18 (18.25, 18.25, 18.25, 19, 16.5, 17, 18.5, 17.5)″
C 16.25 (15.75, 16.5, 16.5, 17.5, 16.25, 16.5, 16.5, 16.25)″
D 8 (8.25, 9, 9.5, 10.25, 11.75, 12, 12.5, 12.75)″
E 3 (3.25, 4, 3.25, 4.25, 4.75, 5, 4.75, 5)″
F 5.5 (6.5, 6.25, 7.75, 7, 7.5, 7.5, 7.75, 7.75)″
G 8.25 (8.25, 8.5, 9, 9.5, 10.5, 11.25, 11.5, 12)″
H 12.5 (13.5, 14.5, 15.5, 18.5, 20, 22, 23.5, 24.5)″

Sleeve

| 46 | 45 | 44 | 43 | 42 | 41 | 40 | 39 | 38 | 37 | 36 | 35 | 34 | 33 | 32 | 31 | 30 | 29 | 28 | 27 | 26 | 25 | 24 | 23 | 22 | 21 | 20 | 19 | 18 | 17 | 16 | 15 | 14 | 13 | 12 | 11 | 10 | 9 | 8 | 7 | 6 | 5 | 4 | 3 | 2 | 1 | |

LEGEND

	No Stitch
	Placeholder—no stitch made

	Knit
	Knit stitch

B	**Knit TBL**
	Knit stitch through the back loop

•	**Purl**
	Purl stitch

	P2tog
	Purl two stitches together as one stitch

	PFB
	Purl into the front and back of the stitch

C2 Over 1 Right P (2/1 LPC)
Sl1 to CN, hold in front. K2, P1 from CN

C2 Over 1 Left P (2/1 RPC)
Sl2 to CN, hold in front. P1, K2 from CN

C2 Over 2 Right (2/2 RC)
Sl2 to CN, hold in back. K2, K2 from CN

C2 Over 2 Left (2/2 LC)
Sl2 to CN, hold in front. K2, K2 from CN

C2 Over 2 Right P (2/2 RPC)
Sl2 to CN, hold in back. K2, P2 from CN

C2 Over 2 Left P (2/2 LPC)
Sl2 to CN, hold in front. P2, K2 from CN

C1 Over 3 Right (1/3 RC)
Sl3 to CN, hold in back. K1, K3 from CN

C1 Over 3 Left (1/3 LC)
Sl1 to CN, hold in front. K3, K1 from CN

	32″
	36″
	40″
	44″
	48″
	52″
	56″
	60″
	64″

Work this st 3 (2, 1, 2, 1, 3, 1, 1, 2) times

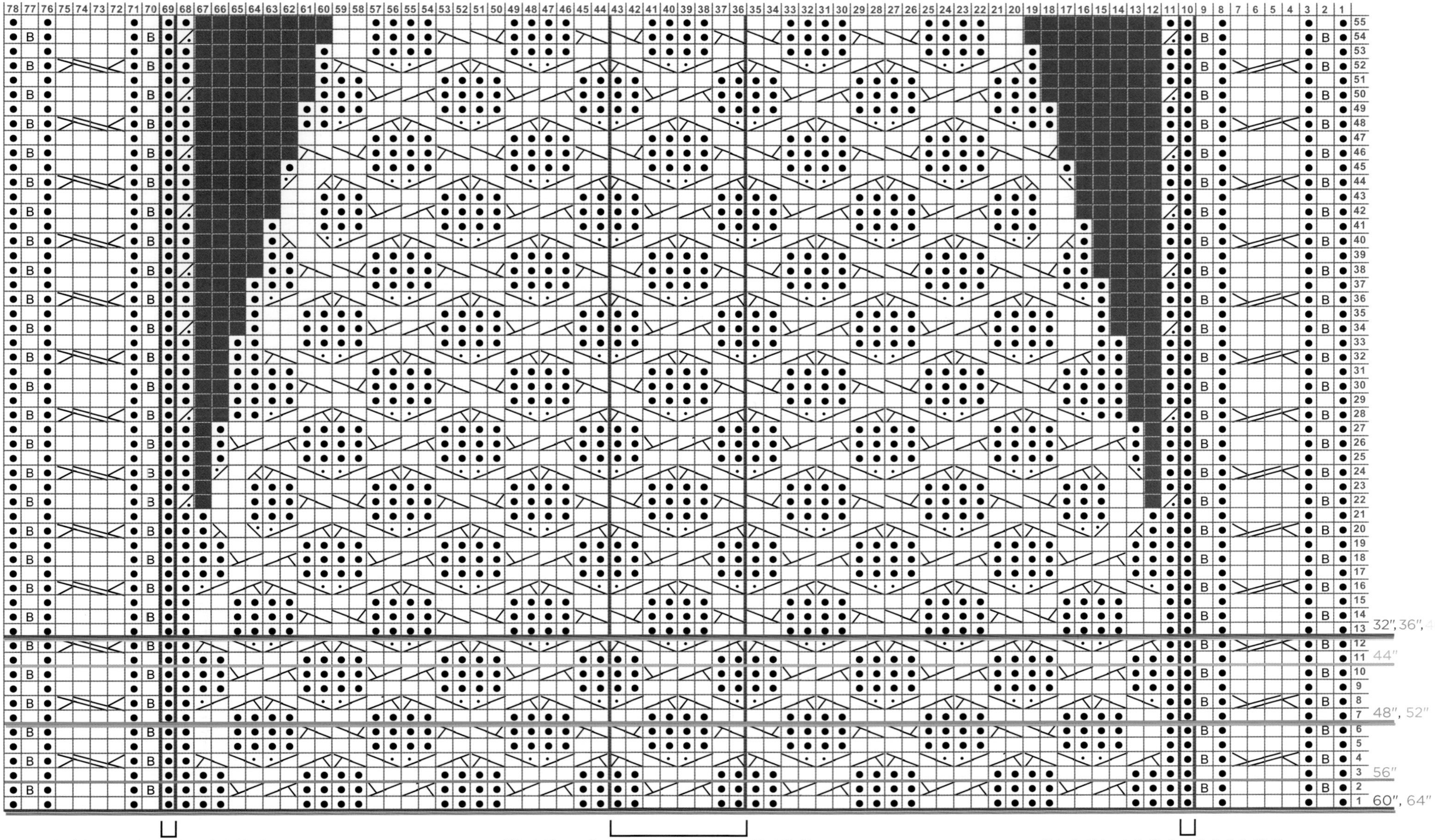

Work these 8 sts 4 (6, 7, 7, 8, 9, 10, 10, 10) times

Work this st 3 (2, 1, 2, 1, 3, 1, 1, 2) times

60", 64"
56"
48", 52"
44"
32", 36", 40"

Work this st 3 (2, 1, 2, 1, 3, 1, 1, 2) times

Work these 8 sts 4 (6, 7, 7, 8, 9, 10, 10, 10) times

Work this st 3 (2, 1, 2, 1, 3, 1, 1, 2) times

Cable Panel (part 3)

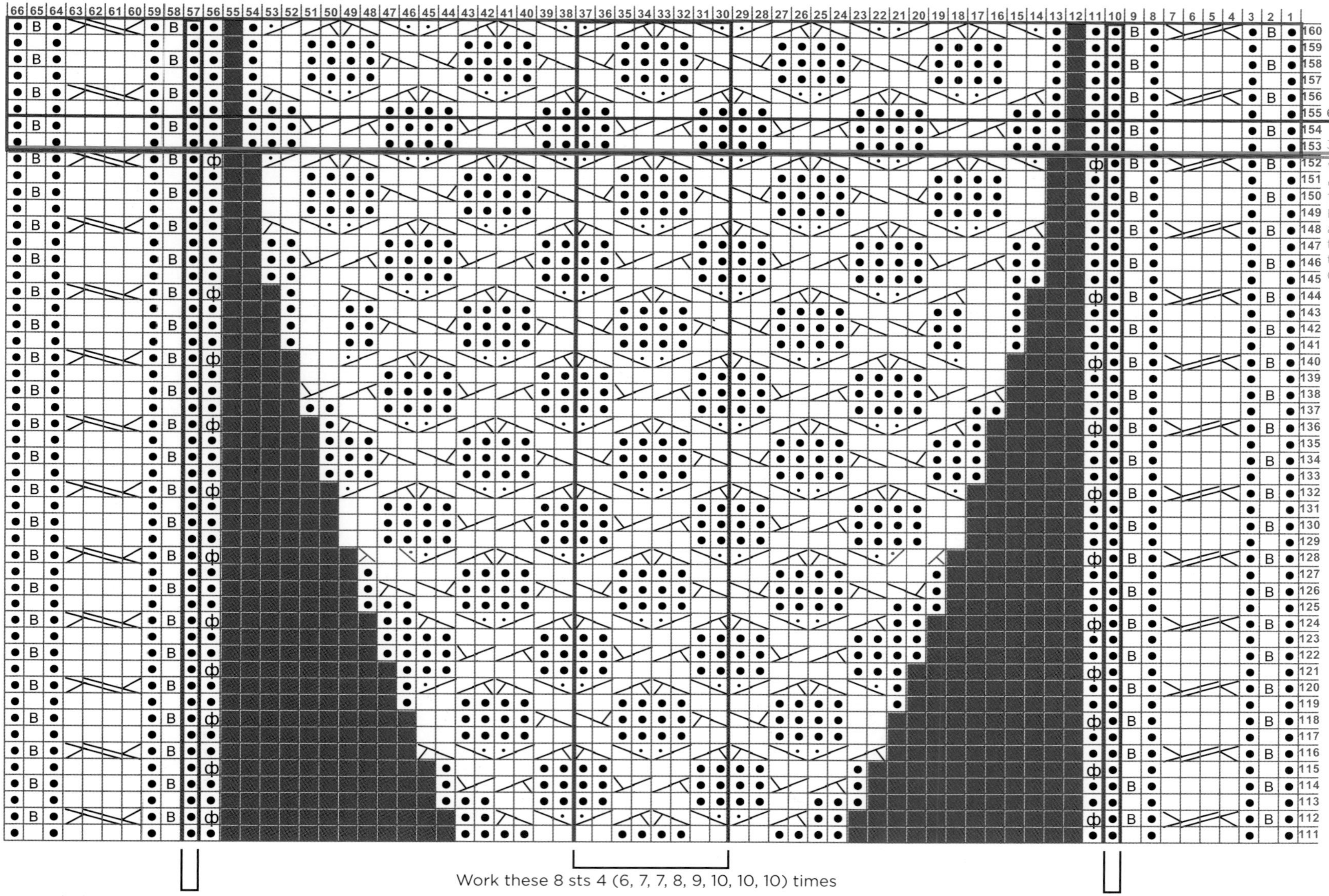

Work this st 3 (2, 1, 2, 1, 3, 1, 1, 2) times

Work these 8 sts 4 (6, 7, 7, 8, 9, 10, 10, 10) times

Work this st 3 (2, 1, 2, 1, 3, 1, 1, 2) times

Work two reps of Rows 153–160, then BO for armholes on first round of third rep (round 169)

Work through Rows 153–160, then BO for armholes on first round of second rep (round 161)

32", 36", 40", 48"

52", 56"

60", 64"

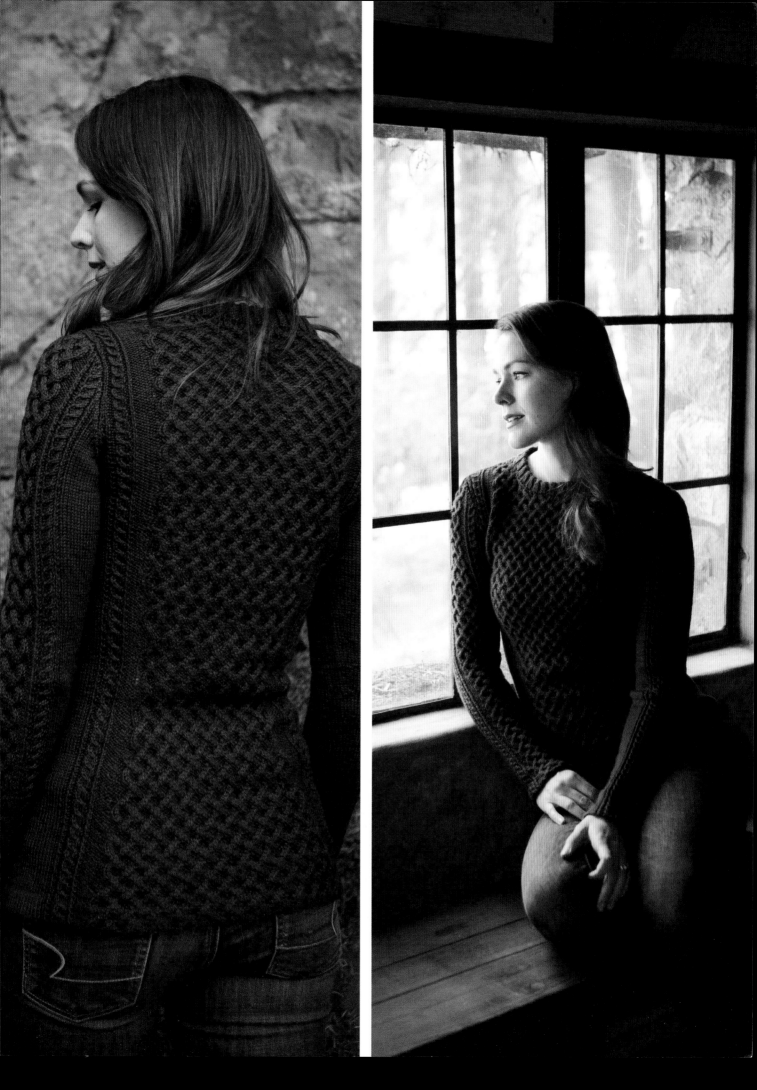

PROFESSOR MEOW PULLOVER

by Claire Slade

FINISHED MEASUREMENTS

32.5 (37, 40.5, 45, 48.5, 53, 57.75, 61, 64.5)" finished bust measurement; garment is meant to be worn with 3-4" of ease

YARN

Knit Picks Wonderfluff™ (bulky weight, 70% Baby Alpaca, 7% Merino, 23% Nylon; 142 yards/50g): MC Finnley 27188, 3 (3, 4, 4, 5, 5, 6, 6, 7) balls, CC Cobblestone 27187, 1 (1, 1, 1, 1, 2, 2, 2, 2) balls

NEEDLES

US 10.5 (6.5mm) straight or 24" circular needles, plus DPNs or 16" circulars, or size to obtain gauge

NOTIONS

Yarn Needle
2 Stitch Markers
Scrap Yarn or Stitch Holder
Optional: Small amount of worsted weight light gray or white yarn for whisker embroidery (MC may be used instead)

GAUGE

14 sts and 18 rows = 4" in Stockinette Stitch, blocked

For pattern support, contact customerservice@knitpicks.com

Professor Meow Pullover

Notes:

This sweater is knit flat, Back and Front pieces worked from the bottoms up, and then seamed; the cat motif is created using the intarsia method. When knitting the cat, use a separate ball of yarn for each section—it is a good idea to wind the yarn into smaller balls before starting.

The charts are read on RS rows (odd numbers) from right to left, and on WS rows (even numbers) from left to right.

DIRECTIONS

Back

Edging
Using MC and straight or longer circular needles, CO 58 (66, 70, 78, 86, 94, 102, 106, 114) sts.

Work in 2x2 Rib until work measures 1.5", ending on a WS row.

Sizes 40.5", 45", and 61" Only: On final Rib row, K1, M1, work in established 2x2 Rib to last st, M1P, P1. 58 (66, 72, 80, 86, 94, 102, 108, 114) sts.

Body
Work in St st until work measures 16 (16, 16.5, 16.5, 17, 17, 17.5, 17.5, 17.5)" from CO edge.

CO 1 (1, 2, 2, 2, 2, 3, 3, 3) sts at beginning of next two rows, for sleeves. 60 (68, 76, 84, 90, 98, 108, 114, 120) sts.

Work in St st until work measures 4.5 (5, 5.5, 6, 6.25, 6.75, 7.25, 7.25, 7.75)" from sleeve CO point, ending on a WS row.

Neckline
Next Row (RS): K22 (26, 29, 33, 36, 40, 44, 47, 50); place these sts on a holder for right back, BO 16 (16, 18, 18, 18, 18, 20, 20, 20) sts, K to end. 22 (26, 29, 33, 36, 40, 44, 47, 50) sts.

Left Back
Row 1 (WS): P across.
Row 2 (RS): SSK, K to end. 1 st dec.
Rep Rows 1-2 until 17 (21, 24, 28, 30, 34, 37, 40, 43) sts remain.

Next Row (WS): BO 3 (3, 4, 5, 5, 6, 6, 7, 7) sts, P to end. 14 (18, 20, 23, 25, 28, 31, 33, 36) sts.
Next Row: K across.
Next Row: BO 3 (3, 4, 5, 5, 6, 6, 7, 7) sts, P to end. 11 (15, 16, 18, 20, 22, 25, 26, 29) sts.
BO remaining sts.

Right Back
With WS facing, return held sts to needle and rejoin yarn.
Row 1 (WS): P across.
Row 2 (RS): K to last 2sts, K2tog. 1 st dec.
Rep Rows 1-2 until 18 (22, 25, 29, 31, 35, 38, 41, 44) sts remain.

Next Row (WS): P across.
Next Row: BO 3 (3, 4, 5, 5, 6, 6, 7, 7) sts, K to last 2 sts, K2tog. 14 (18, 20, 23, 25, 28, 31, 33, 36) sts.
Next Row: P across.

Next Row: BO 3 (3, 4, 5, 5, 6, 6, 7, 7) sts, K to end. 11 (15, 16, 18, 20, 22, 25, 26, 29) sts.
Next Row: P across.
BO remaining sts.

Front

Edging
Work as for Back Edging.

Lower Body
Setup Row (RS): Using MC, K8 (12, 15, 19, 17, 21, 25, 28, 31), join CC and K42 (42, 42, 42, 52, 52, 52, 52, 52), join new MC ball and K to end.

Row 1 (WS): Using MC, P8 (12, 15, 19, 17, 21, 25, 28, 31); using CC, P42 (42, 42, 42, 52, 52, 52, 52, 52); using MC, P to end.
Row 2 (RS): Using MC, K8 (12, 15, 19, 17, 21, 25, 28, 31); using CC, K42 (42, 42, 42, 52, 52, 52, 52, 52); using MC, K to end.
Rep Rows 1-2 until work measures 9.5 (10, 11, 11, 11, 11, 12, 12, 12)" from where CC was joined, ending on a RS row.

Next Row (WS): Using MC, P to 1 st before CC section, PM, P1; using CC, P42 (42, 42, 42, 52, 52, 52, 52, 52); using MC, P1, PM, P to end.

Cat Head
Sts are cast on for Sleeves while chart is being worked—be sure to read through all instructions before proceeding.

For sizes 32.5 (37, 40.5, 45)" use Chart A; for sizes 48.5 (53, 57.75, 61, 64.5)" use Chart B, as follows:
Row 1 (RS): Using MC, K to M, SM, work chart to M, SM; using MC, K to end.
Row 2 (WS): Using MC, P to M, SM, work chart to M, SM; using MC, P to end.
Rep Rows 1-2 until all rows of chart have been worked, and AT THE SAME TIME when work measures 16 (16, 16.5, 16.5, 17, 17, 17.5, 17.5, 17.5)" from CO edge, CO 1 (1, 2, 2, 2, 2, 3, 3, 3) sts at beginning of next two rows, for sleeves. 60 (68, 76, 84, 90, 98, 108, 114, 120) sts.

Once all chart rows have been worked, cont in St st with MC until work measures 4.5 (5, 5.5, 6, 6.25, 6.75, 7.25, 7.25, 7.75)" from sleeve CO point ending on a WS row.

Neckline
Next Row (RS): K22 (26, 29, 33, 36, 40, 44, 47, 50); place these sts on a holder for left front, BO 16 (16, 18, 18, 18, 18, 20, 20, 20) sts, K to end. 22 (26, 29, 33, 36, 40, 44, 47, 50) sts.

Right Front
Row 1 (WS): P across.
Row 2 (RS): SSK, K to end. 1 st dec.
Rep Rows 1-2 until 17 (21, 24, 28, 30, 34, 37, 40, 43) sts remain.

Next Row (WS): BO 3 (3, 4, 5, 5, 6, 6, 7, 7) sts, P to end. 14 (18, 20, 23, 25, 28, 31, 33, 36) sts.
Next Row: K across.

Next Row: BO 3 (3, 4, 5, 5, 6, 6, 7, 7) sts, P to end. 11 (15, 16, 18, 20, 22, 25, 26, 29) sts.
BO remaining sts.

Left Front
With WS facing, return held sts to needle and rejoin yarn.

Row 1 (WS): P across.
Row 2 (RS): K to last 2 sts, K2tog. 1 st dec.
Rep Rows 1-2 until 18 (22, 25, 29, 31, 35, 38, 41, 44) sts remain.

Next Row (WS): P across.
Next Row: BO 3 (3, 4, 5, 5, 6, 6, 7, 7) sts, K to last 2sts, K2tog.
14 (18, 20, 23, 25, 28, 31, 33, 36) sts.
Next Row: P across.
Next Row: BO 3 (3, 4, 5, 5, 6, 6, 7, 7) sts, K to end. 11 (15, 16, 18, 20, 22, 25, 26, 29) sts.
Next Row: P across.
BO remaining sts.

Sew both side seams, from bottom edge up to sleeve and CO edge, then sew both shoulder seams.

Sleeve Edging (work both the same)
Using DPNs or shorter circulars, with RS facing and starting at underarm, PU and K 24 (26, 28, 30, 32, 34, 38, 38, 40) sts up one side of sleeve, then PU and K 24 (26, 28, 30, 32, 34, 38, 38, 40) sts down other side of sleeve, PM, and join in the rnd. 48 (52, 56, 60, 64, 68, 76, 76, 80) sts.
Work 2x2 Rib until Edging measures 1".
BO all sts in pattern.

Neckline Edging
Using DPNs or shorter circulars, starting at top right shoulder seam, PU and K 9 (9, 9, 9, 11, 11, 13, 13, 13) sts down right back neck, 16 (16, 18, 18, 18, 18, 20, 20, 20) sts along neck BO edge, 9 (9, 9, 9, 11, 11, 13, 13, 13) sts up other back side of back neck edge, 9 (9, 9, 9, 11, 11, 13, 13, 13) sts down front left neck, 16 (16, 18, 18, 18, 18, 20, 20, 20) sts along front neck BO edge, and finally 9 (9, 9, 9, 11, 11, 13, 13, 13) sts up front right neck; join in the rnd. 68 (68, 72, 72, 80, 80, 92, 92, 92) sts.
Rnd 1: K all.
BO all sts loosely.

Finishing
Weave in ends, wash, and block to diagram.
Using photo as a guide, with leftover CC yarn, work two Duplicate Stitches over center two sts of each eye. Then, using Running Stitch with lighter yarn or MC, embroider three whiskers on either side of nose.

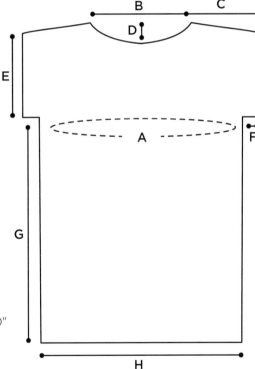

A 32.5 (37, 40.5, 45, 48.5, 53, 57.75, 61, 64.5)"
B 7.5 (7.5, 8, 8, 8.5, 8.5, 9.75, 9.75, 9.75)"
C 4.75 (6, 6.75, 8, 8.5, 9.75, 10.5, 11.5, 12.25)"
D 3 (3, 3, 3, 3.25, 3.25, 3.75, 3.75, 3.75)"
E 7.5 (8, 8.5, 9, 9.5, 10, 11, 11, 11.5)"
F 1.25 (1.25, 1.5, 1.5, 1.5, 1.5, 1.75, 1.75, 1.75)"
G 16 (16, 16.5, 16.5, 17, 17, 17.5, 17.5, 17.5)"
H 16.25 (18.25, 20, 22.5, 24.25, 26.5, 28.75, 30.5, 32.25)"

Chart A

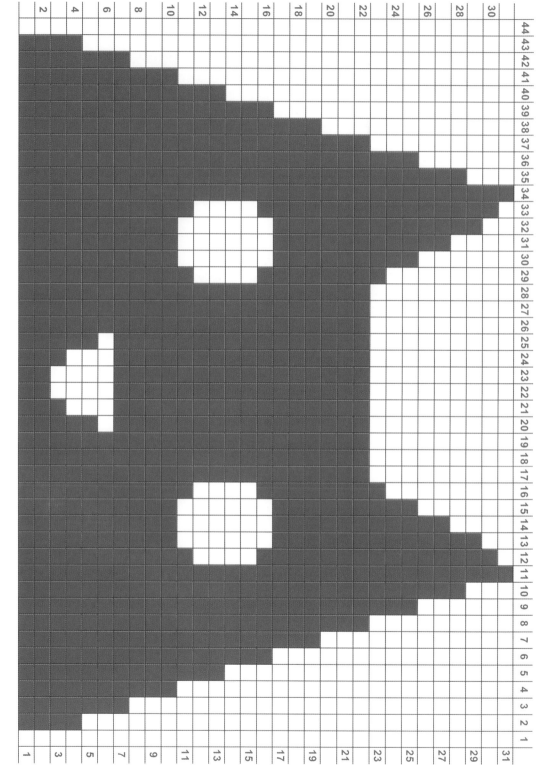

LEGEND

Knit
RS: knit stitch
WS: purl stitch

☐ MC

⬛ CC

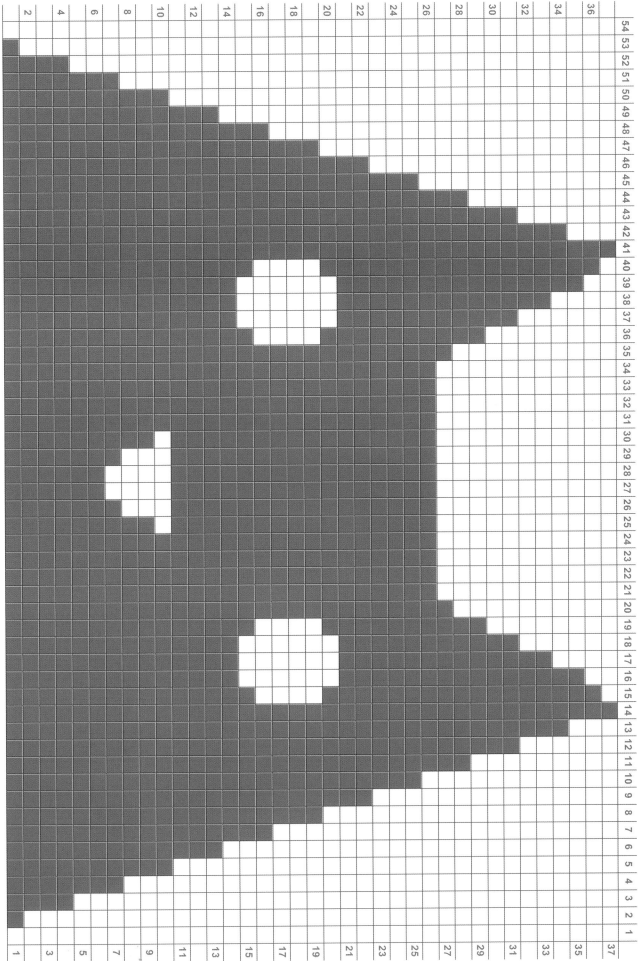

SHADED PULLOVER

by Kerin Dimeler-Laurence

FINISHED MEASUREMENTS

32 (36, 40, 44, 48, 52, 56, 60, 64)" finished bust measurement

YARN

Knit Picks Wool of the Andes™ (worsted weight, 100% Peruvian Highland Wool; 110 yards/50g)

Purple colorway: MC Blackberry 24273, 2 (2, 2, 2, 3, 3, 3, 3, 3) skeins; C1 Indigo Heather 25069, C2 Solstice Heather 25066, C3 Delft Heather 25649, C4 Sprinkle Heather 26159, C5 Haze Heather 26158, C6 Lake Ice Heather 23898, 1 (1, 2, 2, 2, 2, 2, 2, 2) skeins; C7 White 24065, 2 (2, 2, 3, 3, 3, 3, 4, 4) skeins

Neutral colorway: MC Coal 23420, 2 (2, 2, 2, 3, 3, 3, 3, 3) skeins; C1 Onyx Heather 24076, C2 Cobblestone Heather 24283, C3 Marble Heather 25976, C4 Silver 25977, C5 Gosling 25986, C6 Mink Heather 24279, 1 (1, 2, 2, 2, 2, 2, 2, 2) skeins; C7 Almond 25072, 2 (2, 2, 3, 3, 3, 3, 4, 4) skeins

NEEDLES

US 8 (5mm) DPNs or long circular needles for Magic Loop for sleeves and neck, and long circulars for body, or size to obtain gauge
US 7 (4.5mm) DPNs and long circular needles, or one size smaller than those used to obtain gauge

NOTIONS

Yarn Needle
Stitch Markers
Stitch Holders or Scrap Yarn

GAUGE

16 sts and 22 rounds = 4" in Stockinette Stitch in the round on larger needles, blocked

For pattern support, contact customerservice@knitpicks.com

Shaded Pullover

Notes:

This cozy pullover features raglan shaping, a funnel neck, and a longer body and sleeves. A simple stripe sequence gently shifts each color through the sleeves and body.

The sleeves are knit first, beginning at the wrists. They begin with simple ribbed cuffs and are increased to the underarms, then attached to the body. Like the sleeves, the body begins with ribbing. It is shaped to the underarms, where it is joined with the sleeves to work towards the neck. The sweater is then worked up to the neckline. The yoke of the sweater is shaped to the neckline with raglan decreases.

All references to Right and Left are as worn, unless otherwise noted.

Stripe Pattern

Size 32"
Rnds 1-3: Work in MC.
Rnd 4: Work in C1.
Rnds 5-6: Work in MC.
Rnd 7: Work in C1.
Rnd 8: Work in MC.
Rnds 9-14: Rep Rnds 7-8.
Rnds 15-16: Work in C1.
Rnd 17: Work in MC.

Sizes 36" and 40"
Rnds 1-4: Work in MC.
Rnd 5: Work in C1.
Rnds 6-7: Work in MC.
Rnd 8: Work in C1.
Rnd 9: Work in MC.
Rnds 10-15: Rep Rnds 8-9.
Rnds 16-17: Work in C1.
Rnd 18: Work in MC.

Sizes 44" and 48"
Rnds 1-6: Work in MC.
Rnd 7: Work in C1.
Rnds 8-9: Work in MC.
Rnd 10: Work in C1.
Rnd 11: Work in MC.
Rnds 12-17: Rep Rnds 10-11.
Rnds 18-19: Work in C1.
Rnd 20: Work in MC.

Sizes 52" and 56"
Rnds 1-7: Work in MC.
Rnd 8: Work in C1.
Rnds 9-10: Work in MC.
Rnd 11: Work in C1.
Rnd 12: Work in MC.
Rnds 13-18: Rep Rnds 10-11.
Rnds 19-20: Work in C1.
Rnd 21: Work in MC.

Sizes 60" and 64"
Rnds 1-8: Work in MC.
Rnd 9: Work in C1.
Rnds 10-11: Work in MC.
Rnd 12: Work in C1.
Rnd 13: Work in MC.
Rnds 14-19: Rep Rnds 10-11.
Rnds 20-21: Work in C1.
Rnd 22: Work in MC.

All Sizes
Rep the 17 (18, 18, 20, 20, 21, 21, 22, 22) rnd Stripe Pattern sequence, replacing colors on subsequent reps as follows:
Rep 2: Colors C1 and C2.
Rep 3: Colors C2 and C3.
Rep 4: Colors C3 and C4.
Rep 5: Colors C4 and C5.
Rep 6: Colors C5 and C6.
Rep 7: Colors C6 and C7.
Work to the end in color C7 after Rep 7.

DIRECTIONS

Instructions for shaping and Stripe Pattern are written separately but worked at the same time; read both sections before proceeding with both Sleeves and Body.

Sleeves (make 2 the same)
With MC and smaller needles, CO 30 (32, 34, 36, 38, 42, 44, 46, 48) sts. PM and join in the rnd, being careful not to twist sts.
Work in 1x1 Rib for 2.5". Switch to larger needles.

Next Rnd: Begin working from Stripe Pattern, starting on Rnd 1 (1, 1, 1, 3, 4, 10, 10, 9) of first rep of Stripe Pattern, and work Sleeve Increases at the same time.

Sleeve Increases
Inc Rnd: K1, M1L, K to last st, M1R, K1. 2 sts inc.

Sizes 32", 44", 52", 56", and 60" Only: Work an Inc Rnd on the first rnd. 32 (-, -, 38, -, 44, 46, 48, -) sts.

All Sizes: Work an Inc Rnd every 8 (8, 8, 8, 6, 6, 6, 6, 5) rnds 11 (12, 12, 12, 15, 15, 15, 15, 17) times.
Knit 8 (4, 4, 4, 11, 7, 5, 4, 9) rnds plain, continuing Stripe Pattern.
Note final Rnd number and Rep number of Stripe Pattern. 54 (56, 58, 62, 68, 74, 76, 78, 82) sts on needles. Break yarn and place Sleeve sts on scrap yarn or stitch holder.

Body
Ribbing is worked in MC; Stripe Pattern begins on first rnd after ribbing.
With MC and smaller needles, CO 132 (156, 172, 192, 208, 220, 236, 260, 276) sts. PM and join in the rnd, being careful not to twist sts.
Work in 1x1 Rib for 3". PM after 66 (78, 86, 96, 104, 110, 118, 130, 138) sts on last rnd, to mark right underarm.

Switch to larger needles.

Shaping

Work Body Shaping and Stripe Pattern directions at the same time.

Dec Rnd: *K2, SSK, K to 4 sts before M, K2tog, K2, SM; rep from * to end. 4 sts dec.

Inc Rnd: *K2, M1L, K to 2 sts before M, M1R, K2, SM; rep from * to end. 4 sts inc.

Work a Dec Rnd every 10 (7, 8, 7, 9, 9, 9, 8, 8) rnds 5 (7, 7, 8, 7, 7, 7, 8, 8) times. 20 (28, 28, 32, 28, 28, 28, 32, 32) sts dec. 112 (128, 144, 160, 180, 192, 208, 228, 244) sts around body. Work 8 (10, 6, 11, 7, 8, 11, 11, 11) rnds in St st.

Work an Inc Rnd on next rnd, then every 11 (11, 11, 11, 16, 9, 9, 13, 12) rnds 3 (3, 3, 3, 2, 3, 3, 2, 2) times. 128 (144, 160, 176, 192, 208, 224, 240, 256) sts around body. Work 5 (7, 4, 0, 0, 2, 3, 2, 2) rnds in St st.

Join Sleeves

On next rnd, Sleeves are joined to Body. Cont working from Stripe Pattern at the same time as working Raglan Shaping. You should be on the same Rnd and Rep of Stripe Pattern— if not, work additional Body or Sleeve rnds as necessary.

Work across front of Body to 3 (3, 4, 4, 5, 5, 5, 6, 6) sts before right underarm M. PM. Sl next 6 (6, 8, 8, 10, 10, 10, 12, 12) Body sts onto scrap yarn or a stitch holder.

Place a sleeve onto spare needles, leaving first and last 3 (3, 4, 4, 5, 5, 5, 6, 6) sts of rnd on scrap yarn or stitch holder. Knit directly from Body around Sleeve, PM, and work from first live st of back of Body; this joins the sleeve.

Work across back of Body to 3 (3, 4, 4, 5, 5, 5, 6, 6) sts before end of rnd (left underarm). PM. Sl last 3 (3, 4, 4, 5, 5, 5, 6, 6) sts of this rnd and first 3 (3, 4, 4, 5, 5, 5, 6, 6) sts of next rnd onto scrap yarn or a stitch holder.

Place second sleeve onto spare needles, leaving 6 (6, 8, 8, 10, 10, 10, 12, 12) sts on holder as done for first sleeve. Work around Sleeve, PM, marking new BOR. Knit directly into first live st of Body; this joins sleeve and begins next rnd.

Work around all 212 (232, 244, 268, 288, 316, 336, 348, 372) sts for 5 (5, 6, 6, 6, 7, 7, 8, 8) rnds; PM after first 29 (33, 36, 40, 43, 47, 51, 54, 58) sts to mark center front—this M is not noted in Raglan Shaping.

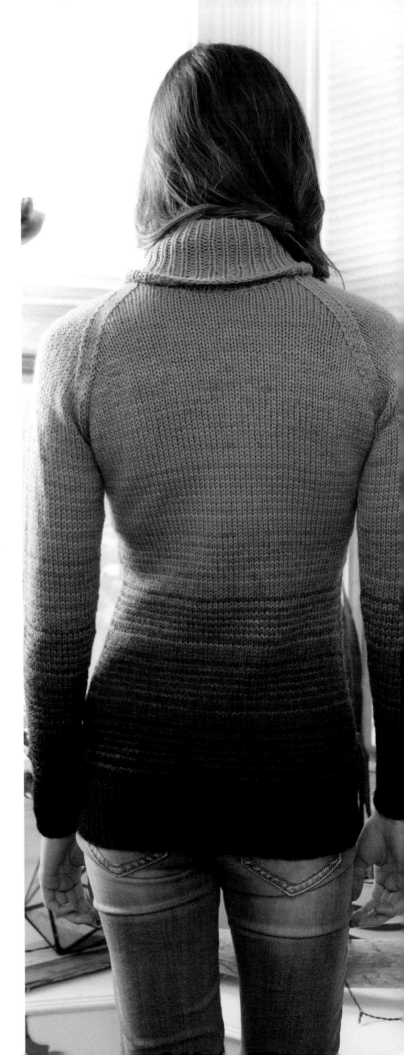

Raglan Shaping

Neckline and decs are worked at the same time—read both sections before proceeding.

Raglan Dec Rnd: *K1, SSK, K to 3 sts before M, K2tog, K1, SM; rep from * around body. 8 sts dec.
Sleeve Dec Rnd: * K to M, SM, K1, SSK, K to 3 sts before M, K2tog, K1, SM; rep from * around body. 4 sts dec.
Body Dec Rnd: *K1, SSK, K to 3 sts before M, K2tog, K1, SM, K to next M, SM; rep from * around body. 4 sts dec.

Each rnd listed in table is a rnd of the yoke. Read from bottom up, working decs on rnds noted and working plain where there is no dec noted. It may be helpful to mark in this chart where Stripe Pattern and Neckline shaping lines up with each rnd.

Neckline

On the row highlighted in the raglan decrease chart, BO for neck: Work to 2 (3, 3, 3, 3, 4, 4, 4) sts before center front M, BO next 4 (4, 6, 6, 6, 6, 8, 8, 8) sts, removing M, cont around in pattern. 96 (100, 110, 118, 130, 134, 144, 140, 144) sts remain at end of BO rnd.

Cont to end of yoke working flat as follows:

Neckline Double Dec Row (RS): K3tog, work to last 3 sts of left neck edge, SSSK. 4 sts dec.
Neckline Double Dec Row (WS): P3tog TBL, work to last 3 sts of right neck edge, P3tog. 4 sts dec.

Neckline Dec Row (RS): K2tog, work to last 2 sts of left neck edge, SSK. 2 sts dec.
Neckline Dec Row (WS): P2tog TBL, work to last 2 sts of right neck edge, P2tog. 2 sts dec.

Continuing Stripe Pattern and Raglan Shaping instructions, Shape Neckline:
Work a Neckline Double Dec Row on next two rows; work a Neckline Dec Row every row 2 (3, 3, 3, 4, 4, 4, 4, 5) times, then every other row 2 (2, 2, 3, 2, 4, 3, 3, 2) times.
After last dec row for your size as shown in raglan table, BO all sts.

Funnel Neck

Funnel neck is picked up around neckline and worked loosely in rib.
With larger needles and C7, and with RS facing, PU and K 20 (22, 24, 24, 26, 30, 30, 30, 30) sts across bound-off sts at back neck, 8 (8, 8, 8, 8, 10, 10, 10, 10) sts across left sleeve, 26 (28, 30, 32, 34, 34, 34, 36, 36) sts around front neck, and 8 (8, 8, 8, 8, 10, 10, 10, 10) sts across right sleeve. 62 (66, 70, 72, 76, 84, 84, 86, 86) sts on needles. PM and join in the rnd. Work in 1x1 Rib for 10-12" or desired length.
BO all sts loosely in Rib.

Finishing

Graft held sts at each underarm closed.
Weave in ends. Wash and block to measurements.

Round/Row	32	36	40	44	48	52	56	60	64
68									R
67								R	
66							B	B	R
65								R	
64						B	B	B	R
63					R	R	R		
62							B		B
61					R	R	R	R	R
60									
59					R	R	B	R	
58									
57					R	R	R	R	
56									
55					R	R	R	R	
54									
53				R	R	R	R	R	
52				B					B
51				R	R	R	R	R	R
50			B						
49				R	R	B	B	B	B
48									
47				R	R	R	R	R	R
46									
45			B	R	R	R	R	R	R
44									
43			R	R	R	R	R	R	R
42									B
41		R	R	R	R	R	R	R	R
40		S							
39		R	R	R	R	B	B	B	B
38									
37	R	R	R	R	R	R	R	R	R
36									
35	R	R	R	R	R	R	R	R	R
34									
33	R	R	R	R	R	R	R	R	R
32									B
31	R	R	R	R	R	R	R	R	R
30									
29	R	R	R	R	R	B	B	B	B
28									
27	R	R	R	R	R	R	R	R	R
26									
25	R	R	R	R	R	R	R	R	R
24									
23	R	R	R	R	R	R	R	R	R
22	S								B
21	R	R	R	R	R	R	R	R	R
20									
19	R	R	R	R	R	B	B	B	B
18									
17	R	R	R	R	R	R	R	R	R
16									
15	R	R	R	R	R	R	R	R	R
14									
13	R	R	R	R	R	R	R	R	R
12									B
11	R	R	R	R	R	R	R	R	R
10									
9	R	R	R	R	R	B	B	B	R
8									
7	R	R	R	R	R	R	R	R	R
6								B	B
5	R	R	R	R	R	R	R	R	R
4		S	B	B			B	B	B
3	R	R	R	B	B	R	R	R	R
2	S	R	B	B	B	R	B	B	B
1	R	R	B	B	B	R	R	R	R
	32	36	40	44	48	52	56	60	64

R	Raglan Decrease Round
B	Body Decrease Round
S	Sleeve Decrease Round
	BO For Neckline on this round

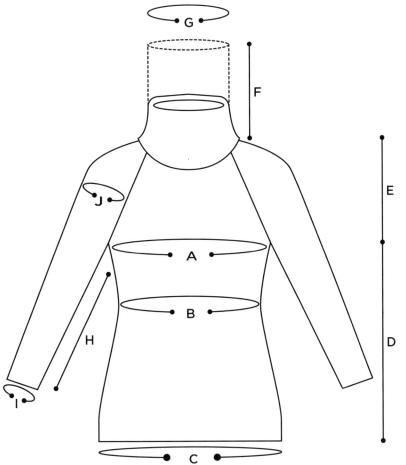

A 32 (36, 40, 44, 48, 52, 56, 60, 64)"
B 28 (32, 36, 40, 45, 48, 52, 57, 61)"
C 33 (39, 43, 48, 52, 55, 59, 65, 69)"
D 20.75 (21.25, 21.25, 21.25, 21.75, 21.75, 22, 22, 22)"
E 7.8 (8.5, 9.25, 10.2, 10.8, 12.9, 12.9, 13.6, 13.8)"
F 10-12"
G 15.5 (16.5, 17.5, 18, 19, 21, 21, 21.5, 21.5)"
H 20.1 (20.7, 20.7, 20.7, 20.7, 20.3, 20, 19.8, 19.6)"
I 7.5 (8, 8.5, 9, 9.5, 10.5, 11, 11.5, 12)"
J 13.5 (14, 14.5, 15.5, 17, 18.5, 19, 19.5, 20.5)"

Glossary

Common Stitches & Techniques

Make 1 Left-leaning Stitch (M1L)
Inserting LH needle from front to back, PU the horizontal strand between the st just worked and the next st, and K TBL.

Make 1 Right-leaning Stitch (M1R)
Inserting LH needle from back to front, PU the horizontal strand between the st just worked and the next st, and K TFL.

Slip, Slip, Knit (SSK)
(Slip 1 knit-wise) twice; insert left-hand needle into front of these 2 stitches and knit them together.

Centered Double Decrease (CDD)
Slip first and second stitches together as if to K2tog; knit 1 stitch; pass 2 slipped stitches over the knit stitch.

Stockinette Stitch (St st, worked flat over any number of sts)
Row 1 (RS): Knit all sts.
Row 2 (WS): Purl all sts.
Rep Rows 1 and 2 for pattern.
St st in the rnd: K every rnd.

Garter Stitch (in the rnd over any number of sts)
Rnd 1: Purl all sts.
Rnd 2: Knit all sts.
Rep Rnds 1 and 2 for pattern.
Garter Stitch flat: K every row.
(One Garter ridge is comprised of two rows/rnds.)

1x1 Rib (worked flat or in the rnd, over an even number of sts)
All Rows/Rnds: *K1, P1; rep from * to end of row/rnd.

2x2 Rib (worked flat over multiples of 4 sts plus 2)
Row 1 (RS): K2, *P2, K2; rep from * to end.
Row 2 (WS): P2, *K2, P2; rep from * to end.
Rep Rows 1-2 for pattern.

2x2 Rib (in the rnd over multiples of 4 sts)
Rnd 1: *K2, P2; rep from * to end.
Rep Rnd 1 for pattern.

Magic Loop Technique
A technique using one long circular needle to knit in the round around a small circumference. A tutorial can be found at https://tutorials.knitpicks.com/wptutorials/magic-loop.

Knitting in the Round with 2 Circular Needles
A technique using two long circulars to knit around a small circumference. A tutorial can be found at https://tutorials.knitpicks.com/knitting-in-the-round-with-2-circular-needles.

Backward Loop Cast On
A simple all-purpose cast on that can be worked mid-row. Also referred to as the loop cast on, the single cast on, or the e-wrap cast on. A tutorial can be found at https://tutorials.knitpicks.com/loop-cast-on.

Long Tail Cast On
Fast and neat once you get the hang of it. Also referred to as the slingshot cast on. A tutorial can be found at https://tutorials.knitpicks.com/long-tail-cast-on.

Cabled Cast On
A strong and nice looking basic cast on that can be worked mid-project. A tutorial can be found at https://tutorials.knitpicks.com/cabled-cast-on.

3-Needle Bind Off
Used to easily seam two rows of live stitches together. A tutorial can be found at https://tutorials.knitpicks.com/3-needle-bind-off.

Abbreviations

approx	approximately	KFB	knit into front and back of stitch	PSSO	pass slipped stitch over	SSP	slip, slip, purl these 2 stitches together through back loop
BO	bind off						
BOR	beginning of round	K-wise	knit-wise	PU	pick up		
CN	cable needle	LH	left hand	P-wise	purl-wise	SSSK	slip, slip, slip, knit these 3 stitches together (like SSK)
C (1, 2...)	color (1, 2...)	M	marker	rep	repeat		
CC	contrast color	M1	make 1 stitch	Rev St st	reverse stockinette stitch	St st	stockinette stitch (*see above*)
CDD	centered double decrease (*see above*)	M1L	make 1 left-leaning stitch (*see above*)	RH	right hand	st(s)	stitch(es)
		M1R	make 1 right-leaning stitch (*see above*)	rnd(s)	round(s)	TBL	through back loop
CO	cast on			RS	right side	TFL	through front loop
cont	continue	MC	main color	Sk	skip	tog	together
dec(s)	decrease(es)	P	purl	SK2P	slip 1, knit 2 together, pass slipped stitch over	W&T	wrap & turn (for short rows; *see next pg*)
DPN(s)	double pointed needle(s)	P2tog	purl 2 stitches together				
inc(s)	increase(s)	P3tog	purl 3 stitches together	SKP	slip, knit, pass slipped stitch over	WE	work even
K	knit			Sl	slip	WS	wrong side
K2tog	knit 2 stitches together	PM	place marker	SM	slip marker	WYIB	with yarn in back
		PFB	purl into front and back of stitch	SSK	slip, slip, knit these 2 stitches together (*see above*)	WYIF	with yarn in front
K3tog	knit 3 stitches together					YO	yarn over

Felted Join (to splice yarn)

One method for joining a new length of yarn to the end of one that is already being used. A tutorial can be found at https://tutorials.knitpicks.com/felted-join.

Mattress Stitch

A neat, invisible seaming method that utilizes the horizontal bars between the first and second rows of the edge of the fabric. A tutorial can be found at https://tutorials.knitpicks.com/mattress-stitch.

Provisional Cast On (crochet method)

Used to cast on stitches that are also a row of live stitches, so they can be put onto a needle and used later.

Directions: Using a crochet hook, make a slipknot, then hold knitting needle in left hand, hook in right. With yarn in back of needle, work a chain st by pulling yarn over needle and through chain st. Move yarn back to behind needle, and rep for the number of sts required. Chain a few more sts off the needle, then break yarn and pull end through last chain. (CO sts may be incorrectly mounted; if so, work into backs of these sts.) To unravel later (when sts need to be picked up), pull chain end out; chain should unravel, leaving live sts. A video tutorial can be found at https://tutorials.knitpicks.com/crocheted-provisional-cast-on.

Provisional Cast On (crochet chain method)

Same result as the crochet method above, but worked differently, so you may prefer one or the other.

Directions: With a crochet hook, use scrap yarn to make a slipknot and chain the number of sts to be cast on, plus a few extra sts. Insert tip of knitting needle into first bump of crochet chain. Wrap project yarn around needle as if to knit, and pull yarn through crochet chain, forming first st. Rep this process until you have cast on the correct number of sts. To unravel later (when sts need to be picked up), pull chain out, leaving live sts. A photo tutorial can be found at https://tutorials.knitpicks.com/crocheted-provisional-cast-on.

Judy's Magic Cast On

This method creates stitches coming out in opposite directions from a seamless center line, perfect for starting toe-up socks.

Directions: Make a slipknot and place loop around one of the two needles; anchor loop counts as first st. Hold needles tog, with needle that yarn is attached to on top. In other hand, hold yarn so tail goes over index finger and yarn attached to ball goes over thumb. Bring tip of bottom needle over strand of yarn on finger (top strand), around and under yarn and back up, making a loop around needle. Pull loop snug. Bring top needle (with slipknot) over yarn tail on thumb (bottom strand), around and under yarn and back up, making a loop around needle. Pull loop snug. Cont casting on sts until desired number is reached; top yarn strand always wraps around bottom needle, and bottom yarn strand always wraps around top needle. A tutorial can be found at https://tutorials.knitpicks.com/judys-magic-cast-on.

Stretchy Bind Off

Directions: K2, *insert LH needle into front of 2 sts on RH needle and knit them tog—1 st remains on RH needle. K1; rep from * until all sts have been bound off. A tutorial can be found at https://tutorials.knitpicks.com/go-your-own-way-socks-toe-up-part-7-binding-off.

Jeny's Surprisingly Stretchy Bind Off (for 1x1 Rib)

Directions: Reverse YO, K1, pass YO over; *YO, P1, pass YO and previous st over P1; reverse YO, K1, pass YO and previous st over K1; rep from * until 1 st is left, then break working yarn and pull it through final st to complete BO.

Kitchener Stitch (also called Grafting)

Seamlessly join two sets of live stitches together.

Directions: With an equal number of sts on two needles, break yarn leaving a tail approx four times as long as the row of sts, and thread through a blunt yarn needle. Hold needles parallel with WSs facing in and both needles pointing to the right. Perform Step 2 on the first front st, then Step 4 on the first back st, then continue from Step 1, always pulling yarn tightly so the grafted row tension matches the knitted fabric:

Step 1: Pull yarn needle K-wise through front st and drop st from knitting needle.

Step 2: Pull yarn needle P-wise through next front st, leaving st on knitting needle.

Step 3: Pull yarn needle P-wise through first back st and drop st from knitting needle.

Step 4: Pull yarn needle K-wise through next back st, leaving st on knitting needle.

Rep Steps 1-4 until all sts have been grafted together, finishing by working Step 1 through the last remaining front st, then Step 3 through the last remaining back st. A tutorial can be found at https://tutorials.knitpicks.com/kitchener-stitch.

Short Rows

There are several options for how to handle short rows, so you may see different suggestions/intructions in a pattern.

Wrap and Turn (W&T) (one option for Short Rows)

Work until the st to be wrapped. If knitting: Bring yarn to front, Sl next st P-wise, return yarn to back; turn work, and Sl wrapped st onto RH needle. Cont across row. If purling: Bring yarn to back of work, Sl next st P-wise, return yarn to front; turn work and Sl wrapped st onto RH needle. Cont across row.

Picking up Wraps: Work to wrapped st. If knitting: Insert RH needle under wrap, then through wrapped st K-wise; K st and wrap tog. If purling: Sl wrapped st P-wise onto RH needle, use LH needle to lift wrap and place it onto RH needle; Sl wrap and st back onto LH needle, and P tog.

A tutorial can be found at https://tutorials.knitpicks.com/short-rows-wrap-and-turn-or-wt.

German Short Rows (another option for Short Rows)

Work to turning point; turn. WYIF, Sl first st P-wise. Bring yarn over back of right needle, pulling firmly to create a "double stitch" on RH needle. If next st is a K st, leave yarn at back; if next st is a P st, bring yarn to front between needles. When it's time to work into double st, knit both strands tog.

Steeking
(Cutting your knitting!)

Preparing a Hand-Sewn Steek

This technique is useful in those cases where the yarn doesn't readily felt to itself or is at a larger gauge than traditional colorwork. The cut line will be directly in the center of the steek; a line of stitching one stitch to each side of this cut line will help to stabilize the cut edge.

It may help to use a contrasting color of thread; this will not be visible in the finished piece. Once the steek has been cut and the edging knit, a sewn-in piece of grosgrain ribbon can help keep the edges from fraying.

Directions:

Hold work so that the steek is in the center of the piece. Reach in and smooth any yarn ends away from these sts. Lay piece on a flat surface to help with sewing.

With sewing needle and thread, sew a running st between the first and second sts to the right of the center cut line. Be sure to catch the floats between every st; sew right through the yarn. Turn work and backstitch down the same column of sts. To backstitch, run the needle under and out as a normal st, but begin the next st halfway between the beginning and end of the first. This will create little loops of thread in the fabric that can't be pulled out. Be sure to make many tiny sts and pierce the yarn with each st if possible. Do not pull the thread so tight as to pucker the fabric. The more time you take in this step, the stronger the edge will be!

Rep the sewn line one st to the left of the center cut line.

Crocheted Steek

A crocheted steek is useful in cases where there is thick fabric. Using a crochet hook appropriate to the weight of the yarn you are using, follow the steps in the diagram to create a crochet chain up the steek.

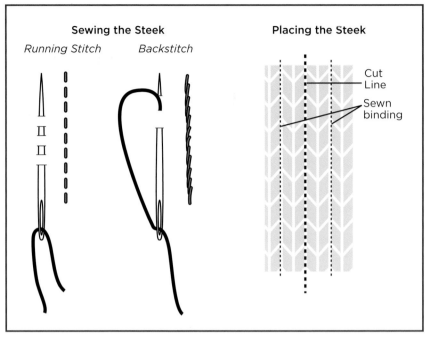

Sewing the Steek

Running Stitch   Backstitch

Placing the Steek

Cut Line

Sewn binding

Crocheted Steek Directions:

Working with the RS facing and yarn held behind work, crochet duplicate sts between two rows of knit sts, 2 sts away from the cut line on both sides of the steek. Work 1 crochet loop for every knit row, pulling work tight. Finish by running final loop over the top of the BO row of knitting.

1. Start by bringing a loop from back of work under CO row to front. Leave a 6″ tail.

2. Insert hook between two sts from front to back, grabbing yarn behind work.

3. Pull a loop through knitted fabric and through loop on hook. Cont in this fashion up the work.

To finish, use a tapestry needle to run ends of crocheted chain through the back of itself; be sure to pierce both the back of the crochet sts as well as the knitted sts, being careful not to let it show on the front side.

THIS COLLECTION FEATURES

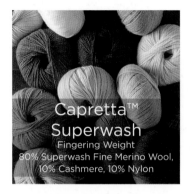

Capretta™
Superwash
Fingering Weight
80% Superwash Fine Merino Wool,
10% Cashmere, 10% Nylon

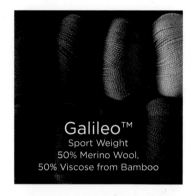

Galileo™
Sport Weight
50% Merino Wool,
50% Viscose from Bamboo

Gloss™ DK
DK Weight
70% Merino Wool, 30% Silk

Palette™
Fingering Weight
100% Peruvian Highland Wool

Swish™ DK
DK Weight
100% Fine Superwash Merino Wool

Wonderfluff™
Bulky Weight
70% Baby Alpaca, 7% Merino
Wool, 23% Nylon

Wool of the
Andes™ Sport
Sport Weight
100% Peruvian Highland Wool

Wool of the
Andes™ Tweed
Worsted Weight
80% Peruvian Highland Wool,
20% Donegal Tweed

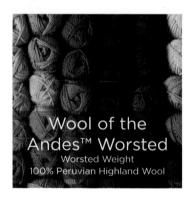

Wool of the
Andes™ Worsted
Worsted Weight
100% Peruvian Highland Wool

KnitPicks®

View these beautiful
yarns and more at
www.KnitPicks.com

Knit Picks yarn is both luxe and affordable—a seeming contradiction
trounced! But it's not just about the pretty colors; we also care
deeply about fiber quality and fair labor practices, leaving you with
a gorgeously reliable product you'll turn to time and time again.

Knit Picks®

From classic pullovers to elaborate colorwork and cables, the *Best of Knit Picks: Pullovers & Cardigans* collection includes ten stunning sweaters that have stood the test of time. These tried-and-true patterns, some updated with new, additional colorways and all featuring refreshed patterns, form a cohesive collection that will inspire you to cast on for years to come. Whether you're new to Knit Picks or a super fan, you'll love having bestselling patterns like Professor Meow, Oakwood Poncho, and Princess Pullover all in one place.

$34.99

ISBN 978-1-62767-240-5

5 3 4 9 9

9 781627 672405

33701

Chapter One

Introduction

LEARNING OBJECTIVES

After studying this chapter, the reader should understand the following concepts and issues:

- Define power and authority. Consider abuse of power and authority within the criminal justice field.
- Consider theories associated with the relationship that exists between criminal justice professionals and those they serve and supervise.
- Define, compare, and contrast the ethics-based theories of deontoloy and utilitarianism.
- Review chapter summaries.

INTRODUCTION

THE CRIMINAL JUSTICE field is made of numerous elements, the central of those being the areas of law enforcement and corrections. Law enforcement agencies operate under the central mission of ensuring obedience to defined societal laws. Corrections agencies function to manage persons convicted of disobedience to said laws. Contemporary civilization depends upon the efficient, effective operation of law enforcement and corrections to achieve and maintain social control. "Social control has come to mean regulation, either in terms of interpersonal relationships with other people; or regulating human behavior in terms of public safety; or enforcing laws and punishing violators of laws" (Chriss, 2013).

To achieve their purpose, law enforcement and corrections professionals are afforded translations of power and authority over the members of society. With this level of influence comes extraordinary responsibility. The relationships that exist between citizens and those tasked with maintaining social control is unique. This relationship is of key importance to the mission of achieving social control within a society and ensuring security and prosperity for citizens. It is incumbent upon the criminal justice professional to maintain a constant awareness of the factors that may influence the critical interaction between themselves and the public and to seek out measures to mitigate negative influences on the relationship between them and the citizens they serve.

The citizens residing within a given community maintain a consciousness of security created by the expectation that law enforcement and corrections professionals are in place to respond to and intercept any threat to their safety or prosperity. This consciousness is merged with a level of deferred authority to criminal justice professionals, or an acceptance of the power and authority that the professionals maintain over the citizen. Likewise, the criminal justice professional maintains a consciousness of professional duty to achieve and maintain social control while simultaneously adhering to the consciousness of service to the citizen.

POWER VS. AUTHORITY

The terms "power" and "authority," commonly used in association with law enforcement and corrections work, are often interpreted as one and the same. The terms actually represent distinct concepts. "Authority is primarily a relational concept. When we speak of a person being an authority, whether we mean that he is an authority on a certain topic, or whether we mean that he is a holder of a certain office or position, we relate him in certain ways to others, to a certain body of knowledge, to certain activities, or to something else of the kind" (Armstrong & Cinnamon, 1976). For example, the position of police chief may maintain authority over the following elements of a police department:

- Oversight of a department's operations and budgeting.
- Oversight of officers, including:
  o Limited disciplinary actions to be addressed on infractions of policy, rules, regulations, laws, or ordinances
  o Full dismissal or heavy sanctioning of officer actions
  o Promotion and rank placement of officers
- Production and development of department policies and regulations.
- Liaison with the governments that oversee and fund the department (City of Willard, 2018).

The authority that the police chief maintains is one of expertise and leadership in relation to the unit overall. The authority that is maintained by the chief translates to the overall successful operation of the agency and to those in its employ and jurisdiction.

Power is a response to the authority that is held or perceived. "Power has been called 'the ability to compel obedience'" (Wolf, 1970). The police chief thus would have the power to enforce obedience to the policy, rules, regulations, laws, or ordinances that are defined under his or her authority. Who else maintains the power to do so, and under whose authority? Although distinctive, power and authority are concepts that are applied simultaneously, particularly within the criminal justice field. Police and corrections officers are tasked with the response to actions that challenge defined authority, and they utilize translations of power to enforce obedience. Let's consider some examples.

BOX 1.1

Within the corrections environment, an incarcerated offender is housed under the institution's operational policies. One of the policies stipulates that an offender must stay within the defined boundaries of the facility's exercise yard at all times during established recreation periods. During those established recreation times, a corrections officer is posted in a tower located above the perimeter fence. The officer is continuously armed with a rifle and is trained to employ force to ensure that the offender stays within the defined boundaries of the exercise yard.

Question: What is the distinction between power and authority in this example?

A police officer stops a speeding motorist who is observed traveling 20 mph over the posted speed limit within the city limits. The officer writes the motorist a citation and communicates a court date. The motorist attends the court date, and the case is heard by the judge. The judge finds the motorist guilty and imposes a fine of $50.

Question: Compare and contrast examples of authority and power in this example.

The power and authority that are afforded those who work within the criminal justice field are unusual, as those persons working within the field are themselves citizens. Thus, they exist under the very authority that they enforce. They also maintain the same expectation of safety, security, and opportunity for prosperity that all citizens maintain. This is an unusual circumstance, and one that requires the advanced consideration of criminal justice professionals.

The work of criminal justice agents often includes distinct morality considerations that are absent in other fields and professions. Sherman (1981) discusses two of them:

> First, criminal justice decisions are made on behalf of society as a whole, a collective moral judgement made in trust by a single person. That would entail a far greater responsibility than what other vocations are assigned. Second, the

decisions criminal justice agents make are not just incidentally, but are primarily, moral decisions. An engineer designs a building that may or may not kill people, but the decision is primarily a physical one and only incidentally a moral one. When a police officer decides to arrest someone … when a judge decides to let that person out on a suspended sentence, the decisions are primarily moral ones (p.14).

THEORETICAL CONSIDERATIONS

Numerous researchers and scholars have considered the relationship that exists between law enforcement professionals and the citizens that they serve. Researchers have also explored the unique factors associated with the criminal justice profession itself—such as cultural dynamics associated with police and corrections work—and defined specific theories. The following sections explore some of the most prominent of these theories.

Theory of Deference Exchange

The theory of deference exchange, posited by Sykes and Clark (1975), focuses on the social positions of both the police officer and the citizen. The researchers contended that the average encounter is impacted by status norms that are interpreted by the two parties. The amount of deference (i.e., the level of humble submission or demonstrated respect) is contingent upon the perceived status of each to the other. Historically, police authority has been generally accepted by citizens, creating a posture of expected deference within society that creates a common assumption that police represent a higher status than citizens. This assumption can be easily explained by the officer's position within society, which is state-conferred power and authority. During police–citizen interactions, an understanding and level of acceptance is ideally adopted among the participants, permitting each to possess an identity that is respected by the other. Sykes and Clark's (1975) theory of deference exchange posed that the difference in the status of one's position influences the quantity and directional flow of deference in police–citizen encounters; thus, perceived context of the position of both the officer and the citizen can have a considerable influence on the rules of deference.

Symbolic Interactionist Theory

Symbolic interactionism theory, formulated by Herbert Blumer (1969), suggests that people are more active in shaping their social world rather than simply responding to it (Herman & Reynolds, 1994). This is particularly applicable to the field of criminal justice, as the unique internal culture present within the police and corrections work setting and the training and professional development of an officer often include powerful behavior influences. The organizational culture and structure can significantly influence officer actions, as the common manner of officer training may "[teach] them to internalize attitudes, values, and beliefs that are used to ensure that appropriate occupational and/or organizational behaviors are adopted" (Fry & Berkes, 1983; Ouchi 1979). The exposure of the officer to the field, merged with the ongoing training and professional development, thus act to internally shape the officer over time.

ETHICS-BASED THEORY

The influence of power and authority on the daily performance of the criminal justice professional can be impactful in both positive and negative ways. The consideration of the impact that negative applications of power and authority can have on the overall mission of the criminal justice agency is essential to maintaining professional ethics. Equally important is the consideration of the impact that positive translations of the concepts can have on meeting the agency mission.

Although criminal justice professionals perform under defined authority, the translation of power is typically situational. When faced with a challenge to defined authority, the officer applies power to elicit obedience. He or she is tasked with the consideration of the most effective and ethical course of action, constantly tempering service and duty with morality. Although often power and authority are translated as the application of force, it does not specifically relate to the application of physical force. The translation of power and authority is far better defined by the manner in which control is achieved. "The decisions of whether to use force, how much to use, and under what conditions are confronted by police officers, juries, judges, prison officials, probation and parole officers, and others. All of them face the paradox … of using harm to prevent harm" (Sherman, 1981). Many times within the criminal justice field, control is applied through nonphysical forms, such as incapacitation, or the simple presence of officers on a scene. Professionals are thus tasked with the consideration of what is most appropriate to gain the control required while using the least amount of control that is necessary. Two principal theories explore the ethical constructs associated with the criminal justice field: deontology and utilitarianism.

Deontology

The deontological ethics approach states that it is the duty of law enforcers to punish those who challenge the well-being of citizens. The word *deontology* comes from the Greek word *deon,* meaning "obligation" or "duty." It is also known as ethical formalism or absolutism (*Making Ethical Decisions Publicly and In Law Enforcement*, 2018). The term "duty" refers to required responsibility. "Deontology (the study of duty) posits that human beings sometimes have duties to perform certain actions, regardless of the consequences" (Braswell, McCarthy, & McCarthy, 2015). Within the field of criminal justice, the consideration of one's duty is constant. Police and corrections professionals' duty to ensure public safety is continuous and often complicated.

Deontology was formulated by Immanuel Kant (1724–1804). Kant believed professionals, such as law enforcement personnel, have duties that are imperative and that those duties must never be abandoned, regardless of the anticipated outcome (McCartney & Parent, 2015). Kant (2006) distinguished two types of duties: hypothetical imperatives and categorical imperatives.

> A hypothetical imperative is a duty that is necessary to accomplish a specific goal. It is something that we do to achieve an end. A categorical imperative is an unconditional rule or duty. Regardless of the impact on you that the decision may cause, the duty remains the same and must be done. In this way, the act is unrelated to the end result; it is a duty regardless of the outcome.

The consideration of what actions and behaviors constitute the duty and responsibility that a criminal justice professional has to members of society can sometimes be confused.

Utilitarianism

The utilitarian ethics approach states that punishing criminals is in the society's overall best interests. In police and corrections work, officers maintain a constant duty to enforce the defined law and maintain a level of obedience and security as defined by that law. To do so, officers may be faced with imposing sanctions or applying levels of power that may challenge their personal principles concerning the distinction between right and wrong or good and bad behavior. The nature of police and corrections work presents the potential for the constant consideration of duty, as it includes continuous response and interaction. The officer's duty is based on personal interaction with people and is thus laden with unique and complex circumstances. It is impossible for the criminal justice professional to maintain a definitive approach to each situation, and he or she is thus challenged to meet each situation with a recognition of the potential challenges to morality and consciousness of duty that is present in the daily work.

> Law enforcement officers possess a great deal of discretion that must be exercised by all officers of every rank, regardless of their experience. When exercising this discretion, officers will be confronted on a daily basis with issues that are complex, and may not be covered in the agency's policy and most certainly would not have been covered in their formal education or police academy or other training (McCartney & Parent, 2015).

For example, a law enforcement officer may deem it his duty to unlawfully arrest a person who he believes to be a sexual predator simply for the purpose of ensuring the protection of the public. However, if an officer fails to adhere to the due process defined by the law, then he has failed in his duty to serve all members of society.

Criminal justice professionals are tasked with the ongoing consideration and application of their duties, with equal attention afforded to rights of citizens and ethical practice.

Consider the following examples:

BOX 1.2

Police officers respond to a reported standoff where they receive reports that a minor, armed with what appears to be a pistol, has barricaded himself within a home. After a period of negotiation, the minor exits the home pointing and firing a pistol in the direction of the officers. The officers return fire. The minor is hit and killed by the shots fired.

Question: What duties or obligations did the officers have in regard to this incident? What possible challenges may exist in regard to the officers' personal principles?

The execution of a death row inmate is scheduled. Policy states that the warden of the facility will be present in the execution area and give the final order to begin the lethal injection.

Question: What duties or obligations did the warden have in regard to this incident? What possible challenges may exist in regard to the warden's personal principles?

The individuality of each situation faced by criminal justice staff requires a level of professionalism that is unique when compared to all other professions. To maintain a professional level of ethics in the application of power and authority, officers must temper duty and morality constantly, and all with a consciousness of service to the community.

ABUSE OF POWER AND AUTHORITY

Each year, police and corrections agencies are faced with instances of abuse of power and authority by employees. Reflective of the situational individuality of the criminal justice work itself, the context of the abuse of power and authority demonstrated by criminal justice staff is extremely unique. To maintain a level of readiness, it is incumbent upon contemporary criminal justice professionals to maintain constant awareness of the challenges to professionalism that are recorded so as to mitigate similar behaviors in their own work life. Police and corrections work is often associated with stereotypical examples of abuse of power and authority, including excessive use of force and racial profiling. Although highly relevant, many additional examples exist. Consider the following examples:

BOX 1.3

An officer enters the home of a person to conduct a search without first obtaining a search warrant. The plain view doctrine states that if the evidence is visible from outside the owner's domain, then the officer can enter without a warrant. The officer later reports observing evidence justifying entry, but no such evidence existed. The judge supports the challenge that was made by the citizen, although similar instances have occurred with this officer in previous incidents.

Question: What examples of abuse of power and authority are presented by this example?

A corrections officer is assigned to the observation and security of the cell house during the night shift. One of the inmates in the cell house has been verbally abusive and disrespectful to the officer over the past few weeks. A different inmate approaches the officer and tells her that he is happy to teach the verbally abusive inmate a lesson if she will let him into that inmate's cell late in the night. During her shift, the officer releases the cell doors of the two inmates. The verbally abusive inmate is physically assaulted by the other inmate.

Question: What examples of abuse of power and authority are presented by this example?

In the chapters that follow, numerous examples of abuse of power and authority within the police and corrections environment will be explored. The examples profile real-world situations in which criminal justice professionals were challenged to maintain a level of professionalism in the translation of power and authority afforded to them by their positions. It is essential to recognize that unethical practice associated with power and authority can be costly to criminal justice professionals, both legally and professionally. Each year, numerous law enforcement and corrections staff are terminated, charged, and even imprisoned for unethical choices and actions within the field. To combat this potential, it is incumbent upon those interested in the field of criminal justice to maintain a high level of consciousness of the authority given them and to review current and potential situations that may challenge professional ethics.

In the chapters that follow, numerous challenges to power and authority within the law enforcement and corrections environment are provided. As you review each profile, consider the factors that may have led to the staff's behavior and different approaches that may have been taken to ensure adherence to professional standards of work. Ask yourself the following questions: What led to the incident? How could it have been different? How can I prevent this from occurring in my own career?

ASSUMING POWER AND AUTHORITY

As individuals progress through their careers within the criminal justice field, they assume numerous assignments and levels of rank within their respective departments. With specific levels of rank come different translations of power and authority, both over those under custody and supervision and over those who are employed within the agency. Ideally, leadership development is introduced to criminal justice staff upon initial hire and then presented to the staff throughout their careers, both through focused training and experience and interaction with peers and supervisors. Consider the following strategies for advancing your own power and authority capability and leadership competency within the criminal justice field:

- Maintain a posture of humility throughout your career. The ability of a professional to continuously learn from those around them requires the conscious acceptance to do so. Be open to the knowledge and experience of others and to the benefits that others can offer your development as a professional.
- Consider the input of others. When assuming a position of power and authority over others, it is often assumed that the persons who are being supervised have a lower level of understanding and intelligence. The operational perspective of those who are under supervision is often greater in many respects, particularly with regard to operational detail.
- Accept the correction and critique of others. Be observant of the impact of high-stress incidents on your own ability to operate effectively. Despite the position of power and authority, criminal justice professionals can continue to be impacted by factors that can lead to incidents such as excessive use of force and coercion. Be accepting of peer efforts to prevent such incidents through correction and critique, and provide the same unbiased assistance to those around you.
- Be observant of situations that may challenge your own professional interpretation and application of power and authority. If you identify areas that may negatively impact your duty to do so, take action to immediately correct or mitigate the situation.
- Be a constant student of the field. Criminal justice is an ever-changing world that requires ongoing consideration of the changes to policy and practice that

may occur throughout the course of your career. In addition to agency-level policy and practice, it is incumbent upon the criminal justice professional to stay informed of state and federal trends, recent research, and current events that may impact you and those under your supervision.

- Seek out opportunities to advance your professional perspective and effectiveness. Agencies often employ numerous practices that present opportunities for ongoing professional development. Examples of practices that provide opportunity for progression of effectiveness in regard to power and authority within the criminal justice field include: completion of agency use of force review; participation on ethics-based agency committees; and participation on operational teams. These examples provide advanced insight into challenges to power and authority that exist within the contemporary field.

TOPICS FOR DISCUSSION

1. How are the power and authority afforded to police and corrections officers different from that afforded to other professions, such as corporate CEO or college dean?
2. Compare and contrast utilitarianism and deontology.
3. Is it impossible for criminal justice professionals to maintain a constant level of professionalism in their jobs, given the nature of their work? Why or why not?

RECOMMENDATIONS FOR READERS

On Combat: The Psychology and Physiology of Deadly Conflict in War and Peace/ Edition 2
  by Dave Grossman, Loren W. Christensen

SOURCES

Armstrong, T. R., & Cinnamon, K. M. (1976). *Power and authority in law enforcement.* Springfield, IL: Charles C. Thomas.

Banks, C. (2013). *Criminal justice ethics.* Thousand Oaks, CA: Sage Publishing.

Blumer, H. (1969). *Symbolic interactionism: Perspective and method.* Englewood Cliffs, NJ: Prentice-Hall.

Braswell, M. C., McCarthy, B. R., & McCarthy, B. J. (2015). *Justice, crime, and ethics.* Waltham, MA: Elsevier.

Chriss, J. (2013). *Social control: An introduction* (2nd ed.). Cambridge, UK: Polity.

City of Willard, Missouri. (n.d.). *Chief of police—duties* [Section 200.010]. Retrieved from https://ecode360.com/28398172

Fry, L. W., & Berkes, L. J. (1983). The paramilitary police model: An organizational misfit. *Human Organization 42*(3): 225–234.

Herman, N., & Reynolds, L. (1994). *Symbolic interaction: An introduction to social psychology.* Dix Hills, NY: General Hall, Inc.

Kant, E. (2006). The categorical imperative. In J. White (Ed.), *Contemporary moral problems* (pp. 14–50). Belmont, CA: Thomson Wadsworth.

Making ethical decisions publicly and in law enforcement. (n.d.). Retrieved from https://opentextbc.ca/ethicsinlawenforcement/chapter/2-3-deontology/

McCartney, S., & Parent, R. (2015). *Ethics in law enforcement.* Victoria, BC: BCcampus. Retrieved from http://opentextbc.ca/ethicsinlawenforcement/

McDermott, J. (1981). *The philosophy of John Dewey.* Chicago, IL: University of Chicago Press.

O'Neill, O. (1986). From *Matters of life and death*, ed. Tom Regan, McGraw-Hill Publishing Company. Excerpted in *Contemporary moral problems*, ed. James E. White. Copyright 1994, West Publishing Company.

Ouchi, W. G. (1979). A conceptual framework for the design of organizational control mechanisms. *Management Science 25,* 833–848.

Sherman, L. W. (1981). *The study of ethics in criminology and criminal justice.* Chicago, IL: Joint Commission on Criminology and Criminal Justice Education and Standards.

Sykes, R., & Clark, J. (1975). A theory of deference exchange in police–citizen encounters. *American Journal of Sociology, 81,* 584–600.

Wolf, R. P. (1970). *In defense of anarchism.* New York: Harper and Row.

CHAPTER TWO

Excessive Use of Force

LEARNING OBJECTIVES

After studying this chapter, the reader should understand the following concepts and issues:

- What is meant by excessive use of force?
- How are agency use of force policies generally designed?
- What are common elements of agency use of force policies?
- Examples of the occurrence of excessive use of force within the corrections and policing professions.

INTRODUCTION

THE USE OF force by law enforcement and corrections staff is a fundamental and necessary practice, as the work generally includes response to and management of the most violent and dangerous situations within our society. Force is utilized for the purpose of enforcing the law, preventing actions that break the law, and gaining control in situations that challenge the safety and security of citizens. The nature of policing and corrections work presents the constant potential for officers to utilize force in the performance of their daily work functions.

The use of force exists as the most significant display of power and authority that is possessed by law enforcement officers and thus requires specific and ongoing consideration (Kinnaird, 2003). When criminal justice staff are introduced to the field, they undergo training on use of force elements including definitions, agency policy, and adopted tactics and weapon systems. Officers are then challenged to apply the training that they have received to the daily circumstances that are faced, utilizing the least amount of force necessary to achieve and maintain compliance from those persons presenting resistance. What is reasonable in one situation may not be in another. The type and amount of force that are appropriate are subject to debate. As new technology is developed (such as electronic stun guns and mobile restraint devices), issues arise as to the applicability to law enforcement and the corrections setting (Hemmens & Atherton, 1999). Although they are not expected to be lawyers, the contemporary law enforcement or corrections officer must be familiar with the legal standard of conduct as they apply to their professional setting if they are to do a good job and avoid acting against the law (Hemmens & Atherton, 1999).

In the following chapter, use of force practice will be discussed, including an overview of contemporary criminal justice policy and practice. We will also consider case studies featuring use of force scenarios that have occurred within the law enforcement and corrections settings, examining elements of staff actions leading to or associated with excessive use of force.

DEFINITIONS

Use of Force – The amount of effort required by law enforcement to gain compliance from an unwilling subject (U.S. Bureau of Justice Statistics, 2018).

Use of Excessive Force – The application of force beyond what is reasonably believed to be necessary to gain compliance from a subject in any given incident (U.S. Bureau of Justice Statistics, 2018).

Non-Deadly or Less-Lethal Force – The level of force required to gain compliance that is not known to or intended to create serious bodily harm or death (U.S. Bureau of Justice Statistics, 2018).

Less-Lethal Weapons – Less-lethal technologies give police an alternative to lethal force. These weapons are especially valuable when lethal force (1) is not necessary, (2) is justified and available for backup, but lesser force may resolve the situation, (3) is justified, but its use could cause serious injury to bystanders or other unacceptable collateral effects. The weapons currently in use include: chemical agents, batons, soft projectiles, and electrical devices such as stun guns and Tasers (U.S. Bureau of Justice Statistics, 2018).

Deadly or Lethal Force – Force that a law enforcement officer uses with the purpose of causing, or that the officer knows to create a substantial risk of causing, death, or serious bodily harm (U.S. Bureau of Justice Statistics, 2018).

POLICY AND PRACTICE

Use of force policy exists as a fundamental tool for law enforcement agencies. The policy is designed to provide guidance to personnel in assessment of force situations, guidance in decision-making, and directives on appropriate application of force (Terrill & Paoline, 2013b). The manner in which an agency defines their use of force policy is of critical importance to the officer's ultimate consideration of power and authority. Officers are directed to perform according to the defined policy, applying their individual perspective of the situation presented to the guidelines of the policy to which they have been trained.

Within law enforcement agencies, policies are outlined that provide direction to staff members on the authority and practice of utilizing force. Policy of this type generally includes a description of the levels of force recognized and authorized within the organization as well as the appropriate application of force to presented types of resistance (National Institute of Justice, 2009).

An example of a use of force continuum follows:

- **Officer Presence — No force is used.** The mere presence of a law enforcement officer is considered a level of force in most use of force policies, and it is often quite effective. Officer presence can work to deter crime or diffuse a situation. During this level of force, one or more officers are simply present at the situation, and officer actions are professional and nonthreatening.
- **Verbalization — Force is not physical.** Use of verbal direction is also considered a level of force, although no physical action is applied.
- **Empty-Hand Control — Officers use bodily force to gain control of a situation.** When empty-hand control is applied, the officer's hands are "empty," or free from any sort of device that might assist in applying force to gain compliance. At this level, the officer utilizes their hands to apply strength or pressure techniques. Policy typically reflects a separation of this level into two distinct categories: soft and hard empty-hand control.
  - o *Soft technique.* When soft empty-hand control techniques are applied, the officer is applying direct pressure to the body. Examples of these techniques include joint lock maneuvers or application of touch pressure to pressure points.
  - o *Hard technique.* When hard empty-hand control techniques are applied, the officer utilizes velocity to apply impact strikes to the body. Examples of these techniques include punching and kicking maneuvers.
- **Less-Lethal Methods — Officers use less-lethal technologies to gain control of a situation.** This term is used to describe weapons that are not fundamentally designed to kill or cause serious bodily injury. However, the munitions deployed from these nonlethal weapons may, in extremely rare cases, injure a person to a degree that may result in death under unique circumstances (Young, 2004). Under normal operating conditions, the less-lethal methods are unlikely to cause a significant injury to the human body. Common outcomes to their use include temporary incapacitation, temporary failure of large muscle mass, and temporary impairment of vision. Based upon a calculated risk factor, the chances of injury meeting the deadly force definition are only

marginal (Young, 2004). Less-lethal methods are extremely common in contemporary law enforcement and corrections environments, and less-lethal weapons are generally carried by uniformed officers on a daily basis. They are designed to allow officers to gain a temporary advantage over resistant subjects, allowing the officer to safely apply restraints, move or transport resistant subjects, or stop assaultive behaviors. Examples of less-lethal methods include:

- o *Blunt impact.* Officers may use a baton (e.g., ASP baton, P-24 baton) or projectile to immobilize a combative person.
- o *Chemical.* Officers may use chemical sprays or projectiles embedded with chemicals (e.g., pepper spray) to restrain an individual.
- o *Conducted Energy Devices (CEDs).* Officers may use CEDs (e.g., Tasers) to immobilize an individual. CEDs discharge a high-voltage, low-amperage jolt of electricity from a distance (Jost, 2002).

- **Lethal Force — Officers use lethal weapons to gain control of a situation.** During this level of force, officers use deadly weapons such as firearms to stop an individual's actions (Jost, 2002).

FIGURE 2.1 Taser

Most contemporary agencies utilize a use of force policy model. The force continuum model acts as the translation of the agency use of force policy to the field application. Specifically, the force continuum is a matrix of the force options available to officers within the agency, progressing from the least amount of force to higher forms. The force continuum is generally communicated to staff through a graphic display of types of force on a sliding scale (Hemmens & Atherton, 1999). The earliest force continuum model was developed in 1984 by Special Agent John Desmedt, who served in the U.S Secret Service Training Division (Stetser, 2001). Since that time, the force continuum model has evolved from linear to nonlinear design.

A linear design of the force continuum resembles a ladder, with the force options flowing in a very specific sequential manner. The linear design presents specific levels of resistance aligned with specific levels

FIGURE 2.2 Pepper Spray

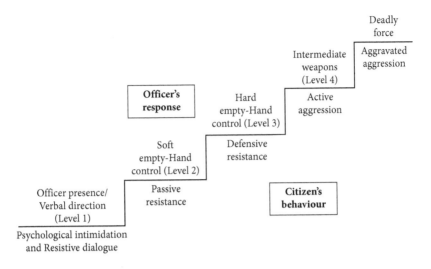

FIGURE 2.3 Linear Use of Force Continuum

of officer control. The model presents the force options available to the officer and associates resistance that may be faced in a situation. Officers are thus directed to identify the resistance that they are presented with and respond with the appropriate level of force. Due to its common presentation as a "ladder," the linear design has been criticized for suggesting that officers must work through the sequential steps of the force continuum before utilization of the appropriate response (Aveni, 2003). The design has also been criticized for its suggestion that a specific type of resistance can only be managed by a specific level of force (Jetelina, Gonzalez, & Bishopp, 2017).

The nonlinear design of the force continuum provides no designation of level of resistance aligned with specific force response. Rather, the nonlinear force continuum presents all of the force options authorized by an agency and all of the potential general levels of resistance that may be encountered. The nonlinear design was developed to enhance decision-making by providing a framework for analyzing the impacting factors involved in situations that required a response. Thus, the officer bases their selection of force based on their individual perspective of the resistance displayed rather than applying a specific, directed level of force. The assumption of the design is that if the responding officer can better assess a situation, they are more likely to select the most reasonable option (Burgess, 2012). The perceived advantage of the nonlinear force continuum is that it allows the officer to consider the totality of the circumstances (Aveni, 2003). The nonlinear design also recognizes the potential for the situation to change. Situations that involve force can often escalate and de-escalate, depending upon numerous factors. Use of force policies that apply the nonlinear design allow for officer discretion in consideration of the situation as it unfolds.

(Guenther, 2016)

In a 2013 examination of utilization of force continuum design, 518 agencies surveyed communicated their use of the force continuum model; 516 of these communicated their use of the linear design (Terrill & Paoline, 2013a). Contemporary researchers have proposed the elimination of the force continuum model altogether and using only the constitutional legal force standards and applicable state law standards—or more specifically, the language of the *Graham v. Connor* (1989) standard (Peters & Brave, 2006). The *Graham v. Connor* (1989) standard communicates that "an officer's use of force on a free person shall be objectively reasonable based upon the totality of circumstances known or perceived by him or her at the time forced was used" (*Graham v. Connor*, 1989).

FIGURE 2.4 Nonlinear Use of Force Continuum

The manner in which the policy is presented to the criminal justice professional through training is critical to their ability to effectively process and apply said policy to daily operations. Officers are typically presented with policy and accepted agency procedures during academy training completed following their initial hiring. An in-depth overview of policy and practice is provided at the time of hire, followed by annual refresher courses throughout the term of employment. This level of training often includes training in specific force options that may be utilized, including certifications on less-lethal methods and firearm qualification. Officers may be required to recertify on less-lethal methods and firearms on an annual or biannual basis throughout their careers to ensure efficiency in their utilization of the methods.

FIGURE 2.5 Pepper Spray Demonstration

Changes in policy and accepted practice may also be presented to staff as needed or as agency changes are adopted into practice. Thus, a higher level of expertise may be observed in an officer employed by an agency for an extended period of time based on the amount of training that has been received. Seasoned staff members may also maintain a significant level of field experience that, merged with ongoing training received, can present a higher expectation of effective and efficient performance in the field. A staff member who is new to the agency may maintain a minimum level of expertise after having received only the initial level of training and minimal field experience.

CASE STUDY 2.1

In 2000, following a conspiracy that unfolded over 30 months (between January 1995 and July 1997), seven federal corrections officers were charged with numerous acts of misconduct during their employment at the U.S. Federal Bureau of Prisons' high-security penitentiary at Florence, Colorado. A 5-year investigation followed, conducted by the FBI and the U.S. Department of Justice's Civil Rights Division. The grand jury indictment listed 55 overt acts of beating, torture, intimidation, deception, and threats. The 9-week trial included more than 60 witnesses (Pendergast, 2004). This prosecution of federal correctional officers was the biggest of its type ever brought by the (U.S. Justice Department's) Civil Rights Division up to that date. The defendants faced prison time of between 4 years and 10 years.

FIGURE 2.6 Jailer

Known collectively as the "Cowboys," the group was accused of being part of a sprawling conspiracy among outlaw corrections officers to systematically assault and abuse prisoners at the high-security penitentiary. The officers were accused of beating approximately 20 inmates. Along with those beatings, reported acts included choking handcuffed inmates, mixing waste into the inmates' food, and threatening other officers who objected to their actions ("Prison Guards Charged in Attacks on Inmates," November 4, 2000).

The investigation and testimony revealed that most of the incidents occurred inside a unit known as the Special Housing Unit, or SHU. The SHU was a unit designated to house the federal system's most disruptive inmates. According to prosecutors, the Cowboys selected prisoners who "needed to be taught a lesson" and proceeded to punch, kick, choke, and otherwise punish them. Prosecutors further noted that they [the Cowboys] also fabricated evidence, including self-inflicted injuries, to make it appear that they were acting in self-defense (Pendergast, 2004).

One of the unit officers testified about details of an incident involving an inmate described as a stalker and compulsive masturbator who was known for writing disgusting letters to female staff. The witness communicated that after one of the inmate's episodes of sexual misbehavior, officers from the unit were directed to "give him the treatment." The inmate was reportedly assaulted while in re-

FIGURE 2.7 Federal Bureau of Prisons high-security U.S. Penitentiary Florence, Colorado

straints, including being picked up, dropped chin-first on the ground, and kicked in the ribs. Following the assault, staff were directed to clean up the bloody area. Testimony further revealed that one of the staff then "slapped her shins repeatedly to raise red spots that would photograph nicely, thus supporting evidence for the official reports, which stated that the offender had kicked the officer" (Pendergast, 2004).

False reporting was commonly referenced throughout the trial; witnesses testified to the common practice of lying on incident report documents and collaborating to ensure consistency in the details that were collectively reported. The investigation revealed observations of staff reports, including identical misspellings of words and use of uncommon words and phrases such as "he began to viciously stab" while "fanatically" screaming (Pendergast, 2004).

The staff assigned to work within the SHU included seasoned veterans and newly trained officers. Testimony portrayed the unit as having a strong internal staff culture. Trial witnesses testified to the common use of unit mottos, including "Lie till you die," "What starts in the SHU stays in the SHU," and "You haven't done anything until you've been suspended one time" (Pendergast, 2004). Misconduct was revealed at numerous levels within the unit, often stemming from pressures to acclimate to the unit culture.

A younger female officer employed at the institution in January 1996 testified that she had discovered one of the defendants in a cell punching an inmate in the torso while the inmate was lying cuffed on the floor (Pendergrast, 2004). In a collective statement, the staff noted:

> The officer (defendant) told her to leave immediately, but instead she entered
> the cell and joined in the assault, testifying that she stepped on the inmate's

head. The woman, who had just started working at the facility, stated in her testimony, "I wanted to be part of the group. I wanted the respect of the other officers, except for the weak and scared ones." Before long, she was kicking prisoners in the groin and squeezing their testicles. She would go on to testify that ultimately her colleagues were congratulating her, she said, and even showed her how not to leave marks (Pendergast, 2004).

Despite the dozens of witnesses, the hundreds of exhibits, and the thousands of pages of documents presented at the Cowboys' trial, the question of motive was scarcely addressed. Motive was irrelevant, prosecutors told the jury; all they had to do was prove that the seven guards conspired to engage in "unnecessary and wanton infliction of pain and suffering under color of law," in violation of the prisoners' constitutional rights (Pendergast, 2004).

After two weeks of jury deliberation in Denver's federal courthouse, three of the officers charged were convicted of violating the civil rights of the inmate by beating him while he was in restraints. The officers were also convicted of engaging in a conspiracy to commit civil rights violations. One of the involved officers died before being sentenced. Two of the involved officers were sentenced to probation in exchange for their testimony, two others were sentenced to 41 months in prison, and one was sentenced to 30 months in prison. Of the 21 crimes charged, the three convicted guards were found guilty of a total of five.

Questions

1. What is meant by the term "under color of law"?
2. In what ways were the officers and staff "provoked" by the offender's behavior displayed?
3. At what points in the scenario were there opportunities for staff to intercede or respond to the observed staff actions?

Topics for Discussion

All staff maintain a responsibility to respond to unethical practices that may be observed or suspected within a corrections environment. Numerous staff are present in a prison unit each day, performing tasks associated with the management of the prison inmates. Consider the different types of staff members who may have had daily contact with the inmates who were involved in this case study.

Discuss the types of daily interactions that occur with the following types of corrections staff:

• Medical/mental health staff

- Legal professionals/attorneys
- Family visitation
- Education/program staff

Inmate behavior within a corrections setting can often include verbal abuse of staff, sexual misconduct, and extreme personal hygiene issues. Staff response to inmate behaviors such as these can be ongoing, requiring extended staff response and observation. Consider the following daily functions that occur within a prison unit. How might they be impacted by extreme inmate behaviors?

- Distribution of inmate medications
- Inmate work crews leaving/returning
- Daily use of inmate showers

Group Exercise

Break into small groups of 5–8 members. Assign each member of the group one of the following positions:

- Cell house officer—new staff
- Cell house officer—experienced staff
- Cell house supervisor
- Unit/facility supervisor
- Unit mental health counselor

Consider the offender behaviors that may be encountered within the prison environment. Discuss the individual perspective that each group member may have in association with the offender behaviors and how they might work together toward the daily operations of the unit. What are the greatest challenges observed? How can these challenges be resolved?

CASE STUDY 2.2

On July 17, 2014, at approximately 3:30 p.m., a man named Eric Garner was approached by a plainclothes police officer in front of a beauty supply store in Tompkinsville, Staten Island, New York. According to bystanders at the scene, Garner had just broken up a fight. Officers reported that Garner was resisting an arrest for illegally selling untaxed cigarettes. Garner, 43, had a history of more than 30 arrests dating back to 1980 on charges including assault and grand larceny. At the time of the incident, Garner was out on bail after being charged with illegally selling cigarettes, driving without a license, marijuana possession, and false impersonation. Garner stood 6-foot-3 and weighed 350 pounds (Meyers, 2014).

The officers on scene engaged in a verbal interaction with Garner, during which time Garner continuously denied his involvement with any wrongdoing. A responding officer approached Garner from behind, attempting to handcuff him. Garner was observed swatting his arms away, saying "Don't touch me, please." A physical altercation ensued, with an officer observed putting Garner in what appeared to be a choke hold from behind—a control maneuver prohibited by NYPD regulations (Scheller & Diehm, 2014). The position of the officer's forearm was of particular interest, as video documentation of the incident seemed to demonstrate the position of the officer's forearm directly over the throat of Garner. Documentation then showed the officer pulling Garner backward in what appeared to be an attempt to bring him to the

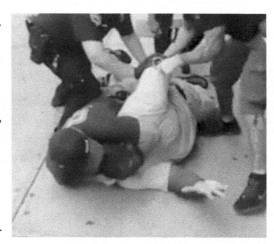

FIGURE 2.8 Garner Use of Force

ground (Steier, 2014). As Garner was being taken to the ground, numerous officers were observed responding to the incident (Goldstein, 2014). Video documentation showed that after approximately 15 seconds, the officers had applied restraints to Garner, and no neck restraint was further observed (Steier, 2014). Garner was documented on the video as saying "I can't breathe" numerous times during the incident (Eversley, 2014).

Garner lay restrained and motionless for several minutes prior to the arrival of the ambulance (Chokshi, 2014). Garner was transported to the local hospital, where he was pronounced dead shortly after the incident (Queally, 2014).

Following the incident, many of the responding staff, including the officer who applied the rear choke hold to Garner and four of the responding EMTs and paramedics who took Garner to the hospital, were suspended for suspected failure to respond to Garner's medical needs during the incident (Margolin, Cliborne, & Crudele, 2014).

Garner's death was ultimately found by the New York City Medical Examiner's Office to be a result of "compression of neck (choke hold), compression of chest and prone positioning during physical restraint by police" (Goldstein & Santora, 2014). Asthma, heart disease, and obesity were cited as contributing factors (Celona & Boniello, 2014). The medical examiner ruled Garner's death a homicide (Calabresi, 2014). The consideration of liability would be considered by a grand jury, which ultimately decided not to indict the officer in the death of Garner (Eversley, 2014).

As a result of Garner's death, an extensive review of the NYPD's training procedures was completed, specifically focusing on the appropriate amount of force that can be used while detaining a suspect. Garner's family filed a wrongful death lawsuit against the city of New York, the police department, and several police officers, seeking $75 million in damages. The parties announced a $5.9 million out-of-court settlement on July 13, 2015 (Goodman, 2015).

Questions

1. What other force options could the officers at the scene have potentially utilized during this situation?

2. How many total officers were present at the scene during the incident, and at what points? Is this impactful to the choices made by officers?

3. Consider areas of the scenario where different force options may have resulted in different outcomes.

4. Was the coroner's ruling of the death as a homicide an accurate ruling? Why?

Topics for Discussion

Law enforcement officers are required to adhere to the defined policies and procedures outlined by their respective agencies in the performance of their work. Consider the following procedures outlined by the agency in this case study as they apply to the following situations:

- Officer is confronted by person armed with a knife

- Officer directs person to exit their vehicle during a traffic stop. Person refuses to do so.

RECOMMENDATIONS FOR READERS

Estelle v. Gamble (1976)

Hudson v. McMillan (1992)

Graham v. Connor (1989)

Whitley v. Albers (1986)

Eric Garner—Citizen recorded video of incident

https://www.youtube.com/watch?v=JpGxagKOkv8

SOURCES

Aveni, T. J. (2003). The force continuum conundrum. *Law & Order, 51*(12), 74–77.

Burgess, M. (2012, September 13). Rethinking use of force. Retrieved from https://www.canadiansecuritymag.com/Guarding/Editorial/Rethinking-use-of-force.html

Calabresi, M. (2014, December 22). Why a medical examiner called Eric Garner's death a Homicide. *Time.*

Celona, L., & Boniello, K. (2014, July 20). Man in chokehold had no throat damage. *The New York Post.*

Chokshi, N. (2014, July 19). New video purports to show aftermath of the chokehold that led to Eric Garner's death. *The Washington Post.*

Eversley, M. (2014, December 3). Lawyer: Cop in chokehold case won't be charged. *USA Today.*

Eversley, M. (2014, December 03). Lawyer: No charges in NYC chokehold death: Federal inquiry launched. *USA Today.*

Goldstein, J. (2014, July 18). Man's death after chokehold raises old issue for the police. *The New York Times.*

Goldstein, J., & Santora, M. (2014, August 01). Staten Island man dies from chokehold during Arrest, autopsy finds. *The New York Times.*

Goodman, J. D. (2015, July 13). Eric Garner case is settled by New York City for $5.9 million. *The New York Times.*

Guenther, T. (2016, August 2). Local police trained in use-of-force guidelines. Retrieved from https://www.pembinavalleyonline.com/local/51525-local-police-trained-in-use-of-force-guidelines

Hemmens, C., & Atherton, E. (1999). *Use of force: Current practice and policy.* Lanham, MD: American Correctional Association.

Jetelina, K., Gonzalez, J., & Bishopp, S. (2017). Gradual escalation of use-of-force reduces police officer injury. *Injury Prevention.*

Jost, K. (2002, April 6). Police misconduct. Retrieved from http://samuelwalker.net/wp-content/uploads/2012/04/CQ-Researcher-Police-Misconduct.pdf

Kinnaird, B. A. (2003). *Use of force: Expert guidance for decisive force response.* Flushing, NY: Looseleaf Law Publications, Inc.

Margolin, J., Cliborne, R., & Crudele, M. (2014). NYPD cop's chokehold may not have caused serious injury to man's throat. *ABC News.*

Meyers, J. (2014, December 04). 11 facts about the Eric Garner case the media won't tell you. Retrieved from ttps://www.newsmax.com/Newsfront/eric-garner.chokehold-grand-jury-police/2014/12/04/id/611058

National Institute of Justice. (2009, August 4). The use of force continuum. Retrieved from https://www.nij.gov/topics/law-enforcement/officer-safety/use-of-force/Pages/continuum.aspx

Pendergast, A. (2004, November 15). Cowboy justice: Bop guards convicted. *Prison Legal News,* 26.

Peters, J., & Brave, M. (2006). Force continuums: are they still needed? *Police and Security News, 22*(1), 1–5.

Prison guards charged in attacks on inmates. (2000, November 4). *New York Times.*

Queally, J. (2014, July 18). Man's death after apparent chokehold by NYPD officer to be probed. *Los Angeles Times.*

Scheller, A., & Diehm, J. (2014, December 05). The chokehold is banned by NYPD, but complaints about its use persist. *The Huffington Post.*

Stetser, M. (2001). *The use of force in police control of violence.* New York: LFB Scholarly Publishing.

Steier, R. (2014, December 08). Ex-NYPD trials chief: Need special prosecutor for cases like Garner. *The Chief.*

Terrill, W., & Paoline, E. A. (2013b). Less lethal force policy and police officer perceptions: A multisite examination. *Criminal Justice and Behavior, 40*(10), 1109–1130. doi: 10.1177/0093854813485074

Terrill, W., & Paoline, E. A. (2013a). Examining less lethal force policy and the force continuum: Results from a national use-of-force study. *Police Quarterly, 16*(1), 38–65. doi: 10.1177/1098611112451262

U.S. Bureau of Justice Statistics. (2018). Terms & definitions: Law enforcement. Retrieved from https://www.bjs.gov/index.cfm?ty=tdtp&tid=7

Young, D. (2004, November 28). Definition and explanation of less lethal. Retrieved from https://www.policeone.com/CERT/articles/94021-Definition-and-explanation-of-less-lethal/

Credits

CHAPTER THREE

Extortion

LEARNING OBJECTIVES

After studying this chapter, the reader should understand the following concepts and issues:

- What is extortion?
- How is extortion different from robbery?
- Consider examples of the occurrence of extortion within the corrections and policing profession.

INTRODUCTION

EXTORTION IS A crime in which one person forces another person to do something against his will (generally to give up money or other property) by threat of violence, property damage, damage to the person's reputation, or extreme financial hardship ("What is Extortion?", 2018).

Extortion is often considered a white-collar crime because it is generally committed in a business setting.

The relationship that exists between criminal justice professionals and those whom they serve and supervise often presents an environment where the opportunity for extortion is present. The power and authority that law enforcement and corrections staff have over persons within society can be misunderstood by both sides, presenting opportunity for manipulation. Extortion within the

FIGURE 3.1 Extortion

criminal justice setting is often represented by the unethical application of control over a person for the purpose of personal gain. Examples of this type of behavior include forcing citizens to provide payment of free services to avoid legal action and manipulating prison inmates for financial gain.

Extortion involves the illegal obtaining of a victim's consent to the crime. Within the criminal justice setting, a person's fear of the power and authority that law enforcement or corrections staff have over them may force consent that would not otherwise be given.

The act of extortion can commonly be confused with robbery. Extortion, however, rarely involves immediate harm. The crimes typically differ in the threat aspects involved. While a robber uses immediate threats and force to steal the victim's property, in extortion the victim willingly hands over his money or personal property in order to avoid future damage or violence ("What is Extortion?", 2018).

It is generally irrelevant whether or not the person actually succeeds in the attempted extortion. Once the threat is made, that person has committed extortion. In some jurisdictions, and under the federal extortion definition, the victim does not even have to hear or receive the threat in order for the offender to be charged with extortion ("What is Extortion?", 2018).

DEFINITIONS

Extortion – Extortion is the crime of obtaining money or property by threat to a victim's property or loved ones, intimidation, or false claim of a right (Free Advice: Legal, 2017).

Robbery – The general elements of robbery are the taking of personal property or money from the person or presence of another, the use of actual or constructive force, the lack of consent on the part of the victim, and the intent to steal on the part of the offender ("Robbery and Extortion," 2018).

POLICY AND PRACTICE

In the criminal justice field, the power and authority that professionals maintain can often be misinterpreted. Members of society may enter into a relationship with law enforcement officers with a preconceived notion based on fear or animosity. Likewise, prison inmates often enter the corrections environment with extreme fear of manipulation or assault, creating an immediate altered posture of concern for staff actions.

The effort to maintain the most productive working relationship possible within the criminal justice setting is largely the responsibility of the criminal justice professional. It is essential that staff recognize the potential for unethical practice that is presented by working situations and maintain a position of integrity.

Many states have specifically recognized the potential for extortion within the criminal justice setting and defined action to the behavior within their law and agency practice. In the California Penal Code, extortion is defined as follows: "Extortion is the obtaining of property from another, with his consent, or the obtaining of an official act of a public officer, induced by wrongful use of force or fear, or under color of official right."

FIGURE 3.2 Extortion 2

There are some instances in policing when the act can be confused or associated with extortion. An example can be gleaned from police ticketing people for jaywalking, speeding, smoking a joint, rolling through a stop sign, breaking curfew, driving without registration, etc. During this process, the officer may hand the victim a piece of paper that states certain terms and compels the recipient to pay a certain amount of money. The ticket may include certain and enforceable threats of more fines or, ultimately, arrest and jail. In this instance, the police are legally allowed to arrest and jail a victim, and they use this threat to extract money. However, this is also an example of an act that is logically indistinguishable from the legal definition of extortion (Sand, 2011).

In daily practice, law enforcement and corrections staff are tasked to apply the highest standards of professionalism possible, adhering to specified agency standards.

CASE STUDY 3.1

In November of 2017, a 16-year veteran police officer pled guilty to charges involving extortion and attempted extortion under color of official right and through the use of threatened force and fear (Department of Justice, U.S. Attorney's Office, District of Massachusetts, 2017). The charge was based on the officer's attempt to use his position as a police officer to extort cocaine from a drug trafficker.

According to prosecutors, the police officer was involved in the purchase of cocaine for approximately one year, during which time he did not identify himself as a police officer (Andersen, 2017). During one of the transactions, the officer displayed his gun and badge, taking the dealer's cocaine and threatening him with arrest if he did not continue to supply the officer with drugs. The drug dealer in the case would ultimately disclose the extortion while acting as an FBI informant while facing drug dealing charges in state court (Andersen, 2017). The drug dealer reported that the officer displayed police identification to him during the transaction, and he communicated his fear that the officer was either "an authentic police officer who would arrest him or a police imposter who intended to rob him" (Harmacinski, 2016). During the incident, the officer reportedly conducted a "pat-down search" of the informant, during which time he took from the dealer a bag of powdered cocaine and two bags of crack cocaine. Following the incident, the officer continued to communicate with the drug trafficker through text messages, telling him, "You will not be arrested at all if you do as I tell you to" (Department of Justice, U.S. Attorney's Office, District of Massachusetts, 2017).

Charges in the incident warranted a sentence of no greater than 20 years in prison, 3 years of supervised release, and a fine of $250,000. (Department of Justice, U.S. Attorney's Office, District of Massachusetts, 2017).

Questions

1. In this case study, what are all of the specific officer behaviors that you recognize as unprofessional?

2. The officer committed much of the extortion behavior while on administrative leave from the agency. Does this impact the level of unethical behavior? Explain your answer.

Topics for Discussion

The work of law enforcement officers can often include the management of situations that are laden with ethical dilemmas. Incidents that include opportunity for extortion often include other challenges to officer professionalism. Consider the following examples:

- Law enforcement officers may respond to situations in which large amounts of money, drugs, or expensive property are involved in criminal activity. During these types of incidents, officers are often tasked to seize, inventory, and process the items as evidence. Officers may have the opportunity to steal items, not including them in the evidence inventory.

- Officers may observe partners or colleagues participating in unethical or illegal activity, such as extortion or theft, and fail to report the incident.

Group Exercise

Break into small groups of 5–8 members. Review Case Study 1. As a group, discuss the following elements and answer the questions that follow.

- You are the officer's partner. Over the last few months, your partner has often communicated to you that he is facing financial bankruptcy due to mounting medical bills. The officer has a young son who is extremely ill.

- You are a rookie officer, focused on maintaining a good record on the job. The officer threatens you that if you report the incident, he will implicate you as well.

1. Does this situation change the way you feel about the officer's behavior?
2. Does this situation change the way you would respond to the officer's behavior?
3. What is the best course of action for you?

CASE STUDY 3.2

In 2017, a former federal prison guard was convicted of extorting money, trucks, security jobs, and sports tickets from wealthy, well-connected inmates in the facility in which he was employed. The officer faced 7 years in prison and $500,000 in fines on three counts of extortion or attempted extortion.

Several inmates at the federal Robert F. Kennedy prison in Morgantown testified that the officer threatened to put them in solitary confinement or strip them of credit for good conduct if they failed to deliver what he wanted. One accused him of assault ("Ex-Guard Convicted of Extortion," 2002).

The accused officer was convicted of extorting money and favors from prisoners in the amount of $90,104. He was sentenced to 41 months in prison ("Guard Properly Convicted, Sentenced for Extorting Prisoners," 2007).

Questions

1. The officer extorted $90,104 dollars from the inmates under his supervision. How do you think the officer was able to receive the funds? What other unethical acts might the officer have done to do so?
2. The officer threatened to place the inmates that he extorted into solitary confinement. What other unethical acts might the officer have done to place the inmates into solitary confinement within the institution?

Topics for Discussion

Despite their incarceration, many prison inmates maintain significant wealth or status within society. Financial wealth is often maintained by the inmate's family. Consider the following points of contact that may be presented to a corrections officer:

- Corrections officer attends church with the wife of an incarcerated inmate who he often observes during inmate visitation.

- Corrections officer distributes mail to inmates, including inmate account statements. The officer observes continuous deposits made to a specific inmate's account by his wife, who writes the inmate letters each week.
- Corrections officer has access to inmate files, including visitation records, inmate phone lists, and inmate qualification for the parole board.

Group Exercise

Break into small groups of 5–8 members. As a group, review the points presented in the *Topics For Discussion* section. Discuss potential practices that may prevent or respond to potential unethical practices that may be presented by each element.

SOURCES

Andersen, T. (2017, August 30). Former Lawrence police officer to plead guilty to extorting drug dealer. *Boston Globe.*

Department of Justice, U.S. Attorney's Office, District of Massachusetts. (2017, August 30). Lawrence police officer agrees to plead guilty to attempted extortion charges. Retrieved from https://www.justice.gov/usao-ma/pr/lawrence-police-officer-agrees-plead-guilty-attempted-extortion-charges

Ex-guard convicted of extortion. (2002, February 13). *Plainview Daily Herald.*

Free Advice: Legal. (2017, December 7). What is Extortion? Retrieved from https://criminal-law.freeadvice.com/criminal-law/violent_crimes/extortion.htm

Guard properly convicted, sentenced for extorting prisoners. (2007, May 15). *Prison Legal News.*

Robbery and extortion. (n.d.). Retrieved from https://www.justanswer.com/law/3usxw-robbery-extortion-often-confused-please-differentiate.html

Sand, G. (2011, October 11). What's the difference between police issuing tickets and the act of extortion? Retrieved from https://www/copblock.org/8972/whats-the-difference-between-police-issuing-tickets-and-the-act-of-extortion/

What is extortion? (n.d.). Retrieved from https://criminal-law.freeadvice.com/criminal-law/violent_crimes/extortion.htm

Credits

CHAPTER 4

Sexual Harassment/Sexual Misconduct

LEARNING OBJECTIVES

After studying this chapter, the reader should understand the following concepts and issues:

- How are sexual harassment and sexual misconduct defined within the criminal justice field?
- Review common practices within the field that can present the opportunity for sexual harassment or sexual misconduct.
- Consider examples of the occurrence of extortion within the corrections and policing profession.

INTRODUCTION

THE CONTINUOUS INTERACTION that exists both among professionals within criminal justice agencies and with the members of society presents the constant potential for ethical dilemmas such as sexual harassment and sexual misconduct. Situations involving this type of unethical behavior have resulted in significant impact to criminal justice agencies. Consider the following statistics:

From January 2010 through September 2010, the National Police Misconduct Statistics and Reporting Project recorded 3,814 unique reports of police misconduct that involved 4,966 sworn law enforcement officers and 5,711 alleged victims. Other statistics noted in the report included:

- 3,814 – Unique reports of police misconduct tracked
- 4,966 – Number of sworn law enforcement officers involved (263 were sheriffs or chiefs)
- 5,711 – Number of alleged victims involved
- 193 – Number of fatalities associated with tracked reports
- $213,840,800 – Estimated amount spent on misconduct-related civil judgments and settlement (*The Cato Institute National Police Misconduct Reporting Project*, 2013).

Within law enforcement and corrections settings, the perception of power and authority that employees maintain for those in their custody or supervision is of key importance in the prevention of this type of unethical practice. Highly relevant to the adherence of professionals to ethical practice in the field is the consideration of the submissive behavior factors that exist between officer and citizen during required interactions and the professional posture that must be maintained during those interactions.

In the following chapter, behaviors leading to sexual harassment and sexual misconduct within the criminal justice setting will be considered, including an overview of contemporary policy. We will also consider case studies featuring scenarios that have occurred within the law enforcement and corrections setting, examining elements of staff actions leading to or associated with sexual harassment and sexual misconduct.

DEFINITIONS

Sexual Harassment – Sexual Harassment: unwelcome sexual advances, requests for sexual favors, and other verbal or physical conduct based on the employee's gender when:

- Submission to such conduct is made either explicitly or implicitly a term or condition of employment.
- Submission to or rejection of such conduct by an employee is used as the basis for employment decisions affecting the employee.
- Such conduct has the purpose or effect of unreasonably interfering with an employee's work performance or creating an intimidating, hostile, or offensive working environment (*Arizona Department of Corrections: Policy 500/0501*).

Sexual Misconduct – The act of sexual misconduct by law enforcement is defined as any action or behavior that includes the misuse of authority and power (including force) by an officer for the purpose of committing a sexual act, initiating sexual contact with another person, or responding to a perceived sexually motivated cue (from a subtle suggestion to an overt action) from another person. It can also include any communication or behavior that could be interpreted as lewd, lascivious, inappropriate, or conduct unbecoming of an officer and violates general principles of acceptable conduct common to law enforcement (*Addressing Sexual Offenses and Misconduct by Law Enforcement: Executive Guide*, 2011).

POLICY AND PRACTICE

Although standard agency policy prohibits the acts of sexual harassment and/or sexual misconduct, officers and staff often work in environments and maintain assignments that are isolated, such as patrol duty or cell house or unit observation. The very nature of the assignment may present situations that can lead to the misuse of designated power and authority or present dynamics that may result in inappropriate actions.

Officers often perform their duties independently, or outside of the direct observation of others. The lack of direct observation by supervisory staff members has historically resulted in the willingness of officers and staff to participate in sexual harassment and misconduct in the work setting.

The fear of arrest or victimization may lead some persons to suggest or submit to sexual activity. For example, a person stopped for speeding may suggest sexual favors in exchange for being excused from any citation. Another example might include a prison work group supervisor threatening to falsely report an inmate for a rule violation if they do not submit to sexual acts while at their work assignment.

Officers and staff also perform numerous duties that present the opportunity for specific challenges to their professionalism, such as pat searches and strip searches. The persons who are under supervision in scenarios such as these are in a posture of submission to the officer. It is incumbent upon the criminal justice professional to maintain awareness of the unique dynamic that is created by submissive behavior presented by persons under custody or supervision or who are engaged in interaction with officers and staff.

Both the authoritative position and the submissive position are held by both males and females within the officer and citizen or inmate interaction. Either gender can

FIGURE 4.1

be involved in the misuse of power and authority leading to victimization and/or unprofessional behavior. Common misconceptions associate sexual harassment within policing with only male staff members and female citizens and sexual misconduct within corrections settings only with female corrections officers and male inmates. These misconceptions are false, with harassment and misconduct behaviors occurring in numerous translations within contemporary criminal justice settings. Most law enforcement and corrections agencies employ a "zero tolerance" position, responding to such behavior with swift action, to include termination and/or criminal or civil charges.

CASE STUDY 4.1

A state prison inmate said she was inside her cell at New Jersey's only women's prison when the officer came to the door during a routine head count, ordering the inmate to touch herself. She said the officer had done this before, asking whether she was "a freak," whether she ever had oral or anal sex, whether he could perform sex acts on her. "No," she said she told him. "Get out of my room." Instead, she claimed, the officer stuck his hand inside her sports bra and, amid a struggle, jammed his arm down her pants, breaking the drawstring. "I didn't know what to do," she said, "whether to say something or scream."

It was December 2008, and she was just starting a 15-year sentence for manslaughter. The senior corrections officer had power over every facet of her life, and she said she feared what he would do with it. So she kept quiet. It would be her word against his.

Over the next 18 months, more than a dozen women at the prison said they, too, had been abused by the officer. A review of the case found:

- At least 16 women claimed they were beaten or sexually abused by the officer between 2008 and 2010. Seven of them formally accused the officer of physical and sexual abuse in two lawsuits filed in state and federal court.
- The Department of Corrections began proceedings to fire the officer in August 2010 for conduct unbecoming of an officer and "undue familiarity," a vague, outdated term that experts say whitewashes serious allegations of sex abuse and keeps the public—and the officers' potential future employers—in the dark.
- Two other officers, including the officer's partner, were fired as a result of the investigation. That partner would swap posts with the officer, giving him unfettered access to inmates in their cells and, according to prison records, warning him when someone else on the staff was headed into their unit.

Continued investigation revealed a rare look inside the women's prison, where inmates say one man turned their unit into a perverted personal playground, hazing, mocking, and sexually abusing them for several years.

The inmates were some of New Jersey's most powerless women and, because of their criminal histories, the least likely to be believed. Many of them were serving time for murder, manslaughter, robbery, and theft. Some had previously been arrested on drug and prostitution charges. Many of the women confided in interviews and depositions that they had been abused in the past by family members, friends, and romantic partners. Most said they were reluctant to report prison abuse, either because they didn't think they'd be believed or feared they would face retaliation for speaking out.

Described by inmates and staff as a large, burly man who could be by turns strict and friendly with prisoners, the officer was assigned to the "cage," an enclosed box roughly the size of a toll booth, from which officers watched the comings and goings through the heavy metal doors of the unit.

The investigation had barely started when letters, written on the forms inmates typically use to file grievances and ask for help, came in defending the officer. Nineteen inmates wrote in June 2010 that the officer was "professional, respectful and that he runs a good unit," according to a report describing the letters' contents. But under questioning by internal investigators, several inmates who defended the officer recanted. At least six who wrote letters on his behalf said they, too, had been targets of his abuse.

Sixteen inmates were identified in the investigatory report as having allegedly suffered some form of sexual or physical abuse. A dozen more said they were not victims themselves but had witnessed the officer wrestle with and grope inmates, throw buckets of ice on them as they showered, slap and spank them with a ruler, and even fart on their beds.

Sex with inmates is a violation of policy for prison staff and is considered sexual assault under New Jersey law, which recognizes that the power imbalance between a corrections officer and an inmate can make it difficult, if not impossible, for the inmate to refuse sexual advances.

The officer, the inmates claimed, liked to play games with the women of North Hall. In internal documents and court records, inmates described the "games" in detail. There was the "ruler game," they said, in which the officer would smack inmates on their hands, heads, or rear ends with a metal ruler. There was the "hot and cold game," in which they claimed he would take commissary items and food from inmates and make them guess where he had hidden them. Often, inmates told investigators, he would make them do pushups to get their food back.

Then there was the "ice game," they said, in which the officer would grab a bucket of ice cubes from a freezer, sneak outside the shower stall, and dump it onto an unsuspecting inmate inside.

The officer would ultimately be terminated from his position based on the allegations.

A deputy attorney general argued in federal court that the administrators conducted a sweeping investigation and ousted three officers accused of wrongdoing. He said prison officials took swift action despite the fact that inmates had never used the formal complaint system to raise the alarm, and he said the inmates had actually hindered the internal investigation by writing letters defending the officer.

Questions

1. Consider standard officer duties such as inmate strip search, inmate pat search, and cell property search. These duties involve personal contact with inmates and also with inmates' personal property. What are ways in which these practices may be misinterpreted as sexual harassment? What are ways that officers can prevent the misinterpretation of duties like these?

Topics for Discussion

Some of the women involved in the incidents submitted statements that supported the innocence of the officer charged. When they recanted their statement, the inmates communicated fear of future victimization as the reason for their actions. Consider the mental control that was maintained over the inmates by the staff member. The staff member directed the actions of the inmates without making direct contact, based on the threat potential that the victimization would occur if the inmates did not support the innocence of the officer.

Consider the mental control that is projected to inmates by corrections staff. Is it a constant factor within a corrections environment? At what point does this control become unprofessional?

Group Exercise 1

Break into small groups of 5–8 members. As a group, discuss and answer the following questions.

- Numerous inmates communicated victimization in this case study. How many inmate complaints of this nature do you believe must be received before administrative action should be taken?

- Multiple staff members participated in the misconduct detailed in the case study, some even "standing guard" for other staff while they engaged in abusive acts. Discuss what measures you would take if you observed this type of abuse of authority within your work environment.

- Discuss agency measures that may be implemented to discourage and/or intercept this type of unprofessional behavior.

Group Exercise 2

Break into small groups of 5–8 members. Review the scenario noted below. As a group, discuss and answer the questions that follow.

Officer Jones has been employed with the police department for 17 years and has a stellar performance record. The agency recently received a formal complaint from a female citizen stating that during a traffic stop, Officer Jones performed a pat search of the female citizen, which she reported as harassing. The female citizen reported that the officer touched her inappropriately during the search. In completion of the search, the officer confiscated a small bag of marijuana and took the appropriate legal action in response to the discovery.

1. What are your initial concerns about this incident?

2. What steps should be taken to confirm the details of the incident? Is it possible to confirm all incident details?

3. What is your suggested response to the formal complaint?

4. As a group, discuss agency measures that may be implemented to discourage and/or intercept potentially unprofessional behavior.

RECOMMENDATIONS FOR READERS

Lopez, K. M., Forde, D. R., & Mitchell Miller, J. (2017). Media coverage of police sexual misconduct in seven cities: A research note. *American Journal of Criminal Justice, 42*(4), 833–844.

Robbins-Johnson, H. (2014). *Predicting staff sexual misconduct in female housing units: Individual versus social climate factors.* (Master's thesis). Retrieved from https://encompass.eku.edu/cgi/viewcontent.cgi?article=1310&context=etd

SOURCES

Arizona Department of Corrections: Policy 500/0501. (n.d.). Retrieved from https://corrections.az.gov/Policies/500/0501.pdf

Cavallier, A. (2016). Former Oklahoma City cop Daniel the officer sentenced to 263 years on rape charges. *CNN.*

De Leon, C. (2015). The trial of Daniel Holtzclaw, the cop charged with sexually assaulting 13 black women. *Glamour.* Retrieved from https://www.glamour.com/story/daniel-holtzclaw-trial

Larimer, S. (2015). Ex-Oklahoma City cop Daniel Holtzclaw found guilty of multiple on-duty rapes. *Washington Post.* Retrieved from https://www.washingtonpost.com/news/morning-mix/wp/2015/12/08/ex-cop-on-trial-for-rape-used-power-to-prey-on-women-prosecutor-says/?utm_term=.9657aa465223

The Cato Institute. *The Cato Institute National Police Misconduct Reporting Project.* (2013). 2010 Annual Report.

Santos, P. (2015). Woman testifies after showing up high to Daniel the officer trial high.

Silverstein, J. (2015). Jury convicts ex-Oklahoma cop Daniel the officer of rape, sodomy charges; faces life in prison. *New York Daily News.* Retrieved from.

Sullivan, S. (2015). Locked up and fighting back. Retrieved from http://www.nj.com/news/index.ssf/page/locked_up.html

Testa, J. (2015). How police caught the cop who allegedly sexually abused black women. *BuzzFeed.* Retrieved from.

IACP (2011). *Addressing Sexual Offenses and Misconduct by Law Enforcement: Executive Guide, June 2011.* Retrieved from http://www.theiacp.org/Portals/0/Addressing_Sexual_Offenses_and_Misconduct_by_LE.pdf

Credit

CHAPTER FIVE

Aiding in Escape

LEARNING OBJECTIVES

After studying this chapter, the reader should understand the following concepts and issues:

- What is the definition of aiding in escape?
- What are common behaviors that lead to aiding in escape within the criminal justice field?
- Consider an example of the occurrence of aiding in escape within the criminal justice profession.

INTRODUCTION

MAINTAINING SUPERVISION OR custody over an individual presents a unique translation of power and authority. Responding to the primary mission of criminal justice agencies—to safeguard public safety—requires that criminal justice professionals maintain accountability of those persons charged and/or convicted of criminal actions. The responsibility of staff to ensure security and accountability of individuals introduces behavior dynamics that are distinct from other interactions that may occur between officers and those in their custody.

In the following chapter, the interaction that commonly occurs between the "keeper and the kept" will be examined to identify areas of potential staff manipulation that occurs within the criminal justice setting. This chapter will also present a consideration of common misconceptions of the professional application of power and authority that occurs during aiding in escape situations. We will also examine a specific case study featuring a scenario involving staff aiding in escape from a U.S. prison environment to consider incident factors.

FIGURE 5.1

DEFINITIONS

Aiding in Escape – Any act that is committed by a jailer or another person that allows a criminal to escape. It is a criminal offense. Assisting escape is a federal crime. Helping a prisoner escape custody is an offense under the federal law. Pursuant to Section 752 under Title 18 of the United States Code, whoever rescues or attempts to rescue or instigates, aids, or assists the escape, or attempt to escape, of any person arrested upon a warrant or other process issued under any law of the United States shall be fined or imprisoned not more than five years, or both, provided that the custody or confinement is an arrest on a charge of felony or conviction of any offense (U.S. Legal.com).

POLICY AND PRACTICE

The specific roles that criminal justice professionals assume when maintaining custody and supervision of inmates is unique. When in this translation of duty, staff assume a posture of ongoing control and accountability for the actions and behaviors presented by the inmate. This distinctive element of the profession involves ongoing awareness of the position and identifiers of those persons directly involved in the officer–inmate relationship. For example, the officer tasked with security and observation performs all of their daily tasks with a consciousness of the potential for challenges to security, such as an inmate's attempt to smuggle unathorized items from a visiting room to an assigned cell. Likewise, the inmate maintains a consciousness that the officer is in a posture of contant investigation and questioning of their actions. The officer maintains an individual perception of power and authority over the actions of the inmate and the security of the environment. The inmate maintiains an invidual perception of submission to the officer's power and authority. When a shift in the indivual perceptions held by the officer and inmate occurs, then a threat to security exists. Often in situations that threaten security, a transition of authority occurs between the officer and inmate, which results in the inmate assuming power and authority over the actions and the security of the environment.

Criminal justice agencies generally outline staff directives associated with employee professionalism, ethics, and conduct procedures within department policy. Staff members are commonly trained in the policy-based agency standards during initial hire and on an annual basis.

FIGURE 5.2

CASE STUDY 5.1

In June of 2015, prison employee Joyce Mitchell assisted two convicted murderers in escaping an upstate New York prison. Joyce Mitchell pled guilty to promoting prison contraband and criminal facilitation. She was sentenced to 2 to 7 years in prison, fined $6,375, and ordered to pay $79,841 in restitution. A tailor at the correctional facility, Mitchell provided inmates with tools they used to cut through cell walls for their escape from the prison.

Following the discovery of the escaped inmates, a manhunt began that ended with law enforcement officers fatally shooting one and recapturing the other. Mitchell had brought a screwdriver and two hacksaw blades into the corrections facility where the inmates were held, smuggling the items into the prison in her personal bag. In collected statements, Mitchell disclosed, "After a couple of days, he told me he and inmate Sweat had cut the holes and were going down in the pipes. I was already bringing stuff in to him and didn't really feel I could stop. I had known about them cutting the hole in the wall for about three or four weeks. The day they were supposed to escape, I was supposed to give my husband, Lyle, two pills. These pills were intended to knock Lyle out so I could leave the house" (Sanchez, Hanna, & Martinez, 2015).

Mitchell communicated that she was unable to follow through with her plan to meet up with the two escapees. "I was to drive my Jeep and bring my cell phone, GPS, clothes, a gun, tents, sleeping bags, hatchet, fishing poles, and money from a package I never picked up. After I picked them up, the plan was to drive to my home and inmate Matt was going to kill my husband. After inmate Matt killed my husband, we were going to drive somewhere. I know I had agreed to help them escape and run away with them, but I panicked and couldn't follow through with the rest of the plan" (Sanchez, Hanna, & Martinez, 2015).

The escape would ultimately result in a $23-million-dollar expense to New York state, primarily in overtime costs associated with the manhunt. During the sentencing of Mitchell, the judge in the case noted that the economic and noneconomic costs were "incalculable" for people affected by the escape and ensuing pursuit (Botelho, 2015).

The judge noted:

> A large portion of the local population were terrorized. Many were forced to flee their homes. Some did not have places to go and had to rent hotel rooms or leave the area. Many residents did not sleep for many nights, afraid that these two extremely violent individuals might be outside their homes. Law enforcement officers came here not just from across New York state but from all over the country. They traversed very inhospitable territory, never knowing if the next step they took in deeply wooded areas might be

their last. And think of their families at home, sick with concern and fright for their loved ones. At any time, you could have stopped the escape from happening (Botelho, 2015).

The following interview was conducted after Mitchell's incarceration.

Interviewer: Did you think that perhaps you were crossing some sort of a line?
Mitchell: I was at first but then I guess I got a little too comfortable.

Interviewer: Did anybody ever stop you and say, "You know Joyce, back off a little bit. Get back behind the desk. Treat them like inmates. Stop being such a nice person. Stop being friends with him."
Mitchell: They never actually told me to stop, but they did say, "You know you're too friendly. You know you're too nice."

Interviewer: When they would say that to you, would you stop?
Mitchell: I would a little bit, but at the time that everything happened I was going through a time where I didn't feel like my husband loved me anymore, and I guess it was just me. I was going through depression, and I guess they saw my weakness and that's how it all started.

Interviewer: So you were looking for something? You were looking for attention?
Mitchell: Yes. Their attention made me feel good.

Interviewer: Both Sweat and Matt were violent offenders. Richard Matt was in prison because he killed a man who was his boss.
Mitchell: Yes.

Interviewer: And then cut his body up?
Mitchell: Yes. And he had no problem telling anybody about that. He actually had a photocopy of the article still showing when he went to court, and he would show it to anybody. In some ways as some sort of street cred(ibility). As to say, "This is what I did and I'm I'm proud of it. A new officer that came in … he'd show him what he was in for."

Interviewer: David Sweat's a guy who shot a sheriff's deputy 15 times. So these are two guys who committed heinous crimes, and these are the guys you allowed yourself to have a friendship with?
Mitchell: Yes. Everybody tells me I'm way too nice.
Interviewer: When did they start asking you for favors?

Mitchell: A few months before they decided to get out they were asking me for things.

Interviewer: What did you bring them?
Mitchell: I would bring cookies and brownies.

Interviewer: Pretending that you were bringing them in for yourself?
Mitchell: Yes.

Interviewer: How often did you do that?
Mitchell: I did it a lot.

Interviewer: Were you ever nervous? Were you afraid you'd get caught doing it?
Mitchell: I actually was, because they're supposed to check our bags every morning when we came in and they're supposed to check them when you go out but they never did. And then they started asking for other things.

Interviewer: Then Richard Matt comes to you and says, "Joyce, I need a star-shaped drill bit." That's a lot different than cookies and brownies.
Mitchell: Yes.

Interviewer: And what did you think?
Mitchell: At first I was like "I can't get you that" but then he said he needed it. At first they didn't tell me, and then after they did it was because they were going to try to escape.

Interviewer: Had you already given it to them at that stage?
Mitchell: Yes, but I gave them the stuff because they had threatened me. It was Matt. He looked at me one day and said, "You know Joyce, I do love you." I said I loved my husband. A little while after that he wanted to get rid of him, meaning kill my husband ("Joyce Mitchell: 'I deserve to be punished' for helping inmates escape," 2015).

Questions

1. In the case study, the officer communicated the ease with which she was able to introduce items into the secure environment of the prison facility during her daily arrival at the institution. This represents a shift from perceived power to maintain security of the prison to perceived power to manipulate the security of the prison. What other shifts in perceived authority can you identify from this case study?

2. At what points did the officer threaten the security of the prison? What strategies might have been instituted to prevent or intercept these threats to the prison security?

Topics for Discussion

When an employee transitions their individual perception from one of power and authority to one of submission to the persons under their custody and supervision, incidents such as aiding in escape become potential threats. Discuss personal strategies that may be instituted to combat the potential for this type of shift in individual perception within the work environment.

RECOMMENDATIONS FOR READERS

"Toward a New Professionalism in Policing."
https://www.ncjrs.gov/pdffiles1/nij/232359.pdf
"Professional Ethics and Corrections, a Professional Responsibility."
http://www.corrections.com/news/article/40952-professional-ethics-and-corrections-a-professional-responsibility

SOURCES

Botelho, G. (2015, November 6). Joyce Mitchell to pay more than $80,000 for her role in murderers' escape. Retrieved from https://www.cnn.com/2015/11/06/us/ny-prison-break-restitution/index.html

Joyce Mitchell: 'I deserve to be punished' for helping inmates escape. (2015, September 14). Retrieved from https://www.today.com/video/joyce-mitchell-i-deserve-to-be-punished-for-helping-inmates-escape-524913219969?v=railb

Sager, I. (2015). Joyce Mitchell tells Matt Lauer in her first-ever interview: 'I just got in over my head'. *The Today Show*. Retrieved from https://www.today.com/news/joyce-mitchell-tells-matt-lauer-her-first-ever-interview-i-t43481

Sanchez, R., Hanna, J., & Martinez, M. (2015, July 29). Joyce Mitchell pleads guilty to helping New York inmates escape. Retrieved from https://www.cnn.com/2015/07/28/us/new-york-prison-break-mitchell/

U.S. Legal.Com. Assisting escape law and legal definition. https://definitions.uslegal.com/a/assisting-escape/

Winter, T., & Connor, T. (2017). Joyce Mitchell, who helped New York inmates escape, denied parole. *NBC News*. Retrieved from https://www.nbcnews.com/storyline/new-york-prison-escape/joyce-mitchell-who-helped-new-york-inmates-escape-denied-parole-n720416

Credits

CHAPTER SIX

Coercion

LEARNING OBJECTIVES

After studying this chapter, the reader should understand the following concepts and issues:

- What is coercion?
- How does coercion compare to interrogation?
- Understand challenges to the consideration of power and authority during unique situations within the field of criminal justice.
- Consider examples of the occurrence of extortion within the corrections and policing profession.

INTRODUCTION

THE POWER AND authority that accompany those employed within the criminal justice field can often be misunderstood, even by those who maintain that authority. This misunderstanding is often associated with law enforcement and corrections staff efforts to maintain public safety through protection. The translation of that protection can sometimes be misinterpreted to mean actions that extend beyond agency policy. An example of this is the use of coercion during police interrogation.

The ability of criminal justice professionals to maintain professional conduct, despite any personal opinions held, is of critical importance to retaining functionality and effectiveness in the field.

DEFINITIONS

Interrogation – Questioning of a suspect or witness by law enforcement authorities. Once a person being questioned is arrested (is a "prime" suspect) he/she is entitled to be informed of his/her legal rights, and in no case may the interrogation violate rules of due process ("Glossary of Some Commonly Used Legal Terms," n.d.).

Police Coercion – Police coercion takes place when officers of the law exert undue pressure to get an individual suspect to admit their involvement in a crime ("Glossary of Some Commonly Used Legal Terms," n.d.).

False Confession – False confessions occur when individuals come forward to law enforcement officers or, during an interrogation, admit their guilt to a crime they were not involved in ("Glossary of Some Commonly Used Legal Terms," n.d.).

POLICY AND PRACTICE

The use of physical or psychological coercion during police interrogation is a forbidden practice in policing and can result in the collection of evidence that is ultimately inadmissible at trial (FindLaw). However, the impact of a confession can often be interpreted by criminal justice professionals as the ultimate application of public safety. An officer may interpret efforts to obtain a confession, using any means necessary, as a service to the community based on their own perception of the guilt of the person being interrogated. Although the officer may feel that their efforts are applied out of service to society, their actions do not represent agency policy. These actions also threaten due process and justice, presenting the potential for the inadmissibility of any evidence obtained in such a manner.

FIGURE 6.1

Coercion has also been observed within corrections environments during staff interviews with inmates. Staff questioning of inmates may occur for various purposes, including investigation into inmate gang affiliation, possession of contraband items, or even inmate participation or knowledge of criminal activity within the prison facility. As with police interrogation scenarios, corrections officers operate under a constant mission to ensure public safety through maintained security of the corrections institution. Officers thus may interpret coercive actions as appropriate in ensuring that mission is upheld.

Common coercive practices that occur within criminal justice agncies include role playing, fabricated evidence, exaggeration of the nature of the offense, misrepresenting identity, and the use of promises. Consider the following examples of each:

Role Playing – Two officers are completing an interrogation of a suspect. One officer speaks to the suspect in a hostile and threatening manner. The other officer privately communicates to the suspect that he understands how unreasonable the other officer is being and that he is on the suspect's side, encouraging the suspect to confide in him, and that he will protect him.

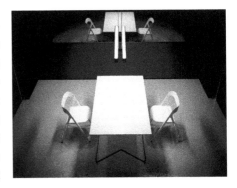

FIGURE 6.2

Fabricated Evidence – Prison officials question an inmate who shares a cell with another inmate. The inmate being questioned is told that a knife has been found in his assigned cell and that if he provides wanted gang intelligence, then the other inmate assigned to the cell will be held responsible for the knife.

Exaggeration of the Nature of the Offense – A suspect being investigated for theft is told that the inhabitants of the house were assualted and that, if found guilty, the suspect would receive a far greater sentence than for that of theft.

Use of Promises – An inmate being questioned for possible association with the Gangster Disciples is told that if he discloses his association and names of other inmates associated with the gang, he will be provided protection for the rest of his life.

The courts have historically relied on three constitutional provisions to insure that confessions are the product of fair procedures.

Fourteenth Amendment Due Process Clause

As we have seen, there is a danger that the pressures of the interrogation process may lead to false confessions. The poor, uneducated, and mentally challenged are particularly vulnerable to trickery and manipulation. Former Supreme Court Justice Arthur Goldberg observed that history teaches that "a system of criminal law enforcement which comes to depend on the 'confession' will, in the long run, be less reliable and more subject to abuses than a system which depends on extrinsic evidence independently secured through skillful investigation" (Escobedo v. Illinois, 378 U.S. 478, 488–489 [1964]).

In the 1930s, the Supreme Court began to rely on the Fourteenth Amendment's Due Process Clause to insure that confessions obtained by state law enforcement officials were voluntary and were not the product of psychological or physical abuse.

The Due Process Clause provides that "[n]o state shall ... deprive any person of life, liberty, or property without due process of law" and continues to be employed by courts to insure that confessions are voluntary. An involuntary confession violates an individual's liberty to make a voluntary choice whether to confess and ultimately may lead to imprisonment and a loss of liberty.

Fifth Amendment Self-Incrimination Clause

Herbert Packer notes that in the American accusatorial system of criminal procedure, the burden is on the prosecution to establish guilt beyond a reasonable doubt at trial, and the defendant may not be compelled to testify against himself or herself. This is distinguished from an inquisitorial system of criminal procedure in which the defendant does not enjoy the privilege against self-incrimination and must answer questions posed by the judge, who typically interrogates witnesses. The drafters of the U.S. Constitution were familiar with the English Star Chamber, a special court established by the English king in the 15th century that was charged with prosecuting and punishing political and religious dissidents. This inquisitorial tribunal employed torture and abuse to extract confessions and was authorized to hand out any punishment short of death. The reign of terror was effectively ended by Puritan John Lillburne, who, in 1637, defied the chamber's order that he confess to spreading dissident religious views. Lillburne was fined, pilloried, whipped, and imprisoned in leg irons in solitary confinement. Parliament ordered his release in 1640, and the House of Lords subsequently vacated Lillburne's sentence, noting that it was "illegal ... unjust ... [and] against the liberty of the subject and law of the land" (Levy, 1968, pp. 272–291). The right against self-incrimination was viewed as sufficiently important that eight of the original American states included provisions that no one may be "compelled to give witness against himself," and the right against self-incrimination subsequently was included in the Fifth Amendment to the U.S. Constitution.

Fifth Amendment to the U.S. Constitution

In 1966, in Miranda v. Arizona, the U.S. Supreme Court concluded that the inherently coercive environment of incommunicado police interrogation overwhelmed individuals' ability to assert their right against self-incrimination. The Supreme Court responded by interpreting the Self-Incrimination Clause requirement that "[n]o person ... shall be compelled in any criminal case to be a witness against himself" to require the police to read individuals their Miranda rights prior to police interrogation (Miranda v. Arizona, 384 U.S. 436 [1966]). The Supreme Court later held that the Sixth Amendment right to counsel protects individuals subjected to interrogation following the "initiation of proceedings against them." The U.S. Supreme Court supplemented the Miranda judgment in a series of cases that held that once the government has taken formal steps to prosecute an individual, he or she possesses a Sixth Amendment right to counsel. At this point, it is clear that the government is determined to prosecute, and the Supreme Court ruled that the police are prohibited by the Sixth Amendment from circumventing the trial process and establishing a suspect's guilt through extrajudicial interrogation. The Court explained that the right to an attorney cannot be limited to the trial itself because the denial of access to a lawyer at this early stage of the prosecutorial process may seal the defendant's fate and reduce the trial to a "mere formality" (Brewer v. Williams, 430 U.S. 387, 398 [1977]) (Interrogations and Confessions).

CASE STUDY 6.1

A common practice for Chicago police commander Jon Burge was to walk into the interrogation room and set down a little black box, according to his alleged victims. The box had two wires and a crank, and Burge would attach one wire to the suspect's handcuffed ankles and the other to his manacled hands. Burge would then place a plastic bag over the suspect's head and crank the little black box as electricity would course through the suspect's body (Miller, 2015).

One of the alleged victims communicated, "When he hit me with the voltage, that's when I started gritting, crying, hollering. . . . It felt like a thousand needles going through my body. And then after that, it just felt like something just burning me from the inside, and I shook, I gritted, I hollered, then I passed out" (Miller, 2015). The man would ultimately provide Burge with a false confession and be convicted of murder. Up to 120 persons would report alleged torture by Burge between 1972 and 1991 (Miller, 2015). Some of the convicted would spend years on death row due to the confessions obtained under duress by Burge. In 2003, the governor of Illinois pardoned four men who had been subjected to torture by Burge.

Some of the men spent years on Illinois's death row because of confessions allegedly obtained by Burge under duress. In 2003, Governor George Ryan pardoned four men on death row who claimed to have been tortured by Burge. Following an extensive and costly effort to investigate Burge's actions, he would ultimately be sentenced to 4½ years in prison for perjury charges (Miller, 2015).

Topics for Discussion

The police commander conducted numerous interrogations that were ultimately deemed coercive based upon those incidents that were communicated by victims or discovered during investigation. Does this imply that all of the interrogations conducted by the individual were coercive? Does it also imply that all interrogations conducted within the agency were possibly coercive? How does the actions of the one individual impact the perception of the agency?

Group Exercise

Break into small groups of 5–8 members. As a group, review the points presented in the *Topics For Discussion* section. As a group, respond to the following questions:

- Is due process more important than justice? If a lack of due process is identified in the criminal justice process, how impactful is it to the ability to seek the truth and ultimate justice for criminal activity?

RECOMMENDATION FOR READERS

Fare v. Michael C., 442 U.S. 707, reh'g den., 444 U.S. 887 (1979)

Johnson v. Zerbst, 304 U.S. 458 (1938)

Lodowski v. State, 307 Md. 233 (1986)

In re Lucas F., 68 Md. App. 97 (1986), cert. den. 307 Md. 433 (1986)

Miranda v. Arizona, 384 U.S. 436 (1966)

Winder v. State, 362 Md. 275 (2001)

Baynor v. State, 355 Md. 726, 738 (1999)

SOURCES

Glossary of some commonly used legal terms. (n.d.). Retrieved August 26, 2018, from
   http://www.padamslawok.com/glossary.html

Miller, M. (2015). Cop accused of brutally torturing black suspects costs Chicago $5.5 million. *Washington Post*.

CHAPTER SEVEN

Policy Examples

Mission and Vision: El Paso County Sheriff's Office Policy Manual

MISSION STATEMENT

MISSION:
Our mission is to provide the citizens of El Paso County effective and efficient public safety services. We deliver them consistently with character, competence, and transparency.

VISION:
Our vision is to ensure El Paso County remains the safest and most enjoyable place to live and visit in the State of Colorado. We are committed to holding the highest standard for public safety to achieve a county free of crime and public disorder.

VALUES:
Honesty—Our personal and professional behavior will be a model for all to follow. Our actions will match our words. We will have the courage to stand up for our beliefs and do what is right.

Loyalty—We are loyal to our Oath to protect the Constitutional Rights of those we serve by empowering our employees to make decisions that support the letter and spirit of the law.

Unity—We have a united commitment to serve our diverse community with fairness, dignity and equality. We commit to excellence in all we do.

LAW ENFORCEMENT AUTHORITY

100.1 PURPOSE AND SCOPE
The purpose of this policy is to affirm the authority of the members of the Sheriff's Office to perform their functions based on established legal authority.

100.2 PEACE OFFICER AUTHORITY
Certified members shall be considered peace officers pursuant to CRS § 16-2.5-101 through CRS § 16-2.5-148 and CRS § 24-7.5-103.

100.2.1 ARREST AUTHORITY WITHIN THE JURISDICTION OF THE EL PASO COUNTY SHERIFF'S OFFICE
The arrest authority within the jurisdiction of the Sheriff's Office includes (CRS § 16-3-102):

a. In compliance with an arrest warrant.
b. When any crime is being, or has been, committed in a peace officer's presence.
c. When there is probable cause to believe that an offense was committed by the person to be arrested.

100.2.2 ARREST AUTHORITY OUTSIDE THE JURISDICTION OF THE EL PASO COUNTY SHERIFF'S OFFICE
The arrest authority of deputies outside the jurisdiction of the Sheriff's Office includes:

a. When a felony or misdemeanor is committed in the deputy's presence in another jurisdiction in the state of Colorado, the local law enforcement agency is notified of the arrest and the arrestee is transferred to that agency (CRS § 16-3-110).
b. When the deputy is in fresh pursuit from within the jurisdiction of the Sheriff's Office and any of the following conditions exist (CRS § 16-3-106):

   1. An arrest warrant has been issued for the person or the deputy knows that such warrant has been issued for the person.
   2. An offense was committed in the deputy's presence.
   3. The deputy has probable cause to believe that the person committed an offense.

c. When deputies are accompanied by law enforcement officers who have the authority to make an arrest in that jurisdiction, are present at the scene of the arrest and participate in the arrest process (CRS § 16-3-202).

d. When another agency has requested temporary assistance during a state of emergency (CRS § 29-5-104).

A deputy making an arrest under this subsection shall, as soon as practicable after making the arrest, notify the agency having jurisdiction where the arrest was made (CRS § 16-3-110).

100.3 INTERSTATE PEACE OFFICER POWERS
Peace officer powers may be extended within other states:

a. As applicable under interstate compacts and memorandums of understanding in compliance with the laws of each state (CRS § 24-60-101; CRS § 29-1-206).

b. When a deputy enters Arizona, Nebraska, New Mexico, Oklahoma or Utah in fresh pursuit of a felony subject (ARS § 13-3832; Neb. Rev. Stat. § 29-416; NMSA § 31-2-1 (New Mexico); 22 O.S. § 221; Utah Code 77-9-1).

c. When a deputy enters Kansas in fresh pursuit of a subject who committed any offense (K.S.A. § 22-2404).

d. When an interstate compact exists with the state of Wyoming that permits a deputy to pursue and arrest an offender who has fled Colorado (Wyo. Stat. § 7-3-103).

Whenever a deputy makes an arrest in another state, the deputy shall take the offender to a magistrate in the county where the arrest occurred as soon as practicable (ARS § 13-3833; K.S.A. § 22-2404; Neb. Rev. Stat. § 29-417; NMSA § 31-2-2 (New Mexico); 22 O.S. § 222; Utah Code 77-9-2).

100.4 CONSTITUTIONAL REQUIREMENTS
All members shall observe and comply with every person's clearly established rights under the United States and Colorado Constitutions.

CHIEF EXECUTIVE OFFICER

101.1 PURPOSE AND SCOPE
The Colorado Peace Officer Standards and Training Board (POST) has mandated that all certified peace officers employed within the State of Colorado shall be certified by POST (CRS § 16-2.5-102).

101.1.1 CHIEF EXECUTIVE OFFICER REQUIREMENTS

Any chief executive officer elected or appointed to the office of Sheriff for the first time shall, as a condition of continued employment, complete the course of training prescribed by POST and obtain the Basic Certificate by POST within one year of taking office, unless POST grants a written extension of not greater than one year (CRS § 30-10-501.6 (1)).

OATH OF OFFICE

102.1 PURPOSE AND SCOPE

The purpose of this policy is to ensure that oaths, when appropriate, are administered to Office members.

102.2 POLICY

It is the policy of the Sheriff's Office that, when appropriate, Office members affirm the oath of their office as an expression of commitment to the constitutional rights of those served by the Office and the dedication of its members to their duties.

102.3 OATH OF OFFICE

All Office members, when appropriate, shall take and subscribe to the oaths or affirmations applicable to their positions. Prior to assuming the duties of a peace officer, certified members shall be required to affirm the oath of office expressing commitment and intent to respect constitutional rights in discharging the duties of a law enforcement officer (Colo. Const. art. XII, § 8).

If a member is opposed to taking an oath, he/she shall be permitted to substitute the word "affirm" for the word "swear," and the words "so help me God" may be substituted with "under the pains and penalties of perjury."

102.3.1 CANON OF ETHICS

All Sheriff's Office deputies shall be required to abide by a code or canon of ethics as adopted by the Office.

102.4 MAINTENANCE OF RECORDS

The oath of office shall be filed in accordance with the established records retention schedule.

Use of Force: Las Vegas Metropolitan Police Department

6/002.00 USE OF FORCE
A.S. 1.2.2, 1.2.7, 1.3.1 THROUGH 1.3.8

I.   *POLICY*
II.   *DEFINITIONS*
III.   *USE OF FORCE TO AFFECT A DETENTION, AN ARREST OR TO CONDUCT A SEARCH*
IV.   *DETERMINING OBJECTIVELY REASONABLE FORCE*
V.   *DUTY TO INTERVENE*
VI.   *LEVELS OF RESISTANCE (see Use of Force Model)*
VII.   *LEVELS OF CONTROL (see Use of Force Model)*
VIII.   *USE OF FORCE MODEL*
IX.   *DE-ESCALATION*
X.   *AUTHORIZED FORCE TOOLS, TECHNIQUES AND EQUIPMENT*
XI.   *REPORTABLE FORCE INCIDENTS*

I. POLICY

THE LAS VEGAS Metropolitan Police Department is committed to protecting people, their property and rights, while providing the best in public safety and service. The proper use of force is essential for policing. There are circumstances where individuals will not comply with the law unless compelled or controlled by the use of force. Yet, officers must also remain mindful that they derive their authority from the community and that unreasonable force degrades the legitimacy of that authority. In a Use of Force Incident, the governmental interest must match the level of force and intrusion upon an individual's constitutional rights.

It is the policy of this department that officers hold the highest regard for the dignity and liberty of all persons, and place minimal reliance upon the use of force. The department respects the value of every human life and that the application of deadly force is a measure to be employed in the most extreme circumstances.

II. DEFINITIONS

  A. *Approved Weapons*—Approved weapons are those weapons meeting department specifications for which officers receive proficiency and safety training. Prior to the use of any approved weapon option, the officer, when practical,

Department of Justice, "The Las Vegas Metropolitan Police Department- Use of Force Policy."

will communicate to other officers and the subject that the use of the option is imminent, and clearly and audibly announce the same to all personnel in the immediate area unless exigent circumstances prevent this from occurring.

B. *Blocking*—Blocking is the positioning of a police vehicle in the path of a suspect vehicle where contact between the vehicles is not anticipated or is anticipated to be minimal. The intent of blocking is to prevent an avenue of escape by the safe placement of a police vehicle.

C. *Cuffing Under Power*—Cuffing under Power is a tactic where a secondary officer handcuffs a subject while the ECD (being deployed by the primary officer) is cycling and the subject is in Neuro-Muscular Incapacitation (NMI).

D. *Deadly Force*—Deadly force is that degree of force, which is likely to produce death or serious bodily injury. Deadly force can also result from a force option being improperly applied. Deadly force is not limited to the use of firearms.

E. *Electronic Control Device (ECD)*—The ECD is a Neuro-Muscular Incapacitation device that stimulates the motor neurons to contract disrupting communication from the brain to the muscles thereby causing temporary motor skill dysfunction.

   1. Spark Display—A non-contact demonstration of the ECD's ability to discharge electricity.
   2. Touch Stun—A secondary function of the ECD intended to administer pain to a subject by making direct contact with the body after the air cartridge has been expended or removed. Note: Use of the ECD in this mode is discouraged.
   3. Probe Mode—The primary function of the ECD, and when the ECD is fired and both probes make contact with a subject. The intent is that the subject be temporarily immobilized for the period of time the ECD is cycled.

F. *Force Transitions*—The movement, escalation/de-escalation, from the application of one force type to another in conjunction with the "objectively reasonable" standard from Graham v. Connor, 490 U.S. 386 (1989). The officer must consider all the factors prior to using force and choose a reasonable option based on the "totality of the circumstances" present.

   The LVMPD Use of Force Policy applies to all commissioned officers, but the legal standard specific to incidents involving use of force within a detention facility are set forth in Hudson v. McMillian, 503 U.S. 1(1992).

G. *Imminent Threat*—"Imminent threat" refers to an impending violent act or resistance that an officer reasonably believes will occur, based on the totality of the circumstances.

H. *Intermediate Force*—The level of force necessary to compel compliance by a subject displaying Aggressive Resistance, which is neither likely nor intended to cause death.

I. *Involved Officer*—A commissioned officer or supervisor, who participated in, directed or influenced the application of the use of force.

J. *Lateral Vascular Neck Restraint (LVNR®)*—LVNR® is a specific method of applying pressure to the side of a subject's neck to overcome resistance and allow safe control. This technique is used only in accordance with official departmental training and policy.

K. *Levels of Control*—Levels of Control are broad categories of influence and or force in identifiable, escalating stages of intensity. They are identified as low level force, intermediate force, and deadly force.

L. *Low Level Force*—Low level force is the level of force that is necessary to interact with a subject that is compliant or displaying Passive or Active Resistance.

M. *Non-Deadly Force*—Non-deadly force is the level of force required to compel compliance, which is not intended to, and is not known to create a substantial risk of causing death or serious bodily harm.

N. *Officer-Involved Shooting*—An officer-involved shooting is an officer's discharge of a firearm at a person, with or without physical injury or the death of the person.

O. *Officer Witness Monitor*—An Officer Witness Monitor is a designated officer who is not involved in the use of deadly force. The responsibilities of the Officer Witness Monitor are to observe and prevent discussions regarding the incident among involved officer(s) and witness(s).

P. *Other Firearm Discharge*—An "other firearm discharge" is an unintentional discharge of a firearm that does not cause injury or death to a person or the intentional shooting at, injuring, or killing animals.

Q. *Precision Intervention Technique (PIT)*—The PIT is a specific manner of intentional contact using a police vehicle against a fleeing vehicle to cause the fleeing vehicle to come to a stop; this technique is used only in accordance with official department training and policy.

R. *Public Safety Statement*—A public safety statement is a series of questions to obtain information and to determine an immediate threat to public safety. It is not an interview. This statement will be obtained by one of the first-responding supervisors and will contain the following questions:

    1. Is anyone injured? If so, where are they located?
    2. Are there any outstanding suspects? If so, what are their descriptions, direction and mode of travel? How long have they been gone? What crime(s) are they wanted for? What weapons are they armed with?

3. Were you involved in an officer-involved shooting?

4. Approximately where were you when you fired the rounds?

5. Approximately how many rounds did you fire and in what direction did you fire them?

6. Do you know if any other officers fired any rounds?

7. Did the suspect fire rounds at you? If so, from what direction were the rounds fired?

8. Are there any weapons or evidence that needs to be secured and/or protected? Where are they located?

9. Are you aware of any witnesses? If so, what is their location?

S. **Ramming**—The use of a vehicle to intentionally hit another vehicle, outside the approved PIT, blocking and stationary vehicle immobilization policies. Ramming is prohibited unless a deadly force situation can be clearly articulated.

T. **Reasonable Force**—Reasonable force is an objective standard of force viewed from the perspective of a reasonable officer, without the benefit of 20/20 hindsight, and based on the totality of the circumstances presented at the time of the incident. See section IV. "Determining Objectively Reasonable Force."

U. **Reportable Force**—Reportable force is any use of force which is required to overcome subject resistance to gain compliance that results in death, injury or complaint of injury, complaint of continuing pain, or any use of force greater than low level force (see Levels of Control) and any application of the LVNR®.

V. **Serious Bodily Injury**—A bodily injury that creates a substantial risk of death; causes serious, permanent disfigurement; or results in a prolonged loss or impairment of the functioning of any bodily member or organ.

W. **Significant Force**—Any force which results in treatment at a medical facility due to injuries or alleged injuries caused by any officer. Examples include, but are not limited to: skeletal fractures; injury or complaint of injury to a person's head or sternum area. All Significant Force is Reportable Force.

X. **Stationary Vehicle Immobilization Technique (Pinching)**—Is a containment tactic whose use is restricted for specialized units. It employs extremely low-speed, intentional vehicle contact with a suspect vehicle. The purpose is to render a vehicle immobile by blocking it in place with police vehicles, so that suspects can be taken into custody.

Y. **Witness Officer**—A commissioned officer or supervisor who did not participate in or directly influence the application of the use of force.

III. USE OF FORCE TO AFFECT A DETENTION, AN ARREST OR TO CONDUCT A SEARCH

A. Officers may use reasonable force:

1. To protect themselves;

2. To protect others;
3. To affect a lawful detention;
4. To affect a lawful arrest;
5. To conduct a lawful search.

B. If it is not already known by the subject to be detained, arrested, or searched, officers should, if reasonable, make clear their intent to detain, arrest or search the subject. When practicable, officers will identify themselves as a peace officer before using force.

IV. DETERMINING OBJECTIVELY REASONABLE FORCE

Under the Fourth Amendment of the United States Constitution a police officer may only use such force as is "objectively reasonable" under all of the circumstances. The standard that courts will use to examine whether a use of force is constitutional was first set forth in Graham v. Connor, 490 U.S. 386 (1989) and expanded by subsequent court cases. The reasonableness of a particular use of force must be judged from the perspective of a reasonable officer on the scene, rather than with 20/20 vision of hindsight. The reasonableness must account for the fact that officers are often forced to make split-second judgments—in circumstances that are tense, uncertain, and rapidly evolving.

The reasonableness inquiry in reviewing use of force is an objective one: the question is whether the officer's actions are objectively reasonable in light of the facts and circumstances confronting them. The officer's perception may be a consideration, but other objective factors will determine the reasonableness of force. These factors may include but are not limited to:

a. The severity of the crime(s) at issue;
b. Whether the subject poses an immediate threat to the safety of the officer(s) or others;
c. Whether the subject is actively resisting arrest or attempting to evade arrest by flight;
d. The influence of drugs/alcohol or the mental capacity of the subject;
e. The time available to an officer to make a decision;
f. The availability of officers/resources to de-escalate the situation;
g. The proximity or access of weapons to the subject;
h. The environmental factors and/or other exigent circumstances.

The officer will use a level of force that is necessary and within the range of "objectively reasonable" options. When use of force is needed, officers will assess each incident to determine, based on policy, training and experience, which use of force option will de-escalate the situation and bring it under control in a safe and prudent manner. Reasonable and sound judgment will dictate the force option to be employed. Therefore, the department examines all uses of force from an objective standard rather than a subjective standard.

The LVMPD Use of Force Policy applies to all commissioned officers, but the legal standard specific to incidents involving use of force within a detention facility are set forth in <u>Hudson v. McMillian</u>, 503 U.S. 1(1992).

LVMPD allows certain classifications of civilian members to carry a firearm and OC spray while on duty. Civilian members have no power of arrest and therefore may only use force consist with Nevada law on self defense or defense of others.

V. DUTY TO INTERVENE

Any officer present and observing another officer using force that is clearly beyond that which is objectively reasonable under the circumstances shall, when in a position to do so, safely intercede to prevent the use of such excessive force. Officers shall promptly report these observations to a supervisor.

VI. LEVELS OF RESISTANCE (SEE USE OF FORCE MODEL)

It is important for officers to bear in mind that there are many reasons a suspect may be resisting arrest or may be unresponsive. The person in question may not be capable of understanding the gravity of the situation. Officers must consider several factors when dealing with a non-compliant subject. A subject may be noncompliant due to a medical condition, mental, physical, or hearing impairment, language barrier, drug interaction or emotional crisis, and have no criminal intent. This may not make the subject any less dangerous but it may require a change in tactics that will be more effective while maintaining officer safety.

    A. *Compliant*—A person contacted by an officer who acknowledges direction or lawful orders given and offers no passive/active, aggressive, or aggravated aggressive resistance.

    B. *Passive Resistance*—The subject is not complying with an officer's commands and is uncooperative, but is taking only minimal physical action to prevent an officer from placing the subject in custody and taking control. Examples include: standing stationary and not moving upon lawful direction, falling limply and refusing to use their own power to move (becoming "dead weight"), holding onto a fixed object, or locking arms to another during a protest or demonstration.

C. **Active Resistance**—The subject's verbal or physical actions are intended to prevent an officer from placing the subject in custody and taking control, but are not directed at harming the officer. Examples include: walking or running away, breaking the officer's grip.

D. **Aggressive Resistance**—The subject displays the intent to harm the officer, themselves or another person and prevent an officer from placing the subject in custody and taking control. The aggression may manifest itself through a subject taking a fighting stance, punching, kicking, striking, attacks with weapons or other actions which present an imminent threat of physical harm to the officer or another.

E. **Aggravated Aggressive Resistance**—The subject's actions are likely to result in death or serious bodily harm to the officer, themselves or another. These actions may include a firearm, use of blunt or bladed weapon, and extreme physical force.

VII. LEVELS OF CONTROL (SEE USE OF FORCE MODEL)

When use of force is needed, officers will assess each incident to determine, based on policy, training and experience, which use of force option is believed to be appropriate for the situation and bring it under control in a safe and prudent manner. Officers must use the amount of force that is objectively reasonable to overcome resistance in order to take lawful police action. The level of control must be proportionate to the circumstances and the level of resistance encountered by the officers.

A. **Low Level Force**—The level of control necessary to interact with a subject that is compliant or displaying Passive or Active Resistance. This level of force is not intended to and has a low-probability of causing injury. Examples are handcuffing a compliant arrestee for transport to detention facility or proning a suspect out on a high-risk vehicle stop.

This level of force includes:
1. Officer Presence
2. Verbal Communication
3. Empty Hand Tactics (Takedowns)
4. Handcuffs/Other LVMPD Approved Restraint Devices
5. Baton (As escort tool)
6. LVNR® (Level One—minimum restraint)
7. K-9—(No bites)
8. Pinching
9. Blocking

B. ***Intermediate Force***—The level of force necessary to compel compliance by a subject displaying Aggressive Resistance, which is neither likely nor intended to cause death.

   This level of force requires a Use of Force Report and includes:
   1. Empty Hand Tactics (Takedown with injury, Strikes, Kicks)
   2. Baton/Impact Weapons (Jabs, Strikes)
   3. LVNR® (Level 2—medium restraint; and 3-maximum restraint)
   4. OC Spray
   5. ECD
   6. Low Lethality Shotgun (five yards or greater)
   7. K-9 (with bites)
   8. P.I.T. (Speeds 40mph or below)

C. ***Deadly Force***—Deadly force is that degree of force, which is likely to produce death or serious bodily injury. Deadly force can also result from a force option being improperly applied. Deadly force is not limited to the use of firearms.
   1. Baton (Striking head, neck, sternum, spine, groin, or kidneys)
   2. Low Lethality Shotgun (Fired at a distance less than five yards)
   3. P.I.T. (More than 40mph)
   4. Ramming
   5. Firearm Use

D. ***Parameters for Use of Deadly Force***
   An officer may use deadly force upon another person only when it is objectively reasonable to:
   1. Protect himself or others from what is reasonably believed to be an imminent threat of death or serious bodily injury;
   2. Prevent the escape of a fleeing felon who the officer has probable cause to believe has committed a violent felony crime and is an imminent threat to human life if escape should occur. (See NRS 171.1455.) Officers will give some warning, if feasible, prior to the use of deadly force.
   Example: *"Police! Stop or I will shoot!"*

E. ***Elements of Deadly Force***
   1. ***Ability***—Ability exists when a person has the means or capability to cause grave injury, serious bodily harm or death to an officer or another. This may include, but is not limited to the following: the suspect's physical ability, size, age, strength, gender, combative skill, level of aggression, and any weapons in their immediate control.
   2. ***Opportunity***—Opportunity exists when a person is in a position to effectively resist an officer's control or to use force or violence upon the officer

or another. Examples which may affect opportunity include: relative distance to the officer or others, and physical barriers between the subject and the officer.

3. ***Imminent Jeopardy***—Based upon all the facts and a circumstance confronting the officer, the officer reasonably believes the subject poses an imminent threat to the life of the officer(s) or other third parties and the officer must act immediately to prevent death or serious bodily injury.

4. ***Preclusion***—All other lesser alternatives have been reasonably considered and exhausted prior to the use of deadly force, to include disengagement. Deadly force in response to the subject's actions must remain reasonable while based upon the totality of the circumstances known to the officer at the time force was applied.

VIII. USE OF FORCE MODEL

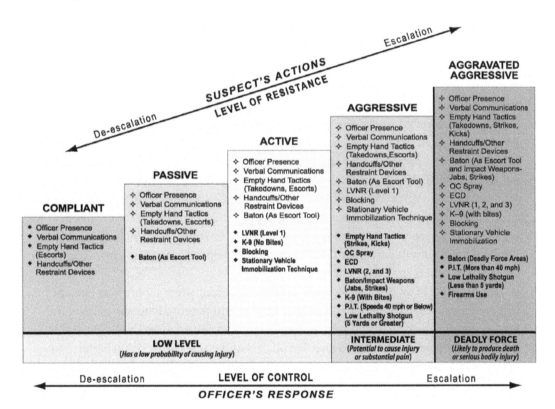

FIGURE 7.1 Each bolded force option within the Levels of Control represents the highest levels of force options available; however, each other force option should be considered to help de-escalate the situation.

This graphic is intended as a general guideline for an officer. The suspect(s) actions will dictate the officer's use of force. Corrections officers will follow their established standard operating procedures in incidents involving use of force within a detention facility.

Force Transition: Force transition is the movement, escalation/de-escalation, from the application of one force type to another in conjunction with the "objectively reasonable" standard.

In use of force incidents, the officer will transition to differing degrees or types of force, including attempts to deescalate. Force situations are dynamic and require an officer to continually assess the suspect's actions to ensure a proportionate response. Officers shall modify their Level of Control in relation to the amount of resistance offered by a subject.

IX. DE-ESCALATION

Policing requires that at times an officer must exercise control of a violent or resisting subject to make an arrest, or to protect the officer, other officers, or members of the community from risk of imminent harm. Clearly, not every potential violent confrontation can be de-escalated, but officers do have the ability to impact the direction and the outcome of many situations they handle, based on their decision making and the tactics they choose to employ.

When reasonable under the totality of circumstances, officers should gather information about the incident, assess the risks, assemble resources, attempt to slow momentum, and communicate and coordinate a response. In their interaction with subjects, officers should use advisements, warnings, verbal persuasion, and other tactics and alternatives to higher levels of force. Officers should recognize that they may withdraw to a position that is tactically more secure or allows them greater distance in order to consider or deploy a greater variety of Force Options. Officers shall perform their work in a manner that avoids unduly jeopardizing their own safety or the safety of others through poor tactical decisions.

The prospect of a favorable outcome is often enhanced when supervisors become involved in the management of an overall response to potential violent encounters by coordinating resources and officers' tactical actions. Supervisors should possess a good knowledge of tactics and ensure that officers under their supervision perform to a standard. As a good practice, supervisors will acknowledge and respond to incidents in a timely manner where police use of force is probable.

X. AUTHORIZED FORCE TOOLS, TECHNIQUES AND EQUIPMENT

With minimal exception, only department-approved weapons and training techniques shall be used. Uniformed officers will carry all tools and equipment required by the policies of this agency. Officers should note that less lethal tools may result in a lethal outcome, or be ineffective even when used appropriately.

Non-uniformed commissioned personnel below the rank of captain are required to carry at least one intermediate force option—baton, OC spray, or ECD—on their person when on-duty unless the requirement is waived, via completion of LVMPD Form 483, by their division commander.

Supervisors of commissioned personnel should ensure their subordinates complete their minimum required hours of training within the calendar year. Officers completing an academy during the calendar year are exempt from the minimum hour requirement. Defensive tactics proficiency testing will be required for the quarter following graduation from an academy.

If the member fails to demonstrate proficiency, the member and/or the member's supervisor will contact the Organizational Development Bureau as soon as practicable for assistance in formulating a remedial training program.

The following are authorized force tools/restraints and techniques which may be used when objectively reasonable and otherwise permitted under this policy. Specialized units may have additional tools that are not covered in this policy.

A. *Presence and Verbal Communication:*
   Level of Control:
   Low Level Force

   Approved Use:
   Officers will, when and to the extent reasonably possible, attempt to use verbal communication skills to control subjects before resorting to physical control methods.

B. *Empty Hand Tactics:*
   Level of Control:
   Low Level Force—takedowns (not likely to cause injury), escorts
   Intermediate Level Force—takedown, strikes, kicking
   Deadly Force—takedown, strikes, kicking

   Certification/POST Requirements:
   a. Entry level training is taught at the LVMPD police and corrections academies.
   b. Annual Training—Two hours of Defensive Tactics training per quarter for lieutenants and below. NV POST requires officers must participate in 8 hours of Defensive Tactics training per year and demonstrate proficiency with each tactic/tool they are authorized to use.

Approved Use:
1. These tactics will be used only in accordance with policy and department training.
2. Members should only use tactics appropriate to the situation which have been taught by department Defensive Tactics instructors.

Post Use of Force Procedures:
Any incident where a subject is injured or complains of injury, or involves strikes, punches or kicks is reportable by completing a Use of Force Report in Blue Team.

C. *Handcuffs, flexible handcuffs, or other restraint devices:*
Level of Control:
Low Level Force
Description:
Officers will only use department-authorized or issued handcuffs.

Certification/POST Requirements:
a. Entry level training is taught at the LVMPD police and corrections academies.
b. Two hours of Defensive Tactics training per quarter for lieutenants and below. NV POST requires officers participate in 8 hours of Defensive Tactics training per year and demonstrate proficiency with each tactic/tool they are authorized to use.

Inspection Requirement:
Handcuffs will be maintained in clean and working order.

Approved Use:
1. This tool will be used only in accordance with policy and department training.
2. In an attempt to minimize the risk of injury to officers and others during arrest situations, officers will handcuff all persons arrested as soon as possible.
3. During investigative detentions ("Terry Stops") where one or more of the following factors is present:
    a. Articulable facts that the subject is physically uncooperative;
    b. Articulable facts that a subject's actions at the scene may present physical danger to themselves or others if not restrained;
    c. Reasonable possibility of flight based on the action of the subject;
    d. Information that the subject is currently armed;

e. The stop closely follows a violent crime and the subject matches specific parts of a description;

f. When there are articulable facts that a crime of violence is about to occur;

g. Care and discretion should be used at extremes of age in handcuffing an individual during an investigative detention.

h. The authority to handcuff during investigatory stops continues for only as long as the circumstances above exist. Investigative detentions cannot exceed 60 minutes pursuant to NRS 171.123.

4. Suicidal persons;

5. During a search warrant service;

a. At a private residence as is reasonably necessary to execute the warrant in safety;

b. At a commercial business open to the public if it reasonably appears that handcuffing is necessary to protect an officer or others from physical harm. Circumstances which may justify initial handcuffing may change and eliminate continued justification;

6. Detoxification clients being transported;

7. By detention personnel moving in-custody subjects.

Disapproved Use:

1. If medical circumstances make it unreasonable to handcuff an arrestee, officers will refrain from handcuffing.

2. When responding to a security office where a subject has already been placed in handcuffs prior to arriving to the scene, officers shall not place LVMPD handcuffs on the subject until they have reasonable suspicion or probable cause based on their independent investigation and/or findings.

Tactical Considerations:

1. Officers will check handcuffs for tightness and double lock as soon as it is safe to do so prior to transport.

2. When a handcuffed subject first complains that handcuffs are too tight and/or are hurting the subject, the officer having custody of the handcuffed subject will, as soon as reasonably possible, check the handcuffs to make sure that they are not too tight. If they are too tight (per training), they will be loosened and relocked.

3. Officers will transport subject to the detention facility in a timely manner and booked. Under no circumstances will a person under

arrest be held in a transport vehicle longer than two (2) hours before being transported to the detention facility and booked.

Post Use of Force Procedures:
This is a low level force option. Any incident where a subject is injured or complains of injury is reportable by completing a Use of Force Report in Blue Team.

D. **Baton/Impact Weapons:**
Level of Control:
Low Level Force—when used as an escort tool
Intermediate Force—when used for jabbing or striking
Deadly Force—striking suspects on the head, neck, sternum, spine, groin, or kidneys

Description:
1. A baton is a department-authorized expandable straight baton or side handle baton.
2. All commissioned police personnel the rank of lieutenant and below must obtain certification training and carry the baton when in an approved LVMPD uniform (see 4/107.00).
3. Plain clothes officers are required to carry either OC spray, an ECD, or an expandable straight baton.

Certification/POST Requirements:
a. Entry level training is taught at the LVMPD police and corrections academies.
b. All officers, in the rank of lieutenant and below, shall complete the following requirements:
   a. Receives initial baton training in the academy; or
   b. Receives a minimum of eight (8) hours of initial PR-24 (AL or FX) or a minimum of four (4) hours of initial expandable straight baton training by an LVMPD certified Defensive Tactics Instructor.
3. Annual Training—Two hours of Defensive Tactics training per quarter for lieutenants and below. NV POST requires officers participate in 8 hours of Defensive Tactics training per year and demonstrate proficiency with each tactic/tool they are authorized to use.

Inspection Requirement:
Batons will be maintained in clean and working order.

Approved Use:
1. This tool will be used only in accordance with policy and department training.
2. Blocking, jabbing, to apply control holds, or passive/active escort techniques (Example: stirring the pot).

Disapproved Use:
1. A subject who poses no imminent threat will not be struck with a baton or impact tool.
2. Officers are discouraged from using their firearm as an impact tool due to the possibility of an unintentional discharge.
3. During non-deadly force incidents, officers will use reasonable care to avoid striking suspects on the head, neck, sternum, spine, groin, or kidneys, as these strikes may constitute deadly force.
4. The use of instruments as a weapon for the purpose of striking or jabbing (i.e., flashlights, radio, etc.) other than department-authorized batons, is strongly discouraged and acceptable only when other authorized force responses have been exhausted and are either unavailable or ineffective.
5. Officers must be able to articulate a compelling need to use any other device or object other than an authorized baton as an impact weapon.

Post Use of Force Procedures:
Any use of the baton, other than for escort/control hold or "stirring the pot," and any incident where a subject is injured or complains of injury, is reportable.

E. *Oleoresin Capsicum Spray:*
Level of Control:
Intermediate Force

Description:
1. OC spray is a non-lethal agent which acts as an inflammatory and has a natural base as opposed to a chemical base.
2. All commissioned police personnel the rank of lieutenant and below must obtain certification training and carry OC spray when in an approved LVMPD uniform (see 4/107.00).
3. Plain clothes officers are required to carry OC spray, an ECD, or an expandable straight baton.

Certification/POST Requirements:

1. Entry level training is taught at the LVMPD police and corrections academies.
2. Annual Training—Two hours of Defensive Tactics training per quarter for lieutenants and below. NV POST requires officers participate in 8 hours of Defensive Tactics training per year and demonstrate proficiency with each tactic/tool they are authorized to use.

Inspection Requirement:
OC spray expiration date and serviceability will be checked.

Deployment Requirement:
1. When deploying, an officer will, if practical, announce a warning to the subject and other officers of the intent to deploy the OC spray if the subject does not comply with your commands.
   Example, *"Do what I am telling you to do, or I will spray you with pepper spray."*
2. Officer shall give the subject a reasonable opportunity to voluntarily comply.

Approved Use:
1. OC Spray will be used only in accordance with policy and department training.
2. OC spray may be used when subject is engaging or displays the intent to engage in aggressive resistant behavior which may cause injury.
3. OC spray may be used on vicious or aggressive animals when those animals interfere with the safety of the officers or citizens.
4. OC spray may only be used in a protest or demonstration situation when authorized by an incident commander in response to imminent threat of harm.
5. Correction Officers will follow their standard operating procedures regarding the use of OC Spray.

Disapproved Use:
1. Shall not be used on a subject inside a closed vehicle, unless an officer is attempting to secure an aggressive resistant suspect in a patrol vehicle. OC is not intended to be used to force extraction from an enclosed area, unless utilized in a detention facility.
2. Shall not be used on passive resistant protestors.
3. Shall not be used other than as an aerosol/stream.

   4. Shall not be used on a handcuffed subject unless the subject is displaying Aggressive Resistance.

Tactical Considerations:
   1. Whenever possible, should be used upwind and relatively close to the subject.
   2. High capacity OC spray may be used as an intermediate level of control; however, officers will assess the effect the device will have on subjects in the general area due to the volume of agent dispersed.

Supervisory Responsibility:
   Incident commander may authorize use in a protest or demonstration incident in response to imminent threat of harm.

Post Use of Force Procedures:
   1. An officer using OC spray will:
      a. Request medical attention to the scene, as soon as possible, to wash and treat affected skin/eye area whenever a subject is directly exposed to OC spray in the facial area, or to treat any underlying condition that could be aggravated by the OC spray;
      b. Inform detention personnel during the booking process of prisoner exposure to OC spray;
      c. Take prisoner to the nurse's station;
      d. Use of this tool is reportable and will be reported by completing a Use of Force Report in Blue Team.
   2. A civilian department member using OC spray on-duty will:
      a. Request medical attention to the scene to wash and treat affected skin/eye area whenever a subject is directly exposed to OC spray in the facial area, or to treat any underlying condition that could be aggravated by the OC spray;
      b. Request a field unit to respond and notify immediate supervisor;
      c. Field unit personnel responding to civilian use of OC spray will:
         1) Take appropriate enforcement action;
         2) Assist the civilian in completing the appropriate paperwork, including a Use of Force Report;
         3) Inform detention personnel during booking process of prisoner exposure to OC spray;
         4) Take prisoner to the medical section.

F. ***Lateral Vascular Neck Restraint®:***
There are three levels to applying the LVNR®. Level One begins with Low Level Force and may progress to the Intermediate based on the suspect's actions.

Level of Control:
 Low Level Force—LVNR® Level One—minimum restraint
 Intermediate Force—LVNR® Level Two—medium restraint;
         Level Three—maximum restraint.

Description:
 The LVNR® is a control technique in which the carotid arteries on the sides of the neck are compressed, restricting blood flow to the brain, causing the subject to pass out.

Certification/POST Requirements:
1. Entry Level Training is provided in the LVMPD police and corrections academies. No officer will use the LVNR® without first completing the 12-hour certification course provided in the academy.
2. Training will be provided by certified LVNR® instructors only.
3. All commissioned officers below the rank of captain will receive training in the LVNR®.
4. Officers certified in the LVNR® will be required to complete an annual four-hour recertification course.
   a. Any officer requesting an exemption from LVNR® training due to medical reasons must obtain a medical exemption from their physician.
   b. This exemption must be obtained immediately upon requesting the exemption and at the beginning of each calendar year thereafter, and be forwarded to the Director of Risk Management.

Approved Use:
1. This tool will be used only in accordance with policy and department training.
2. The LVNR® is a defensive tactic to quickly and safely stop active/aggressive resistance.

Disapproved Use:
1. Will not be used on subjects that have been exposed to OC spray or who are experiencing difficulty breathing.
2. Officers will not use any other arm bar technique that involves a neck restraint.

Tactical Considerations:
1. When applying the LVNR®, only the amount of force necessary to bring the subject under control will be used.
2. Upon the subject being brought under control the LVNR® will be relaxed.

Post Use of Force Procedures:
1. All uses of the LVNR® will be reported by completing a Use of Force Report in Blue Team.
2. The arresting or transporting officer will:
   a. Notify his immediate supervisor when the LVNR® is attempted or used;
   b. Summon medical attention immediately when a subject is rendered unconscious, injured or claims injury as a result of the LVNR®;
   c. Transport prisoner to the appropriate detention facility;
   d. Inform the detention facility on-duty supervisor that the LVNR® has been applied earlier to the subject.

G. ***Electronic Control Device:***
   All commissioned personnel at the rank of lieutenant and below must obtain ECD certification training. Sergeants and below must carry the ECD when in an approved LVMPD uniform (see 4/107.00), excluding NYE, 9/11 or any other Special Events as stated in the IAP for the Event.

Level of Control:
   Intermediate Force

Description:
1. The ECD is a neuro-muscular incapacitation (NMI) device that disrupts the body's ability to communicate messages from the brain to the muscles thereby causing temporary NMI.
   a. An air cartridge is a replaceable cartridge for the ECD which uses compressed nitrogen to fire two barbed probes on thin connecting wires, sending a high voltage/low current signal into a subject.
2. Use of the ECD Camera
   a. Some ECDs are equipped with a video camera and audio recording device. The camera will allow recordings in high resolution black and white imagery, and stores up to 90 minutes of video in a looping format. Additionally, the camera has audio capabilities.
   b. Any and all images, video, and/or audio generated by the ECD camera are the sole property of the Las Vegas Metropolitan

Police Department. No video and/or audio may be downloaded unless obtained in the course of official duties. No material produced by the ECD cameras may be reproduced, uploaded to non-departmental websites, or otherwise disseminated without authorization from the Sheriff or his designee.

c. When an officer leaves the Patrol Division, the ECD camera must be turned into the Supply Section.

Certification/POST Requirements:

1. Entry Level Training is taught at the LVMPD police and corrections academies.
2. Defensive Tactics instructors who have been certified as ECD instructors will be the only authorized persons to instruct on the ECD.
3. Officers authorized to use an ECD must successfully complete an initial eight-hour certification training course, to include written and practical tests.
4. Once certified, officers must annually attend four-hour recertification training.
    a. All commissioned personnel at the rank of lieutenant and below must obtain certification training.
    b. All sergeants and below must carry the ECD when in an approved LVMPD uniform (see 4/107.00), excluding NYE or any other Special Events as stated in the IAP for the Event.
    c. All officers, regardless of issuance of an ECD, will maintain their certification by attending the annual recertification class through the AOST Staff.
    d. DSD personnel will continue to follow their established SOPs regarding ECD deployment.
5. If the member fails to demonstrate proficiency after additional training has been given, the member and/or the member's supervisor will contact the Training Section for assistance in formulating a remedial training program.

Inspection Requirement:

1. Officers will use only authorized ECD equipment issued by the LVMPD. The ECD will be inspected for damage and cleanliness, and batteries and cartridges replaced by the officer when required. The battery display will be checked on the CID at the beginning of each shift. A reading of 20% or less will require the battery pack be changed. The battery pack will not be removed from the ECDs except when the reading is 20% or less or to conduct a data download. The

ECD will never be stored more than 48 hours without the battery pack attached. When off duty, ECDs must be stored and secured in a climate-controlled area (i.e. locker), not in a vehicle.

2. Officers must conduct a spark check, outside the public view, at the beginning of shift to ensure the ECD will function properly. It is conducted by removing the cartridge, test firing the ECD and observing the electrical arc. This spark check does not require completion of a Use of Force Report. When spark checking or replacing cartridges, officers will not mask the ECD or point it in the direction of others.

3. Uniformed officers will carry the ECD in a department approved holster. The holster will be carried on the duty belt, on the side opposite the duty firearm. Cross-draw position is optional. Plain clothes officers will carry the ECD on their weak side. Officers have the option of carrying the standard DPM or the X-DPM which is an extended version, capable of carrying a spare ECD cartridge.

Deployment Requirement:

1. When displaying an ECD, officers will give a warning, when practical, to the subject and other officers before firing the ECD.

Example: ***"Do what I am telling you to do or I will taze you and it will hurt."***

2. Officer shall give the subject a reasonable opportunity to voluntarily comply.

Approved Use:

1. This tool will be used only in accordance with policy and department training.

2. The ECD is an Intermediate Level of Control and may be used when there is an imminent threat of physical harm.

Disapproved Use:

1. Officers are not authorized to draw or display the ECD except for training and inspection, unless the circumstances create a reasonable belief that use may be necessary. The ECD will be handled in the same manner as a firearm and will be secured prior to entering any detention facility.

2. The intentional use of more than one ECD simultaneously on the same subject is prohibited.

3. The ECD will not be used:

a. When the officer knows a subject has come in contact with flammable liquids or is in a flammable atmosphere;

b. When the subject is in a position where a fall may cause injury or death;

c. Punitively for purposes of coercion or in an unjustified manner;

d. To escort or jab individuals;

e. To awaken unconscious or intoxicated individuals;

f. When the subject is visibly pregnant, unless deadly force is the only other option;

g. When the subject is in handcuffs or waist restraints;

h. When a subject displays solely Passive or Active Resistance (i.e. peaceful protest, refusal to stand, non-aggressive verbal resistance, etc.);

i. When a subject is fleeing as the sole justification for use of the ECD.

4. The ECD should not be used in the following circumstances unless there are compelling reasons to do so which can be clearly articulated:

a. When the subject is operating a motor vehicle;

b. When the subject is holding a firearm;

c. When the subject is at the extremes of age (elderly and young children) or physically disabled;

d. In a situation where deadly force is clearly justifiable unless another officer is present and capable of providing deadly force to protect the officers and/or others as necessary.

5. Use of the ECD Camera:

a. The ECD camera will not be used as a simple recording device whether pointed at or away from subject(s), or while the officer is blocking or obscuring the lens or microphone (the unit displays a flashing "88" symbol advising that the lens is blocked).

b. The ECD camera may only be used for official police business. Any use of the ECD camera video or audio that is not in the performance of official duties is strictly prohibited.

Tactical Considerations:

1. There are three types of reportable ECD applications:

a. Spark Display—A non-contact demonstration of the ECD's ability to discharge electricity.

b. Touch Stun—(without a cartridge)—A secondary function of the ECD intended to administer pain to a subject by making direct contact with the body after the air cartridge has been expended or removed. Note: Use of the ECD in this mode is discouraged.

    c. Probe Mode—When the ECD is fired and both probes make contact with a subject with the intent that the subject be temporarily immobilized for the period of time the ECD is cycled. Proper application will result in temporary immobilization of the subject and provide the officer a "window of opportunity" in which to take the subject safely into custody.

2. For a frontal shot, reasonable effort should be made to target lower center mass and avoid intentionally targeting the head, neck, groin and chest. It is recognized that the dynamics of each situation and officer safety may not permit the officer to limit the application of the ECD probes to a precise target area. Back shots are the preferred target area when practical.

3. Medical Considerations:

    a. Personnel should be aware that there is a higher risk of sudden death in subjects under the influence of drugs and/or exhibiting symptoms associated with excited delirium. In addition, positional asphyxia—a death that occurs when a subject's body position interferes with breathing, either when the chest is restricted from expanding properly or when the position of the subject's head obstructs the airway—may exacerbate the condition of any individual who has received an ECD application.

4. When deploying an ECD, officers will:

    a. When encountering subjects wearing heavy or loose clothing on the upper body, consider the legs as a target;

    b. Initial use of the ECD shall be a standard five-second cycle, and then the officer will evaluate the need to apply a second five-second cycle after providing the subject a reasonable opportunity to comply. Each subsequent five-second cycle requires separate justification. Once the subject has been exposed to three cycles, the ECD shall be deemed ineffective and another use of force option will be considered, unless exigent circumstances exist;

    c. Assess the suspect's actions after each application of the ECD;

    d. Control and restrain immediately. Begin control and restraint procedures, including cuffing under power, as soon as is reasonably safe and practical to do so in order to minimize the total duration of ECD exposure(s). The device user, and those assisting the user, should avoid touching the probes, wires, and the areas between the probes to avoid accidental shock during the electrical discharge;

    e. The use of "touch stun" mode should only be used to supplement Probe Mode to complete the Neuro-Muscular Incapacitation

(NMI) effect. The ECD "touch stun" mode requires the same level of justification as probe deployment. Each "touch stun" must be separately justified and documented on the Use of Force Report.

Post Use of Force Procedures:

1. All ECD activations are reportable with the exception of conducting a spark check. Unintentional activations will be reported on an Officer's Report.

2. Following an ECD deployment, the officer will:
   a. Notify immediate supervisors that an ECD has been used as soon as reasonably possible after deployment. Summon medical attention when subject is injured or claims injury;
   b. Ensure the probes are removed from the subject's skin by an ECD certified officer. If one or more probes strike the head, neck, or groin, officers shall take prompt care to monitor the condition of the subject and ensure probes penetrating these areas are removed by medical personnel;
   c. Handle the probes in the same manner as contaminated needles and sharps in accordance with department bio-hazard disposal procedures (see 5/110.10), and impound all probes, wires and cartridges as evidence. In cases of deadly force or in-custody death CSI will impound the probes;
   d. Complete Use of Force Report in Blue Team;
   e. Present deployed ECD to supervisor for data upload prior to end of shift, if a reportable use of force incident occurred;
   f. Forward a copy of the Use of Force Report, via Blue Team, to the supervisor;
   g. Notify detention personnel, at the time of booking, that the subject has been struck with ECD probes or received a touch stun.

3. The officer's supervisor will:
   a. Respond to the scene when a ECD has been used and notify the area lieutenant and/or watch commander that an ECD has been used;
   b. Conduct an investigation of the ECD usage to determine justification and adherence to procedure, as well as to correct any identifiable training deficiencies (NOTE: Acting supervisors are not authorized to complete this investigation);
   c. Assist with the completion of the Use of Force Report in Blue Team as necessary;
   d. Ensure the data record of the ECD and/or the video in which a reportable use of force incident occurs into Blue Team prior to

the end of shift. (X26 uploads must be attached in either a .pdf or .rtf format);

    e. Ensure photographs are taken of the site of the puncture/probe impacts and any related injuries. Attach to the Use of Force Report in Blue Team;

    f. Verify the probes, wires and cartridges are properly impounded and arrange for replacement cartridges. Accidental discharges will not require impounding of the probes, wires and cartridges unless there has been an injury.

4. The area lieutenant/watch commander will respond to the scene if serious bodily injury resulted from the use of the ECD.

5. Following an ECD deployment, the bureau/area commander will:

    a. Ensure that the video has been viewed, if there is any, prior to completing the Blue Team administrative review;

    b. Ensure the Use of Force Report is complete, accurate and forwards the report to the Internal Affairs Section via Blue Team;

    c. Ensure a control log is maintained for ECD/cartridge check-out and check-in, and repairs.

Use of the ECD Camera

After an officer fires an ECD, the video evidence must be uploaded by the officer's supervisor into Blue Team prior to the end of shift (X26 uploads must be attached in either a .pdf or .rtf format). The supervisor will also upload video that did not result in the officer firing the ECD if the video has sufficient evidentiary value, and attach an event number.

H. *Low Lethality Shotguns*

Level of Control:

1. Intermediate Force—when fired at a distance of five yards or greater.
2. Deadly Force—when fired at a distance less than five yards.

Description of Tool:

1. Low lethality shotguns are department-issued Remington 870 shotguns with the fore end and stock colored orange.
2. The ammunition is a 12 gauge, drag stabilized, less lethal round. The shell is clear/translucent, containing a 40 grain tear-shaped yellow beanbag with # 9 shot. The round has "drag stabilized beanbag" imprinted on the side.

Certification/POST Requirements:

1. Entry level training is taught at the LVMPD police and corrections academies.
2. Officers must re-qualify annually with the low lethality shotgun.

Inspection Requirement:

Officers will inspect their shotgun prior to the start of each shift to verify that it is only loaded with department-issued low lethality munitions.

Deployment Requirement:

1. Prior to firing a low lethality shotgun, when feasible, the officer will announce a warning to the subject and other officers of the intent to deploy the low lethality shotgun if the subject does not comply with commands.

    For example, *"Police! Do what I am telling you to do, or I will shoot you with a bean bag, and it will hurt."*
2. Officer shall give the subject a reasonable opportunity to voluntarily comply.
3. Two officers must be present if a low lethality shotgun is deployed.
4. Correction officers will continue to follow their standard operating procedures regarding the use of the low lethality shotgun.

Approved Use:

1. This tool will be used only in accordance with policy and department training.
2. The low lethality shotgun should only be used against persons who are armed with a weapon that could cause serious injury or death to themselves or others, or when a subject poses an imminent threat to the safety of the officer or other persons. This includes, but is not limited to: an edged weapon, club, pipe, bottle, brick, etc.
3. Officers are cautioned that the target area for impact munitions substantially differs from a deadly force target area. Instead of aiming for center mass of the body, the low lethality shotgun is aimed at abdomen, thighs or forearms. The head, neck, and groin should be avoided.
4. It may be used as an option to deadly force only when circumstances allow the officer involved to bring an incident to a safe conclusion without unnecessary risk to the officers.

Disapproved Use:

1. The low lethality shotgun will not be used in the following circumstances

    a. Against persons who are holding a firearm unless there are compelling reasons to do so which can be clearly articulated.

    b. In a civil unrest situation unless authorized by a lieutenant or above, and each application must have a specific targeted individual who presents an imminent threat; and it must be reasonably assured that other individuals in the crowd who pose no threat of violence will not be struck by the munitions.

    c. When the subject is visibly pregnant, unless deadly force is the only other option.

2. The low lethality shotgun should not be used in the following circumstances unless there are compelling reasons to do so which can be clearly articulated:

    a. When the subject is at the extremes of age (elderly and young children) or physically disabled;

    b. When a suspect is in an elevated position where a fall is likely to cause serious injury or death;

    c. When subject is handcuffed or otherwise restrained;

    d. As a breeching tool.

Tactical Considerations:

Officers should not fire the low lethality shotgun through mediums, such as glass or chain link fences, because the bag may tear and lead shot may be released.

Supervisory Responsibility:

1. In use of force incidents the area supervisor will:

    a. Proceed immediately to the incident involving the low lethality shotgun deployment and assume tactical control;

    b. Ensure that low lethality shotgun deployment is appropriate for the incident;

    c. If low lethality shotgun deployment is inappropriate for the incident, modify or countermand deployment.

Post Use of Force Procedures:

1. After firing the low lethality shotgun, an officer must immediately notify his supervisor and summon medical attention for the subject.

2. If a deadly force incident has occurred, the area supervisor will notify dispatch, and request appropriate notifications be made.

3. The area/watch commander will respond when a subject has been struck with the low lethality shotgun projectile, and conduct a preliminary interview with the officer to determine who will investigate the use of force. If the low lethality shotgun was fired at a distance

of closer than 5 yards, the incident shall be investigated as a deadly force incident and require a FIT and CIRT response. If the distance is determined to be 5 yards or greater, the supervisor will conduct the use of force investigation, and ensure a crime scene analyst responds.

4. The supervisor will document the scene and situation, and conduct interviews with other witnesses, if any. The documentation will be entered into Blue Team by the involved officer.

5. The officer will advise detention facility supervisor at the time of booking that the subject has been struck with the low lethality shotgun projectile and what medical attention has been administered to the subject.

I. *Use of Canine*

Level of Control:
Low Level—No bites
Intermediate Force—With bites

Certification/POST Requirements:
1. All police service dogs and detector dogs (explosive, narcotic and cadaver detection) will be initially certified.
2. Police service dogs will be re-certified on a quarterly basis, while detector dogs will be re-certified on a semi-annual basis.

Inspection Requirement:
Maintenance training with the K-9 team should occur on a daily basis to ensure the training standards are maintained.

Deployment Requirement:
K9 teams can be requested through Communications, 24 hours a day, 7 days a week. A K-9 team may need to be called out upon the approval of the section lieutenant or his designee.

Approved Use:
1. Canine will be used only in accordance with policy and department training.
2. LVMPD's police canine provides many valuable services, including searches and criminal apprehension, evidence and contraband searches and detection, locating missing persons, and public relations activities.
3. K-9 may be used in searches for misdemeanor suspects when the dog is maintained on a leash.

4. Canines are available to assist in searches, crowd control (only when approved by a lieutenant or above, and in accordance with policy 2/113.01, Use of Police Dogs), explosive and narcotic detection, in addition to regular patrol duties and special assignments.
5. A police service dog may be used by the handler to perform a search or apprehension and in compliance with this policy.
6. Canine is approved when there is probable cause to believe the suspect has committed a crime or is a danger to themselves or others, and when the suspect is actively evading efforts to take them into custody and the use of a canine would reduce risk to officers or the public.

Disapproved Use:
The use of canines in crowd control is highly discouraged, and this tactic will only be employed in accordance with policy 2/113.01, Use of Police Dogs.

Tactical Considerations:
1. In police operations, canine handlers are in charge and responsible for their dogs' deployment.
2. When it is believed a suspect may be armed with a weapon likely to cause injury or death to the police service dog, the handler may exercise his/her discretion before deploying the dog.
3. Risk to Third Parties: In using police service dogs, the canine handler shall exercise reasonable care to avoid unnecessary risk of injury to persons who are not the subject of a search or apprehension.

Post Use of Force Procedures:
1. The use of force scene will be immediately secured.
2. The canine officer/handler will immediately request medical assistance for any person who is injured or complains of injury.
3. The injuries will be photographed.
4. The incident will be documented on a Use of Force Report.
5. All uses of force by a K-9 handler team will be immediately investigated by the member's immediate supervisor or another K-9 Detail supervisor. This investigation will include interviews of the witnesses and the suspect, if appropriate, and if the interview will not compromise any criminal investigation.
6. Injuries caused by the police service dog to persons who were not the subject of the search will be documented in an Officer's Report, and will require a supervisor response.

J. *Precision Intervention Technique:*
   Level of Control:

   Intermediate Force—PIT may be used to apprehend violators at speeds 40mph or below. Deadly Force—PIT is considered deadly use of force in the following instances:
   1. At speeds of more than 40mph;
   2. When used on motorcycles;
   3. When used to stop a vehicle with deflated tires;
   4. When used on high center of gravity vehicles likely to roll over, such as vans, SUVs, and jeeps;
   5. In circumstances creating a substantial risk of death or serious bodily injury.

   Description:

   PIT is a specific manner of intentional contact using a police vehicle against a fleeing vehicle to cause the fleeing vehicle to come to a stop.

   Certification/POST Requirements:
   1. Entry level training is taught at the LVMPD police and corrections academies.
   2. Officers are trained on the PIT and when its use is permissible.
   3. Only commissioned officers who maintain current certification may use this stopping technique.

   Deployment Requirement:
   1. Prior to initiating a PIT, officers will use their emergency equipment (red lights and sirens) and will give the operator of the suspect vehicle a reasonable opportunity to stop.
   2. Officers will broadcast through dispatch the intent to use PIT if circumstances permit. Otherwise, notification will be made after the fact.
   Approved Use:
   1. This tool will be used only in accordance with policy and department training.
   2. Circumstances warranting the use of PIT as deadly force are as follows:
      a. Continued movement of the pursued vehicle would place others in danger of serious bodily injury or death; and/or
      b. Apparent risk of harm, to other than the occupants of the pursued vehicle, is so great as to outweigh the risk of harm in making the forcible stop; and

   c. Other means of apprehension have been considered and rejected as impractical, i.e., continue to follow, stop sticks, call for the air unit.

Disapproved Use:
   1. PIT will not be used unless the suspect demonstrates he/she is attempting to evade police and the elements necessary for an approved Vehicular Pursuit (6/014.00) are present (i.e., violent felony offense or suspect presents a clear and immediate danger to the public).
   2. Officers driving department truck or SUV-type vehicles are not authorized to use PIT.

Tactical Considerations:
   1. It is important that the PIT is applied within the parameters of the law and department policies to ensure the safety of persons and property, while enforcing the law by bringing a fleeing vehicle to a stop and taking suspects into custody for their criminal charges.
   2. Officers will consider other means of apprehension before attempting forcible stops and will use a reasonable amount of force.
   3. Officers will consider the safety of the public and suspects before executing this technique. The following locations and hazards should be evaluated:
      a. Areas with pedestrians;
      b. Other vehicle traffic;
      c. Parked vehicles;
      d. Telephone/utility poles;
      e. Bridges;
      f. Areas adjacent to paved roads with a large elevation change.

Supervisory Responsibility:
   1. Immediately acknowledge notification over the radio, and assume responsibility for controlling PIT;
   2. Order discontinuation of the PIT when the necessity for apprehension is outweighed by the dangers of the PIT;
   3. Consider use of other options.

Post Use of Force Procedures:
   Where there is contact with another vehicle, the incident will be investigated as either an accident or a Use of Force.

1. PIT (successful uses, attempts and/or declared uses) is considered reportable force and must be reported by completing the Use of Force Report in Blue Team;
2. A Pursuit Report in Blue Team will also be completed when the PIT was used during a pursuit;
3. The field supervisors shall respond to the PIT location and assume responsibility for the scene ensuring all applicable reports are completed and required notifications made.
4. The Communications supervisor shall notify a commissioned supervisor and a Traffic supervisor whenever PIT and/or vehicle ramming has been used to terminate a pursuit. They will advise a Traffic supervisor and the Director of Risk Management whenever the use of PIT and/or vehicle ramming results in property damage, injury, or death. The Traffic supervisor will respond, evaluate and determine Traffic's response. If it has been determined that the PIT has been a use of deadly force, the Fatal Detail, CIRT, and FIT will respond.
5. Traffic officers shall respond to assist with the traffic investigation. Since PIT is a planned enforcement technique, an accident report will not be required. In the event of third-party property damage, the responding traffic officer will complete the LVMPD 42, Vehicle Incident Report.
6. The on duty supervisor shall review the PIT to determine if procedures were followed. They will forward the report up through their chain to the bureau/area commander for review, and initiate any necessary corrective actions.
7. The bureau/area commander will ensure that the necessary investigative and corrective actions have been followed. He or she will record the comments/actions and forward the report to the Internal Affairs Bureau, via Blue Team.
8. If a vehicle belonging to an uninvolved citizen is damaged, the watch commander will respond to:
   a. Offer the citizen alternative transportation, if available and necessary;
   b. Offer to tow the damaged vehicle at department expense using the duty service to an LVMPD contract repair facility, or if the citizen insists, to a facility of the citizen's choice, for repair/replacement at the earliest opportunity;
   c. Inform Risk Management, via Communications, of the damage and location where the vehicle will be towed. Risk Management will determine if a response is necessary;
   d. Instruct the citizen to contact Risk Management the next work day.

K. *Blocking:*

Level of Control:

Low Level Force

Description:

Blocking is the positioning of a police vehicle in the path of a suspect vehicle where contact between the vehicles is not anticipated or is anticipated to be minimal. In circumstances where the officer initiates contact it is a reportable use of force. In the use of blocking, the potential for injuries and vehicle damages are low. If the suspect initiates contact, the incident will be investigated as an incident.

Approved Use:
1. This tactic will be used only in accordance with policy.
2. The intent of blocking is to prevent the escape of a suspect by utilizing a vehicle to block the path of the suspect vehicle when contact is not anticipated or probable.

Tactical Considerations:

Officers will consider the safety of the public and suspects before executing this technique. The following locations and hazards should be evaluated:
   a. Seriousness of the crime;
   b. The number of suspects;
   c. If the suspect(s) are known to have weapons;
   d. The potential of the suspect using their vehicle as a weapon;
   e. The potential tactical disadvantage due to the close proximity of the suspect;
   f. The potential for creating a crossfire situation.

Post Use of Force Procedures:
1. This is a reportable use of force whenever contact is made between vehicles.
   a. If the officer initiates contact with the suspect vehicle with his patrol vehicle the contact will be reported as a Use of Force in Blue Team; if the suspect vehicle is unoccupied, contact will be reported as a vehicle incident.
   b. If the suspect vehicle unintentionally touches the patrol vehicle, the contact will be reported as a traffic incident. If the suspect intentionally strikes the patrol vehicle while it is occupied, the contact will be investigated as a potential crime.

L. *Stationary Vehicle Immobilization Technique (Pinching)*
Level of Control:
Low Level Force

Description:
Pinching is a pre-planned containment tactic that uses low-speed, intentional vehicle contact with a suspect's vehicle. This tactic is limited for use by specialized units with Bureau Commander's approval and training. The purpose is to render a vehicle immobile so that suspects can be taken into custody. Patrol officers may use a blocking technique.

Certification/POST Requirements:
1. Personnel assigned to an approved unit intending to use this technique for a preplanned apprehension, must re-certify each year by attending EVOC training in conjunction with PIT training.
2. Approval necessary for specialized units to train in and use this technique must be given by the specialized unit's bureau commander, and the ODB commander.
3. Training records for personnel certified in this technique will be maintained by the Training Section of ODB.

Deployment Requirement:
The officer has a reasonable belief that the suspect has committed a crime and has been attempting to evade, or has the potential to harm themselves or others.

Approved Use:
1. This pre-planned tactic is not approved for use by Patrol.
2. This tactic will be used only in accordance with policy and department training.
    a. Pinching may be used as an apprehension technique when it is necessary and reasonable to do so under the circumstances.
    b. It is authorized for specialized units who have gathered intelligence information on a specific suspect(s), and can articulate the need for the application of the technique based on the suspects' potential for violence, and the need to prevent a vehicular pursuit.

Tactical Considerations:
Officers will consider the safety of the public and suspects before executing this technique. The following locations and hazards should be evaluated:
1. Seriousness of the crime;

2. The number of suspects;
3. If the suspect(s) are known to have weapons;
4. The potential of the suspect using their vehicle as a weapon;
5. The potential tactical disadvantage due to the close proximity of the suspect;
6. The potential for creating a crossfire situation;
7. The size/weight of the suspect vehicle compared to the police vehicle.

Supervisory Responsibility:
1. Supervisors assigned to units authorized to use this technique will ensure all personnel operating LVMPD vehicles in a Stationary Vehicle Immobilization employment are current on annual certifications.
2. Order discontinuation of the pinch when the necessity for apprehension is outweighed by the dangers of the pinch.
3. Ensure this is the best tactic and that other reasonable options have been considered.

Post Use of Force Procedures:
1. This is a reportable use of force whenever contact is made between vehicles.
2. This technique is not considered an accident.

D. *Firearm Use:*
Level of Control:
    Deadly Force—Shots fired

Description:
    See policy 5/208.02 Authorized Firearms and Associated Equipment

Certification/POST Requirements:
    See policy 5/108.14 Firearms Training

Inspection Requirement:
1. Ensure weapon is clean and functional at all times;
2. Ensure weapon is loaded with department duty ammunition and not mixed with practice ammunition;
3. Officer is responsible to know how many rounds are loaded in each magazine.

Deployment Requirement:
1. Before using a firearm, officers will, whenever feasible, identify themselves and state their intention to shoot.

Example: *"Police! Stop or I'll shoot!"*
2. Officer shall give the subject a reasonable opportunity to voluntarily comply.

Approved Use:
1. This tool will be used only in accordance with policy and department training.
2. Officers are to fire their weapons only to stop and incapacitate an assailant from completing a potentially deadly act. Officers should shoot at the "center mass" for maximum stopping effectiveness and minimal danger to innocent bystanders.
3. Protect the officer or others from what is reasonably believed to be an imminent threat of death or serious bodily injury.
4. Prevent the escape of a fleeing felon who the officer has probable cause to believe has committed a violent felony crime and is an imminent threat to human life if escape should occur (See NRS 171.1455 and Tennessee v. Garner, 471 U.S. 1(1985)).
5. Destroying Injured or Dangerous Animals—Officers may destroy an injured or dangerous animal under the following circumstances:
   a. In self-defense;
   b. To prevent serious harm to the officer or others; or
   c. When the animal is so badly injured as to require humane relief from further suffering.

NOTE: A seriously wounded or injured animal may be destroyed only after all attempts have been made to request assistance from the agency (Humane Society, animal control, game warden, etc.) responsible for the disposal of animals. The destruction of vicious animals involves the same rules set forth for self-defense and the defense and safety of others. (See policy 5/109.08 for an exception regarding the Humane Disposal of Animals at Resident Locations.) Also, if the animal's owner is present, the owner will be allowed, at his option, to transport the animal to veterinary care.

Disapproved Use:
   a. Officers are not authorized to draw or display their firearms, except for training at an approved firearms range, unless the circumstances create reasonable belief that it may be necessary to use the firearm in the performance of their duty.
   b. Officers are not authorized to discharge their firearm:
      a. As warning shots;
      b. If it appears likely that an innocent person may be injured;

    c. Either at or from a moving vehicle, unless it is absolutely necessary to do so to protect against imminent threat to the life of the officer or others. The imminent threat must be by means other than the vehicle, itself:
1) Officers will attempt to move out of the path of an oncoming vehicle, if possible, rather than discharge their firearms;
2) Officers will not intentionally place themselves in the path of an oncoming vehicle and attempt to disable the vehicle by discharging their firearms;
3) Officers will not discharge their firearms at a fleeing vehicle (a vehicle moving away from the officer) or its driver.

Tactical Considerations:
1. An officer's decision to draw or exhibit a firearm should be based on the tactical situation at hand and the officer's reasonable belief there is a substantial risk that the situation will escalate to the point where deadly force may be justified. Unnecessarily drawing or exhibiting a firearm may limit an officer's alternatives in controlling a situation, create unnecessary anxiety on the part of citizens, and result in an unwarranted or accidental discharge of the firearm.
2. Officers are to fire their weapons only to stop and incapacitate an assailant from completing a potentially deadly act or causing serious bodily injury.
3. Officers should shoot at the "center mass" for maximum stopping effectiveness and minimal danger to innocent bystanders.
4. Flashlights mounted to firearms will be used only for the purposes authorized and intended and will not be used routinely in the place of a hand-held flashlight.

N. *Deployment of Rifles*
Level of Control:
Deadly Force—Shots fired

Description:
See policy 5/208.02 Authorized Firearms and Associated Equipment

Certification/POST Requirements:
See policy 5/108.14 Firearms Training

Inspection Requirement:
1. Ensure weapon is clean and functional at all times;

2. Ensure weapon is loaded with department duty ammunition and not mixed with practice ammunition;

3. Officer is responsible to know how many rounds are loaded in each magazine.

Deployment Requirement:

1. If there is a potential for deadly force an officer may deem an approved rifle is appropriate based on distance, available cover, and tactical situation presented. It is important for an officer to understand terminal ballistic capabilities and limitations of the rifle to be deployed.

2. It is incumbent on the officer to use discretion when deploying and displaying the rifle, and to only deploy the rifle when the situation dictates. The officer must be aware of the number of rifles already deployed.

3. Officer(s) deploying rifle(s) will:

   a. Announce intent to deploy the rifle via the radio and receive an acknowledgment from dispatch;

   b. Whenever possible, deploy the rifle using a two-officer team consisting of a single rifle carrier supported by a cover officer to ensure security of the scene;

   c. Advise dispatch, via the radio, of deployment location and update dispatch and others assigned to the event whenever deployment location changes, thus providing situational awareness to all personnel on-scene of location of deployed rifle(s);

   d. Advise dispatch, via the radio, of whether or not deploying officer is accompanied by a cover officer.

4. Communications will re-broadcast that a rifle has been deployed and notify the area supervisor of the deployment.

Approved Use:

1. This tool will be used only in accordance with policy and department training.

Supervisory Responsibility:

1. It is the supervisor's responsibility to ensure proper deployment of rifles and address over-deployment.

2. Area supervisor will:

   a. Proceed immediately to the incident involving the rifle deployment and assume tactical control, when possible;

   b. Ensure that rifle deployment is appropriate for the incident;

    c. If rifle deployment is inappropriate for the incident, modify or countermand deployment.

Post Use of Force Procedures:
1. Upon completion of the incident the deploying officer's supervisor will ensure that officer(s) who deployed a rifle complete a rifle deployment report via Blue Team.
2. The report will detail the following:
    a. Details of the incident;
    b. Justification for the rifle deployment, including the nature of the threat resulting in decision to deploy rifle.
3. When multiple officers deploy rifles at a single incident, the sergeant should designate one of the officers to complete the Rifle Deployment Report, listing all officers that deployed a rifle as "involved officers" in the report.
4. Rifle deployment reports are not required when a rifle(s) is deployed as part of training or a tactical drill exercise (i.e., MACTAC tests).
5. SWAT is exempt from rifle deployment reporting procedures.
6. Corrections officers will follow their standard operation procedures when conducting a high risk transport, and are exempt from rifle deployment reporting procedures.
7. Supervisor of the deploying officer will:
    a. Conduct a review of the deployment and make appropriate comments in the Rifle Deployment Report in Blue Team, to include any supervisory decisions countermanding or modifying original deployment;
    b. Forward the report to the supervising lieutenant for review;
6. Lieutenant reviewing will:
    a. Conduct a review of the Rifle Deployment Report and make appropriate comments;
    b. Forward Rifle Deployment Report to the bureau/area commander;
7. Bureau/Area Commander will review Rifle Deployment Report and concur or disagree with deployment. If deployment was not in compliance with policy, take appropriate corrective action to include timely notification of the Division Commander.

XI. REPORTABLE FORCE INCIDENTS

Reportable force incidents which require the completion of a Use of Force Report in Blue Team include, but are not limited to:
1. Empty Hand Tactics (Takedown with injury, Strikes, Kicks)

2. Baton/Impact Weapons (Jabs, Strikes)
3. OC Spray
4. ECD (To include spark display)
5. LVNR® (Level 1, 2 and 3)
6. K-9 (With bites)
7. Blocking (With intentional contact)
8. Stationary Vehicle Immobilization Technique (Pinching—With contact between vehicles)
9. P.I.T. (Used or attempted)
10. Ramming
11. Low Lethality Shotgun
12. Firearm Use (Shots fired—outside the firearm's range, excluding off-duty situations such as hunting or participating in competitive shooting)
13. Deployment of Rifles (Excluding SWAT/SERT)

Supervisors will respond without necessary delay to all potential reportable uses of force. (See policy 5/109.01, Post Use of Force, for supervisor responsibilities. (2/11, 6/22/12)

5/109.00 USE OF FORCE
A.S. 26.1.1
See Critical Policies/Procedures 6/002.00

5/109.01 POST USE OF FORCE PROCEDURES

I. USE OF FORCE INVESTIGATION AND REPORT

A. The department reviews or investigates all reportable use of force incidents to determine their justification, as well as to correct any identifiable training deficiencies. Members involved in reportable use of force incidents will immediately notify their supervisor or, if unavailable, another on-duty supervisor, and complete the Use of Force Report in Blue Team prior to the end of shift. The report should distinguish which force option was selected and why it was selected to the exclusion of other options. Supervisors will respond to each use of force incident in which reportable force is used, conduct an investigation and assist with the completion of the use of force report. (NOTE: Acting supervisors are not authorized to complete this investigation). The report will be required by each member involved in a use of force incident when reportable force is used.

B. A Use of Force Report is not required when no injury or complaint of injury occurs as a result of:
   1. Low Profile Pat Down/High Profile Pat Down/Arm Lock/Standing Search;
   2. Routine Handcuffing;
   3. Felony Prone Handcuffing (Front and Rear);
   4. Felony Prone Search Felony Kneeling;
   5. Baton Escort Technique;
   6. Takedown;
C. The following Use of Force Options do require a Use of Force Report:
   1. Any use of force greater than "restraint;"
   2. Any takedown which causes injury or verbal complaint of injury;
   3. Use of OC Spray;
   4. Lateral Vascular Neck Restraint;
   5. Use of an Electronic Control Device or a Spark Demonstration;
   6. Baton Takedowns;
   7. Baton Strikes and Jabs;
   8. Empty Hand Strikes, Punches, and Kicks;
   9. Use of a Low Lethality Shotgun;
   10. A use of force results in death or serious bodily injury;
   11. A citizen or person arrested complains that an injury has been inflicted as the result of the use of force; or
   12. PIT and/or ramming is used, attempted, or declared.
D. The following incidents require a Firearm Discharge Report:
   1. A firearm is discharged outside the LVMPD Range or other designated shooting range;
   2. A firearm is discharged resulting in death or serious bodily injury;
      a. FIT will complete the Firearm Discharge Report in these incidents.
   3. A Non-Injury or Property Damage Intentional Discharge of a Firearm Incident (which includes an intentional discharge at anything other than a person, such as a dog)
      a. CIRT will complete the Firearm Discharge Report in these incidents.

II. INVESTIGATIVE RESPONSIBILITIES: USE OF NON-DEADLY FORCE

A. Non-Deadly Force requiring a Use of Force report but not resulting in death or serious bodily injury will be investigated by the members' chain of command (excluding the low lethality shotgun).

1. The Member will:

   a. Request that Communications notify the respective immediate supervisor when a reportable non-deadly use of force occurs;
   b. If needed, request medical assistance and provide information on injuries;
   c. Complete the Use of Force Report and all other required reports connected to the incident;
   d. Forwards the Use of Force Report through the chain of command.

2. The member's Supervisor will:

   a. Respond to the scene without unnecessary delay and, if unable to respond, request an alternate supervisor at the same level or higher respond to the scene;
   b. Interview the subject(s) and member(s) involved and document their statements;
   c. Locate and interview any witnesses and on-scene medical personnel (when applicable) and document their statements and/or log the names of any potential witnesses who claim no first-hand knowledge;
   d. Collect evidence and ensure photographs are taken of the subject(s), the scene and member(s) involved when possible and appropriate;
   e. Ensure all reports are completed and that the incident is properly documented;
   f. Notify the area lieutenant or watch commander when an Electronic Control Device has been used;
   g. Notify Communications and the area lieutenant/DSD lieutenant or watch commander when significant force was used or alleged.

3. The Area Lieutenant/Watch Commander will:

   a. Personally examine and interview the subject regarding the incident when significant force is used and if unable to respond, request an alternate supervisor at the same level respond to the scene;
   b. Ensure interviews, photographs and reports are properly completed;
   c. Notify Internal Affairs Section Lieutenant if significant force is used;
   d. If the incident rises to the level of serious bodily injury, ensure all notifications are made and all appropriate action is being taken.

4. The Bureau/Area Commander will:

   a. Complete the Use of Force administrative review and forward to IAB.

III. INVESTIGATIVE RESPONSIBILITIES: USE OF DEADLY FORCE OR FORCE INVOLVING SERIOUS BODILY INJURY

It is the policy of this department to conduct a fair, impartial and thorough investigation of all uses of deadly force for the interest of the officer, the department and the community alike. The following procedures shall apply to all deadly force investigations:

A. *Primary Responsibilities in a Deadly Force Investigation*
   1. Major Crimes or Violent Crimes details: When available, detectives from the Major Crimes or Violent Crimes details will respond immediately to the scene, contact the Incident Commander for direction and to provide assistance.
   2. Force Investigation Team (FIT) of the Homicide Detail: The criminal investigation will seek to determine whether the use of deadly force was legally justified under criminal law. FIT also directs the investigation against a suspect who either committed crimes which led to the use of deadly force or who has committed crimes against an officer.
   3. Critical Incident Review Team (CIRT): Conducts non-criminal, administrative examinations of uses of deadly force or other high-risk police operations as directed by the Sheriff. The purpose of this review is to improve individual and agency performance through the evaluation of decision making, tactics used, supervision and the actual use of force. CIRT will then make recommendations to the Sheriff that may identify possible training needs (for the individual, squad, unit, section or department) and/or changes to policies and practices.
   4. Crime Scene Investigations Section (CSI): CSI responds to a deadly force incident to complete crime scene documentation. The ranking member of the CSI Section at the scene shall be in charge of the processing of the crime scene. Prior to commencing the crime scene investigation, the ranking FIT detective and ranking member of the CSI Section shall confer to determine the actions to be taken by those persons assigned to the scene, including which officers, detectives, and crime scene analysts shall be authorized to enter the crime scene perimeter.

B. *Involved/Witness Officer(s)*
   1. When an officer intentionally discharges a firearm at a human being, uses deadly force, has an unintentional discharge of a firearm, causes serious bodily injury or becomes aware of an incustody death, the officer will:
      a. Ensure life safety of others;
      b. Ensure the scene is safe and secure;

      c.   Notify both Communications (via radio if on-duty) and a supervisor without delay;

         1)   If needed, will request medical assistance and provide information on injuries;

         2)   Include suspect description and location.

2.   In addition, off-duty officers or plain-clothes personnel will:

      a.   Be aware of the particular danger of a potential police-on-police confrontation when first-responding officers arrive to the scene;

      b.   Make certain they are readily identifiable as officers; Off-duty officers or plain-clothes personnel should display their badges and/or identification prominently and identify themselves frequently;

      c.   Inform Communications via radio (or if off-duty and no radio available, they should call 9-1-1) if they have taken action, are armed or are wearing plainclothes;

      d.   When confronted by first-responding officers, off-duty officers or plain-clothes personnel should be aware of and obey first-responding officers' verbal commands.

3.   In deadly force investigations, FIT detectives shall be briefed, by the first-responding supervisor or supervisor in charge of the event, on the names and locations of the Involved Officer and potential Witness Officers.

      a.   When there is concern that an officer is not a Witness Officer, but an Involved Officer, the ranking FIT supervisor will make the final determination regarding the status of the officers(s).

4.   Officer statements:

      a.   Involved Officer: An officer or supervisor, who participated in, directed or influenced the application of the use of force.

         1)   Involved Officers _may_ provide a recorded statement to FIT investigators. If given, involved officer statements will be taken at least 48 hours after the incident by FIT investigators.

      b.   Witness Officer: An officer or supervisor who did not participate in or directly influence the application of the use of force.

         1)   Witness Officers are required to provide a recorded statement to FIT investigators. Witness Officer statements will be taken at a date, time and location determined by FIT investigators.

C. *Incident Responsibilities*

1.   Any officer or supervisor assigned, involved, or arrived on the scene of a use of force investigation shall not leave until released by the supervisor in charge of the event.

2.   The supervisor first on scene will act as Incident Commander (per 5/213.06) until relieved by an area lieutenant or watch commander and will:

    a.   Ensure medical attention is provided for those in need;

    b.   Coordinate the search for outstanding suspects;

    c.   Ensure the immediate crime scene is secured and protected;

    d.   Oversee the identification and isolation of witnesses;

    e.   Ensure witness officer(s) and involved officer(s) are separated and placed in a secure and safe environment.

    f.   Contact Communications and advise the type of incident and request that notifications be made;

    g.   Obtain a Public Safety Statement (PSS) from the officer(s) who have discharged a firearm or who have used deadly force to determine:

        1)   Is anyone injured? If so, where are they located?

        2)   Are there any outstanding suspects? If so, what are their description, direction and mode of travel? How long have they been gone? What crime(s) are they wanted for? What weapon(s) are they armed with?

        3)   Were you involved in an Officer Involved Shooting?

        4)   Approximately where were you when you fired the rounds?

        5)   Approximately how many rounds did you fire and in what direction did you fire them?

        6)   Do you know if any other officers fired any rounds?

        7)   Is it possible the suspect fired rounds at you? If so, from what direction were the rounds fired?

        8)   Are there any weapons or evidence that needs to be secured/protected? Where are they located?

        9)   Are you aware of any witnesses? If so, what is their location?

NOTE: The Public Safety Statement is not an interview, and must be timely. The PSS will be documented and maintained by the supervisor to relay to responding FIT investigators. If circumstances permit, the PSS will not be made in front of other participant officers. The supervisor must take appropriate action based on the information received from the PSS.

3. The Watch Commander (or an area lieutenant) will:

    a.   Respond immediately to the scene of the use of deadly force.

4. The Incident Commander will:

    a.   Designate a Command Post;

    b.   Establish the outer perimeter, the staging area, and the media staging area;

    c.   Identify and separate civilian witnesses;

    d.   Identify and separate officer witnesses;

e. Assign an Officer Witness Monitor(s).
   1) The monitor will limit the number of auxiliary and incidental contact(s) an officer may have with others.
   2) The monitor will assist the officer in contact with PEAP, chain of command, legal representative and a representative from their collective bargaining unit.
   3) The monitor will attempt to provide food, drink, restroom, and phone and allow the officer to contact family members to advise them of their welfare.

5. Major Crimes or the Violent Crimes details will:
   a. Respond immediately to begin a preliminary investigation;
   b. Ensure the Major Incident Log has been assigned and is being completed.
   c. Assist in the early management of the crime scene, the identification and separation of witnesses, and the canvass.

6. Communications will:
   1) Assign at least one additional sergeant to the scene;
      1) If sergeants are unavailable for the particular area command in which the use of deadly force occurred, the dispatcher will assign sergeants from other area commands or units other than Patrol.
   2) Ensure the proper notifications are made immediately by utilizing the Critical Incident/OIS Group Page via the note page method.

The following guidelines for notifications are to be made by Communications dependent upon the type of incident:

1. Use of Deadly Force or Force Involving Serious Bodily Injury
   a. The officer's immediate supervisor;
   b. The watch commander;
   c. The officer's bureau commander;
   d. Major Crimes or Violent Crimes detail;
   e. FIT;
   f. CIRT;
   g. Crime Scene Investigations Section;
   h. Risk Manager.

2. A Non-Injury or Property Damage Intentional Discharge of a Firearm Incident (which includes an intentional discharge at anything other than a person, such as a dog; see Department Manual Section 5/109.08 for an exception regarding Humane Disposal of Animals at Resident Locations):
   a. The officer's immediate supervisor;
   b. The watch commander;

     c. The officer's bureau commander;

     d. Major Crimes or Violent Crimes details;

     e. Crime Scene Investigations Section;

     f. CIRT;

     g. Risk Manager.

3. Unintentional Discharge or Accidental Discharge of a Firearm:

     a. The officer's immediate supervisor;

     b. The watch commander;

     c. The officer's bureau commander;

     d. CIRT;

        1) CIRT will investigate any unintentional discharge of a firearm that occurs during a police operation, such as the inadvertent discharge of a shotgun while deploying it in response to a high-risk call.

     e. Internal Affairs;

        1) IA will investigate any accidental discharges that occur not as the result of a police operation, such as an unintentional discharge of a shotgun while inspecting it at an area command parking lot.

     f. Crime Scene Investigations Section;

     g. Risk Manager, when injury or property damage result.

4. Vehicle Accident/Incident that causes death or serious bodily injury:

     a. The officer's immediate supervisor;

     b. The watch commander;

     c. The officer's bureau commander;

     d. CIRT;

     e. FIT;

     f. Traffic Bureau/Fatal Detail.

5. The Use of PIT at speeds above 40mph when contact is made, or the deliberate ramming/intentional contact of a police vehicle with a suspect or another vehicle to stop or apprehend a suspect:

     a. The officer's immediate supervisor;

     b. The watch commander;

     c. The officer's bureau commander;

     d. CIRT;

     e. FIT;

     f. Traffic Bureau/Fatal Detail.

6. The Use of PIT at speeds below 40mph when contact is made:

     a. The officer's immediate supervisor;

     b. The watch commander;

     c. An on-duty Traffic supervisor;

> 1) If any questions or concerns arise from this PIT investigation, FIT and/or the Traffic Section/Fatal Detail shall be notified.

7. PEAP and the officer's bargaining association will be notified whenever the actions of an officer did or could have resulted in serious injury/death (including any intentional discharge of a firearm at a human being).

D. *Initial Briefing*

1. The Incident Commander will:

   a. Designate a location for the initial briefing as to provide a secure place where operational security measures can be met. The briefing location will not compromise the integrity of the immediate crime scene. Interruptions to the briefing should be kept to a minimum. Lighting and noise factors should be considered;

   b. Conduct the initial briefing; the time of the briefing will be logged. Only essential personnel will attend the briefing. This procedure supports the integrity of the FIT's investigation. Essential personnel are identified as:

      1) The supervisor who obtained the Public Safety Statement;
      2) Major Crimes or Violent Crimes personnel;
      3) Investigative Services Division Commander;
      4) FIT personnel;
      5) CSI personnel;
      6) CIRT personnel;
      7) Traffic Bureau/Fatal Detail.

      All other personnel are deemed non-essential and will be excluded from the briefing.

   c. Initiate a documented roll call of essential personnel announcing their names and positions. A FIT detective will complete a log of the roll call and note the briefing times. The ISD Commander, or his designee, will monitor the roll call to check that only essential personnel are included in the brief and he or she will address any divergences from this protocol;

   d. List any safety concerns, such as firearms evidence, bio-hazards, and potential security issues at a medical facility which may surround the incident;

   e. Brief personnel on the circumstances and surrounding details of the department's response to the incident, including the steps to secure the scene, identification of witnesses, and the progression of the canvass of the surrounding area; the involved officer's location, welfare and who is accompanying them shall also be briefed; and the supervisor who received the Public Safety Statement from the involved officer(s) will relay this information in the initial briefing;

    f.   At the close of the brief, designates control of the scene and investigation to the FIT lieutenant or supervisor. This transition will be communicated to Dispatch via the radio.

  2. The Investigative Services Division Commander or his designee will:

    a.   Brief the involved officer's chain of command on the circumstances surrounding the incident. In addition, the Force Investigation Team will brief the Office of Public Information prior to any media release.

E. *Scene Walkthrough with the Officer Involved*

  1. The purpose of the scene walkthrough with an officer involved is to help investigators develop an understanding of the scene and identify potential physical evidence. The walkthrough is voluntary and it is not an interview. Detailed narratives shall be avoided. If more than one officer is involved in the incident, their walkthroughs will be conducted independently of each other. Walkthroughs will be conducted by FIT personnel. The personnel observing the walkthrough shall be limited to:

    a.   The officer involved or witness officer;

    b.   A representative of the officer or legal counsel;

    c.   FIT detectives (2);

    d.   FIT sergeant and/or lieutenant;

    e.   CSA Supervisor.

  2. Witness officers will provide information as needed and directed either by supervisory personnel or the FIT. FIT will provide a timely briefing on the walkthrough to CIRT.

  3. Upon release of the crime scene by FIT to CSI, subsequent walkthroughs of the immediate crime scene will be limited to personnel who demonstrate an investigatory purpose, including CIRT personnel, and will be conducted at the discretion and at the direction of Crime Scene Investigations supervisory personnel only after initial documentation, primarily the overall photography, of the scene has been completed and potential areas containing physical evidence have been identified and protected.

  4. Crime Scene Investigations personnel will collect, preserve, and book physical evidence within the identified crime scenes. The FIT supervisor is responsible for determining the steps taken in the handling of any potential video surveillance. Such video surveillance evidence shall be seized and booked in accordance with LVMPD Search and Seizure Policy, Section 4.

5. No photographs of the crime scene shall be taken independent of the Crime Scene Investigations Section. If other photographs, audio or video recordings have been taken, such evidence will be reported to the Force Investigation Team by any officer who has such knowledge.

F. *Media Release*
   1. Media inquiries shall be referred to the Robbery/Homicide Bureau Commander, or their designee. The bureau commander will provide liaison with the on-scene and follow-up inquires from the media. At the close of the scene investigation, the FIT lieutenant will prepare the written media release. The Office of Public Information will also be an available resource in deadly-force incidents.
   2. The identity of officers involved in deadly force incidents will not be released to the public or media for 48 hours. The Office of Public Information will collect media coverage of deadly force incidents and will provide the coverage to FIT and to CIRT. Such coverage may be a resource for both the investigative and administrative review.

G. *Countdown of Firearms and Photographs of Officer Involved*
   1. The FIT Supervisor will:
      a. Ensure the involved officer relinquishes custody of the discharged firearm to the Crime Scene Investigations Section;
      b. Provide a replacement if the firearm used was a handgun for which there is a department-issued replacement available;
         1) No immediate replacement will be provided for any department-issued or personally-owned long guns, such as an AR-15 rifle or shotgun.
   2. The CSI Supervisor will:
      a. Ensure, in an officer-involved shooting, that the officer's firearm(s) are not modified, operated, loaded or unloaded in any fashion following the shooting prior to countdown.
      b. Direct the documentation of the officer's immediate condition. Standard documentation will include, but is not limited to:
         1) Photographs of at least four full-length views of the officer (front, back, right and left sides) in a standing position;
         2) Items of evidence or injuries to show general location and condition;
         3) Items of evidence or injuries (with and without scale) so they can be recognized and identified;

      4) Items or areas (patterned injuries, bloodstains, bite marks, etc.) where it is necessary to document class and individual characteristics for future comparison, and at least one facial view.

   3. Ensure the officer's equipment is photographed in place (on the person) prior to examination to show the location, presence, and condition of any tools (firearm, ECD, baton, etc.) available during the incident;

   4. Direct the countdown of a officer's firearm. It is preferable the countdown occurs at the Force Investigation Team's office; however, circumstances may dictate another location is utilized.

     a. Prior to handling specialized weapons or an unfamiliar firearm, Crime Scene Investigations personnel will permit an officer who is familiar with the firearm to unload the firearm, under supervision, to ensure a safe countdown.

H. *Force Investigation Team's Interview Guidelines*

   1. The involved officers have the same rights and privileges regarding criminal investigation interviews that other citizens have.

   2. When practical, involved officers will be interviewed last to ensure investigators have as complete a picture as possible prior to the interview.

   3. FIT will conduct a voluntary interview, a minimum of 48 hours after the incident, with the officer whose use of force resulted in death. Since the interviews are voluntary, involved officers have the power to decline to be interviewed. A pre-interview which discusses details of the incident prior to recording a statement shall be avoided.

   4. If any involved officer refuses to provide a voluntary statement, the Force Investigation Team may submit the case to the District Attorney's Office without such a statement. If any officer refuses to provide a voluntary statement or decides to wait before giving one, he or she will be admonished not to discuss the incident with any other officers involved in the incident. In those cases where an officer declines to provide a timely interview, investigators shall document their efforts to obtain the interview, including when the request was made and to whom it was directed. A subsequent compelled interview, conducted by the Critical Incident Review Team, may be scheduled at a later date and in compliance with the rights and obligations set out in NRS 289.

I. *Reporting Procedures*

   1. If a surviving suspect has committed a crime, FIT detectives will complete the arrest report and arrest package. FIT will be responsible for investigating any crimes committed against an officer by a suspect. FIT may delegate any other crimes that occurred prior to the use-of-deadly-force incident, or were learned of afterwards, to the appropriate investigative detail.

2. The Involved Officer's Immediate Supervisor will:
    a. Complete LVMPD 117, Notice of Relief of Duty, thus placing the involved officer in relief of duty status for any incident involving the use of deadly force or wherein serious bodily injury results. Supervisors will place other officers in relief of duty status at the direction of PEAP. This will be done based on all the facts and circumstances known to the PEAP personnel and only for the well-being of that officer.
    b. After the initial response and preliminary investigation, if an officer's supervisor or chain of command becomes aware of either an allegation of misconduct or performance issues so egregious if proven true will most likely result in punitive actions against the officer, a Statement of Complaint will be completed by the supervisor. The notification of the internal investigation will be communicated and coordinated with FIT, CIRT and the Internal Affairs Bureau prior to contacting the officer. Under most circumstances, the internal investigation will not proceed until the criminal investigation by FIT has been completed.
3. The FIT Supervisor will:
    a. Complete the Use of Force Report in Blue Team and forward it to Internal Affairs for uses of deadly force. If an officer refuses to give a voluntary statement to FIT, the officer will be required to complete a Use of Force Report in Blue Team per department policy.
    b. Ensure the following forms are completed and provided to the Force Investigation Team to be memorialized in the case file of a use of deadly force incident:
        1) The Public Safety Statement form;
        2) Inner Perimeter Log;
        3) Major Incident Log;
4. The Investigative Services Division Commander, or his designee, will brief Executive Staff at various stages of the investigation. This may include the following:
    a. After the initial briefing at the scene;
    b. An update upon the conclusion of the preliminary investigation;
    c. At a 72-hour briefing to the Sheriff;
    d. An investigative status update as requested.

J. *Police Employee Assistance Program (PEAP) Involvement*
    1. PEAP personnel respond to use of force incidents resulting in death, serious injury, or where death could have resulted or any intentional discharge of a firearm at a human being. PEAP arranges for psychological

counseling of involved officers by a qualified psychologist and advises the appropriate chain of command of the officer's readiness to return to duty.

2. Upon PEAP personnel's arrival to the scene they will contact the FIT supervisor. After conferring with the FIT supervisor, PEAP will provide assistance to the officers involved in the incident.

3. PEAP personnel will not become involved in the investigative process, nor will personnel discuss any details of the incident with the involved officer prior to the officer providing a statement to FIT. PEAP personnel will be able to interact with involved officers and can explain the investigative process to them while the officer is under the observation of the Officer Witness Monitor.

4. If PEAP personnel believe a Critical Incident Stress Debriefing is appropriate after a deadly force incident, PEAP will seek prior approval of such a forum with the FIT lieutenant and the Critical Incident Review Team lieutenant.

K. *Contact with Suspect or Person to Whom Force Was Applied*

1. If a suspect or person to whom force was applied is transported for emergency medical treatment, an officer shall accompany the subject to the hospital. This will guarantee the chain of evidence is preserved and memorialized and spontaneous statements can be documented. The escorting officer will verify that medical personnel are aware the subject's clothing and personal effects must be secured as evidence.

2. Interviews with a suspect or person involved in a use of deadly force will be tape recorded. If a suspect has been transported to a hospital, a FIT detective will arrange for a timely interview when it becomes permissible. Additional evidence from the suspect, such as blood or ballistic evidence will be collected at the hospital.

3. In circumstances such as an unintentional discharge or an inappropriate use of deadly force, if no reasonable suspicion or probable cause exists to warrant an investigative detention, the subject is free to leave. Timely and consensual efforts will be made to attempt to identify the subject and investigators will seek the subject's cooperation. Subjects will be told their cooperation is voluntary and such interaction will then be documented.

L. *The Administrative and Tactical Review*

1. The CIRT will verbally report to the Organizational Development Bureau Commander on preliminary review of tactical, training, and administrative issues at the 72-hour briefing.

2. During the criminal investigation conducted by the Force Investigation Team, timely copies of reports will be made available to CIRT. The criminal investigation can and will share its information freely with the administrative/tactical examination, but CIRT may not share information with the criminal investigation that was compelled under "Garity."

Upon completion of the criminal review for non-fatal incidents, the closure will be documented in a memorandum to the lieutenant of the CIRT. After receiving written notice by FIT that the criminal investigation is complete, CIRT will begin their review process. See the Critical Incident Review Team and the Use of Force Review Board policies for further information.

IV. ADMINISTRATIVE REVIEW

The Professional Standards Division will complete a documented annual use of force analysis. (2/11, 4/12)

Aiding in Escape: Arizona Department of Corrections

PURPOSE

THIS DEPARTMENT ORDER ensures that the optimum level of professionalism is maintained by Department employees and that qualified persons are recruited, selected and employed based upon bona fide occupational qualifications. The Department expects the highest ethical standards of honesty, integrity, impartiality and conduct of its employees in their interaction with inmates, offenders, former inmates/offenders, other employees and the general public. To merit the public's continued respect and confidence, employees shall observe all laws while at and away from work.

Department Order #527, Sexual Harassment and Employment Discrimination, as related to "Employee Professionalism, Ethics and Conduct" issues have been placed in a separate Department Order in order to emphasize their importance.

PROCEDURES

501.01 GENERAL RESPONSIBILITIES

1.1   All employees shall:

    1.1.1   Accept responsibility and delegated authority to efficiently and effectively perform their assigned duties in a courteous, considerate and prompt manner.

    1.1.2   Ensure their personal conduct is in accordance with this Department Order at all times.

    1.1.3   Immediately report misconduct to their chain of command.

    1.1.4   Cooperate with Department's official investigations.

    1.1.5   Ensure they maintain a professional demeanor at all times.

    1.1.6   Abide by the Department's Code of Ethics, Attachment A.

1.2   Approving authorities shall:

1.2.1 Consider knowledge and application of laws, rules, policies and procedures in Performance Appraisal for Correctional Employees (PACE) file preparation.

1.2.2 Ensure their subordinates are held accountable for compliance with this Department Order, and allegations of employee misconduct at any level are thoroughly investigated and resolved.

1.2.3 Investigate allegations of misconduct and administer appropriate corrective discipline for sustained employee misconduct, in accordance with Department Order #601, Administrative Investigations and Employee Discipline.

1.2.4 Take prompt and appropriate administrative action and/or corrective disciplinary action regarding criminal charges filed against subordinate staff, and related allegations of misconduct.

1.2.5 Seek, when appropriate, the prosecution of employees for:

    1.2.5.1 Failing to discharge their custodial responsibility, provided the failure resulted in the escape of an inmate or the serious physical injury or death of another person or inmate, pursuant to A.R.S. 13-2513.

    1.2.5.2 Engaging in sexual contact and/or intercourse with inmates or offenders under Department supervision, pursuant to A.R.S. 13-1419 and the Prison Rape Elimination Act of 2003.

        1.2.5.2.1 Department employees and offenders on release status are exempt from this restriction, provided employees were legally married to the offenders prior to sentencing.

    1.2.5.3 Other violations of law.

501.02 STAFF RELATIONSHIPS WITH INMATES, OFFENDERS AND FORMER INMATES/OFFENDERS—

Employees shall limit their relationships with inmates and inmates' families to officially authorized activities. Employees shall refrain from personal relationships with current or former inmates, offenders and inmates'/offenders' family members. Employees are required at all times to maintain a professional distance from current or former inmates/offenders and deal with them in a courteous and professional manner.

1.1 Department employees shall:

    1.1.1 Avoid being placed in situations that may compromise their professional integrity; compromise security; or cause embarrassment to the Department or the State of Arizona.

    1.1.2 Avoid undue familiarity.

    1.1.3 Report in writing all family relationships with current or former inmates/offenders to their Warden or Bureau Administrator.

    1.1.4 Immediately report, both verbally and in writing, to their immediate supervisor any request to engage in an unauthorized activity, including, but not limited to:

        1.1.4.1 Bribery.

        1.1.4.2 Attempted bribery.

        1.1.4.3 Solicitation of bribery.

        1.1.4.4 Any attempt to jeopardize accepted employee-inmate relationships and/or any unauthorized contact.

    1.1.5 Take corrective action on all inmate rule violations and offender violations of Conditions of Supervision to ensure impartiality and fairness with all inmates and offenders.

    1.1.6 Address an inmate as "inmate" followed by their surname, for example "Inmate Smith" or "Inmate Jones."

1.2 Department employees shall not:

    1.2.1 Establish personal relationships unless a prior family relationship existed and notification of relationship has been provided to their chain of command.

1.2.2   Engage in intimate contact or other inappropriate behavior with a current or former inmate/offender.

1.2.3   Engage in sexual contact or sexual intercourse with an inmate or offender.

    1.2.3.1   Employees and offenders on release status are exempt from section 1.2.2 through 1.2.3 above, provided the employee and offender were married prior to sentencing.

1.2.4   Engage in horseplay or wager with current or former inmates/offenders.

1.2.5   Enter any area, to which they are not assigned, except as is necessary in the performance of their assigned duties, or with the prior approval of the Warden, Deputy Warden, Bureau Administrator or Inspector General of the involved institution/location.

1.2.6   Take or send, except as required as part of their assigned duties, inmate or offender letters, writings, verbal or written messages, literature or reading matter or any other item without the written permission of the Warden, Deputy Warden or Bureau Administrator.

1.2.7   Have contact or communication beyond their duties without prior written Warden or Bureau Administrator approval.

1.2.8   Give inmates or offenders any food or beverage not part of their job responsibilities including food and beverages from inside or outside institutions without prior written Warden or Bureau Administrator approval.

1.2.9   Barter or deal with current or former inmates/offenders. Employees may purchase inmate arts and crafts or business products in accordance with Department Order #906, Inmate Recreation/Arts & Crafts.

1.2.10   Lend, borrow, exchange, give, take or take gifts, presents, cash or property to or from current or former inmates/offenders, or their family/friends without prior written Warden or Bureau Administrator approval.

1.2.11   Deal directly with, be involved in, or sponsor personal activities (e.g., taking inmates or offenders to a show, shopping or other activities) without official approval.

1.2.12 Discuss personal information and issues with current or former inmates/offenders or with other employees while in the presence of current or former inmates/offenders.

1.2.13 Submit verbal or written recommendations on the behalf of current or former inmates/offenders.

1.2.14 Be placed in situations where personal obligation and/or official favors are expected.

1.2.15 Periodic rotation of employees in accordance with Department Order #524, Employee Assignments and Staffing may occur to prevent over-familiarity with individual inmates or offenders.

1.2.16 The Staff Development and Training Bureau Administrator shall ensure comprehensive training is provided to employees regarding appropriate relations.

501.03 STAFF ARRESTS/NEGATIVE LAW ENFORCEMENT CONTACT

1.1 Department employees shall report immediately upon return to work/duty to their supervisor, a designee within their chain of command, or the institution Duty Officer, all contacts with law enforcement authorities that may cause embarrassment to the Department or the state of Arizona by submitting an Information Report (IR), Form 105-2. This includes, but is not limited to:

1.1.1 Arrests.

1.1.2 Citations for other than minor traffic violations.

Coercion: Model Policies for Law Enforcement in Maryland
INTERVIEWS AND INTERROGATIONS

I. Purpose:
The purpose of this policy is to provide standards and general guidelines for law enforcement interviews and interrogations that are accurate, credible and professionally accomplished.

II. Policy:
    A. It is the policy of _____ that, the conduct of police interviews and interrogations should be fair, competent, and totally objective. It is extremely important that this practice should also be perceived as non-coercive and unbiased by the courts and the general public.

    B. It is the policy of _____ that, interviews and interrogations comply with all constitutional requirements, applicable state and local laws and strictly adhere to agency investigative procedures.

    C. It is the policy of _____ to accurately and completely record or otherwise document the conditions, content, and conclusions of any interview or interrogations. This agency acknowledges the advantages of electronic recording whenever investigative and environmental conditions allow.

III. Definitions:
    A. Interview: A purposeful and non-accusatory conversation with a victim, a complainant, a witness, or even a possible criminal suspect. The atmosphere is non-custodial and the interviewee should feel that he/she is free to end or terminate the interview and leave at any time.

    B. Interrogation: During an interrogation, the person being questioned by the police is not free to leave, and police questioning or conduct is specifically designed to elicit incriminating responses implicating the person in criminal activity. All custodial interrogations shall be preceded by issuance of the *Miranda* warning.

    C. Electronic Recording: The practice of audio recording and/or videotaping an interview or interrogation. It is a violation of Maryland law to audio-tape any conversation without the consent of all parties.

D. Custody: A suspect is considered to be in custody if, under similar circumstances, a reasonable person in the suspect's position would feel that his/her liberty to move about freely or leave was being restrained in any way.

IV. Guiding Principles—Interviews:

A. Interviews are critical components of a police investigation. Most police interviews are conducted with victims, complainants and witnesses to a criminal act. Interviews may be conducted in the field, in police facilities, in vehicles, or in any other convenient location.

B. Officers should give clear notification, followed by acknowledgment by the person being interviewed that the questioning is non-custodial and that the person being questioned is free to discontinue and leave at any time.

C. A fact-finding interview of a possible criminal suspect is not an interrogation. Thus the *Miranda* warnings are not required.

D. If, at any time during an interview, a person's responses incriminate, or tend to incriminate him/her in the commission of a crime, the questioning officer shall give the *Miranda* warnings before continuing the interrogation, regardless of whether the person has been arrested. The warnings indicate that the person is now a suspect and that he/she is not at liberty to leave.

E. Whenever possible and practical, officers should prepare a typed (or written) statement of an interview and have it reviewed, acknowledged as accurate and signed by the interviewee.

F. While electronic recording may be appropriate for interrogation of criminal suspects, non-custodial interviews of crime victims, witnesses and associated individuals may also be electronically recorded.

G. Any interview that is electronically recorded must have the express consent of all parties. Persons being interviewed should sign a consent form.

V. Guiding Principles—Interrogations:

A. Custodial interrogations of criminal suspects shall always be preceded by *Miranda* warnings, using the agency pre-printed form. If at any stage of the custodial questioning, the suspect indicates that s/he wants to stop talking or to consult with an attorney before continuing, the questioning shall stop.

B. Interrogations should be pre-planned and investigating officers should have a clear understanding of the issues to be covered. This ordinarily includes an understanding of the evidence available, victim/witness accounts, offense elements, possible alibis and defenses, and applicable laws.

C. Interrogations should, whenever possible, be conducted by two officers. Prior to the interrogation each officer should have a clear understanding of the respective roles each will perform.

D. If a confession to a criminal act is obtained, officers should prepare a written statement to that effect and endeavor to have it reviewed, acknowledged as accurate, and signed by the suspect.

E. Where practical and when available, consideration should be given to recording the entire interrogation on videotape. This consideration should be given regardless of whether the interrogation is conducted in the field or in a police facility.

F. If the interrogation is to be electronically recorded, the suspect should first sign a consent form. Covert or surreptitious electronic audio recordings of interviews and interrogations are prohibited by Maryland law.

G. Under no circumstances are interrogating officers allowed to utilize physical force or any physically inhumane or abusive coercion against a suspect to make him or her provide incriminating information. The use of physical force or employment of torture techniques or psychological coercion during an interrogation is unconstitutional.

H. Officers have no authority to offer promises of leniency or special consideration as inducements for admissions or cooperation. This subtle form of coercion is prohibited.

I. Information developed through interrogations and/or confessions should be corroborated to the fullest extent possible by information and evidence available through other investigative means.

J. If there is more than one suspect, any incriminating statements or information supplied by one suspect against another must be independently substantiated.

VI. Special Cases—Juveniles:

A. Juveniles have the same *Miranda* rights as adults. A juvenile suspect may waive *Miranda* and make a voluntary statement during a custodial interrogation, but whether the statement is voluntary depends on factors such as: age; experience; education; background; intelligence; capacity to understand his or her rights and the consequences of waiving them; and presence of a parent during the interrogation.

B. Although police are not specifically required to tell a juvenile that he or she has a right to speak to his or her parents, it is advisable to do so. Parents' absence from the interrogation does not automatically invalidate the statement, but at least one Maryland court has held that a 10-year old is entitled to parental guidance, unless the State could demonstrate he had the mental capacity to understand the significance of his *Miranda* rights and the consequences of waiving them.

C. Interrogation of juveniles should be limited to a reasonable time-duration with opportunities for periodic rest breaks. The number of officers participating in the interrogation of a juvenile should be limited.

Policing Policy and Procedure: Eau Claire Police Department Policy and Procedure

305.4 THE INVESTIGATION PROCESS

The following procedures are guidelines for use in the investigation of an officer-involved shooting.

305.4.1 Duties of Initial [officer_deputy] Arriving On-Scene

Upon arrival at the scene of an officer-involved shooting, the first uninvolved officer will be the officer-in-charge and assume the duties of a supervisor until relieved by the responding supervisor, and should:

    a.   Secure the scene, identify and eliminate hazards for all those involved.
    b.   Take all reasonable steps to obtain emergency medical attention for all apparently injured individuals.
    c.   Coordinate a perimeter or pursuit of suspects as appropriate.
    d.   Request additional resources, units or agencies as appropriate.
    e.   Brief the supervisor upon arrival.

305.4.2 Duties of Initial On-Scene Supervisor

Upon arrival at the scene of an officer-involved shooting, the first uninvolved supervisor should continue and complete the duties as outlined above, plus:

    a.   Ensure the scene is secure and as safe as possible for other responders.
    b.   Manage the pursuit of suspects.
    c.   Ensure reasonable steps are taken to obtain emergency medical attention for all apparently injured individuals.
    d.   Attempt to obtain a brief overview of the situation from any non-shooter officers. In the event that there are no non-shooter officers, the supervisor should attempt to obtain a brief voluntary overview from one shooter officer.
    e.   If necessary, the supervisor may administratively order any officer from this department to immediately provide the information necessary to secure the scene and pursue suspects. This would include such things as outstanding suspect information, number and direction of shots fired, parameters of the incident scene, identity of known witnesses and similar information.

f. Absent a voluntary statement from any officer, the initial on-scene supervisor should not attempt to order any officer to provide any information other than public safety information.

g. Provide all available information to the Shift Commander and the Communications Center. If feasible, sensitive information should be communicated over secure networks.

h. Take command of and secure the incident scene with additional personnel until relieved by a DetectiveDivision supervisor or other assigned personnel.

i. As soon as practicable, shooter officers should respond or be transported (separately, if feasible) to the station or away from the scene to a designated location free from the distractions of the investigative process for further direction.

1. Each involved officer should be given an administrative order not to discuss the incident with other involved officers pending further direction from a supervisor.

2. When an officer's weapon is taken or left at the scene (e.g., evidence), the officer will be provided with a comparable replacement weapon or transported to the station by other officers.

305.4.3 [watchcommander] Duties

Upon learning of an officer-involved shooting, the Shift Commander shall be responsible for coordinating all aspects of the incident until relieved by the Chief of Police or a Deputy Chief.

305.4.4 Notifications

The following persons shall be notified as soon as practicable:

- Chief of Police
- Detective Deputy Chief
- Patrol Deputy Chief
- Use of Force Coordinator
- Outside agency investigators (if appropriate)
- City Risk Manager
- Psychological/peer support personnel
- Medical Examiner (if necessary)
- Officer representative (if requested)
- Public Information Officer

All outside inquiries about the incident shall be directed to the public information officer.

305.4.5 Media Relations

A media release shall be prepared with input and concurrence from the supervisor and the agency representative responsible for each phase of the investigation. This release will be available to the DetectiveDeputy Chief and Records Technician in the event of inquiries from the media.

It is the policy of this department to not release the identities of involved officers absent their consent or as required by law. Moreover, no involved officer shall be subjected to contact from the media and no involved officer shall make any comments to the press unless authorized by the Chief of Police or a Deputy Chief.

Employees receiving inquiries regarding incidents occurring in other agency jurisdictions shall refrain from public comment and will direct those inquiries to the agency having jurisdiction and primary responsibility for the investigation.

305.4.6 Involved [officers_deputies]

Once the involved officers have arrived at the station, the Shift Commander should admonish each officer that the incident shall not be discussed except with authorized personnel or representatives. The following shall be considered for the involved officer:

a. Any request for a representative will be accommodated (Wis. Stat. § 164.02(1)(b)).

b. While discussions with licensed attorneys will be considered privileged as attorney-client communications, no involved officers shall be permitted to meet collectively or in a group with an attorney prior to providing a formal interview or report.

c. Discussions with department representatives (e.g., employee association) will be privileged only as to the discussion of non-criminal information. However, no involved officers shall be permitted to meet collectively or in a group with a representative or attorney prior to providing a formal interview or report.

d. A psychologist or other psychotherapist shall be provided by the Department to each involved officer or any officer upon request.

   1. Interviews with a licensed psychotherapist will be considered privileged and will not be disclosed except to the extent that a report is required to determine whether the officer is fit for return to duty.

   2. If an interview or session with a licensed psychotherapist takes place prior to the involved officer providing a formal interview or report, the involved officers shall not be permitted to consult or meet collectively or in a group with a licensed psychotherapist prior to providing a formal interview or report.

e. Although the Department will honor the sensitivity of communications with peer counselors, there is no legal privilege to such. Peer counselors are cautioned not to discuss the facts of any incident with an involved or witness officer.

Care should be taken to preserve the integrity of any physical evidence present on the officer's equipment or clothing, such as blood or fingerprints, until investigators or lab personnel can properly retrieve it.

Investigators shall make reasonable accommodations to the officer's physical and emotional needs. The investigator should ask the officer whether he/she wishes notification to be made to family and friends and how notification should be made. If an officer has been seriously injured or killed, the supervisor in charge of the incident shall obtain the line of duty death packet to help determine how to make notification to the officer's family and friends.

Each involved officer shall be given reasonable paid administrative leave following an officer-involved shooting. It shall be the responsibility of the Shift Commander to make schedule adjustments to accommodate such leave.

Involved officers should be informed of the availability of counseling options as outlined in the Fitness for Duty Policy. Such counseling may include Department and/or involved employee debriefing.

305.5 SHOOTING INCIDENT CRIMINAL INVESTIGATION

305.5.1 Investigative Personnel

Once notified of an officer-involved shooting, it shall be the responsibility of the Detective Division supervisor to assign appropriate personnel to handle the investigation of related crimes. Investigators will be assigned to work with those from an outside agency should the investigation be assumed by another agency, and may be assigned to separately handle the investigation of any related crimes that are not being investigated by the outside agency.

All related reports, except reports deemed confidential and/or administrative, will be forwarded to the designated supervisor for approval. Confidential reports shall be maintained exclusively by personnel who are authorized for such access. Administrative reports will be forwarded to the appropriate Deputy Chief.

305.5.2 Criminal Investigation

This department may utilize an outside agency to conduct an independent criminal investigation into the circumstances of any officer-involved shooting involving bodily harm or death.

If available, investigations personnel from this department may be assigned to partner with investigators from the outside agency to avoid duplicate efforts in related criminal investigations.

Once public safety issues have been addressed, criminal investigators will be given the next opportunity to interview officers in order to give them the opportunity to give a voluntary statement. The following shall be considered for the involved officer:

a. If requested, any involved officer will be afforded the opportunity to consult individually with a representative of his/her choosing or an attorney prior to speaking with criminal investigators.
b. Any voluntary statement provided by the officer will be made available for inclusion in the administrative or other related investigations.
c. Absent consent from the involved officer or as required by law, no administratively coerced statement will be provided to any criminal investigators.

305.5.3 Reports By Involved [officers_deputies]

In the event that suspects remain outstanding or are subject to prosecution for related offenses, this department shall retain the authority to require involved officers to provide sufficient information for related criminal reports to facilitate the apprehension and prosecution of those individuals.

While the involved officer may write the report, it is generally recommended that such reports be completed by assigned investigators, who should interview the involved officers as victims/witnesses. Since the purpose of these reports will be to facilitate criminal prosecution, statements of involved officers should focus on evidence to establish the elements of criminal activities by the involved suspects. Care should be taken not to duplicate information provided by involved officers in other reports.

Nothing in this section shall be construed to deprive an involved officer of the right to consult with legal counsel prior to completing any such criminal report.

Reports related to the prosecution of criminal suspects will be processed according to normal procedures and should also be included for reference in the investigation of the officer-involved shooting.

305.6 WITNESS IDENTIFICATION AND INTERVIEWS

Because potential witnesses to an officer-involved shooting or other major incident may become unavailable or the integrity of their statements compromised with the passage of time, a supervisor should take reasonable steps to promptly coordinate with criminal investigators to utilize available personnel for the following:

   a. Identifying all persons present at the scene and in the immediate area.
      1. When feasible, a recorded statement should be obtained from persons who claim they did not witness the incident but were present at the time it occurred.
      2. Any potential witness who is unwilling or unable to remain available for a formal interview should not be detained absent reasonable suspicion to detain or probable cause to arrest. Without detaining the individual for the sole purpose of identification, an officer should attempt to identify the witness prior to his/her departure.
   b. Witnesses who are willing to provide a formal interview should be asked to meet at a suitable location where criminal investigators may obtain a recorded statement. Such witnesses, if willing, may be transported by department personnel.
      1. A written, verbal or recorded statement of consent for transportation should be obtained prior to transporting a witness in a department vehicle. When the witness is a minor, consent should be obtained from the parent or guardian, if available, prior to transportation.
   c. Assigning available personnel to promptly contact the suspect's known family and associates to obtain any available and untainted background information about the suspect's activities and state of mind prior to the suspect's contact with officers.

305.7 ADMINISTRATIVE INVESTIGATION

In addition to all other investigations associated with an officer-involved shooting, this department can conduct a separate internal administrative investigation, pursuant to the Personnel Complaints Policy, to determine conformance with department policy. This investigation will be conducted under the supervision of the Supervisor or as designated the by the Chief of Police.

   a. Any officer involved in a shooting may be administratively compelled to provide a blood sample for alcohol/drug screening. Absent consent from the officer, such compelled samples and the results of any such testing shall not be disclosed to any criminal investigative agency.
   b. If any officer has voluntarily elected to provide a statement to criminal investigators, the assigned administrative investigator should review that statement before proceeding with any further interview of the involved officer.
      1. If a further interview of the officer is deemed necessary to determine policy compliance, care should be taken to limit the inquiry to new areas with minimal, if any, duplication of questions addressed in the voluntary

statement. The involved officer shall be provided with a copy of his/her prior statement before proceeding with any subsequent interview.

c.   In the event that an involved officer has elected not to provide criminal investigators with a voluntary statement, the assigned administrative investigator shall conduct an administrative interview to determine all relevant information.

   1.   Although this interview should not be unreasonably delayed, care should be taken to ensure that the officer's physical and psychological needs have been addressed before commencing the interview.

   2.   If requested, the officer shall have the opportunity to select an uninvolved representative which may include legal representation, to be present during the interview (Wis. Stat. § 164.02(1)(b)).

   3.   In order to maintain the integrity of each individual officer's statement, involved officers shall not consult or meet with a representative or attorney collectively or in groups prior to being initially interviewed.

   4.   Administrative interviews should be recorded by the investigator. The officer may also record the interview.

   5.   The officer shall be informed of the nature of the investigation and shall be informed of all constitutional Miranda rights. Assuming there is no voluntary waiver, he/she will then be given his/her *Garrity* rights, and assuming there is no voluntary waiver, will then be given an administrative order to provide full and truthful answers to all questions (Wis. Stat. § 164.02(1)(a)).

   6.   The administrative interview shall be considered part of the officer's administrative investigation file.

   7.   The Supervisor shall compile all relevant information and reports necessary for the Department to determine compliance with applicable policies.

   8.   The completed administrative investigation shall be submitted to the Use of Force Review Board, which will restrict its findings as to whether there was compliance with the Use of Force Policy.

   9.   Any other indications of potential policy violations shall be determined in accordance with standard disciplinary procedures.

   10.   The administrative investigator may ask the employee to submit to a polygraph examination, but only when a statement is made by the involved employee that differs from other information relating to the investigation, and reconciling the differences is necessary to complete the investigation. No notation or reference to a request or refusal to submit to such an examination may be made in any file or report (Wis. Stat. § 111.37).

305.8 CIVIL LIABILITY RESPONSE

A member of this department may be assigned to work exclusively under the direction of the legal counsel for the Department to assist in the preparation of materials deemed necessary in anticipation of potential civil litigation.

All materials generated in this capacity shall be considered attorney work product and may not be used for any other purpose. The civil liability response is not intended to interfere with any other investigation. However, persons preparing the response shall be given reasonable access to all other investigations.

305.9 AUDIO AND VIDEO RECORDINGS

Any officer involved in an incident may be permitted to review available Mobile Audio Video (MAV) or other video or audio recordings prior to providing a recorded statement or completing reports.

Upon request, non-law enforcement witnesses who are able to verify their presence and their ability to contemporaneously perceive events at the scene of an incident may also be permitted to review available MAV or other video or audio recordings with approval of assigned investigators or a supervisor.

Any MAV and other known video or audio recordings of an incident should not be publicly released during an ongoing investigation without consulting the District Attorney or City Attorney's Office as appropriate.

Rules of Conduct: San Diego County Sheriff's Department

2.1 RULES OF CONDUCT FOR MEMBERS OF THE SAN DIEGO COUNTY SHERIFF'S DEPARTMENT

All employees shall conform to Federal, State, and Local laws, as well as to the policies of this Department. It shall be the responsibility of all employees to familiarize themselves and comply with all such policies, orders, directives, rules and regulations of this Department. (02-12-13)

2.2 APPLICABILITY

These Rules of Conduct apply to all classifications of employees, including Reserve, 960 hour Rehires, student workers, interns, contract professionals and Volunteer employees, except when a rule, by its very nature, does not apply to a given classification of employee. (06-24-14)

2.3 VIOLATION OF RULES

Employees shall not commit or omit any acts which constitute a violation of any of the rules, regulations, directives, orders or policies of this Department, whether stated in these Rules of Conduct or elsewhere. Employees shall be responsible for their own acts, and they shall not shift to others the burden, or responsibility, for executing or failing to execute a lawful order or duty. (Reviewed 1-11-2011)

2.4 UNBECOMING CONDUCT

Employees shall conduct themselves at all times, both on and off duty, in such a manner as to reflect most favorably on this Department. Unbecoming conduct shall include that which tends to bring this Department into disrepute or reflects discredit upon the employee as a member of this Department, or that which tends to impair the operation and efficiency of this Department or employee. (Reviewed 1-11-2011)

2.5 IMMORAL CONDUCT

Employee shall maintain a level of moral conduct in their personal and business affairs which is in keeping with the highest standard of the law enforcement profession. Employees shall not participate in any incident involving moral turpitude which tends to impair their ability to perform their duties or causes this Department to be brought into disrepute. (Reviewed 1-11-2011)

2.6 CONFORMANCE TO LAWS

Employees shall obey all laws of the United States, of this state, and of local jurisdictions.

The acts of employees giving rise to an indictment, information or complaint, filed against an employee, or a conviction for violating any law, including a conviction following a plea of nolo contendere, may be cause for disciplinary action, temporary or permanent reassignment (excluding minor traffic).

Employees shall immediately inform their immediate supervisor of any and all circumstances where non-conformance to laws has been, or may be, alleged by any law enforcement agency.

The supervisor receiving such notification shall immediately notify Internal Affairs. (7-30-03) (Reviewed 1-11-2011)

2.7 SEEKING OR ACCEPTING GIFTS, GRATUITIES, BRIBES, OR REWARDS

It is prohibited for employees to directly or indirectly solicit or accept from any person, business, or organization any gift, gratuity, bribe, or reward for the benefit of the employee, if it may reasonably be inferred that the person, business, or organization:

Seeks to influence action of an official nature or seeks to affect the performance or non-performance of an official duty, or

Has an interest which may be substantially affected directly or indirectly by the performance or non-performance of an official duty.

Food and Other Services: When making purchases, whether on or off duty, employees shall pay the posted price(s) for food, services or any other consideration. Discounts will not be accepted nor solicited where the employee's official position is used to effect same, or the discount can be reasonably shown to be as a result of any official position. A discount may be accepted where it has been negotiated by a recognized employee group sanctioned by the Sheriff.

For the purpose of this rule, the words "gifts", "gratuity", "bribe", and "reward", shall include money, food, tangible or intangible personal property, loan, promise, service, entertainment, or any other consideration. (Reviewed 1-11-2011)

2.8 VISITING PROHIBITED ESTABLISHMENTS

Employees shall not knowingly enter or frequent any establishment (house of prostitution, gambling house, etc.) wherein the laws of the United States, the state, or the local jurisdiction are regularly violated except in the performance of duty or while acting under proper and specific orders from a supervisor. (Reviewed 1-11-2011)

2.9 ASSOCIATIONS

Employees shall not associate on either a personal or business basis or have dealings with persons whom they know, or should know, or have reason to believe are, or have been racketeers, sexual offenders, drug dealers, illegal drug users, illegal gamblers, persons whom the employee suspects, or should suspect, are involved in felonious activities, convicted felons, persons held in county custody, felons serving or who have served time in custody, or persons under criminal investigation or indictment, except as necessary to the performance of official duties, or where unavoidable because of other personal relationships. (09-21-04) (Reviewed 1-11-2011)

2.10 GAMBLING

Employees shall not engage or participate in any form of illegal gambling at any time, except in the performance of duty and while acting under proper and specific orders from a supervisor. (Reviewed 1-11-2011)

2.11 USE OF DRUGS

Employees shall not use any controlled substances, narcotics, or hallucinogens except when prescribed in the treatment of employees by one legally authorized to prescribe such medication. When controlled substances, narcotics, or hallucinogens are prescribed, and the employee is taking these substances while on duty or in such close proximity to going on duty that it would create an effect, employees shall notify their supervisor. (NOTE: Controlled substance is defined under Section 11007 and Sections 11054 through 11058 of the Health and Safety Code.) (10-24-05) (Reviewed 1-11-2011)

2.12 ALCOHOLIC BEVERAGES IN SHERIFF'S OFFICE FACILITIES

Employees shall not bring into or store alcoholic beverages in any Sheriff's facility or County vehicle except those being held as evidence or for an approved instructional program. (Reviewed 12-18-2010)

2.13 USE OF ALCOHOL/ON DUTY

Employees shall not drink intoxicating beverages while on duty except in the performance of official duties. Employees shall not appear for duty, or be on duty, while under the influence of intoxicants or any degree whatsoever, or have an odor of intoxicants on their breath. (Reviewed 12-18-2010)

2.14 USE OF ALCOHOL/OFF DUTY

Employees, while off duty, shall refrain from consuming intoxicating beverages to the extent that it results in unlawful impairment (such as driving under the influence or being unable to care for their own safety or the safety of others), public intoxication, or obnoxious or offensive behavior in public which would tend to discredit them or this Department, or render the employee unfit to report for their next regular tour of duty. (Reviewed 12-19-2010)

2.15 INSUBORDINATION

Insubordination is the willful refusal to obey a reasonable and lawful order given and understood. A reasonable and lawful order given to a subordinate shall be followed regardless of the method of conveyance. The willful failure to obey orders constitutes grounds for discipline (including termination). (Reviewed 12-19-2010)

2.16 CONFLICTING OR ILLEGAL ORDERS

Employees who are given an otherwise proper order which is in conflict with a previous order, regulation, directive or manual, shall respectfully inform the supervisor issuing the order of the conflict. If the supervisor issuing the order does not alter or retract the conflicting order, the order shall stand. Under these circumstances, the responsibility shall be upon the supervisor. Employees shall obey the conflicting order and shall not be held responsible for disobedience of the order previously issued. However, employees shall not obey any order which they reasonably believe would require them to commit any illegal act. If in doubt as to the legality of the order, employees shall request that the person issuing the order confer with higher authority or clarify the order. (Reviewed 12-27-2010)

2.17 PUBLIC APPEARANCES AND STATEMENTS

Employees shall not publicly criticize or ridicule this Department, its policies, or employees, by speech, writing or other expression, where such expression is defamatory, obscene, unlawful, tends to undermine the effectiveness of this Department, interferes with the maintenance of discipline, or is made with reckless disregard for truth or falseness. This rule is not intended to apply to political activities by a candidate for public office. Such activity is fully covered under Policy and Procedure Section 2.43 (Political Activity).

Employees shall not address public gatherings, appear on radio or television, prepare any articles for publications, act as correspondents, release or divulge investigative information, or any other matter of this Department, while holding themselves out as having an official capacity in such matters without having obtained official sanction or authority.

Any speech, writing or other expression made where the listener or reader may reasonably assume that the employee is acting as a spokesperson on behalf of the Department will be governed by the above guidelines. (Reviewed 12-27-2010)

2.18 ABUSE OF POSITION

Use of Official Position or Identification
Employees are prohibited from using their official position, official identification cards or badges; (1) for personal or financial gain, (2) for obtaining privileges not otherwise available to them except in the performance of duty, or (3) for avoiding consequences of illegal acts (such as traffic citations, driving under the influence, etc.). Employees may not lend their identification cards or badges to another person, or permit them to be photographed or reproduced.

Use of Name, Photograph or Title
Employees shall not permit or authorize the use of their names, photographs, or official titles which identify them as members of the Sheriff's Department, in connection with testimonials or advertisements of any commodity of commercial enterprise.

Use of C.C.W. License by Non-Peace Officer
Employees who in their capacity as private citizens, have applied for and received concealed weapons licenses are not authorized to, nor shall they represent to any person that they are carrying or utilizing such weapon within the course and scope of their employment. Nor shall any employee who has obtained a concealed weapons license misrepresent himself/herself to any person as being a Deputy Sheriff. (Reviewed 1-4-2011)

2.19 ENDORSEMENTS AND REFERRALS
Employees shall not recommend or suggest in any manner, when acting in their official capacity, the employment or procurement of a particular product, professional or commercial service (such as an attorney, ambulance service, towing service, bondsman, mortician, etc.). When any such service is necessary, employees shall proceed in accordance with established Departmental procedures. (Reviewed 1-4-2011)

2.20 IDENTIFICATION
Sworn employees shall carry their identification cards on their persons at all times, except when impractical or dangerous to their safety or to an investigation. While on duty, all employees shall furnish their first and last name and ARJIS number to any person requesting that information, except when the withholding of such information is necessary for the performance of police duties. (2-12-13)

2.21 CITIZEN COMPLAINTS
Employees shall courteously and promptly accept and record in writing any complaint made by a citizen against any employee or any Department policy or procedure. Employees may attempt to resolve the complaint, but shall never attempt to dissuade any citizen from lodging a complaint. Employees shall immediately notify their supervisor of a complaint as required by Department procedures. (Refer to Policy and Procedure Section 3.2 for procedure for handling citizen complaints. (Reviewed 1-11-2011)

2.22 COURTESY
Employees shall be courteous to the public and fellow employees. They shall be tactful in the performance of their duties, shall control their tempers, exercise patience and discretion even in the face of extreme provocation. Except when necessary to establish control during a violent or dangerous situation, no member shall use coarse, profane or violent language. Employees shall not use insolent language or gestures in the performance of his or her duties. (04-02-14)

2.23 REQUEST FOR ASSISTANCE
When any person requests assistance or advice, or makes complaints or reports, either by telephone or in person, all pertinent information will be obtained in an official and courteous manner, and will be properly and judiciously acted upon consistent with established Department procedures. (Reviewed 12-5-2010)

2.24 REPORTING FOR DUTY
Employees shall report for duty at the time and place required by assignment or orders and shall be physically and mentally fit to perform their duties. They shall be properly equipped and cognizant of information required for the proper performance of duty so that they may immediately assume their duties. Judicial subpoenas and training assignments shall constitute an order to appear under this section. (Reviewed 12-5-2010)

2.25 SLEEPING ON DUTY

Employees shall remain awake while on duty. If unable to do so, they shall so report to their immediate supervisor who shall determine the proper course of action. (Reviewed 12-5-2010)

2.26 MEALS

Sworn employees assigned to uniformed patrol or detentions shall be permitted to suspend patrol or other assigned activity, subject to immediate call at all times, for the purpose of having meals during their tours of duty, but only for such period of time, and at such time and place, as established by Departmental procedures. (Reviewed 12-5-2010)

2.27 NEGLECT OF DUTY

Employees shall not read, play games, watch television or movies or otherwise engage in entertainment while on duty, except as may be required in the performance of duty. They shall not engage in any activities or personal business, which would cause them to neglect or be inattentive to duty. (Reviewed 12-5-2010)

2.28 TELEPHONES, NAMES, ADDRESSES

Sworn employees shall have telephones in their residences, and all employees shall immediately report any changes of telephone numbers, names, or residence addresses (post office boxes will not be acceptable for this purpose) to their supervisor and to such other persons as may be required by this Department (use Form AS 1/25).

Employees should be aware that, under certain circumstances, they are subject to call back to ensure the efficient operation of the Department. (12-11-02) (Reviewed 12-5-2010)

2.29 FICTITIOUS ILLNESS OR INJURY REPORTS

Employees shall not feign illness or injury, falsely report themselves ill or injured, or otherwise deceive or attempt to deceive any official of this Department as to the condition of their health. (Reviewed 12-5-2010)

2.30 FAILURE TO MEET STANDARDS

Employees shall properly perform their duties and assume the responsibilities of their positions. Employees shall perform their duties in a manner which will tend to establish and maintain the highest standards of efficiency in carrying out the mission, functions, and objectives of this Department. Failure to meet standards may be demonstrated by a lack of knowledge of the application of laws required to be enforced; an unwillingness or inability to perform assigned tasks; the failure to conform to work standards established for the employee's position; the failure to take appropriate action on the occasion of a crime, disorder, or other condition deserving police attention; absence without leave; unauthorized absence from the assignment during a tour of duty; the failure to submit complete and accurate reports on a timely basis when required or when directed by a supervisor. (Reviewed 1-27-2011)

2.31 PERSONAL APPEARANCE

Employees on duty shall wear uniforms or other clothing appropriate to their assignment in accordance with established Departmental procedures.

Employees on duty shall maintain a neat, well-groomed appearance and shall style their hair according to established Departmental regulations. Reference Sections 3.11 "Hair and Grooming Standards for Sworn Personnel", of the Departmental Policy and Procedure Manual.

Employees having occasion to visit any Sheriff's Department facility, while off-duty, shall be neat and clean in their appearance. (Reviewed 1-27-2011)

2.32 USE OF TOBACCO

Employees shall not smoke or use smokeless tobacco when they: (1) are in formation, (2) have to leave their assignment or post for the sole purpose of doing so, (3) are engaged in traffic control or direction, or (4) are dealing in person with the public. Smoking or use of smokeless tobacco at all other times will be in compliance with the County Smoking Ordinance (Chapter 8 S.D.C.C. and Section 3.38 Policy and Procedure Manual). (Reviewed 12-5-2010)

2.33 EMPLOYMENT OUTSIDE OF DEPARTMENT

Employees may engage in off-duty employment subject to the following limitations: (1) such employment shall not interfere with the employee's employment with this Department; (2) employees shall submit a written request for off-duty employment to his/her Facility Captain/Division Manager, whose approval must be granted prior to engaging in such employment.

Approval may be denied where it appears that the outside employment might: (1) render the employee unavailable during an emergency; (2) physically or mentally exhaust the employee to the point that their performance may be affected; (3)

require that any special consideration be given to scheduling of the employee's regular duty hours.

Approval shall be denied where it appears that the outside employment might involve: (1) the sale or distribution of alcoholic beverages as the primary business or produce; (2) investigative work for insurance agencies; (3) work for private guard services, collection agencies, attorneys or bail bond agencies, or (4) work for an employer who has been convicted of a felony or who openly associates with convicted felons.

Reference Section 3.7 "Outside Employment", of the Department Policy and Procedure Manual. (4-19-06) (Reviewed 2-18-2011)

2.34 CARRYING OF FIREARMS

Employees who are authorized to carry firearms shall carry them in accordance with the law and established Department policy and procedure. Sworn Peace Officers (830.1 P.C.) and Court Service Officers (830.36) who are authorized to carry a firearm, may (optional) carry a firearm, when off duty, except:

1. When consuming intoxicating beverages.
2. When under a doctor's care for a mental or physical illness which requires the officer to ingest any medication that would impair his normal reactions.
3. While suspended from duty or during the loss of police powers.

When authorized for off-duty carry, firearms shall be concealed from public view when the employee is wearing civilian attire. When a firearm is displayed in an on-duty status, the sworn employee shall wear their uniform badge in a position plainly visible from the employee's front and shall have their Department Identification Card on their person to present upon request.

Employees are responsible for securing firearms left in unattended vehicles to minimize theft/loss.

Aside from using Department-installed locking devices, the preferred method of securing a handgun in an unattended vehicle is locked in the glovebox. If this is not possible, handguns and firearms shall be locked in the trunk. (08-16-12)

2.35 OPERATION OF VEHICLES

Employees shall operate all county owned or maintained vehicles, or any vehicle being operated in the performance of their official duties, in a careful and prudent manner, and shall obey all laws of the state and all Departmental orders pertaining to such operation. Employees shall set a proper example for other persons by the manner in which they operate all vehicles in an official capacity. Loss or suspension of an employee's driver's license shall be reported to the Department immediately and may be cause for reassignment, suspension, or termination. When employees drive any vehicle requiring other than a regular driver's license (Class C) they shall possess the required class endorsement. (10-10-07) (Reviewed 12-31-2010)

2.36 USE OF DEPARTMENT EQUIPMENT

Employees shall utilize Department equipment only for its intended purpose, in accordance with established Departmental procedures and shall not abuse, damage or lose Department equipment. All Department equipment issued to employees, including manuals, shall be maintained in proper order. (Reviewed 12-31-2010)

2.37 DISSEMINATION OF INFORMATION

Employees shall treat the official business of this Department as confidential. Information regarding official business shall be disseminated only to those for whom it is intended, in accordance with established Departmental procedures. Employees may remove or copy official records or reports from any law enforcement installation only in accordance with established Departmental procedures. Employees shall not divulge the identity of persons giving confidential information, except to their supervisors. (Reviewed 12-31-2010)

2.38 INTERVENTION

Employees shall not use their position, or knowledge gained by employment with this Department, to intervene in, or interfere with any case, or investigation being handled by this Department, or any other agency. (Reviewed 12-31-2010)

2.39 PROCESSING PROPERTY

Property which has been discovered, gathered or received in connection with Departmental responsibilities will be processed in accordance with established Departmental procedures. Employees shall not convert to their own use, manufacture, conceal, falsify, destroy, remove, tamper with or withhold any property found or obtained in connection with the performance of their duties, except in accordance with Department procedures. (Reviewed 12-31-2010)

2.40 ABUSE OF PROCESS/WITHHOLDING EVIDENCE

Employees shall not convert to their own use, manufacture, conceal, falsify, destroy, remove, tamper with, or withhold evidence or information, or make false accusations of a criminal or traffic charge. (Reviewed 12-31-2010)

2.41 DEPARTMENTAL REPORTS

Employees shall submit all necessary reports on time and in accordance with established Departmental procedures. Reports submitted by employees shall be truthful and complete; no employee shall knowingly enter or cause to be entered any inaccurate, false, or improper information, nor omit pertinent information reasonably expected to be included. (Reviewed 12-31-2010)

2.42 PAYMENT OF DEBTS

Employees shall not undertake any financial obligations which they know or should know they will be unable to meet. An isolated instance of financial irresponsibility will not be grounds for discipline, except in unusually severe cases. Repeated instances of financial difficulty may be cause for disciplinary action. Filing for voluntary bankruptcy petition shall not, by itself, be cause for discipline. Financial difficulties stemming from unforeseen causes (such as medical expenses or personal disaster) shall not be cause for discipline, provided that a good faith effort, to settle all accounts, is being undertaken. (Reviewed 12-31-2010)

2.43 POLITICAL ACTIVITY

Employees shall be permitted to:

- Register and vote in any election;
- Be candidates for elective public office, including Office of the Sheriff.
- Communicate through the mail or by other means, requests for political funds or contributions to a significant segment of the public which may include officers or employees of the county; however, employees shall not solicit political funds or contributions solely from other employees of the County of San Diego. (Govt. Code '3205.)
- Express opinions as individuals privately and publicly on political issues and candidates;
- Attend political conventions, rallies, and similar political gatherings;
- Actively engage in any non-partisan political functions;
- Sign political petitions as individuals;
- Make financial contributions to political organizations;

- Serve as election judges or clerks in performance of non-partisan duties as prescribed by state or local laws;
- Hold membership in a political party and participate in its functions to the extent consistent with the law and consistent with this section;
- Participate fully in public affairs to the extent that such endeavors do not impair efficient performance of official duties, or create real or apparent conflicts of interest.

Employees are prohibited from:

- Using their official capacity to influence, interfere with or affect the results of an election;
- Directly or indirectly, using, promising, threatening or attempting to use any official influence in aid of any political activity, or to affect the result of any election to political office, or upon any other corrupt condition or consideration;
- Engaging in political activity of any kind while in uniform prescribed for any employee of the County of San Diego or during any hours in which they have been directed to perform their assigned duties, or in any Sheriff's facility or on any property leased or controlled by the Sheriff's Department. (Govt. Code ''3206, 3207.) (Reviewed 12-31-2010)

2.44 LABOR ACTIVITIES

Employees shall have the right to join labor organizations, but nothing shall compel this Department to recognize or to engage in collective bargaining with any such labor organizations, except as provided by law.

Employees shall not engage in any strike. "Strike" includes the concerted failure to report for duty, willful absence from one's position, unauthorized holidays, sickness unsubstantiated by a physician's statement, the stoppage of work, or the abstinence in whole or in part from the full, faithful and proper performance of the duties of employment for the purposes of inducing, influencing or coercing a change in conditions, compensation, rights, privileges or obligations of employment. (Reviewed 12-31-2010)

2.45 USE OF LIE DETECTORS, MEDICAL EXAMINATION, PHOTOGRAPHS, LINEUPS

Lie Detectors

Employees may voluntarily submit to a lie detector test (as defined in Government Code section 3307(b)) when the examinations are specifically directed and narrowly related to a particular investigation being conducted by this Department (see Section 3307 Government Code).

Medical Examinations; Tests; Photographs; Lineups

Upon the order of the Sheriff or the Sheriff's designee, employees shall submit to any medical, ballistics, chemical or other tests, photographs, or lineups. All procedures carried out under this section shall be specifically directed and narrowly related to a particular administrative investigation being conducted by this Department.

Excerpt from Government Code for reference:

3307. (a) No public safety officer shall be compelled to submit to a lie detector test against his or her will. No disciplinary action or other recrimination shall be taken against a public safety officer refusing to submit to a lie detector test, nor shall any comment be entered anywhere in the investigator's notes or anywhere else that the public safety officer refused to take, or did not take, a lie detector test, nor shall any testimony or evidence be admissible at a subsequent hearing, trial, or proceeding, judicial or administrative, to the effect that the public safety officer refused to take, or was subjected to a lie detector test.

(b) For the purpose of this section, "lie detector" means a polygraph, deceptograph, voice stress analyzer, psychological stress evaluator, or any other similar device, whether mechanical or electrical, that is used, or the results of which are used, for the purpose of rendering a diagnostic opinion regarding the honesty or dishonesty of an individual. (03-21-12)

2.46 TRUTHFULNESS

When asked by the Sheriff, the Sheriff's designee or any supervisor, employees will always answer questions, whether orally or in writing, truthfully and to the fullest extent of their knowledge. All written and verbal reports shall be truthful and complete. (Reviewed 1-27-2011)

2.47 FINANCIAL DISCLOSURE

Employees shall submit financial disclosures and responsibility statements in a prescribed manner if required by the Sheriff in connection with an investigation in which this information is material to that investigation. (Reviewed 1-27-2011)

2.48 TREATMENT OF PERSONS IN CUSTODY

Employees shall not mistreat, nor abuse physically or verbally, persons who are in their custody. Employees shall handle such persons in accordance with law and established Departmental procedures. (Reviewed 1-16-2011)

2.49 USE OF FORCE

Employees shall not use more force in any situation than is reasonably necessary under the circumstances. Employees shall use force in accordance with law and established Departmental procedures, and report all use of force in writing. (Reviewed 1-16-2011)

2.50 USE OF LETHAL/LESS LETHAL WEAPONS

Employees shall not use or handle lethal or less lethal weapons (including chemical agents, saps, batons, taser guns, etc.,) in a careless or imprudent manner. Employees shall use these weapons in accordance with law and established Departmental procedures. (Reviewed 1-16-2011)

2.51 ARREST, SEARCH AND SEIZURE

Employees shall not make any arrest, search or seizure, nor conduct any investigation or official Department business, in a manner which they know or ought to know is not in accordance with law and established Department policies and procedures. (Reviewed 1-16-2011)

2.52 CONFLICTS OF INTEREST

No employee shall make, participate in making or in any way attempt to use his or her official position to influence a governmental decision in which the employee knows, or has reason to know, that he or she has a financial interest. (Govt. Code ''1090, 87100 et seq.). (Reviewed 1-16-2011)

2.53 DISCRIMINATION

Employees shall not express any prejudice or harassment concerning race, religious creed, color, national origin, ancestry, physical or mental disability, medical condition, pregnancy, marital status, gender, age, political beliefs, sexual orientation, lifestyle or similar personal characteristics.

Examples of discriminatory acts which will not be tolerated include the use of verbal derogatory comments, slurs, or jokes, derogatory pictures, cartoons or posters and actions which result in a person being treated unequally. (Reviewed 1-27-2011)

2.54 SEXUAL HARASSMENT

Employees shall not participate in or allow behaviors or situations that they know or should know, constitute sexual harassment as outlined in state and federal law.

Employees shall take swift action to stop the offensive behavior or correct the situation. Employees shall not retaliate in any way against a complaining party or witness involved in sexual harassment allegations. (08-18-97) (Reviewed 1-16-2011)

2.55 NON-BIASED BASED POLICING

A. All investigative detentions, traffic stops, arrests, searches, and seizures of property by employees will be based on a standard of reasonable suspicion or probable cause as required by the Fourth Amendment of the U.S. Constitution and relevant statutory authority. Employees must be able to articulate specific facts and circumstances, which support probable cause or reasonable suspicion for an arrest, traffic stop, investigation, detention or search.

B. Except as provided in this procedure, employees shall not consider race, ethnicity, religion, national origin, sexual orientation, gender, or lifestyle in establishing either reasonable suspicion or probable cause.

Appropriate consideration of race, ethnicity, origin, sexual orientation, and gender shall be used for purposes of housing, classification, transportation or any other matters affecting an inmate's status when necessary for the safety and security of the inmate or the institution. Consideration of the above-mentioned personal characteristics shall not be used for purposes of inmate discipline.

C. Employees may take into account a reported descriptor such as race, ethnicity, religion, national origin, sexual orientation, gender, or lifestyle of a specific suspect or suspects based on credible, reliable and locally relevant information that links a person(s) of a specific descriptor to a particular criminal incident(s). Race, ethnicity, religion, national origin, sexual orientation, gender, or lifestyle can never be the sole factor in establishing reasonable suspicion or probable cause, but can, in the restricted circumstances described above, be one factor of the totality of the circumstances. (10-21-02) (Reviewed 1-27-2011)

2.56 OFF DUTY INTERVENTION

In determining whether or not to intervene, the off duty peace officer should consider the totality of the situation. In a case where action is considered necessary, to prevent death, the possibility of death or serious bodily injury, significant property damage or loss, the off duty peace officer should consider the offense involved, the difficulty that being off duty tactically and operationally presents, and/or other factors as articulated and observed by the off duty peace officer.

If an off duty peace officer intervenes in the criminal conduct, he/she must, if reasonably possible, identify themselves, their agency and their intent to stop the criminal conduct. Any law enforcement action taken by the peace officer will be governed by the policies and procedures, rules and regulations that apply to on duty personnel.

When outside the limits of their jurisdiction, but within the State of California, off duty peace officers may assist any law enforcement officer who appears to be in need of immediate assistance and may assist in the prevention of the commission of any crime involving the immediate danger to persons or property, or of the escape of the perpetrator of the offense.

Off duty peace officers outside the state of California, do not have police officer powers/status and therefore have only the rights and obligations of private citizens of that state. (07-11-08) (Reviewed 1-27-2011)

Mission and Vision of the Michigan Department of Corrections

As Department of Corrections' employees, we maintain high standards of professional conduct. We treat each other, citizens and offenders with respect. Our mission defines the way we perform our jobs and demonstrates our commitment to "expecting excellence every day" in everything we do.

Our mission is to create a safer Michigan through effective offender management and supervision in our facilities and communities while holding offenders accountable and promoting their rehabilitation.

Our vision is based on the following principles:

1. We will remain committed to the protection of the public, safety of our staff, and security of offenders.
2. We will actively engage in the development of effective criminal justice policy.
3. We will ensure sound management using proven fiscal practices and outcome-oriented strategies.
4. We will hire, train, equip, support, and mentor a high quality staff and hold them to the highest professional standards.
5. We will provide humane and protective custodial care, rehabilitative opportunities, and reentry assistance for offenders under our supervision.
6. We will establish meaningful partnerships with public and private entities to assist us in successfully accomplishing our mission.
7. We will conduct all of our duties and responsibilities with the highest degree of integrity, expectations for excellence, and respect for the value and dignity of human life.

DEFINITIONS

For purposes of this document, the following definitions shall be used:

Contraband: any article not specifically authorized by policy including an employee's personal property.

Department: Michigan Department of Corrections.

Discipline: actions taken upon substantiating a rule violation including written reprimands, suspensions without pay, involuntary demotions, discharges or unsatisfactory service ratings.

Discriminatory Harassment: unwelcome advances, requests for favors, and other verbal or non-verbal communication or conduct (e.g. comments, innuendo, threats, jokes, pictures, gestures) based on race, color, national origin, disability, sex, sexual orientation, age, height, weight, marital status, religion, genetic information or partisan considerations.

Employee: any classified or unclassified employee of the State of Michigan in the Department of Corrections excluding any independent contractor or their employees.

Facility: any property owned, leased, or occupied by the Department (e.g. hospitals, public works assignments, etc.).

Offender: a prisoner or parolee under the jurisdiction of the Michigan Department of Corrections or housed in a Department facility, a probationer who is supervised by an employee of the Department, or any person referred to the Department by the courts for investigation or supervision.

Overfamiliarity: conduct which has resulted in or is likely to result in intimacy; a close personal or non-work related association.

Over-the-Counter Medication: medication which can be purchased without a prescription in the United States.

Prescription Medication: medication which cannot be purchased without authorization from a licensed health care authority.

Sexual Harassment of Offenders: sexual harassment includes verbal statements or comments of a sexual nature to an offender, demeaning references to gender or derogatory comments about body or clothing, or profane or obscene language or gestures of a sexual nature.

Sexual Conduct with Offenders: the intentional touching, either directly or through clothing, of a prisoner's genitals, anus, groin, breast, inner thigh, or buttock with the intent to abuse, arouse or gratify the sexual desire of any person. Invasion of privacy for sexual gratification, indecent exposure, or voyeurism. An attempted, threatened, or requested sexual act or helping, advising, or encouraging another employee to engage in a sexual act with an offender.

NOTE: The language of an applicable Collective Bargaining Agreement or Civil Service Commission Rules and Regulations supersede the provisions of the Employee Handbook where in conflict.

GENERAL INFORMATION

1. EQUAL EMPLOYMENT OPPORTUNITY
The Department is committed to equal employment opportunity. For more information, refer to PD 02.06.100 "Equal Employment Opportunity."

2. DISCRIMINATION
An employee shall not discriminate against a person on the basis of religion, sex, sexual orientation, race, color, national origin, age, weight, height, disability, marital status, genetic information or partisan considerations.

3. POLITICAL ACTIVITIES
Classified employees are restricted from certain political activities by Civil Service Commission Rules. Refer to Section 1-12 "Political Activities" of the Civil Service Commission Rules and PD 02.03.107 "Code of Ethics and Conduct-Employees" for details on these restrictions.

4. CONFLICT OF INTEREST
Employees are restricted from engaging in actions which may constitute a conflict of interest with employment with the Department. Refer to Section 2-8 "Ethical Standards and Conduct" of the Civil Service Commission Rules and PD 02.03.105 "Outside Employment" for further details.

5. PUBLIC INFORMATION
Employees speaking as a representative of the Department are responsible for the accuracy of their statements, are expected to reflect the position of the Department, and are to contact the Office of Public Information and Communications for current information and the Department's position on issues.

Employees making presentations on correctional issues in a capacity other than as a representative of the Department shall inform the audience that their remarks are not made in their official capacity as an employee. Employees are to be guided by PD 02.03.106 "External Communications by Employees" and PD 01.06.130 "Media Relations" when speaking to the public or the media.

6. EMPLOYEE SERVICES PROGRAM

The Employee Services Program (ESP) provides services to active State employees who are experiencing problems or personal concerns that are affecting their work. ESP also offers assessment and referral for employees' family members when appropriate. ESP counselors provide assistance in the identification and resolution of personal problems. For additional guidance refer to PD 02.04.107 "Employee Services Program," or contact ESP at 1-800-521-1377 in Lansing or 1-800-872-5563 in Detroit.

7. EMPLOYEE GRIEVANCE PROCEDURE

The Civil Service Commission has established a grievance procedure for employees not covered by a labor agreement. Refer to the Civil Service Grievances, Technical Complaints, and Appeals Procedure for more information. This procedure is available in Department Human Resources Offices and/or on the Civil Service Web Site, Regulations, Chapter 8.

Employees covered by a labor agreement should refer to the applicable collective bargaining agreement to determine the grievance procedure which applies to them.

8. CHANGES IN EMPLOYMENT STATUS

a. Separation: Voluntary/Involuntary

An employee is expected to give at least two weeks advance notice before resigning, retiring, or transferring. Such notice shall be provided to the employee's supervisor and Human Resources Office.

If an employee is not rated satisfactory at the end of his or her initial probationary period (including any extensions), the employee will be separated as provided for in Civil Service Commission Rules and/or applicable collective bargaining agreements. Initial probationary employees are afforded grievance rights within the Department as specified in the applicable Civil Service Commission Rules or collective bargaining agreement.

An employee may be involuntarily separated or discharged for various reasons as specified by the Civil Service Commission Rules, Department policies, and/or applicable collective bargaining agreement. An employee with status may have a review of the discharge through the appropriate grievance procedure.

An employee will receive payment for any unused leave credits as authorized by the Civil Service Commission Rules or applicable collective bargaining agreement after separation.

b. Transfers

Transfer requests within the Department must be provided to the appropriate Human Resources Office and in accordance with any applicable collective bargaining agreement.

c. Promotion/Demotion

Any promotion or advancement within the Department is determined by the employee's past and present job performance, knowledge, skills, abilities, and eligibility. Some positions have residency requirements as identified in PD 02.02.112 "Duty Schedules, Business Hours and Residence Requirements."

A demotion is an authorized movement of an employee with status to a lower classification level. Voluntary or involuntary demotions are governed by the Civil Service Commission Rules, Department policies, and/or the applicable collective bargaining agreement. An employee with status may have a review of an involuntary demotion through the appropriate grievance procedure.

d. Position Classification Review

It may become necessary to review the class titles or levels of positions due to changes that have taken place in duties and responsibilities involved that may impact the proper classification of a position. These reviews are made by the Civil Service Commission. If an employee feels their current classification and level does not reflect their present duties, an employee may initiate a review of his or her position. Refer to Civil Service Commission Rules, Section 4-2 "Position Classification Review."

e. Retirement

The Department has employees covered under various retirement programs. There are several options as to how your benefits will be paid upon retirement or provided to a survivor. A description of these options is found in the information published by the Department of Technology, Management and Budget, Office of Retirement Services. Contact the Office of Retirement Services at 1-800-381-5111 for more information.

EMPLOYMENT REQUIREMENTS

Employees shall comply with the following employment requirements. Failure to comply will generally result in corrective action, up to and including discharge.

1. ROLE MODELS

One of the major objectives of the Department is to influence and persuade offenders to become law-abiding citizens. The on-duty and off-duty conduct of Department employees must serve as an example of proper conduct.

2. FITNESS FOR DUTY

Employees are required to be physically and mentally fit to perform regular and emergency duties.

An employee, whose primary responsibility is a custody or security function and who incurs a duty or non-duty injury or temporary disability, may be required to submit medical information that s/he is able to perform regular and emergency duties before returning to active duty.

Employees who do not have primary custody or security responsibilities must also be physically and mentally fit to perform their duties. If a non-custody employee incurs a duty or non-duty injury or temporary disability, s/he will be permitted to work unless it is determined that the injury/illness will interfere with the performance of their essential job duties.

The Department may require a second medical opinion in accordance with the applicable collective bargaining agreement, Family and Medical Leave Act (FMLA), and/or Civil Service Commission Rules.

Reasonable accommodations will be considered on a case-by-case basis for qualified persons with specific needs under the Americans with Disabilities Act.

3. USE OF LEAVE

Use of leave (e.g. annual, sick, compensatory, school/community and banked leave time) is governed by Department policy, Civil Service Commission Rules and collective bargaining agreements. An employee may use annual leave, compensatory time, school/community or banked leave time only if prior approval has been obtained from the proper supervisor. Advance approval can be any time prior to actual use of leave credits. Leave may not be used before it is earned. Employees are responsible to ensure they have appropriate leave credits to cover the absence. Refer to PD 02.02.100, "Time Utilization and Compensation" for more information.

Administrative leave may be granted only in accordance with PD 02.02.101 "Administrative Leave."

All sick leave used must be certified by the employee. The appointing authority may require verification as provided by applicable Civil Service Commission Rules or collective bargaining agreements.

Medical verification will be required under the following conditions and may be required under other conditions:

- When an employee has been counseled for excessive use or abuse of sick leave within the preceding six (6) months (1,044 actual work hours).
- When the employee has been hospitalized for any reason.
- When an employee has been on sick leave for five (5) or more consecutive work days.
- When an employee has been absent as a result of an accident, injury, or outpatient surgery.
- When an employee has requested annual leave and been denied and subsequently requests use of sick leave for the corresponding time.
- When an employee claims illness on the day of a change of assignment.

- When an employee's sick leave credits have been reduced to sixteen (16) hours or less for reasons other than leaves of absence, FMLA, workers' compensation, or death in the family.
- When the absence of a considerable number of employees on a shift indicates a concerted effort among the employees at the work site, the appointing authority shall immediately request medical verification of each employee.
- When an employee establishes a pattern of absences and/or emergency leave requests such as absence on a regular continuing basis on a given day of the week, before or after a regular day off, a payday, or a holiday.

Employees must be notified of the requirement to submit medical verification of their temporary disability at the time of call-in or in advance if possible. Employees must contact their Human Resources Office to obtain the necessary requirements for medical verification. Medical verification must be submitted prior to a return to work and may be submitted as applicable directly to the Human Resources Office or the Disability Management Unit. Failure to provide requested medical verification at the time of the return to work may result in the employee not being able to work. Authorization of leave credits does not prohibit the issuance of corrective or disciplinary action for unsatisfactory time and attendance.

Refer to applicable collective bargaining agreements, Civil Service Commission Rules, and PD 02.02.102 "Leave of Absence" regarding absence due to the Family and Medical Leave Act or unpaid leave of absence.

4. PUNCTUALITY

Regular attendance and punctuality are required of all employees. All employees are expected to adhere to the work schedule approved by their supervisor and to be at their assignment at the start of their shift or work day. In addition, all employees must adhere to specific facility procedures for attendance accountability.

5. PROPER NOTICE OF ABSENCE

Any employee, who provides service to offenders or with duties involving the direct management or observation of offenders, must personally notify his/her supervisor or a designated person of an unscheduled absence no earlier than 30 minutes prior to the start of the employee's shift but no later than the start of the shift, or in accordance with the applicable collective bargaining agreement. For example, an employee with duties involving the direct management or observation of offenders whose shift begins at 8:00 a.m., must call in between 7:30 a.m. and 8:00 a.m.

Health care employees with duties involving the direct management or observation of offenders must call in their absence as soon as possible, but no later than 30 minutes prior to the start of the employee's shift.

All other employees must notify the proper authority of an unscheduled absence as soon as possible, but no later than 30 minutes after their normal starting time.

An employee who does not report for duty on their regularly scheduled workday without proper leave approval, will be considered absent without leave. That employee shall receive lost time and be subject to corrective action. The notice of an unscheduled absence shall be made personally by the employee, unless physically unable to do so. Unauthorized absence by an employee for three (3) or more consecutive workdays may result in separation for unauthorized absence.

The employee is responsible for providing updated medical documentation prior to the expiration of any previously submitted documentation for which s/he is absent from work for an extended time or on a medical leave of absence. Failure to provide updated medical documentation within the expiration of the previously submitted documentation may result in separation for vacating a position.

6. JAIL TIME OR OTHER RESTRICTED SUPERVISION

No employee shall be allowed to work while under any electronic monitoring supervision or device, house arrest, or sentenced to jail time for any reason, including weekends, even if granted a work release pass. Employees must use available annual leave, BLT, personal leave, or compensatory time while serving jail time or under other restricted supervision before being placed on lost time or requesting and being considered for approval for an unpaid leave of absence consistent with Civil Service Commission Rules and/or applicable collective bargaining agreement.

7. LICENSE, CERTIFICATION OR SIMILAR REQUIREMENT

Employees are responsible for maintaining any license, certification or similar requirement necessary to per-form the duties of their assignment. Employees shall not be allowed to work in that position, and may be subject to immediate non-disciplinary separation or disciplinary action up to and including discharge, if a necessary license, certification or similar requirement has expired, been suspended or revoked.

8. TRAINING REQUIREMENTS

Employees are required to attend and successfully complete new employee and in-service training sessions in accordance with PD 02.05.100 "New Employee Training Program," and PD 02.05.101 "In-Service Training."

New employees who do not successfully complete the required training program will be separated.

Employees who are authorized to carry a concealed weapon or use any firearm on duty must take and satisfactorily complete training instruction in accordance with policy on a prescribed time schedule. Employees will only be assigned to armed duties after meeting the qualifying standard for each individual type of firearm and chemical agent necessary for that assignment. As required by Department policy, in order to continue employment in such positions, employees must periodically re-qualify with the appropriate firearm(s) and chemical agents. Refer to PD 03.03.100 "Firearms and Chemical Agents" (Exempt) for additional information on weapon possession and use.

9. PERSONAL INFORMATION

To assist the Human Resources Offices in maintaining complete and accurate personnel files, an employee must immediately supply a written report to the Human Resources Office regarding any change in personal status. Some changes may require completion of forms that are available in the Human Resources Offices or through MI HR Self Service.

Immediate reporting of changes in personal information will help avoid inaccurate payroll deductions, loss of insurance benefits for dependents, delays in payroll processing, or the Department's inability to contact family members in emergencies.

Supervisors and employees whose primary responsibility is the custody, security, medical care, supervision, or investigation of offenders are required to have a working telephone by which they can be contacted. All other employees must provide their work location with a means to contact them within a reasonable period of time.

Current telephone numbers for employees as well as the home and street address of all employees must be on file at their Human Resources Office and work location. All employees are required to comply with residency and telephone requirements as specified in PD 02.02.112 "Duty Schedules, Business Hours and Residence Requirements."

DEPARTMENT WORK RULES

In accordance with PD 02.03.100 "Employee Discipline," OP 02.03.100-A "Employee Discipline" and the applicable collective bargaining agreement, an employee who violates Department or Civil Service Commission Rules, regulations, policies, procedures, post orders, work statements or conditions of employment will be subject to disciplinary action.

Conduct violating any of the following rules will subject an employee to disciplinary action up to and including discharge. Refer to PD 02.03.100 "Employee Discipline" and the applicable collective bargaining agreement for information relating to an employee's right to representation.

Any violation of rules occurring prior to the effective date of this handbook will continue to be disciplined based on the rule and policy in effect at the time of the infraction.

Employees are prohibited from retaliating against any person who reports rule violations. Employees shall not disclose to anyone that a work rule violation report has been filed, the details of the report, and/or the status of any investigation, except as required to comply with Department policy or to provide information to their representative in an administrative, civil or criminal proceeding.

1. HUMANE TREATMENT OF INDIVIDUALS

Employees are expected to treat individuals in a humane manner in the workplace or while on duty.

Examples of actions of an employee in violation of this rule are described below. This is not an exhaustive list of behavior which may be in violation of this rule.

- Displaying a weapon (firearm, taser, etc.) or object for the purpose of intimidating an offender, visitor, volunteer, employee or citizen, except in the performance of an employee's duties. See PD 04.05.100 "Disturbance Control" (Exempt), PD 04.05.110 "Use of Force" (Exempt) and PD 04.05.112 "Managing Disruptive Prisoners" (Exempt) for direction regarding control of offenders.
- Using speech, action, gesture, or movement that causes physical or mental intimidation or humiliation.
- Failing to try to secure necessary medical or other assistance in instances of medical emergencies, injury, assault or attempted suicide.
- Making unnecessary or unreasonable rules for an employee, visitor, volunteer or an offender to follow.
- Using abusive or profane language or actions which degrade or belittle another person or group.

2. USE OF POSITION FOR PERSONAL GAIN

Employees shall not engage in actions that could constitute the use of their position for personal gain.

Examples of actions of an employee in violation of this rule are described below. This is not an exhaustive list of behavior which may be in violation of this rule.

- Displaying his/her Department-issued identification card or badge, or referencing their employment or position with the Department for other than a work-related reason.
- Obtaining goods or services that would otherwise not be available or offered to the employee if not for his/her position.
- Obtaining information, assistance or leniency from another law enforcement or criminal justice agency.

Examples are not intended to restrict an employee from taking advantage of such things as retail discounts, which a business may offer to all members of a group, such as law enforcement or criminal justice professionals.

For additional information refer to PD 02.03.107 "Code of Ethics and Conduct—Employees" and Civil Service Commission Rule 2-8 "Ethical Standards and Conduct."

3. DISCRIMINATORY HARASSMENT

Employees shall not discriminate or engage in discriminatory harassment. Discriminatory harassment includes unwelcome advances, requests for favors and other verbal and non-verbal communication or conduct based on race, color, national origin, disability, sex, sexual orientation, age, height, weight, marital status, religion, genetic information or partisan considerations.

Employees must report any incidents of such conduct to the designated discriminatory harassment counselor or to the appropriate supervisor. For specific information pertaining to confidentiality and reporting requirements, refer to PD 02.03.109 "Discriminatory Harassment."

Employees are prohibited from retaliating against a person because the person has made a complaint, either orally or in writing, of discrimination or discriminatory harassment based on race, color, national origin, disability, sex, sexual orientation, age, height, weight, marital status, religion, genetic information or partisan considerations.

4. MISUSE OF STATE OR OTHER AGENCY PROPERTY OR EQUIPMENT

Employees shall not misuse State or other agency property.

Examples of actions of an employee in violation of this rule are described below. This is not an exhaustive list of behavior which may be in violation of this rule.

- Using State or agency property for personal purposes or purposes beyond that of their official job duties without proper authorization.
- Use of computers, printers, faxes, etc., for non-work related activities.

- Inappropriate use of the internet.
- Removing items from State or other agency premises without proper authorization.

In addition to any disciplinary action that may be imposed, an employee who misuses State or other agency property will be responsible for any consequences resulting from that misuse (e.g. civil or criminal charges or penalties), and may be required to reimburse the affected agency for its value. Property must be kept clean and in good condition at all times and immediately returned upon leaving the Department.

State-operated recreation facilities and equipment may be used by off-duty personnel for physical fitness or rehabilitation purposes with the approval of the appropriate Warden or Administrator. Such activity is voluntary and the Department will not be responsible for accidents or injuries.

5. CONDUCT UNBECOMING

Employees shall not behave in an inappropriate manner or a manner which may harm or adversely affect the reputation or mission of the Department. Employees have a special responsibility to serve as role models. Employees must also support and uphold the law through their own actions and personal conduct.

If an employee is arrested for or charged with a criminal offense, the behavior shall be investigated to determine whether such activity violates this rule. Violation of this rule is not contingent upon whether or not an employee has been arrested or charged with a criminal offense. If the investigation establishes a violation of this rule, whether it occurred on or off duty, disciplinary action up to and including discharge may result regardless of any prosecutorial action or court disposition.

Any conduct by employees involving theft shall result in discharge.

6. PHYSICAL CONTACT

Inappropriate physical contact is prohibited. Examples include, but are not limited to, inappropriate placing of hands on another person, horseplay, or other types of body contact, including body contact with an object.

Examples of appropriate physical contact include, but are not limited to, a handshake at an offender's graduation; at the beginning or end of a meeting; or during times of accomplishment and achievement.

7. CONFIDENTIAL NATURE OF RECORDS

Employees shall respect the confidentiality of employee, offender and health care information (including electronic records). Employees shall not share confidential information, other official information, or reports with unauthorized persons. Information is not to be divulged for other than legitimate authorized business purposes. Refer to PD 02.01.140 "Human Resources Files," PD 03.02.100 "Health Services" and PD 03.04.108 "Prisoner Health Information."

No offender file may be removed from a facility without the approval of the Director or respective Deputy Director, Regional Prison Administrator, Warden or Field Operations Administration Regional Administrator unless required as part of the employee's official job duties. Offender health care information can only be released with a proper release of information signed by the offender, pursuant to a subpoena or court order, or under PD 03.04.108 "Prisoner Health Information."

8. USE OF HEALTH CARE SERVICES

Employees shall only use the facility health care services in cases of emergency, medical stabilization for serious on-the-job injuries, and Department authorized services, such as TB tests and Hepatitis B vaccinations. When the clinic facilities are used for an emergency or on-the-job injury, the employee is to be transferred as soon as practical to a physician or hospital. A written report must be made by the clinic staff in each of these instances and sent to the appropriate Warden, Human Resources Office and the Administrator of the Bureau of Health Care Services.

9. CLASS II INSUBORDINATION

Willful acts of employees contrary to management directives that may compromise the Department's ability to carry out its responsibilities, such as operation of safe and secure facilities or protection of the public, are prohibited. Violation of this rule shall result in discharge.

10. CLASS I INSUBORDINATION

Insubordination is the disregard of authority or refusal to immediately follow management directives. Employees are prohibited from actions or inactions showing disregard of authority or failing to immediately follow management directives.

11. SEARCHES WHILE ON FACILITY PROPERTY

All employees are subject to authorized searches while on facility property. Employees who refuse to submit to an authorized search will be suspended immediately pending investigation. Violation of this rule shall result in discharge.

12. RESPONDING OR ASSISTING DURING AN EMERGENCY

All employees of the Department, regardless of classification, have security responsibility. Employees shall immediately respond to any request for assistance during an emergency, including emergency preparedness drills and mobilizations. An employee shall come to the assistance of another employee, offender, visitor, volunteer, etc., who is in distress or any other emergent situation.

13. ENFORCING RULES, REGULATIONS, POLICIES, PROCEDURES, POST ORDERS AND WORK STATEMENTS

All employees shall be familiar with, enforce and follow all Department rules, regulations, policies, procedures, post orders and work statements. An employee shall not undermine or interfere with the Department's efforts to enforce rules, regulations, policies, procedures, post orders and work statements.

14. MAINTAINING ORDER

Any action or inaction by an employee that may detract from maintaining order of Department operations is prohibited.

15. CHAIN OF COMMAND

Employees shall follow their chain of command. Proper morale and discipline require a recognition of authority within the various units and divisions of the Department. It is important to know the immediate supervisory official in charge so that all work-related questions are addressed to the proper person. Complaints and concerns shall be submitted to the immediate supervisor for resolution before going to a higher level, or to an outside source.

An employee may bypass an immediate supervisor only in an emergency or in accordance with specific Department policies. Supervisors shall inform their employees whom they should contact in cases of emergency, questions or problems. If the chain of command is not followed, issues should be sent back to the proper supervisor by the recipient.

The requirement to follow chain of command is not intended to abrogate the ability of employees to file complaints under their respective collective bargaining agreement or under the Whistleblowers' Protection Act, PA 469 of 1980, as amended, or other State or federal law, to report a violation or suspected violation of the law.

CRIMINAL ACTS, CONTRABAND AND CONTROLLED SUBSTANCES

Work Rule #5 and Work Rules #16 through #22 prohibit behavior involving criminal acts, contraband, and controlled substances both on and off duty. Controlled substances are defined in the Michigan Public Health Code. The Department has a zero-tolerance policy regarding employees possessing, using, or introducing controlled substances into a facility where offenders are housed or assigned. Zero tolerance means if a preponderance of evidence demonstrates that an employee has used, possessed, attempted to introduce, or otherwise involved themselves with controlled substances, s/he will be discharged.

The presence of contraband within correctional facilities and other settings where offenders are housed presents a safety and security risk and is therefore prohibited. For this reason, employees are responsible for any item within their area of control which includes, but is not limited to, the automobile they have driven, their clothing, and within purses and briefcases.

Employees are subject to drug and alcohol testing pursuant to Civil Service Commission Rules or the provisions of an applicable collective bargaining agreement.

16. CRIMINAL ACTS—FELONY

Employees shall not engage in any conduct, whether on one's own time or in connection with official duties, which results in a felony conviction, whether by guilty plea, no contest plea, delayed or deferred sentence or trial. A felony conviction shall result in discharge.

Felonious behavior not resulting in a felony conviction may still result in disciplinary action up to and including discharge for violation of Work Rule #5 "Conduct Unbecoming."

Employees shall provide a verbal report to their immediate supervisor, or if unavailable to the next available manager in their chain of command, within 24 hours after any felony citation or arrest. This verbal report shall be followed up within 72 hours with a written report by the employee to the appropriate Deputy Director, Administrator or Warden.

Employees shall also provide written reports to their immediate supervisor within 24 hours after any stage or phase of an arrest or prosecution including but not limited to: issuance of any warrant, any arraignments, any pre-trial conferences, pleas of any kind, preliminary examination, trial, conviction, sentencing, delay, deferral, diversion, or dismissal. Employees charged with a felony will be suspended without pay pending the outcome of the criminal charges.

Failure to report as required by this rule shall result in disciplinary action for violation of Work Rule #38 "Reporting Requirements."

17. CONTROLLED SUBSTANCE/INTOXICANT—POSSESSION, INTRODUCTION OR ATTEMPTED INTRODUCTION

Possessing, introducing, or attempting to introduce controlled substances or intoxicants into any facility where offenders are supervised shall result in discharge and possible referral for prosecution. This does not include items brought in by a clergy as allowed per PD 04.04.110 "Search and Arrest in Correctional Facilities" and/or MCL 800.281.

Employees shall not possess, introduce, or attempt to introduce into any facility where offenders are supervised any other substances, such as yeast, which can be used to manufacture a prohibited or illegal substance.

18. USE OF ALCOHOL OR CONTROLLED SUBSTANCE

Employees are subject to random, reasonable suspicion, pre-appointment, post accident, and followup drug and alcohol testing in accordance with Civil Service Commission Rule 2-7 or applicable collective bargaining agreement. An employee who reports for duty with alcohol on his/her breath, or when suspected of being under the influence of alcohol or a controlled substance, will be required to submit to an evidential breath test or appropriate drug test.

Employees shall comply with all requirements of the Civil Service Commission Rule, the applicable collective bargaining agreement, and this work rule. A violation of Provision **A** below shall result in disciplinary action up to and including discharge. A violation of **B, C, D, E, F** or **G** below shall result in discharge and the employee will not be eligible for rehire with the Department.

The following are prohibited activities for all employees:

A. Consuming alcohol while on duty, or reporting for duty or being on duty with a blood alcohol concentration of .02 or greater percent by weight in the blood but less than .08.

B. Reporting for duty or being on duty with a blood alcohol level of .08 or higher.

C. Using a controlled substance on duty unless used as prescribed by a physician except as addressed in Provision G below.

D. Reporting for duty or being on duty with a prohibited level of a controlled substance.

E. Refusing to submit to a required drug test or alcohol test. Refusal to submit to a drug and/or alcohol test means any of the following: 1) failing to provide an adequate sample without medical explanation, 2) engaging in conduct that obstructs the testing process, or 3) refusing to be tested.

F. Interfering with any testing procedure or tampering with any test sample.

G. Using medical marihuana (marijuana) is prohibited.

19. RULE RESCINDED IN 2000. NUMBER INTENTIONALLY NOT REUSED

20. INTRODUCTION OR POSSESSION OF CONTRABAND ITEMS

Employees shall not introduce or possess unauthorized items such as escape paraphernalia, weapons, facsimiles of weapons, ammunition, wireless communication devices, cell phones, tobacco or facsimiles of tobacco products (e.g. electronic vapor cigarettes), lighters or any other item not specifically authorized by PD 04.04.100 "Custody, Security and Safety Systems" (Exempt) or facility operating procedure in any facility where offenders are housed.

21. CONTRABAND IN VEHICLE ON THE PREMISES OF A FACILITY HOUSING OFFENDERS

Employees shall lock or properly secure any vehicle (including jeeps, motorcycles, bicycles, etc.) brought onto the premises of a facility housing offenders. Employees are responsible for ensuring that unauthorized items such as alcohol, controlled substances, weapons, ammunition, or facsimiles thereof are not in the vehicle. It will be assumed the employee was aware of the presence of the prohibited item if it is found in the vehicle. Violations of this rule may result in criminal prosecution. See PD 03.03.100 "Firearms and Chemical Agents" (Exempt) regarding the proper handling and storage of weapons.

22. MISDEMEANOR OR OTHER RESTRICTIONS

Any conduct by an employee, whether on one's own time or in connection with official duties, which results in a misdemeanor conviction (including diversion programs), whether by guilty plea, no contest plea, delayed or deferred sentence, or trial, is prohibited.

Behavior not resulting in a misdemeanor conviction may still result in disciplinary action up to and including discharge for violation of Work Rule #5 "Conduct Unbecoming." Traffic offenses that are not misdemeanors do not need to be reported.

Employees shall provide a verbal report to their immediate supervisor or, if unavailable, to the next available manager in their chain of command within 24 hours after any stage or phase of an arrest or prosecution including but not limited to: issuance of any warrant, any arraignments, any pre-trial conferences, pleas of any kind, preliminary examination, trial, conviction, sentencing, delay, diversion or dismissal. Each verbal report shall be followed up within 72 hours with a written report by the employee to the appropriate Deputy Director, Administrator or Warden.

Restrictions, such as a restricted or suspended driver's license or a personal protection order, must be verbally reported to the employee's immediate supervisor within 24 hours of becoming aware of the action to determine whether the restriction or personal protection order has an adverse impact on the employee's ability to perform his/her work assignment. Each verbal report shall be followed up within 72 hours with a written report by the employee to the appropriate Deputy Director, Administrator or Warden.

In addition to Work Rule #22 "Misdemeanor or Other Restrictions," failure to report as required by this rule shall result in disciplinary action for violation of Work Rule #38 "Reporting Requirements."

A misdemeanor conviction for a violation of the Controlled Substance Act or criminal sexual conduct shall result in discharge.

An employee who is discharged for violation of this rule or who resigns in lieu of termination during an investigation will not be eligible for rehire with the Department.

23. POSSESSION AND/OR USE OF MEDICATION

Employees shall immediately notify their supervisor if taking prescribed medication which may interfere with the employee's work responsibilities.

In addition, an employee who has duties involving the direct management or observation of offenders shall immediately provide written notice to the Warden or appropriate Administrator, through the Human Resources Office, of a prescribed medication that could reasonably be expected to affect the work performed. Such medication includes, but is not limited to: narcotic pain medication, psychotropic medication, mood altering medication, and antihistamines.

Employees must submit the "Employee Medication Request" form (CAJ-555) when taking prescribed medication which may interfere with their work responsibilities. If there is a question on the effects of the medication, the employee shall be required to provide medical clarification from a licensed physician. If the medication does not adversely affect job performance and needs to be taken at work, the Warden or appropriate Administrator will provide a way for the employee to take the medication by approving the CAJ-555 form.

24. RULE RESCINDED IN 2000. NUMBER INTENTIONALLY NOT REUSED

25. RULE RESCINDED IN 2000. NUMBER INTENTIONALLY NOT REUSED

26. ENTRY INTO A FACILITY

Employees shall not visit non-public areas of a facility where offenders are housed for non-work related purposes without prior approval of the Warden, appropriate Administrator, or designee. Off-duty employees are required to receive permission to enter or be present at any secure area of a facility.

Employees visiting any facility where offenders are housed shall sign the facility visitor's log.

An employee may visit an offender only if that offender is an immediate family member and is housed at a facility other than where the employee works. For purposes of this rule "immediate family member" is defined as grandparent, parent, stepparent, spouse, mother-in-law, father-in-law, child, stepchild, grandchild, sibling, stepbrother and stepsister. An aunt and uncle may be included if adequate verification is provided that they served as a surrogate parent.

Visitation at an institution shall take place in accordance with PD 05.03.140 "Prisoner Visiting."

Visiting an immediate family member who is an offender housed in a facility requires prior permission of both the appointing authority where the offender is housed and the employee's appointing authority. Visiting an immediate family member who is an offender housed in a jail and under Department supervision or jurisdiction requires prior written approval from the employee's appointing authority, and an approved "Offender Contact Exception Request" form (CAJ-202) on file. If the immediate family member is not under Department supervision or jurisdiction, prior written approval is not required.

27. DERELICTION OF DUTY

Employees shall fully perform their job duties. Any action or omission of an employee indicating neglect of his/her job duties, including but not limited to the safe and proper care and control of offenders, failure to make all required rounds, required field agent contacts, or participation in recreational activities with offenders while on duty, will be considered dereliction of duty.

28. USE OF FORCE

Employees shall use the least amount of force necessary to perform their duties consistent with the provisions of PD 04.05.110 "Use of Force" (Exempt) and PD 04.05.112 "Managing Disruptive Prisoners" (Exempt). Excessive use of force shall result in discharge.

29. EXCHANGE OF DUTIES-CUSTODY/SECURITY

Employees shall not exchange duties or responsibilities without prior explicit permission from the immediate supervisor.

30. DUTY RELIEF

Employees shall not leave an assignment without proper relief or authorization.

31. SECURITY PRECAUTIONS

Any action or inaction by an employee which jeopardizes the safety or security of employees, the public or offenders is prohibited.

Examples of actions of an employee in violation of this rule are described below. This is not an exhaustive list of behavior which may be in violation of this rule.

- Failure to keep assigned weapons properly secured, clean and in working order, properly loaded and at hand for immediate use.
- Loss of security equipment (e.g. keys, handcuffs, radios, ERT equipment, etc.).
- Failure to follow specific security detail instructions.
- Failure to follow PD 04.04.110 "Search and Arrest in Correctional Facilities."
- Failure to follow critical/dangerous tool policy as indicated in PD 04.04.120 "Tool Control."
- Propping open security doors or doors that should remain locked.
- Allowing unknown or unidentified individuals into buildings.
- Unauthorized distribution of exempt policy directives or operating procedures.
- Failure to follow security precautions as outlined in PD 03.03.100 "Firearms and Chemical Agents" (Exempt).

32. ATTENTION TO DUTY

Employees shall remain alert while on duty. Sleeping or failure to properly observe an assigned area or offenders, including missing post checks, are examples of inattention to duty.

Items that detract from the alertness of an employee are not allowed. Employees with duties involving the direct management or observation of offenders shall not have unauthorized electronic devices, computer games, books, pamphlets, newspapers, or other reading materials while on duty, except for post orders, a copy of the applicable collective bargaining agreement, and information specific to the performance of job-related duties.

All other employees may possess such items at their work site but are prohibited from using them while on duty except when they fall within the scope of their assigned duties.

33. REPORTING VIOLATIONS

Employees shall immediately report behavior which is in violation of Departmental rules, policies, procedures, work statements or post orders, etc., to supervisory staff.

Failure to report conduct involving drugs, escape, sexual misconduct, sexual harassment, workplace safety or excessive use of force will aggravate the penalty up to and including discharge.

34. REPORTING APPROACH TO INTRODUCE CONTRABAND, VIOLATE RULES, POLICIES, PROCEDURES, POST ORDERS AND WORK STATEMENTS

Employees shall report each time they are approached to introduce contraband or violate rules, policies, procedures, post orders or work statements. A verbal report of the approach shall be made immediately to the employee's supervisor and a complete written report of the approach must be made no later than the end of the employee's work day.

35. RULE RESCINDED IN 2000. NUMBER INTENTIONALLY NOT REUSED

36. RULE RESCINDED IN 2000. NUMBER INTENTIONALLY NOT REUSED

37. RULE RESCINDED IN 2012. NUMBER INTENTIONALLY NOT REUSED

38. REPORTING REQUIREMENTS

Employees shall timely submit accurate and complete oral and written reports when required by Department policy, procedure, post order or work statement, or when requested by a supervisor or other authorized personnel. Failure to provide reports that are accurate and complete is a violation of this work rule.

39. RULE RESCINDED IN 2012. NUMBER INTENTIONALLY NOT REUSED

40. RULE RESCINDED IN 2000. NUMBER INTENTIONALLY NOT REUSED

41. RULE RESCINDED IN 2000. NUMBER INTENTIONALLY NOT REUSED

42. EMPLOYEE UNIFORM REQUIREMENTS

Employees shall not wear a Department uniform except in the performance of duty, while representing the Department in an official capacity, or direct travel to and from the work site. Refer to PD 02.03.103 "Employee Uniforms" for additional restrictions.

Employees required to be in uniform must wear and return the entire uniform as provided in PD 02.03.103 "Employee Uniforms" and PD 02.03.121 "Special Alternative Incarceration Program—Employee Uniforms." Substitution of other types of clothing for parts of the uniform or alterations of the uniform are permitted only when clearly authorized under policy or contractual guidelines. The uniform shall be clean and neat at all times.

43. RULE RESCINDED IN 2000. NUMBER INTENTIONALLY NOT REUSED

44. RULE RESCINDED IN 2000. NUMBER INTENTIONALLY NOT REUSED

45. RULE RESCINDED IN 2000. NUMBER INTENTIONALLY NOT REUSED

46. RULE RESCINDED IN 2006. NUMBER INTENTIONALLY NOT REUSED

47. FALSIFYING, ALTERING, DESTROYING, REMOVING DOCUMENTS OR FILING FALSE REPORTS

Employees shall not falsify, alter, destroy or remove documents, including but not limited to, employment applications, data entries, log book entries, door card entries, rounds, OMNI entries, investigative reports, time and attendance records (both electronic and hard copy), misconduct reports, health care provider statements, receipts, travel vouchers or databases. Fraudulent reporting of an employee's time through the time clock or the State's automated payroll system is expressly prohibited. Violation of this rule shall result in discharge.

Employees who file a false complaint will be considered to have violated this rule.

48. GIVING OR RECEIVING GIFTS OR SERVICES

Employees are forbidden from exchanging with, giving to, or accepting gifts or services from an offender, including but not limited to: food and beverage items; shoe shines or any other item neither necessary for, nor related to, the performance of their official work-related responsibilities.

49. RULE RESCINDED IN 2012. NUMBER INTENTIONALLY NOT REUSED.

50. OVERLY-FAMILIAR OR UNAUTHORIZED CONTACT

OVERFAMILIARITY PROHIBITED

Employees are prohibited from engaging in overfamiliarity with an offender, or a family member or listed visitor of an offender.

It is prohibited for employees to have a nonprofessional relationship with an offender, the offender's family or their listed visitors. This rule gives examples of prohibited conduct, but is not intended to be all inclusive. Employees shall avoid any appearance of impropriety with offenders, offenders' family members and their listed visitors. However, contact with an offender, his/her family, or support system in the community is permitted in the performance of their duties in order to develop professional relationships with individuals who are part of the offender's support system. This contact shall be narrowly focused on the offender's success, with activities being documented in OMNI case notes for active offenders.

For purposes of this rule, "Listed Visitor" means a person on an offender's approved visitors list as provided in PD 05.03.140 "Prisoner Visiting."

Non-work relationships with offenders, other than an employee with his/her approved family member, are prohibited regardless of when the relationship began.

Relationships with an offender which existed prior to offender status involving children of the employee and the offender will be evaluated on a case-by-case basis through submission of an "Offender Contact Exception Request" form (CAJ-202).

Relationships with an offender's family member or visitor which existed prior to offender status occurring will be reviewed on a case-by-case basis through submission of a CAJ-202 form.

Unless approved by the appropriate Executive Policy Team member, an employee shall not live with, nor provide lodging for, an offender except if the offender is a family member of the employee, including a spouse where the employee's marriage to the offender existed prior to the employment date or where the spouse became an offender after the employment date. In all cases where the employee lives with or provides lodging to an offender who is a family member, this must be immediately reported in writing to the employee's Warden or appropriate Administrator.

PERMISSIBLE CONTACT

Employees may have contact with another employee of the Department who is the family member of an offender. Approval from the appropriate Executive Policy Team member or designee, or an "Offender Contact Exception Request" form is not required for such contact.

Employees may have contact with their immediate family, which is defined as spouse, parent(s), children or step-children, brother(s), sister(s), parent(s)-in-law, grandparent(s), grandchild(ren) and any person(s) whose financial or physical care the employee is principally responsible. The CAJ-202 form is not required for employees to have contact with an offender who is a member of that employee's immediate family. However, the employee is required to immediately provide written notice of the contact to the Warden or appropriate Administrator.

REPORTING REQUIREMENTS AND APPROVAL PROCESS

If contact is made with an offender, a family member of an offender or a listed visitor of an offender outside the course of an employee's job duties, such contact must be reported in writing to the employee's immediate supervisor or, if unavailable, to the next available supervisor in their chain of command by the end of the employee's next regularly scheduled workday. Such reporting is not required if a written exception (CAJ-202 form) has been granted.

Employees shall not make any contact with any offender, any family member of an offender, or a listed visitor of an offender outside the regular performance of the employee's job duties unless approval has been granted in writing by the appropriate Executive Policy Team member or designee. Employees shall use form CAJ-202 "Offender Contact Exception Request" to request such an exception. Offender Contact Exception Requests must be renewed whenever a change in the offender's status occurs, the employee's classification or worksite changes, or relationship to the offender, family member of offender, or visitor changes. A copy of all requests shall be retained in the employee's personnel file.

EXAMPLES

Unless the contact is work related or an exception has been granted pursuant to this rule, examples of behavior which presume overfamiliarity include, but are not limited to:

- Giving or receiving non-work related letters, messages, money, personal mementos, pictures, telephone numbers, legal or other services to or from an offender or a family member or a listed visitor of an offender.
- Being at the residence of an offender or a family member or listed visitor of an offender or them being at an employee's residence.
- Non-work related contact or visits with an offender or a family member or listed visitor of an offender without authorization.
- Any relationship with an offender, their family member or listed visitors that begins after offender status occurred.
- Conversation of a sexual or romantic nature.
- Sexual misconduct or sexual harassment of an offender's family members or listed visitors.
- Financial involvement with offenders, family members of offenders, or listed visitors.
- Working for or employing an offender or their family member(s).
- Visiting or corresponding with an offender or their family, or listed visitors.
- Having knowledge of or assisting another employee to engage in overfamiliarity.
- Renting property to an offender or an offender's family member or listed visitors.

Failure to report unauthorized contact until such contact is detected shall be considered an aggravating factor for determining the level of discipline issued. Any violation of this rule will be grounds for discharge.

An employee who is discharged for violation of this rule or who resigns during an investigation for over-familiarity and other conduct prohibited by policies established pursuant to these topics or failure to report a violation of Department policy or work rules in these areas will not be eligible for rehire with the Department.

51. SEXUAL CONDUCT WITH OFFENDER

Employees shall not engage in sexual conduct with an offender. Examples of actions of an employee in violation of this rule are described below. This is not an exhaustive list of behavior which may be in violation of this rule.

- An attempted, threatened, or requested sexual act or helping, advising, or encouraging another employee to engage in a sexual act. This includes assisting the violator in avoiding discovery.
- The intentional touching, either directly or through clothing, of an offender's genitals, anus, groin, breast, inner thigh, or buttocks with the intent to abuse, arouse, or gratify the sexual desire of any person. This conduct is a criminal offense under Michigan Penal Code 750.520c.
- Invasion of privacy for sexual gratification, indecent exposure or voyeurism.

An employee shall not be eligible for rehire with the Department, who:

A. Is discharged for any violation of this rule.
B. Resigns during an investigation for sexual conduct, sexual harassment, or other conduct prohibited by policies established pursuant to these topics.
C. Fails to report a violation of Department policy or work rules in these areas.

For additional information, refer to PD 03.03.130 "Humane Treatment and Living Conditions for Prisoners" and PD 03.03.140 "Prohibited Sexual Conduct Involving Prisoners."

Any violation of this work rule shall result in discharge and may lead to criminal prosecution.

52. SEXUAL HARASSMENT OF OFFENDER

Employees shall not engage in sexual harassment of an offender. Employees shall not assist, advise or encourage another to engage in sexual harassment, nor shall they assist the violator in avoiding discovery. Sexual harassment can include, but is not limited to:

A. Verbal or written statements of a sexual nature.
B. Demeaning references to gender or derogatory verbal or written statements about body or clothing.
C. Profane or obscene language or gestures of a sexual nature.

For additional information, refer to PD 03.03.130 "Humane Treatment and Living Conditions for Prisoners" and PD 03.03.140 "Prohibited Sexual Conduct Involving Prisoners."

Employees are required to report any incidents of sexual harassment to a supervisor. Incidents must be reported whether witnessed by the employee or reported to the employee by an offender.

53. WORKPLACE SAFETY

Threats by employees such as bomb threats, death threats, threats of assault, acts of physical violence, etc., are expressly prohibited.

Employees shall not carry or possess a firearm, explosive, weapon or facsimile of a weapon at a facility or while on duty except as authorized by Department policy.

Employees shall not physically fight or assault any person on facility grounds. Employees may act to reasonably defend themselves against violence in accordance with custody and security policies and procedures.

If an employee becomes aware of a threat of violence or an act of violence, the employee shall immediately report the threat or act to their immediate supervisor, or if unavailable, to the next available supervisor in his/her chain of command. This verbal report shall be followed up by the end of the shift with a written report by the employee to the appropriate management representative.

Failure to report a threat or act of physical violence will be considered a violation of Work Rule #33 "Reporting Requirements."

Violation of this rule shall result in discharge.

54. MISUSE OF RECORDING DEVICES OR RECORDED INFORMATION

Using any type of recording device to record, transmit, or transcribe audio conversations, electronic information or video images without the consent of all parties being recorded is prohibited. The only exceptions to this rule are:

A. Recordings which are authorized, routinely recorded, and/or monitored as part of the daily operations of the Department.
B. Recordings made with prior approval of the appropriate Administrator.
C. Recording devices used during investigatory interviews as part of an administrative investigation. Such recordings shall be disclosed to all members present at the time of its use, except in the case of prisoner interviews.

In addition, employees are prohibited from making copies or removing copies of communications without authorization which are routinely recorded and/or monitored as part of the daily operations of the Department (logbooks, security tapes, etc.).

Policy Directives (PDs) and Civil Service Commission Rules referenced in this Handbook are available for review at all work sites as well as electronically through Document Access System (DAS). If not available, contact your supervisor.

2012

Michigan Department of Corrections

Employee Handbook

Acknowledgement and Receipt

I certify that I have received, and understand that it is my responsibility to read and familiarize myself with, the Michigan Department of Corrections' work rules and employment requirements. I understand my signature below indicates that I have received the MDOC Employee Handbook. I recognize that I will be held to the standards contained within and that violation of any of those standards or any rule violations can result in corrective action up to and including discharge. I am aware that a copy of this document will be placed in my personnel file.

_____

NAME (Please Print: Last, First, Middle Initial)
DATE

_____

SIGNATURE
DATE

(perforated for easy detachment)

INDEX